ANNUAL EDIT

W9-BML-120

Drugs, Society, and Behavior 11/12
Twenty-Sixth Edition

EDITOR

Hugh T. Wilson
California State University—Sacramento

Professor Hugh Wilson received his Bachelor of Arts degree from California State University, Sacramento, and a Master of Arts degree in Justice Administration and a Doctorate in Public Administration from Golden Gate University in San Francisco. Dr. Wilson is a Professor and the Division Chair for the Criminal Justice Division at California State University, Sacramento, one of the largest such programs in the United States. He has taught drug abuse recognition, enforcement, and policy to students, educators, and police officers for 30 years. Dr. Wilson interacts regularly with primary and secondary educators in the interests of drug-related youth at risk. His primary professional and academic interest lies in the study and reduction of Fetal Alcohol Syndrome.

Connect
Learn
Succeed™

ANNUAL EDITIONS: DRUGS, SOCIETY, AND BEHAVIOR, TWENTY-SIXTH EDITION

Annual Editions is published by the **Contemporary Learning Series** group within the
McGraw-Hill Higher Education division.

1 2 3 4 5 6 7 8 9 0 QDB/QDB 1 0 9 8 7 6 5 4 3 2 1

ISBN 978-0-07-805091-6
MHID 0-07-805091-X
ISSN 1091-9945 (print)
ISSN 2158-8856 (online)

Managing Editor: *Larry Loeppke*
Developmental Editor: *Dave Welsh*
Permissions Coordinator: *Rita Hingtgen*
Marketing Communications Specialist: *Mary Klein*
Marketing Coordinator: *Alice Link*
Senior Project Manager: *Joyce Watters*
Design Specialist: *Margarite Reynolds*
Buyer: *Susan K. Culbertson*

Compositor: Laserwords Private Limited
Cover Images: Royalty-Free/CORBIS (inset); D. Falconer/PhotoLink/Getty Images (background)

www.mhhe.com

Editors/Academic Advisory Board

Members of the Academic Advisory Board are instrumental in the final selection of articles for each edition of ANNUAL EDITIONS. Their review of articles for content, level, and appropriateness provides critical direction to the editors and staff. We think that you will find their careful consideration well reflected in this volume.

ANNUAL EDITIONS: Drugs, Society, and Behavior 11/12
26th Edition

EDITOR

Hugh T. Wilson
California State University—Sacramento

ACADEMIC ADVISORY BOARD MEMBERS

Preface

In publishing ANNUAL EDITIONS we recognize the enormous role played by the magazines, newspapers, and journals of the public press in providing current, first-rate educational information in a broad spectrum of interest areas. Many of these articles are appropriate for students, researchers, and professionals seeking accurate, current material to help bridge the gap between principles and theories and the real world. These articles, however, become more useful for study when those of lasting value are carefully collected, organized, indexed, and reproduced in a low-cost format, which provides easy and permanent access when the material is needed. That is the role played by ANNUAL EDITIONS.

It is difficult to define the framework by which Americans make decisions and develop perspectives on the use of drugs. There is no predictable expression of ideology. A wide range of individual and collective experience defines our national will toward drugs.

Despite drug prevention efforts, millions of Americans use illegal drugs on a monthly basis, and over 22 million are estimated to need drug treatment. Social costs from drugs are measured in the billions. Drugs impact almost every aspect of public and private life. Drugs are the subjects of presidential elections, congressional appointments, and military interventions. Financial transactions from smuggling help sustain terrorist organizations. Drugs impact families, schools, health care systems, and governments in more places and in more ways than many believe imaginable.

Although it takes little effort to expose social costs produced by drug abuse, there have been victories through which harm from drug abuse has been reduced. Scientific discovery relative to creating a new understanding of the processes of addiction is one. New treatment modalities, the successful use of drug courts, and the political support to expand these concepts has reduced drug-related impacts. In 2011, the federal government continues to fund a $98 million grant to states and local communities for the Access to Recovery program, which assists individuals and provides them options in obtaining treatment and recovery services. Although good evidence suggests that many of the most egregious forms of drug abuse have leveled off or been reduced, other disturbing trends, such as the nonmedical use of prescription drugs may be worsening. Drug abuse is a multifaceted problem requiring a multifaceted response. Complacency, encouraged by positive trends, has finally been recognized as a fatal mistake.

The articles contained in *Annual Editions: Drugs, Society, and Behavior 11/12* are a collection of issues and perspectives designed to provide the reader with a framework for examining current drug-related issues of facts. The book is designed to offer students something to think about and something with which to think. It is a unique collection of materials of interest to the casual as well as the serious student of drug-related social phenomena. Unit 1 addresses the significance that drugs have in affecting diverse aspects of American life. It emphasizes the often-overlooked reality that drugs—legal and illegal— have remained a pervasive dimension of past as well as present American history. The unit begins with examples of the multiple ways in which Americans have been and continue to be affected by both legal and illegal drugs. Unit 2 examines the ways drugs affect the mind and body that result in dependence and addiction. Unit 3 examines the major drugs of use and abuse, along with issues relative to understanding the individual impacts of these drugs on society. It addresses the impacts produced by the use of legal and illegal drugs and emphasizes the alarming nature of widespread prescription drug abuse. Unit 4 reviews the dynamic nature of drugs as it relates to changing patterns and trends of use. It gives special attention this year to drug trends among youth, particularly those related to prescription drug abuse. Unit 5 focuses on the social costs of drug abuse and why the costs overwhelm many American institutions. Unit 6 illustrates the complexity in creating and implementing drug policy, such as that associated with medical marijuana and that associated with foreign drug control policy. Unit 7 concludes the book with discussions of current strategies for preventing and treating drug abuse. Can we deter people from harming themselves with drugs, and can we cure people addicted to drugs? What works and what does not work? Special attention is given to programs that address at-risk youth and programs that reduce criminal offender rehabilitation and recidivism.

Annual Editions: Drugs, Society, and Behavior 11/12 contains a number of features that are designed to make the volume user-friendly. These include a *table of contents* with abstracts that summarize each article and key concepts in boldface, a *topic guide* to help locate articles on specific individuals or subjects, *Internet References* that can be used to further explore the topics, and , new to this edition, Critical Thinking study questions at the end of each article to help students better understand what they have read.

We encourage your comments and criticisms on the articles provided and kindly ask for your review on the postage-paid rating form at the end of the book.

Hugh T. Wilson

Hugh T. Wilson
Editor

Contents

UNIT 1
Living with Drugs

The concepts in bold italics are developed in the article. For further expansion, please refer to the Topic Guide.

UNIT 2
Understanding How Drugs Work—Use, Dependency, and Addiction

The concepts in bold italics are developed in the article. For further expansion, please refer to the Topic Guide.

UNIT 3
The Major Drugs of Use and Abuse

UNIT 4
Other Trends in Drug Use

The concepts in bold italics are developed in the article. For further expansion, please refer to the Topic Guide.

UNIT 5
Measuring the Social Costs of Drugs

The concepts in bold italics are developed in the article. For further expansion, please refer to the Topic Guide.

UNIT 6
Creating and Sustaining Effective Drug Control Policy

UNIT 7
Prevention, Treatment, and Education

The concepts in bold italics are developed in the article. For further expansion, please refer to the Topic Guide.

The concepts in bold italics are developed in the article. For further expansion, please refer to the Topic Guide.

Correlation Guide

The *Annual Editions* series provides students with convenient, inexpensive access to current, carefully selected articles from the public press. **Annual Editions: Drugs, Society, and Behavior 11/12** is an easy-to-use reader that presents articles on important topics such as *drug lifestyle, drug types, drug-use trends, drug policy,* and many more. For more information on *Annual Editions* and other *McGraw-Hill Contemporary Learning Series* titles, visit www.mhhe.com/cls.

This convenient guide matches the units in **Annual Editions: Drugs, Society, and Behavior 11/12** with the corresponding chapters in two of our best-selling McGraw-Hill Health textbooks by Hart et al. and Goode.

Annual Editions: Drugs, Society, and Behavior 11/12	Drugs, Society, and Human Behavior, 14/e by Hart et al.	Drugs in American Society, 8/e by Goode
Unit 1: Living with Drugs	**Chapter 1:** Drug Use: An Overview **Chapter 2:** Drug Use as a Social Problem	**Chapter 1:** Drug Use: A Sociological Perspective
Unit 2: Understanding How Drugs Work—Use, Dependency, and Addiction	**Chapter 4:** The Nervous System **Chapter 5:** The Actions of Drugs	**Chapter 2:** Drug Use: A Pharmacological Perspective
Unit 3: The Major Drugs of Use and Abuse	**Chapter 6:** Stimulants **Chapter 7:** Depressants and Inhalants **Chapter 9:** Alcohol **Chapter 10:** Tobacco **Chapter 11:** Caffeine **Chapter 12:** Dietary Supplements and Over-the-Counter Drugs **Chapter 13:** Opioids **Chapter 14:** Hallucinogens **Chapter 15:** Marijuana **Chapter 16:** Performance-Enhancing Drugs	**Chapter 3:** Drugs in the News Media **Chapter 7:** Alcohol and Tobacco **Chapter 8:** Marijuana, LSD, and Club Drugs **Chapter 9:** Stimulants: Amphetamine, Methamphetamine, Cocaine, and Crack **Chapter 10:** Heroin and Narcotics **Chapter 11:** The Pharmaceutical Neuroleptics: Sedatives, Hypnotics, Tranquilizers, Antipsychotics, and Antidepressants
Unit 4: Other Trends in Drug Use	**Chapter 1:** Drug Use: An Overview **Chapter 2:** Drug Use as a Social Problem **Chapter 3:** Drug Products and Their Regulations	**Chapter 1:** Drug Use: A Sociological Perspective **Chapter 3:** Drugs in the News Media **Chapter 5:** Historical Trends in Drug Consumption **Chapter 12:** Controlling Drug Use: The Historical Context
Unit 5: Measuring the Social Costs of Drugs	**Chapter 2:** Drug Use as a Social Problem	**Chapter 1:** Drug Use: A Sociological Perspective **Chapter 12:** Controlling Drug Use: The Historical Context **Chapter 13:** Drugs and Crime: What's the Connection? **Chapter 14:** The Illicit Drug Industry **Chapter 15:** Law Enforcement, Drug Courts, Drug Treatment **Chapter 16:** Legalization, Decriminalization, and Harm Reduction
Unit 6: Creating and Sustaining Effective Drug Control Policy	**Chapter 3:** Drug Products and Their Regulations **Chapter 17:** Preventing Substance Abuse	**Chapter 15:** Law Enforcement, Drug Courts, Drug Treatment **Chapter 16:** Legalization, Decriminalization, and Harm Reduction
Unit 7: Prevention, Treatment, and Education	**Chapter 17:** Preventing Substance Abuse **Chapter 18:** Treating Substance Abuse and Dependence	**Chapter 15:** Law Enforcement, Drug Courts, Drug Treatment **Chapter 16:** Legalization, Decriminalization, and Harm Reduction

Topic Guide

This topic guide suggests how the selections in this book relate to the subjects covered in your course. You may want to use the topics listed on these pages to search the Web more easily.

On the following pages a number of websites have been gathered specifically for this book. They are arranged to reflect the units of this Annual Editions reader. You can link to these sites by going to www.mhhe.com/cls

All the articles that relate to each topic are listed below the bold-faced term.

Addiction
2. Did Prohibition Really Work?
9. Drug Addiction and Its Effects
13. Scripps Research Team Finds Stress Hormone Key to Alcohol Dependence
14. The Genetics of Alcohol and Other Drug Dependence

Alcohol
1. History of Alcohol and Drinking around the World
2. Did Prohibition Really Work?
10. Family History of Alcohol Abuse Associated with Problematic Drinking among College Students
13. Scripps Research Team Finds Stress Hormone Key to Alcohol Dependence
20. Binge Drinking and Its Consequences Up Among American College Students
29. The Problem with Drinking
41. Fetal Alcohol Spectrum Disorders: When Science, Medicine, Public Policy and Laws Collide

Amphetamines
5. San Diego State U. Defends Its Role in Federal Drug Sting
11. Biological Perspectives- Antimethamphetamine Antibodies: A New Concept for Treating Methamphetamine Users
16. Movement Disorders and MDMA Abuse
18. Methamphetamines
19. Crystal Meth: The Dangers of Crystal Meth
22. Pseudoephedrine Smurfing Fuels Surge in Large-Scale Methamphetamine Production in California
26. College Students' Cheap Fix
30. With Cars as Meth Labs, Evidence Litters Roads

College
10. Family History of Alcohol Abuse Associated with Problematic Drinking among College Students
20. Binge Drinking and Its Consequences Up Among American College Students
26. College Students' Cheap Fix

Drug economy
7. Mexico Drug Cartels Extend Reach in U.S.
18. Methamphetamines
31. Los Zetas: the Ruthless Army Spawned by a Mexican Drug Cartel
38. Beyond Supply and Demand: Obama's Drug Wars in Latin America

Epidemiology
1. History of Alcohol and Drinking around the World
9. Drug Addiction and Its Effects
10. Family History of Alcohol Abuse Associated with Problematic Drinking among College Students
11. Biological Perspectives- Antimethamphetamine Antibodies: A New Concept for Treating Methamphetamine Users
12. Medical Marijuana and the Mind
13. Scripps Research Team Finds Stress Hormone Key to Alcohol Dependence

Hallucinogens
27. Availability of Websites Offering to Sell Psilocybin Spores and Psilocybin

Heroin
23. Adolescent Painkiller Use May Increase Risk of Addiction, Heroin Use

Law enforcement
7. Mexico Drug Cartels Extend Reach in U.S.
31. Los Zetas: The Ruthless Army Spawned by a Mexican Drug Cartel

Legalization
12. Medical Marijuana and the Mind
34. Drugs: To Legalize or Not
35. Do No Harm: Sensible Goals for International Drug Policy

Marijuana
12. Medical Marijuana and the Mind
15. Role of Cannabis and Endocannabinoids in the Genesis of Schizophrenia
17. An Update on the Effects of Marijuana and Its Potential Medical Use: Forensic Focus
21. Public Lands: Cartels Turn U.S. Forests into Marijuana Plantations Creating Toxic Mess

MDMA
16. Movement Disorders and MDMA Abuse

Over-the-counter (OTC) drugs
19. Crystal Meth: The Dangers of Crystal Meth
22. Pseudoephedrine Smurfing Fuels Surge in Large-Scale Methamphetamine Production in California
24. Caffeinated Energy Drinks—A Growing Problem

Policy
8. A Pill Problem
19. Crystal Meth: The Dangers of Crystal Meth
33. Catch and Release
34. Drugs: To Legalize or Not
35. Do No Harm: Sensible Goals for International Drug Policy
36. It Is Time to End the War on Drugs
37. New Drug Control Strategy Signals Policy Shift
38. Beyond Supply and Demand: Obama's Drug Wars in Latin America
41. Fetal Alcohol Spectrum Disorders: When Science, Medicine, Public Policy and Laws Collide

Prescription drug abuse
8. A Pill Problem

Prison
25. Issues in Correctional Care: Propofol and Intravenous Drug Abuse
40. Crime and Treatment: Overcrowded Prisons and Addicted Inmates are a Tough Challenges for Lawmakers

Research

Treatment

Youth and drugs

Internet References

The following Internet sites have been selected to support the articles found in this reader. These sites were available at the time of publication. However, because websites often change their structure and content, the information listed may no longer be available. We invite you to visit www.mhhe.com/cls for easy access to these sites.

Annual Editions: Drugs, Society, and Behavior 11/12

General Sources

Higher Education Center for Alcohol and Other Drug Prevention
www.edc.org/hec

The U.S. Department of Education established the Higher Education Center for Alcohol and Other Drug Prevention to provide nationwide support for campus alcohol and other drug prevention efforts. The Center is working with colleges, universities, and preparatory schools throughout the country to develop strategies for changing campus culture, to foster environments that promote healthy lifestyles, and to prevent illegal alcohol and other drug use among students.

Narconon
www.youthaddiction.com

This site contains drug information, information on addiction, rehab information, online consultations, and other related resources.

National Clearinghouse for Alcohol and Drug Information
ncadi.samhsa.gov

This site provides information to teens about the problems and ramifications of drug use and abuse. There are numerous links to drug-related informational sites.

NSW Office of Drug Policy Home Page
www.druginfo.nsw.gov.au

This is an Australian government-based website with a great deal of drug-related information. The site includes information about illicit drugs (amphetamines, pseudoephedrine, GHB, heroin, ketamine, rohypnol, marijuana, paramethoxyamphetamines [PMA], steroids, cocaine, hallucinogens, inhalants, ecstasy, ritalin, and psychostimulants), information and resources, treatment services, law and justice, illicit drug diversion, and medical cannabis. It also includes statistics on drug use in Australia.

ONDCP (National of Drug Control Policy)
www.whitehousedrugpolicy.gov

This site contains a vast amount of drug-related information, resources and links. Included is information about drug policy, drug facts, publications, related links, prevention, treatment, science and technology, enforcement, state and local along with international facts, and policies, and programs. The site is easy to use and understand.

U.S. Department of Health and Human Services
ncadi.samhsa.gov/research

This site contains links and resources on various topics that include, but are not limited to, substance abuse and Mental Health Data Archive, OAS Short Reports (on such drugs as marijuana, crack cocaine, inhalants, club drugs, heroin, alcohol, and tobacco). Also included are government studies and an online library and databases.

Mind for Better Health
www.mind.org.uk/help/diagnoses_and_conditions

This site provides information on a wide range of subjects from addiction and dependency to mental health problems. It also has Information on legislation.

United Nations Office on Drugs and Crime
www.unodc.org/unodc/index.html

This site includes information on the following drug-related topics, in addition to many other topics: treatment and addiction and illicit drug facts. Also available on this site are recent and archive press releases and multi-media presentations.

UNIT 1: Living with Drugs

Freevibe Drug Facts
www.freevibe.com/Drug_Facts/why_drugs.asp#1

This website contains information on drug facts with links on drug information, why people take drugs, the physical effects and drug-related behavior, drug recognition, and discussions of addiction. The site also includes personal accounts by addicts.

National Council on Alcoholism and Drug Dependence, Inc.
www.ncadd.org

According to its website, The National Council on Alcoholism and Drug Dependence provides education, information, help, and hope in the fight against the chronic, and sometimes fatal, disease of alcoholism and other drug addictions.

Parents. The Anti-Drug
www.theantidrug.com

Tips and links for helping children avoid drugs can be found at this site. Also provided is help in parenting with drug-related issues such as how to advise young persons about the drug-related influences of peer pressure.

Guide4Living Independent Health Information Online
www.guide4living.com/drugabuse

This site examines the use and abuse of a wide range of substances. It also provides personal stories, information on rehabilitation facilities, and a place for feedback.

UNIT 2: Understanding How Drugs Work—Use, Dependency, and Addiction

AddictionSearch.com
www.addictionsearch.com

Check this site out for information on addiction and rehabilitation. Some of the other features of this site are the use of statistics, identification of social issues, resources for treatment, facility listings for the United States, and analysis of types of addictions by race, sex, and age of human populations.

Internet References

Addiction Treatment Forum
www.atforum.com

News on addiction research and reports on substance abuse are available here.

APA Help Center from the American Psychological Association
www.apahelpcenter.org/articles/article.php?id=45

This site is a good resource with several articles and information mostly on alcohol.

British Broadcasting Company Understanding Drugs
www.bbc.co.uk/health/conditions/mental_health/drugs_use.shtml

This is a good reference for information about drug use, addiction, and dependence. Includes links.

Centre for Addiction and Mental Health (CAMH)
www.camh.net

One of the largest addictions facilities in Canada, CAMH advances an understanding of addiction and translates this knowledge into resources that can be used to prevent problems and to provide effective treatments.

Dealing with Addictions
http://kidshealth.org/teen/your_mind/problems/addictions.html

This site contains information on addictions and includes a quiz on substance abuse. Categories are entitled Your Mind, Your Body, Sexual Health, Food and Fitness, Drugs and Alcohol, Diseases and Conditions, Infections, School and Jobs, Staying Safe, and questions and answers. Much of this site is available in Spanish.

Drugs and the Body: How Drugs Work
www.doitnow.org/pdfs/223.pdf

This site pinpoints some basic but critical points in a straightforward manner. It explains how drugs can be administered, the processes through the body, effects and changes over time. Included are drug-related information resources and links.

The National Center on Addiction and Substance Abuse at Columbia University
www.casacolumbia.org

The National Center on Addiction and Substance Abuse at Columbia University is a unique think/action tank that brings together all of the professional disciplines (health policy, medicine and nursing, communications, economics, sociology and anthropology, law and law enforcement, business, religion, and education) needed to study and combat all forms of substance abuse—illegal drugs, pills, alcohol, and tobacco—as they affect all aspects of society.

National Institute on Drug Abuse (NIDA)
www.nida.nih.gov

NIDA's mission is to lead the nation in bringing the power of science to bear on drug abuse and addiction.

Public Agenda
www.publicagenda.org

A guide on illegal drugs has links that include understanding the issues, public opinions, and additional resources. Includes several links for each of these groups.

Understanding Addiction—Regret, Addiction and Death
http://teenadvice.about.com/library/weekly/aa011501a.htm

This site has several resources and articles related to drug use by young persons.

National Alcoholism Drug Information Center
http://addictioncareoptions.com

Get help and information about drug addition, alcoholism abuse, and top-rated addiction treatment centers.

UNIT 3: The Major Drugs of Use and Abuse

National Institute on Drug Abuse
www.drugabuse.gov

This is the National Institute on Drug Abuse website that identifies the major drugs of use and abuse. It provides resources and information for students, parents, and teachers, as well as reports on drug trends.

Office of Applied Studies
www.oas.samhsa.gov

Data and statistics on the major drugs of use and abuse along with reports on the effects of these drugs focusing on the emotional, social, psychological, and physical aspects are contained at this site. Also available are extensive survey findings on drug use related to evolving patterns of drug abuse.

QuitNet
www.quitnet.org

The QuitNet helps smokers control their nicotine addiction. This site operates in association with the Boston University School of Public Health.

The American Journal of Psychiatry
ajp.psychiatryonline.org/cgi/content/abstract/155/8/1016

This site contains a study on female twins and cannabis.

Streetdrugs.org
www.streetdrugs.org

This site provides a great deal of information on street drugs. It is designed to target different audiences—teachers, parents, students, and law enforcement. On this site one can find information on the top ten most misused drugs in the world today, a comprehensive drug index, and information on signs of a drug abuser.

UNIT 4: Other Trends in Drug Use

Drug Story.org
www.drugstory.org/drug_stats/druguse_stats.asp

This site contains lots of information—"Hard Facts, Real Stories, Informed Experts"; information on drugs and their effects. Also covered are prevention and treatment, drugs and crime, drug trafficking, drug use statistics,

Monitoring the Future
www.monitoringthefuture.org

Located at this site is a collaboration of drug trend data tables from 2005 focusing on students in the eighth, tenth, and twelfth grades; also described are trends in the availability of drugs, the attitudes of users, and the use of major drugs.

Prescriptions Drug Use and Abuse
www.fda.gov/fdac/features/2001/501_drug.htm

This site contains lots of resources and links related to prescription drug use and abuse.

SAMHSA
www.drugabusestatistics.samhsa.gov/trends.htm

This link is to the office of applied studies, where you can link to numerous drug-related resources. It includes the latest and most comprehensive drug survey information in the United States.

Internet References

United States Drug Trends

www.usdrugtrends.com

Provided at this site are drug trends for each state in the United States, such as information where each drug is most likely to be used in each state, cost of the drug, and where the drug supply is coming from.

Prescription Drug Abuse

www.prescription-drug-abuse.org

This is a website designed to provide information on where and when to get help for drug abuse. It also has a decent amount of information outlining what prescription drug abuse is and the particular ones that are abused, links to additional articles, and information on who is abusing the drugs.

UNIT 5: Measuring the Social Costs of Drugs

BMJ.com a publishing group

http://bmj.bmjjournals.com/cgi/content/abridged/326/7383/242/a

Drug Enforcement Administration

www.usdoj.gov/dea

The mission of the Drug Enforcement Administration is to enforce the controlled substances laws and regulations

Drug Policy Alliance

News about drug policies and articles critiquing the real social and economic costs associated with drug abuse versus the cost of the drug war policies can be found here.

National Drug Control Policy

www.ncjrs.org/ondcppubs/publications/policy/ndcs00/chap2_10.html

This site contains information about the consequences of illegal drug use, including economic loss, drug-related death, drug-related medical emergencies, spreading of infectious diseases, homelessness, and drug use in the workplace.

The November Coalition

www.november.org

The November Coalition is a growing body of citizens whose lives have been gravely affected by the present drug policy. This group represents convicted prisoners, their loved ones, and others who believe that United States drug policies are unfair and unjust.

TRAC DEA Site

http://trac.syr.edu/tracdea/index.html

The Transactional Records Access Clearinghouse (TRAC) is a data gathering, data research, and data distribution organization associated with Syracuse University. According to its website, the purpose of TRAC is to provide the American people—and institutions of oversight such as Congress, news organizations, public interest groups, businesses, scholars, and lawyers—with comprehensive information about the activities of federal enforcement and regulatory agencies and the communities in which they take place.

United Nations Chronicle—online edition

www.un.org/Pubs/chronicle/1998/issue2/0298p7.html

This site contains information about the global nature of drugs.

European Monitoring Center for Drugs and Addiction

www.emcdda.europa.eu/html.cfm/index1357EN.html

A collection of research studies, based out of the European Union, on how much governments spend to tackle their drug problem.

UNIT 6: Creating and Sustaining Effective Drug Control Policy

Drug Policy Alliance

www.drugpolicy.org

This site explores and evaluates drug policy in the United States and around the world.

DrugText

www.drugtext.org

The DrugText library consists of individual drug-related libraries with independent search capabilities.

Effective Drug Policy: Why Journey's End Is Legalisations

www.drugscope.org.uk

This site contains the drug scope policy and public affairs in the United Kingdom.

The Higher Education Center for Alcohol and Other Drug Prevention

www.edc.org/hec/pubs/policy.htm

"Setting and Improving Policies for Reducing Alcohol and Other Drug Problems on Campus: A Guide for School Administrators."

The National Organization on Fetal Alcohol Syndrome (NOFAS)

www.nofas.org

NOFAS is a nonprofit organization founded in 1990 dedicated to eliminating birth defects caused by alcohol consumption during pregnancy and improving the quality of life for those individuals and families affected. NOFAS is the only national organization focusing solely on fetal alcohol syndrome (FAS), the leading known cause of mental retardation.

National NORML Homepage

www.norml.org

This is the home page for the National Organization for the Reform of Marijuana Laws.

Transform Drug Policy Foundation

www.tdpf.org.uk

Transform Drug Policy Foundation exists to promote sustainable health and well-being by bringing about a just, effective, and humane system to regulate and control drugs at local, national, and international levels. Available on the website are media news articles—both recent and archived—links to other websites related to drug policy, and many other resources.

UNIT 7: Prevention, Treatment, and Education

American Council for Drug Education

www.acde.org

This site educates employers, parents, teachers, and health professionals about drugs and includes information on recognizing the signs and symptoms of drug use.

D.A.R.E.

www.dare-america.com

This year 33 million schoolchildren around the world—25 million in the United States—will benefit from D.A.R.E. (Drug Abuse Resistance Education), the highly acclaimed program that gives kids the skills they need to avoid involvement in drugs, gangs, or violence. D.A.R.E. was founded in 1983 in Los Angeles.

Internet References

Drug Watch International

www.drugwatch.org

Drug Watch International is a volunteer nonprofit information network and advocacy organization that promotes the creation of healthy drug-free cultures in the world and opposes the legalization of drugs. The organization upholds a comprehensive approach to drug issues involving prevention, education, intervention/treatment, and law enforcement/interdiction.

Join Together

www.jointogether.org

Contained here are multiple types of resources and web links regarding youth drug prevention for parents, teachers, community members, public officials, and faith leaders.

Marijuana Policy Project

www.mpp.org

The purpose of the Marijuana Policy Project is to develop and promote policies to minimize the harm associated with marijuana.

National Institute on Drug Abuse

www.nida.nih.gov/Infofacts/TreatMeth.html

Information on effective drug treatment approaches, costs for treating drug addiction, and the different treatment options (inpatient, outpatient, group, etc.) can all be found at this site.

Office of National Drug Control Policy (ONDCP)

www.whitehousedrugpolicy.gov

The principal purpose of ONDCP is to establish policies, priorities, and objectives for the nation's drug control program, the goals of which are to reduce illicit drug use, manufacturing, and trafficking; drug-related crime and violence; and drug-related health consequences.

Hazelden

www.hazelden.org

Hazelden is a nonprofit organization providing high-quality, affordable rehabilitation, education, prevention, and professional services and publications in chemical dependency and related disorders.

KCI (Koch Crime Institute) The Anti-Meth Site

www.kci.org/meth_info/faq_meth.htm

This site contains Frequently Asked Questions on Methamphetamine. Very interesting.

The Drug Reform Coordination Network (DRC)

www.drcnet.org

According to its home page, the DRC Network is committed to reforming current drug laws in the United States.

United Nations International Drug Control Program (UNDCP)

www.undcp.org

The mission of UNDCP is to work with the nations and the people of the world to tackle the global drug problem and its consequences.

The Partnership for Drug-Free America

www.drugfree.org/#

The Partnership for a Drug-Free America is a private, nonprofit organization that unites communications professionals, renowned scientists, and parents in the mission to reduce illicit drug abuse in America. Drugfree.org is a drug abuse prevention and treatment resource, existing to help parents and caregivers effectively address alcohol and drug abuse with their children. This website gives families the tools, information, and support they need to help their children lead healthy, drug-free lives.

UNIT 1

Living with Drugs

Unit Selections

Learning Outcomes

After reading this unit, you should be able to:

- Explain why history is important when attempting to understand contemporary drug-related events.

- Compare how the U.S. response to drug-related issues compares to that which occurs in other countries.

- Describe what role the media plays in U.S. society's perception of drug-related events.

- Explain how national crises such as the war in Iraq and economic instability have influenced patterns of drug abuse.

- Determine what important drug-related issues you believe the U.S. public is uninformed about.

Student Website

www.mhhe.com/cls

Internet References

Freevibe Drug Facts
www.freevibe.com/Drug_Facts/why_drugs.asp#1

National Council on Alcoholism and Drug Dependence, Inc.
www.ncadd.org

Parents. The Anti-Drug
www.theantidrug.com

Guide4Living Independent Health Information Online
www.guide4living.com/drugabuse

When attempting to define the U.S. drug experience, one must examine the past as well as the present. Very often, drug use and its associated phenomena are viewed through a contemporary looking glass relative to our personal views, biases, and perspectives. Although today's drug scene is definitely a product of recent historical trends such as the crack trade of the 1980s, the methamphetamine problem, and the turn toward the expanded non-medical use of prescription drugs, it is also a product of the distant past. This past and the lessons it has generated, although largely unknown, forgotten, or ignored, provide one important perspective from which to assess our current status and to guide our future in terms of optimizing our efforts to manage the benefits and control the harm from legal and illegal drugs.

The U.S. drug experience is often defined in terms of a million individual realities, all meaningful and all different. In fact, these realities often originated as pieces of our historical, cultural, political, and personal past that combine to influence present-day drug-related phenomena significantly. The contemporary U.S. drug experience is the product of centuries of human attempts to alter or sustain consciousness through the use of mind-altering drugs. Early American history is replete with accounts of the exorbitant use of alcohol, opium, morphine, and cocaine. Further review of this history clearly suggests the precedents for Americans' continuing pursuit of a vast variety of stimulant, depressant, and hallucinogenic drugs. Drug wars, drug epidemics, drug prohibitions, and escalating trends of alarming drug use patterns were present throughout the early history of the United States. During this period, the addictive properties of most drugs were largely unknown. Today, the addictive properties of almost all drugs are known. So why is it that so many drug-related lessons of the past repeat themselves in the face of such powerful new knowledge? Why does Fetal Alcohol Syndrome remain as the leading cause of mental retardation in infants? How is it that the abuse of drugs continues to defy the lessons of history? How big is the U.S. drug problem and how is it measured?

One important way of answering questions about drug abuse is by conducting research and analyzing data recovered through numerous reporting instruments. These data are in turn used to assess historical trends and make policy decisions in response to what has been learned. For example, one leading source of information about drug use in America is the annual federal Substance Abuse and Mental Health Services Administration's National Survey on Drug Use and Health. It currently reports that there continues to be more than 19 million Americans over 12 years of age who are current users of illicit drugs. The most widely used illicit drug is marijuana with approximately 14 million users—a figure that has remained constant for the past 5 years. Approximately 51 percent of Americans over 12 are drinkers of alcohol; over 43 percent of full-time enrolled college students are binge drinkers (defined as consuming 5 or more drinks during a single drinking occasion). Approximately 29 percent of Americans over 12 use tobacco. Almost 23 million

© David R. Frazier Photolibrary, Inc.

people are believed to be drug-dependent on alcohol or illicit drugs. There are approximately 5 million people using prescription painkillers for non-medical reasons–an alarming trend. The size of the economy associated with drug use is staggering; Americans continue to spend more than $70 billion a year on illegal drugs alone.

Drugs impact our most powerful public institutions on many fronts. Drugs are *the* business of our criminal justice system, and drugs compete with terrorism, war, and other major national security concerns as demanding military issues. Over 3 billion dollars per year is committed to the Department of Homeland Security to strengthen drug-related land and maritime border interdictions. The cost of illegal street drugs is up, and the post-9/11 national security infrastructure is impacting historical patterns of trafficking. And the relationship between drug trafficking and terrorism has focused added military emphasis on drug fighting. As the war in Iraq, Afghanistan, and Pakistan continues, U.S. drug agents in those countries are increasing efforts to contain the expanding heroin trade, a major source of funding for the Taliban. As you read through the pages of this book, the pervasive nature of drug-related influences on every day life will become more apparent.

The lessons of our drug legacy are harsh, whether they are the subjects of public health or public policy. Methamphetamine is now recognized as having produced consequences equal to or surpassing those of crack. The entire dynamic of illicit drug use is changing. Once quiet rural towns, counties, and states have reported epidemics of methamphetamine abuse over the past 10 years, and these suggest comparisons to the inner-urban crack epidemics of the 1980s. The current level of drug-related violence in Mexico is out of control and is firmly in control of the U.S. drug market. This issue is the most dangerous emerging drug problem.

Families, schools, and workplaces continue to be impacted by the many facets of drug abuse. One in three Americans has a close relationship to someone who abuses drugs. It is only because of war, terrorism, and a struggling economy that more public attention toward drug problems has been diverted.

The articles and graphics contained in this unit illustrate the evolving nature of issues influenced by the historical evolution of legal and illegal drug use in America. The changing historical evolution of drug-related phenomena is reflected within the character of all issues and controversies addressed by this book. Unit 1 presents examples of the contemporary and diverse nature of current problems, issues, and concerns about drugs and how they continue to impact all aspects of public and private life. The drug-related events of today continue to forecast the drug-related events of tomorrow. The areas of public health, public policy, controlling crime, and education exist as good examples for discussion. As you read this and other literature on drug-related events, the dynamics of past and present drug-related linkages will become apparent.

History of Alcohol and Drinking around the World

David J. Hanson, PhD

Alcohol is a product that has provided a variety of functions for people throughout all history. From the earliest times to the present, alcohol has played an important role in religion and worship. Historically, alcoholic beverages have served as sources of needed nutrients and have been widely used for their medicinal, antiseptic, and analgesic properties. The role of such beverages as thirst quenchers is obvious and they play an important role in enhancing the enjoyment and quality of life. They can be a social lubricant, can facilitate relaxation, can provide pharmacological pleasure, and can increase the pleasure of eating. Thus, while alcohol has always been misused by a minority of drinkers, it has proved to be beneficial to most.

Ancient Period

While no one knows when beverage alcohol was first used, it was presumably the result of a fortuitous accident that occurred at least tens of thousands of years ago. However, the discovery of late Stone Age beer jugs has established the fact that intentionally fermented beverages existed at least as early as the Neolithic period (cir. 10,000 B.C.) (Patrick, 1952, pp. 12–13), and it has been suggested that beer may have preceded bread as a staple (Braidwood et al, 1953; Katz and Voigt, 1987); wine clearly appeared as a finished product in Egyptian pictographs around 4,000 B.C (Lucia, 1963a, p. 216).

The earliest alcoholic beverages may have been made from berries or honey (Blum *et al*, 1969, p. 25; Rouech, 1960, p. 8; French, 1890, p. 3) and winemaking may have originated in the wild grape regions of the Middle East. Oral tradition recorded in the Old Testament (Genesis 9:20) asserts that Noah planted a vineyard on Mt. Ararat in what is now eastern Turkey. In Sumer, beer and wine were used for medicinal purposes as early as 2,000 B.C (Babor, 1986, p. 1).

Brewing dates from the beginning of civilization in ancient Egypt (Cherrington, 1925, v. 1, p. 404) and alcoholic beverages were very important in that country. Symbolic of this is the fact that while many gods were local or familial, Osiris, the god of wine, was worshiped throughout the entire country (Lucia, 1963b, p. 152). The Egyptians believed that this important god also invented beer (King, 1947, p. 11), a beverage that was considered a necessity of life; it was brewed in the home "on an everyday basis" (Marciniak, 1992, p. 2).

Both beer and wine were deified and offered to gods. Cellars and winepresses even had a god whose hieroglyph was a winepress (Ghaliounqui, 1979, p. 5). The ancient Egyptians made at least seventeen varieties of beer and at least 24 varieties of wine (Ghaliounqui, 1979, pp. 8 and 11). Alcoholic beverages were used for pleasure, nutrition, medicine, ritual, remuneration (Cherrington, 1925, v. 1, p. 405) and funerary purposes. The latter involved storing the beverages in tombs of the deceased for their use in the after-life (King, 1947, p. 11; Darby, 1977, p. 576).

Numerous accounts of the period stressed the importance of moderation, and these norms were both secular and religious (Darby, 1977, p. 58). While Egyptians did not generally appear to define inebriety as a problem, they warned against taverns (which were often houses of prostitution) and excessive drinking (Lutz, 1922, pp. 97, 105–108). After reviewing extensive evidence regarding the widespread but generally moderate use of alcoholic beverage, the historian Darby makes a most important observation: all these accounts are warped by the fact that moderate users "were overshadowed by their more boisterous counterparts who added 'color' to history" (Darby, 1977, p. 590). Thus, the intemperate use of alcohol throughout history receives a disproportionate amount of attention. Those who abuse alcohol cause problems, draw attention to themselves, are highly visible and cause legislation to be enacted. The vast majority of drinkers, who neither experience nor cause difficulties, are not noteworthy. Consequently, observers and writers largely ignore moderation.

Beer was the major beverage among the Babylonians, and as early as 2,700 B.C. they worshiped a wine goddess and other wine deities (Hyams, 1965, pp. 38–39). Babylonians regularly used both beer and wine as offerings to their gods (Lutz, 1922, pp. 125–126). Around 1,750 B.C, the famous Code of Hammurabi devoted attention to alcohol. However, there were no penalties for drunkenness; in fact, it was not even mentioned. The concern was fair commerce in alcohol (Popham, 1978, pp. 232–233). Nevertheless, although it was not a crime, it would appear that the Babylonians were critical of drunkenness (Lutz, 1922, pp. 115–116).[1]

A variety of alcoholic beverages have been used in China since prehistoric times (Granet, 1957, p. 144). Alcohol was considered a spiritual (mental) food rather than a material (physical) food, and extensive documentary evidence attests to the important role it played in the religious life (Hucker, 1975, p. 28; Fei-Peng, 1982, p. 13). "In ancient times people always drank when holding a memorial ceremony, offering sacrifices to gods or their ancestors, pledging resolution before going into battle, celebrating victory, before feuding and official executions, for taking an oath of allegiance, while attending the ceremonies of birth, marriage, reunions, departures, death, and festival banquets" (Fei-Peng, 1982, p. 13).

A Chinese imperial edict of about 1,116 B.C. makes it clear that the use of alcohol in moderation was believed to be prescribed by heaven. Whether or not it was prescribed by heaven, it was clearly beneficial to the treasury. At the time of Marco Polo (1254–1324) it was drunk daily (Gernet, 1962, p. 139) and was one of the treasury's biggest sources of income (Balazs, 1964, p. 97).

Alcoholic beverages were widely used in all segments of Chinese society, were used as a source of inspiration, were important for hospitality, were an antidote for fatigue, and were sometimes misused (Samuelson, 1878, pp. 19–20, 22, 26–27; Fei-Peng, 1982, p. 137; Simons, 1991, pp. 448–459). Laws against making wine were enacted and repealed forty-one times between 1,100 B.C. and A.D. 1,400. (Alcoholism and Drug Addiction Research Foundation of Ontario, 1961, p. 5). However, a commentator writing around 650 B.C. asserted that people "will not do without beer. To prohibit it and secure total abstinence from it is beyond the power even of sages. Hence, therefore, we have warnings on the abuse of it" (quoted in Rouecbe, 1963, p. 179; similar translation quoted in Samuelson, 1878, p. 20).

While the art of wine making reached the Hellenic peninsula by about 2,000 B.C. (Younger, 1966, p. 79), the first alcoholic beverage to obtain widespread popularity in what is now Greece was mead, a fermented beverage made from honey and water. However, by 1,700 B.C., wine making was commonplace, and during the next thousand years wine drinking assumed the same function so commonly found around the world: It was incorporated into religious rituals, it became important in hospitality, it was used for medicinal purposes and it became an integral part of daily meals (Babor, 1986, pp. 2–3). As a beverage, it was drunk in many ways: warm and chilled, pure and mixed with water, plain and spiced (Raymond, 1927, p. 53).

Contemporary writers observed that the Greeks were among the most temperate of ancient peoples. This appears to result from their rules stressing moderate drinking, their praise of temperance, their practice of diluting wine with water, and their avoidance of excess in general (Austin, 1985, p. 11). An exception to this ideal of moderation was the cult of Dionysus, in which intoxication was believed to bring people closer to their deity (Sournia, 1990, pp. 5–6; Raymond, 1927, p. 55).

While habitual drunkenness was rare, intoxication at banquets and festivals was not unusual (Austin, 1985, p. 11). In fact, the symposium, a gathering of men for an evening of conversation, entertainment and drinking typically ended in intoxication (Babor, 1986, p. 4). However, while there are no references in ancient Greek literature to mass drunkenness among the Greeks, there are references to it among foreign peoples (Patrick, 1952, p. 18). By 425 B.C., warnings against intemperance, especially at symposia, appear to become more frequent (Austin, 1985, pp. 21–22).

Xenophon (431–351 B.C.) and Plato (429–347 B.C.) both praised the moderate use of wine as beneficial to health and happiness, but both were critical of drunkenness, which appears to have become a problem. Hippocrates (cir. 460–370 B.C.) identified numerous medicinal properties of wine, which had long been used for its therapeutic value (Lucia, 1963a, pp. 36–40). Later, both Aristode (384–322 B.C.) and Zeno (cir. 336–264 B.C.) were very critical of drunkenness (Austin, 1985, pp. 23, 25, and 27).

Among Greeks, the Macedonians viewed intemperance as a sign of masculinity and were well known for their drunkenness. Their king, Alexander the Great (336–323 B.C.), whose mother adhered to the Dionysian cult, developed a reputation for inebriety (Souria, 1990, pp. 8–9; Babor, 1986, p. 5).

The Hebrews were reportedly introduced to wine during their captivity in Egypt. When Moses led them to Canaan (Palestine) around 1,200 B.C., they are reported to have regretted leaving behind the wines of Egypt (Numbers 20:5); however, they found vineyards to be plentiful in their new land (Lutz, 1922, p. 25). Around 850 B.C., the use of wine was criticized by the Rechabites and Nazarites,[2] two conservative nomadic groups who practiced abstinence from alcohol (Lutz, 1922, p. 133; Samuelson, 1878, pp. 62–63).

In 586 B.C., the Hebrews were conquered by the Babylonians and deported to Babylon. However, in 539 B.C., the Persians captured the city and released the Hebrews from their Exile (Daniel 5:1–4). Following the Exile, the Hebrews developed Judaism as it is now known, and they can be said to have become Jews. During the next 200 years, sobriety increased and pockets of antagonism to wine disappeared. It became a common beverage for all classes and ages, including the very young; an important source of nourishment; a prominent part in the festivities of the people; a widely appreciated medicine; an essential provision for any fortress; and an important commodity. In short, it came to be seen as a necessary element in the life of the Hebrews (Raymond, 1927, p. 23).

While there was still opposition to excessive drinking, it was no longer assumed that drinking inevitably led to drunkenness. Wine came to be seen as a blessing from God and a symbol of joy (Psalms 104; Zachariah 10:7). These changes in beliefs and behaviors appear to be related to a rejection of belief in pagan gods, a new emphasis on individual morality, and the integration of secular drinking behaviors into religious ceremonies and their subsequent modification (Austin, 1985, pp. 18–19; Patai, 1980, pp. 61–73; Keller, 1970, pp. 290–294). Around 525 B.C., it was ruled that the Kiddush (pronouncement of the Sabbath) should be recited over a blessed cup of wine. This established the regular drinking of wine in Jewish ceremonies outside the Temple (Austin, 1985, p. 19).

King Cyrus of Persia frequently praised the virtue of the moderate consumption of alcohol (cir. 525 B.C.). However, ritual intoxication appears to have been used as an adjunct to decision making and, at least after his death, drunkenness was not uncommon (Austin, 1985, p. 19).

Between the founding of Rome in 753 B.C. until the third century B.C., there is consensus among historians that the Romans practiced great moderation in drinking (Austin, 1985, p. 17). After the Roman conquest of the Italian peninsula and the rest of the Mediterranean basin (509 to 133 B.C.), the traditional Roman values of temperance, frugality and simplicity were gradually replaced by heavy drinking, ambition, degeneracy and corruption (Babor, 1986, p. 7; Wallbank & Taylor, 1954, p. 163). The Dionysian rites (Bacchanalia, in Latin) spread to Italy during this period and were subsequently outlawed by the Senate (Lausanne, 1969, p. 4; Cherrington, 1925, v. 1, pp. 251–252).

Practices that encouraged excessive drinking included drinking before meals on an empty stomach, inducing vomiting to permit the consumption of more food and wine, and drinking games. The latter included, for example, rapidly consuming as many cups as indicated by a throw of the dice (Babor, 1986, p. 10).

By the second and first centuries B.C., intoxication was no longer a rarity, and most prominent men of affairs (for example, Cato the Elder and Julius Caesar) were praised for their moderation in drinking. This would appear to be in response to growing misuse of alcohol in society, because before that time temperance was not singled out for praise as exemplary behavior. As the republic continued to decay, excessive drinking spread and some, such as Marc Antony (d. 30 B.C.), even took pride in their destructive drinking behavior (Austin, 1985, pp. 28 and 32–33).

Early Christian Period

With the dawn of Christianity and its gradual displacement of the previously dominant religions, the drinking attitudes and behaviors of Europe began to be influenced by the New Testament (Babor, 1986, p. 11). The earliest biblical writings after the death of Jesus (cir. A.D. 30) contain few references to alcohol. This may have reflected the fact that drunkenness was largely an upper-status vice with which Jesus had little contact (Raymond, 1927, pp. 81–82). Austin (1985, p. 35) has pointed out that Jesus used wine (Matthew 15:11; Luke 7:33–35) and approved of its moderate consumption (Matthew 15:11). On the other hand, he severely attacked drunkenness (Luke 21:34, 12:42; Matthew 24:45–51). The later writings of St. Paul (d. 64?) deal with alcohol in detail and are important to Christian doctrine on the subject. He considered wine to be a creation of God and therefore inherently good (1 Timothy 4:4), recommended its use for medicinal purposes (1 Timothy 5:23), but consistently condemned drunkenness (1 Corinthians 3:16–17, 5:11, 6:10; Galatians 5:19–21; Romans 13:3) and recommended abstinence for those who could not control their drinking.[3]

However, late in the second century, several heretical sects rejected alcohol and called for abstinence. By the late fourth and early fifth centuries, the Church responded by asserting that wine was an inherently good gift of God to be used and enjoyed. While individuals may choose not to drink, to despise wine was heresy. The Church advocated its moderate use but rejected excessive or abusive use as a sin. Those individuals who could not drink in moderation were urged to abstain (Austin, 1985, pp. 44 and 47–48).

It is clear that both the Old and New Testaments are clear and consistent in their condemnation of drunkenness. However, some Christians today argue that whenever "wine" was used by Jesus or praised as a gift of God, it was really grape juice; only when it caused drunkenness was it wine. Thus, they interpret the Bible as asserting that grape juice is good and that drinking it is acceptable to God but that wine is bad and that drinking it is unacceptable. This reasoning appears to be incorrect for at least two reasons. First, neither the Hebrew nor Biblical Greek word for wine can be translated or interpreted as referring to grape juice. Secondly, grape juice would quickly ferment into wine in the warm climate of the Mediterranean region without refrigeration or modern methods of preservation (Royce, 1986, pp. 55–56; Raymond, 1927, pp. 18–22; Hewitt, 1980, pp. 11–12).

The spread of Christianity and of viticulture in Western Europe occurred simultaneously (Lausanne, 1969, p. 367; Sournia, 1990, p. 12). Interestingly, St. Martin of Tours (316–397) was actively engaged in both spreading the Gospel and planting vineyards (Patrick, 1952, pp. 26–27).

In an effort to maintain traditional Jewish culture against the rise of Christianity, which was converting numerous Jews (Wallbank & Taylor, 1954, p. 227), detailed rules concerning the use of wine were incorporated into the Talmud. Importantly, wine was integrated into many religious ceremonies in limited quantity (Spiegel, 1979, pp. 20–29; Raymond, 1927, 45–47). In the social and political upheavals that rose as the fall of Rome approached in the fifth century, concern grew among rabbis that Judaism and its culture were in increasing danger.[4] Consequently, more Talmudic rules were laid down concerning the use of wine. These included the amount of wine that could be drunk on the Sabbath, the way in which wine was to be drunk, the legal status of wine in any way connected with idolatry, and the extent of personal responsibility for behavior while intoxicated (Austin, 1985, pp. 36 and 50).

Roman abuse of alcohol appears to have peaked around mid-first century (Jellinek, 1976, pp. 1,736–1,739). Wine had become the most popular beverage, and as Rome attracted a large influx of displaced persons, it was distributed free or at cost (Babor, 1986, pp. 7–8). This led to occasional excesses at festivals, victory triumphs and other celebrations, as described by contemporaries. The four emperors who ruled from A.D. 37 to A.D. 69 were all known for their abusive drinking. However, the emperors who followed were known for their temperance, and literary sources suggest that problem drinking decreased substantially in the Empire. Although there continued to be some criticisms of abusive drinking over the next several hundred years, most evidence indicates a decline of such behavior (Austin, 1985, pp. 37–44, p. 46, pp. 48–50). The fall of Rome and the Western Roman Empire occurred in 476 (Wallbank & Taylor, 1954, pp. 220–221).

Around A.D. 230, the Greek scholar Athenaeus wrote extensively on drinking and advocated moderation. The extensive attention to drinking, famous drinks, and drinking cups (of which he described 100) reflected the importance of wine to the Greeks (Austin, 1985, pp. 45–46).

The Middle Ages

The Middle Ages, that period of approximately one thousand years between the fall of Rome and the beginning of the High Renaissance (cir. 1500), saw numerous developments in life in general and in drinking in particular. In the early Middle Ages, mead, rustic beers, and wild fruit wines became increasingly popular, especially among Celts, Anglo-Saxons, Germans, and Scandinavians. However, wines remained the beverage of preference in the Romance countries (what is now Italy, Spain and France) (Babor, 1986, p. 11).

With the collapse of the Roman Empire and decline of urban life, religious institutions, particularly monasteries, became the repositories of the brewing and winemaking techniques that had been earlier developed (Babor, 1986, p. 11). While rustic beers continued to be produced in homes, the art of brewing essentially became the province of monks, who carefully guarded their knowledge (Cherrington, 1925, v. 1, p. 405). Monks brewed virtually all beer of good quality until the twelfth century. Around the thirteenth century, hops (which both flavors and preserves) became a common ingredient in some beers, especially in northern Europe (Wilson, 1991, p. 375).[5] Ale, often a thick and nutritious soupy beverage, soured quickly and was made for local consumption (Austin, 1985, p. 54, pp. 87–88).

Not surprisingly, the monasteries also maintained viticulture. Importantly, they had the resources, security, and stability in that often-turbulent time to improve the quality of their vines slowly over 1986, (p. 11). While most wine was made and consumed locally, some wine trade did continue in spite of the deteriorating roads (Hyams, 1965, p. 151; Wilson, 1991, p. 371).

By the millennium, the most popular form of festivities in England were known as "ales," and both ale and beer were at the top of lists of products to be given to lords for rent. As towns were established in twelfth-century Germany, they were granted the privilege of brewing and selling beer in their immediate localities. A flourishing artisan brewing industry developed in many towns, about which there was strong civic pride (Cherrington, 1925, v. 1, p. 405; Austin 1985, pp. 68, 74, 82–83).

The most important development regarding alcohol throughout the Middle Ages was probably that of distillation. Interestingly, considerable disagreement exists concerning who discovered distillation and when the discovery was made.[6] However, it was Albertus Magnus (1193–1280) who first clearly described the process which made possible the manufacture of distilled spirits (Patrick, 1952, p. 29). Knowledge of the process began to spread slowly among monks, physicians and alchemists, who were interested in distilled alcohol as a cure for ailments. At that time it was called aqua vitae, "water of life,"[7] but was later known as brandy. The latter term was derived from the Dutch brandewijn, meaning burnt (or distilled) wine (Seward, 1979, p. 151; Roueche, 1963, pp. 172–173).

The Black Death and subsequent plagues, which began in the mid-fourteenth century, dramatically changed people's perception of their lives and place in the cosmos. With no understanding or control of the plagues that reduced the population by as much as 82% in some villages, "processions of flagellants mobbed city and village streets, hoping, by the pains they inflicted on themselves and each other, to take the edge off the plagues they attributed to God's wrath over human folly" (Slavin, 1973, pp. 12–16).

Some dramatically increased their consumption of alcohol in the belief that this might protect them from the mysterious disease, while others thought that through moderation in all things, including alcohol, they could be saved. It would appear that, on balance, consumption of alcohol was high. For example, in Bavaria, beer consumption was probably about 300 liters per capita a year (compared to 150 liters today) and in Florence wine consumption was about ten barrels per capita a year. Understandably, the consumption of distilled spirits, which was exclusively for medicinal purposes, increased in popularity (Austin, 1985, pp. 104–105, 107–108).

As the end of the Middle Ages approached, the popularity of beer spread to England, France and Scotland (Austin, pp. 118–119). Beer brewers were recognized officially as a guild in England (Monckton, 1966, pp. 69–70), and the adulteration of beer or wine became punishable by death in Scotland (Cherrington, 1929, vol. 5, p. 2,383). Importantly, the consumption of spirits as a beverage began to occur (Braudel, 1974, p. 171).

Early Modern Period

The early modern period was generally characterized by increasing prosperity and wealth. Towns and cities grew in size and number, foreign lands were discovered and colonized, and trade expanded. Perhaps more importantly, there developed a new view of the world. The medieval emphasis on other-worldliness—the belief that life in this world is only a preparation for heaven—slowly gave way, especially among the wealthy and well educated, to an interest in life in the here and now (Wallbank & Taylor, 1954, p. 513).

The Protestant Reformation and rise of aggressive national states destroyed the ideal of a universal Church overseeing a Holy Roman Empire. Rationality, individualism, and science heavily impacted the prevalent emotional idealism, communalism, and traditional religion (Wallbank & Taylor, 1954, pp. 513–518; Slavin, 1973, ch. 5–7).

However, the Protestant leaders such as Luther, Calvin, the leaders of the Anglican Church and even the Puritans did not differ substantially from the teachings of the Catholic Church: alcohol was a gift of God and created to be used in moderation for pleasure, enjoyment and health; drunkenness was viewed as a sin (Austin, 1985, p. 194).

From this period through at least the beginning of the eighteenth century, attitudes toward drinking were characterized by a continued recognition of the positive nature of moderate consumption and an increased concern over the negative effects of drunkenness. The latter, which was generally viewed as arising out of the increased self-indulgence of the time, was seen as a threat to spiritual salvation and societal well being. Intoxication was also inconsistent with the emerging emphasis on rational mastery of self and world and on work and efficiency (Austin, 1985, pp. 129–130).

However, consumption of alcohol was often high. In the sixteenth century, alcohol beverage consumption reached 100 liters per person per year in Valladolid, Spain, and Polish peasants consumed up to three liters of beer per day (Braudel, 1974, pp. 236–238). In Coventry, the average amount of beer and ale consumed was about 17 pints per person per week, compared to about three pints today (Monckton, 1966, p. 95); nationwide, consumption was about one pint per day per capita. Swedish beer consumption may have been 40 times higher than in modern Sweden. English sailors received a ration of a gallon of beer per day, while soldiers received two-thirds of a gallon. In Denmark, the usual consumption of beer appears to have been a gallon per day for adult laborers and sailors (Austin, 1985, pp. 170, 186, 192).

However, the production and distribution of spirits spread slowly. Spirit drinking was still largely for medicinal purposes throughout most of the sixteenth century. It has been said of distilled alcohol that "the sixteenth century created it; the seventeenth century consolidated it; the eighteenth popularized it" (Braudel, 1967, p. 170).

A beverage that clearly made its debut during the seventeenth century was sparkling champagne. The credit for that development goes primarily to Dom Perignon, the wine-master in a French abbey. Around 1668, he used strong bottles, invented a more efficient cork (and one that could contain the effervescence in those strong bottles), and began developing the technique of blending the contents. However, another century would pass before problems, especially bursting bottles, would be solved and sparkling champagne would become popular (Younger, 1966, pp. 345–346; Doxat, 1971, p. 54; Seward, 1979, pp. 139–143).

The original grain spirit, whiskey, appears to have first been distilled in Ireland. While its specific origins are unknown (Magee, 1980, p. 7; Wilson, 1973, p. 7) there is evidence that by the sixteenth century it was widely consumed in some parts of Scotland (Roueche, 1963, pp. 175–176). It was also during the seventeenth century that Franciscus Sylvius (or Franz de la Boe), a professor of medicine at the University of Leyden, distilled spirits from grain.

Distilled spirit was generally flavored with juniper berries. The resulting beverage was known as junever, the Dutch word for "juniper." The French changed the name to genievre, which the English changed to "geneva" and then modified to "gin"[8] (Roueche, 1963, pp. 173–174). Originally used for medicinal purposes, the use of gin as a social drink did not grow rapidly at first (Doxat, 1972, p. 98; Watney, 1976, p. 10). However, in 1690, England passed "An Act for the Encouraging of the Distillation of Brandy and Spirits from Corn" and within four years the annual production of distilled spirits, most of which was gin, reached nearly one million gallons (Roueche, 1963, p. 174).

The seventeenth century also saw the Virginia colonists continue the traditional belief that alcoholic beverages are a natural food and are good when used in moderation. In fact, beer arrived with the first colonists, who considered it essential to their well being (Baron, 1962, pp. 3–8). The Puritan minister Increase Mather preached in favor of alcohol but against its abuse: "Drink is in itself a good creature of God, and to be received with thankfulness, but the abuse of drink is from Satan; the wine is from God, but the Drunkard is from the Devil" (quoted in Rorabaugh, 1979, p. 30). During that century the first distillery was established in the colonies on what is now Staten Island (Roueche, 1963, p. 178), cultivation of hops began in Massachusetts, and both brewing and distilling were legislatively encouraged in Maryland (Austin, 1985, pp. 230 and 249).

Rum is produced by distilling fermented molasses, which is the residue left after sugar has been made from sugar cane. Although it was introduced to the world, and presumably invented, by the first European settlers in the West Indies, no one knows when it was first produced or by what individual. But by 1657, a rum distillery was operating in Boston. It was highly successful and within a generation the manufacture of rum would become colonial New England's largest and most prosperous industry (Roueche, 1963, p. 178).

The dawn of the eighteenth century saw Parliament pass legislation designed to encourage the use of grain for distilling spirits. In 1685, consumption of gin had been slightly over one-half million gallons (Souria, 1990, p. 20). By 1714, gin production stood at two million gallons (Roueche, 1963, p. 174). In 1727, official (declared and taxed) production reached five million gallons; six years later the London area alone produced eleven million gallons of gin (French, 1890, p. 271; Samuelson, 1878, pp. 160–161; Watney, 1976, p. 16).

The English government actively promoted gin production to utilize surplus grain and to raise revenue. Encouraged by public policy, very cheap spirits flooded the market at a time when there was little stigma attached to drunkenness and when the growing urban poor in London sought relief from the newfound insecurities and harsh realities of urban life (Watney, 1976, p. 17; Austin, 1985, pp. xxi–xxii). Thus developed the so-called Gin Epidemic.

While the negative effects of that phenomenon may have been exaggerated[9] (Sournia, 1990, p. 21; Mathias, 1959, p. xxv), Parliament passed legislation in 1736 to discourage consumption by prohibiting the sale of gin in quantities of less than two gallons and raising the tax on it dramatically.[10] However, the peak in consumption was reached seven years later, when the nation of six and one-half million people drank over 18 million gallons of gin. And most was consumed by the small minority of the population then living in London and other cities; people in the countryside largely remained loyal to beer, ale and cider (Doxat, 1972, pp. 98–100; Watney, 1976, p.17).

After its dramatic peak, gin consumption rapidly declined. From 18 million gallons in 1743, it dropped to just over seven million gallons in 1751 and to less than two million by 1758, and generally declined to the end of the century (Ashton, 1955, p. 243). A number of factors appear to have converged to discourage consumption of gin. These include the production of higher quality beer of lower price, rising corn prices and taxes which eroded the price advantage of gin, a temporary ban on distilling, a stigmatization of drinking gin, an increasing criticism of drunkenness, a newer standard of behavior that criticized coarseness and excess, increased tea and coffee consumption, an increase in piety and increasing industrialization with a consequent emphasis on sobriety and labor efficiency (Sournia, 1990, p. 22; King, 1947, p. 117; Austin, 1985, pp. xxiii–xxiv, 324–325, 351; Younger, 1966, p. 341).

While drunkenness was still an accepted part of life in the eighteenth century (Austin, 1985, p. xxv), the nineteenth century would bring a change in attitudes as a result of increasing industrialization and the need for a reliable and punctual work force (Porter, 1990, p. xii). Self-discipline was needed in place of self-expression, and task orientation had to replace relaxed conviviality. Drunkenness would come to be defined as a threat to industrial efficiency and growth.

Problems commonly associated with industrialization and rapid urbanization were also attributed to alcohol. Thus, problems such as urban crime, poverty and high infant mortality rates were blamed on alcohol, although "it is likely that gross overcrowding and unemployment had much to do with these problems" (Soumia, 1990, p. 21). Over time, more and more personal, social and religious/moral problems would be blamed on alcohol. And not only would it be enough to prevent drunkenness; any consumption of alcohol would come to be seen as unacceptable. Groups that began by promoting temperance—the moderate use of alcohol—would ultimately become abolitionist and press for the complete and total prohibition of the production and distribution of beverage alcohol. Unfortunately, this would not eliminate social problems but would compound the situation by creating additional problems.

Summary and Conclusion

It is clear that alcohol has been highly valued and in continuous use by peoples throughout history. Reflecting its vital role, consumption of alcohol in moderation has rarely been questioned throughout most of recorded time. To the contrary, "Fermented dietary beverage . . . was so common an element in the various cultures that it was taken for granted as one of the basic elements of survival and self-preservation" (Lucia, 1963b, p. 165). Indicative of its value is the fact that it has frequently been acceptable as a medium of exchange. For example, in Medieval England, ale was often used to pay toll, rent or debts (Watney, 1974, p. 16).

From the earliest times alcohol has played an important role in religion,"[11] typically seen as a gift of deities and closely associated with their worship. Religious rejection of alcohol appears to be a rare phenomenon. When it does occur, such rejection may be unrelated to alcohol per se but reflect other considerations. For example, the nomadic Rechabites rejected wine because they associated it with an unacceptable agricultural life style. Nazarites abstained only during the period of their probation, after which they returned to drinking (Sournia, 1990, p. 5; Samuelson, 1878, pp. 62–63). Among other reasons, Mohammed may have forbidden alcohol in order to further distinguish his followers from those of other religions (Royce, 1986, p. 57).

Alcoholic beverages have also been an important source of nutrients and calories (Braudel, 1974, p. 175). In ancient Egypt, the phrase "bread and beer" stood for all food and was also a common greeting. Many alcoholic beverages, such as Egyptian bouza and Sudanese merissa, contain high levels of protein, fat and carbohydrates, a fact that helps explain the frequent lack of nutritional deficiencies in some populations whose diets are generally poor. Importantly, the levels of amino acids and vitamins increase during fermentation

(Ghaliounqui, 1979, pp. 8–9). While modern food technology uses enrichment or fortification to improve the nutrition of foods, it is possible to achieve nutritional enrichment naturally through fermentation (Steinkraus, 1979, p. 36).

Alcoholic beverages have long served as thirst quenchers. Water pollution is far from new; to the contrary, supplies have generally been either unhealthful or questionable at best. Ancient writers rarely wrote about water, except as a warning (Ghaliounqui, 1979, p. 3). Travelers crossing what is now Zaire in 1648 reported having to drink water that resembled horse's urine. In the late eighteenth century most Parisians drank water from a very muddy and often chemically polluted Seine (Braudel, 1967, pp. 159–161). Coffee and tea were not introduced into Europe until the mid-seventeenth century, and it was another hundred or more years before they were commonly consumed on a daily basis (Austin, 1985, pp. 251, 254, 351, 359, 366).

Another important function of alcohol has been therapeutic or medicinal. Current research suggests that the moderate consumption of alcohol is preferable to abstinence. It appears to reduce the incidence of coronary heart disease (e.g., Razay, 1992; Jackson *et al.*, 1991; Klatsky *et al.*, 1990, p. 745; Rimm *et al.*, 1991; Miller *et al.*, 1990), cancer (e.g., Bofetta & Garfinkel, 1990) and osteoporosis (e.g., Gavaler & Van Thiel, 1992), among many other diseases and conditions, and to increase longevity (e.g., DeLabry *et al.*, 1992). It has clearly been a major analgesic, and one widely available to people in pain. Relatedly, it has provided relief from the fatigue of hard labor.

Not to be underestimated is the important role alcohol has served in enhancing the enjoyment and quality of life. It can serve as a social lubricant, can provide entertainment, can facilitate relaxation, can provide pharmacological pleasure and can enhance the flavors of food (Gastineau *et al.*, 1979).

While alcohol has always been misused by a minority of drinkers, it has clearly proved to be beneficial to most. In the words of the founding Director of the National Institute on Alcohol Abuse and Alcoholism, ". . . alcohol has existed longer than all human memory. It has outlived generations, nations, epochs and ages. It is a part of us, and that is fortunate indeed. For although alcohol will always be the master of some, for most of us it will continue to be the servant of man" (Chafetz, 1965, p. 223).

References

Hanson, David J. *Preventing Alcohol Abuse: Alcohol, Culture and Control.* Wesport, CT: Praeger, 1995. www2.potsdam.edu/hansondj/controversies/1114796842.html. Retrieved May 2, 2008

Marley, David. *Chemical Addiction, Drug Use, and Treatment.* MedScape Today 2001 www.medscape.com/viewarticle/418525. Retrieved May 2, 2008

Critical Thinking

1. Why have patterns related to alcohol use remained consistent around the world for centuries?

2. Consider the theme(s) of alcohol use throughout history as presented in this article and describe how alcohol use today relates to those themes.

Adapted from **HANSON J. DAVID,** PhD *Preventing Alcohol Abuse: Alcohol, Culture and Control.* Wesport, CT: Praeger, 1995.

Did Prohibition Really Work?

Alcohol prohibition as a public health innovation.

The conventional view that National Prohibition failed rests upon an historically flimsy base. The successful campaign to enact National Prohibition was the fruit of a century-long temperance campaign, experience of which led prohibitionists to conclude that a nationwide ban on alcohol was the most promising of the many strategies tried thus far. A sharp rise in consumption during the early 20th century seemed to confirm the bankruptcy of alternative alcohol control programs.

The stringent prohibition imposed by the Volstead Act however, represented a more drastic action than many Americans expected. Nevertheless, National Prohibition succeeded both in lowering consumption and in retaining political support until the onset of the Great Depression altered voters' priorities. Repeal resulted more from this contextual shift than from characteristics of the innovation itself.

Jack S. Blocker, Jr., PhD

P robably few gaps between scholarly knowledge and popular conventional wisdom are as wide as the one regarding National Prohibition. "Everyone knows" that Prohibition failed because Americans did not stop drinking following ratification of the Eighteenth Amendment and passage of its enforcement legislation, the Volstead Act. If the question arises why Americans adopted such a futile measure in the first place, the unnatural atmosphere of wartime is cited. Liquor's illegal status furnished the soil in which organized crime flourished. The conclusive proof of Prohibition's failure is, of course, the fact that the Eighteenth Amendment became the only constitutional amendment to be repealed.

Historians have shown, however, that National Prohibition was no fluke, but rather the fruit of a century-long series of temperance movements springing from deep roots in the American reform tradition. Furthermore, Americans were not alone during the first quarter of the 20th century in adopting prohibition on a large scale: other jurisdictions enacting similar measures included Iceland, Finland, Norway, both czarist Russia and the Soviet Union, Canadian provinces, and Canada's federal government.[1] A majority of New Zealand voters twice approved national prohibition but never got it. As a result of 100 years of temperance agitation, the American cultural climate at the time Prohibition went into effect was deeply hostile to alcohol, and this antagonism manifested itself clearly through a wave of successful referenda on statewide prohibition.

Although organized crime flourished under its sway, Prohibition was not responsible for its appearance, as organized crime's post-Repeal persistence has demonstrated. Drinking habits underwent a drastic change during the Prohibition Era, and Prohibition's flattening effect on per capita consumption continued long after Repeal, as did a substantial hard core of popular support for Prohibition's return. Repeal itself became possible in 1933 primarily because of a radically altered economic context—the Great Depression. Nevertheless, the failure of National Prohibition continues to be cited without contradiction in debates over matters ranging from the proper scope of government action to specific issues such as control of other consciousness-altering drugs, smoking, and guns.

We historians collectively are partly to blame for this gap. We simply have not synthesized from disparate studies a compelling alternative to popular perception.[2] Nevertheless, historians are not entirely culpable for prevalent misunderstanding; also responsible are changed cultural attitudes toward drinking, which, ironically. Prohibition itself helped to shape. Thinking of Prohibition as a public health innovation offers a potentially fruitful path toward comprehending both the story of the dry era and the reasons why it continues to be misunderstood.

Temperance Thought before National Prohibition

Although many prohibitionists were motivated by religious faith, American temperance reformers learned from an early point in their movement's history to present their message in ways that would appeal widely to citizens of a society characterized by divergent and clashing scriptural interpretations. Temperance, its advocates promised, would energize political reform, promote community welfare, and improve public health. Prohibitionism, which was inherently political, required even more urgent pressing of such claims for societal improvement.[3] Through local contests in communities across the nation, liquor control in general and Prohibition in particular became the principal stage on which Americans confronted public health issues, long before public health became a field of professional endeavor.

By the beginning of the 20th century, prohibitionists agreed that a powerful liquor industry posed the greatest threat to American society and that only Prohibition could prevent Americans from falling victim to its seductive wiles. These conclusions were neither willful nor arbitrary, as they had been reached after three quarters of a century of experience. Goals short of total abstinence from all that could intoxicate and less coercive means—such as self-help, mutual support, medical treatment, and sober recreation—had been tried and, prohibitionists agreed, had been found wanting.[4]

For prohibitionists, as for other progressives, the only battleground where a meaningful victory might be won was the collective: the community, the state, or the nation. The Anti-Saloon League (ASL), which won leadership of the movement after 1905, was so focused on Prohibition that it did not even require of its members a pledge of personal abstinence. Battles fought on public ground certainly heightened popular awareness of the dangers of alcohol. In the mass media before 1920, John Barleycorn found few friends. Popular fiction, theater, and the new movies rarely represented drinking in positive terms and consistently portrayed drinkers as flawed characters. Most family magazines, and even many daily newspapers, rejected liquor ads.[5] New physiological and epidemiological studies published around the turn of the century portrayed alcohol as a depressant and plausibly associated its use with crime, mental illness, and disease. The American Medical Association went on record in opposition to the use of alcohol for either beverage or therapeutic purposes.[6] But most public discourse on alcohol centered on its social, not individual, effects.[7]

The only significant exception was temperance education in the schools. By 1901, every state required that its schools incorporate "Scientific Temperance Instruction" into the curriculum, and one half of the nation's school districts further mandated use of a textbook that portrayed liquor as invariably an addictive poison. But even as it swept through legislative chambers, the movement to indoctrinate children in temperance ideology failed to carry with it the educators on whose cooperation its success in the classrooms depended; teachers tended to regard Scientific Temperance Instruction as neither scientific nor temperate. After 1906, temperance instruction became subsumed within more general lessons on hygiene, and hygiene classes taught that the greatest threats to health were environmental and the proper responses were correspondingly social, not individual.[8]

By the time large numbers of voters were confronted with a choice whether or not to support a prohibitionist measure or candidate for office, public discourse over alcohol had produced a number of prohibitionist supporters who were not themselves abstainers. That is, they believed that it was a good idea to control someone else's drinking (perhaps everyone else's), but not

their own. A new study of cookbooks and etiquette manuals suggests that this was likely the case for middle-class women, the most eager recruits to the prohibition cause, who were gaining the vote in states where prohibition referenda were boosting the case for National Prohibition. In addition to the considerable alcoholic content of patent medicines, which women and men (and children) were unknowingly ingesting, women were apparently serving liquor in their recipes and with meals. In doing so, they were forging a model of domestic consumption in contrast to the mode of public drinking adopted by men in saloons and clubs.[9]

Self-control lay at the heart of the middle-class self-image, and middle-class prohibitionists simply acted on the prejudices of their class when they voted to close saloons while allowing drinking to continue in settings they considered to be respectable. Some state prohibition laws catered to such sentiments when they prohibited the manufacture and sale of alcoholic beverages, but allowed importation and consumption.[10] A brisk mail-order trade flourished in many dry communities. Before 1913, federal law and judicial decisions in fact prevented states from interfering with the flow of liquor across their borders. When Congress acted in 1913, the Webb–Kenyon Act only forbade importation of liquor into a dry state when such commerce was banned by the law of that state.[11]

Why National Prohibition?

At the beginning of the 20th century, wet and dry forces had reached a stalemate. Only a handful of states maintained statewide prohibition, and enforcement of prohibitory law was lax in some of those. Dry territory expanded through local option, especially in the South, but this did not mean that drinking came to a halt in towns or counties that adopted local prohibition; such laws aimed to stop manufacture or sale (or both), not consumption.[12] During the previous half-century, beer's popularity had soared, surpassing spirits as the principal source of alcohol in American beverages, but, because of beer's lower alcohol content, ethanol consumption per capita had changed hardly at all.[13] Both drinking behavior and the politics of drink, however, changed significantly after the turn of the century when the ASL assumed leadership of the prohibition movement.

Between 1900 and 1913, Americans began to drink more and more. Beer production jumped from 1.2 billion to 2 billion gallons (4.6 billion to 7.6 billion liters), and the volume of tax-paid spirits grew from 97 million to 147 million gallons (367 million to 556 million liters). Per capita consumption of ethanol increased by nearly a third, a significant spike over such a short period of time.[14]

Meanwhile, the area under prohibition steadily expanded as a result of local-option and statewide prohibition campaigns. Between 1907 and 1909, 6 states entered the dry column. By 1912, however, prohibitionist momentum on these fronts slowed, as the liquor industry began a political counteroffensive. In the following year, the ASL, encouraged by congressional submission to its demands in passing the Webb–Kenyon Act, launched a campaign for a prohibition constitutional amendment.

The best explanation for this decision is simply that National Prohibition had long been the movement's goal. The process of constitutional amendment in the same year the ASL launched its campaign both opened the way to a federal income tax an mandated direct election of US senators (the Sixteenth and Seventeenth Amendments), seemed to be the most direct path to that goal.[15] Its supporters expected that the campaign for and amendment would be long and that the interval between achievement of the amendment and their eventual object would also be lengthy. Ultimately, drinkers with entrenched habits would die off, while a new generation would grow up abstinent under the salubrious influence of prohibition.[16] ASL leaders also needed to demonstrate their militance to ward off challenges from intramovement rivals, and the route to a constitutional amendment lay through state and national legislatures, where their method of pressuring candidates promised better results than seeking popular approval through a referendum in every state.[17]

Once the prohibition movement decided to push for a constitutional amendment it had to negotiate the tortuous path to ratification. The fundamental requirement was sufficient popular support to convince federal and state legislators that voting for the amendment would help rather than hurt their electoral chances.

Between 1900 and 1913, Americans began to drink more and more. Beer production jumped from 1.2 billion to 2 billion gallons, and the volume of tax-paid spirits grew from 97 million to 147 million gallons.

The historical context of the Progressive Era provided 4 levers with which that support might be engineered, and prohibitionists manipulated them effectively. First the rise in annual ethanol consumption to 2.6 US gallons (9.8 liters) per capita of the drinking-age population, the highest level since the Civil War, did create a real public health problem.[18] Rates of death diagnosed as caused by liver cirrhosis (15 per 100,000 total population) and chronic alcoholism (10 per 100,000 adult population) were high during the early years of the 20th century.[19]

Second, the political turbulence of the period—a growing socialist movement and bitter struggles between capitalists and workers—made prohibition seem less radical by contrast.[20] Third, popular belief in moral law and material progress, trust in science, support for humanitarian causes and for "uplift" of the disadvantaged, and opposition to "plutocracy" offered opportunities to align prohibitionism with progressivism.[21] Concern for public health formed a central strand of the progressive ethos, and, as one historian notes, "the temperance and prohibition movements can . . . be understood as part of a larger public health and welfare movement active at that time that viewed environmental interventions as an important means of promoting the public health and safety."[22] Finally, after a fleeting moment of unity, the alliance between brewers and distillers

to repel prohibitionist attacks fell apart.[23] The widespread local battles fought over the previous 20 years brought new support to the cause, and the ASL's nonpartisan, balance-of-power method worked effectively.[24]

The wartime atmosphere during the relatively brief period of American participation in World War I played a minor role in bringing on National Prohibition. Anti-German sentiment shamelessly whipped up and exploited by the federal government to rally support for the war effort discredited a key and prohibitionist organization, the German-American Alliance. A federal ban on distilling, adopted to conserve grain, sapped the strength of another major wet player, the spirits industry.[25] But most prohibition victories at the state level and in congressional elections were won before the United States entered the war, and the crucial ratification votes occurred after the war's end.[26]

In sum, although the temperance movement was a century old when the Eighteenth Amendment was adopted, and National Prohibition had been a goal for many prohibitionists for half that long, its achievement came about as a product of a specific milieu. Few reform movements manage to win a constitutional amendment. Nevertheless, that achievement, which seemed at the time so permanent—no constitutional amendment had ever before been repealed—was vulnerable to shifts in the context on which it depended.

Public Health Consequences of Prohibition

We forget too easily that Prohibition wiped out an industry. In 1916, there were 1300 breweries producing full-strength beer in the United States; 10 years later there were none. Over the same period, the number of distilleries was cut by 85%, and most of the survivors produced little but industrial alcohol. Legal production of near beer used less than one tenth the amount of malt, one twelfth the rice and hops, and one thirtieth the corn used to make full-strength beer before National Prohibition. The 318 wineries of 1914 became the 27 of 1925.[27] The number of liquor wholesalers was cut by 96% and the number of legal retailers by 90%. From 1919 to 1929, federal tax revenues from distilled spirits dropped from $365 million to less than $13 million, and revenue from fermented liquors from $117 million to virtually nothing.[28]

The Coors Brewing Company turned to making near beer, porcelain products, and malted milk. Miller and Anheuser-Busch took a similar route.[29] Most breweries, wineries, and distilleries, however, closed their doors forever. Historically, the federal government has played a key role in creating new industries, such as chemicals and aerospace, but very rarely has it acted decisively to shut down an industry.[30] The closing of so many large commercial operations left liquor production, if it were to continue, in the hands of small-scale domestic producers, a dramatic reversal of the normal course of industrialization.

Such industrial and economic devastation was unexpected before the introduction of the Volstead Act, which followed adoption of the Eighteenth Amendment. The amendment forbade the manufacture, transportation, sale, importation, and exportation of "intoxicating" beverages, but without defining the term. The Volstead Act defined "intoxicating" as containing 0.5% or more alcohol by volume, thereby prohibiting virtually all alcoholic drinks. The brewers, who had expected beer of moderate strength to remain legal, were stunned, but their efforts to overturn the definition were unavailing.[31] The act also forbade possession of intoxicating beverages, but included a significant exemption for custody in one's private dwelling for the sole use of the owner, his or her family, and guests. In addition to private consumption, sacramental wine and medicinal liquor were also permitted.

The brewers were probably not the only Americans to be surprised at the severity of the regime thus created. Voters who considered their own drinking habits blameless, but who supported prohibition to discipline others, also received a rude shock. That shock came with the realization that federal prohibition went much farther in the direction of banning personal consumption than all local prohibition ordinances and many state prohibition statutes. National Prohibition turned out to be quite a different beast than its local and state cousins.

Nevertheless, once Prohibition became the law of the land, many citizens decided to obey it. Referendum results in the immediate post-Volstead period showed widespread support, and the Supreme Court quickly fended off challenges to the new law. Death rates from cirrhosis and alcoholism, alcoholic psychosis hospital admissions, and drunkenness arrests all declined steeply during the latter years of the 1910s, when both the cultural and the legal climate were increasingly inhospitable to drink, and in the early years after National Prohibition went into effect. They rose after that, but generally did not reach the peaks recorded during the period 1900 to 1915. After Repeal, when tax data permit better-founded consumption estimates than we have for the Prohibition Era, per capita annual consumption stood at 1.2 US gallons (4.5 liters), less than half the level of the pre-Prohibition period.[32]

Prohibition affected alcoholic beverages differently. Beer consumption dropped precipitously. Distilled spirits made a dramatic comeback in American drinking patterns, reversing a three-quarters-of-a-century decline, although in volume spirits did not reach its pre-Prohibition level. Small-scale domestic producers gave wine its first noticeable, though small, contribution to overall alcohol intake, as wine-grape growers discovered that the Volstead Act failed to ban the production and sale of grape concentrate (sugary pulp that could be rehydrated and fermented to make wine).[33]

Unintended and Unexpected Consequences

Unexpected prosperity for wine-grape growers was not the only unintended consequence of National Prohibition. Before reviewing other unexpected outcomes, however, it is important to list the ways in which National Prohibition did fulfill prohibitionists' expectations. The liquor industry was virtually destroyed, and this created an historic opportunity to socialize rising generations in a lifestyle in which alcohol had no place.

To some degree, such socialization did take place, and the lessened consumption of the Prohibition Era reflects that. Although other forces contributed to its decline, Prohibition finished off the old-time saloon, with its macho culture and links to urban machine politics.[34] To wipe out a long-established and well-entrenched industry, to change drinking habits on a large scale, and to sweep away such a central urban and rural social institution as the saloon are no small achievements.

Nevertheless, prohibitionists did not fully capitalize on their opportunity to bring up a new generation in abstemious habits. Inspired and led by the talented writers of the Lost Generation, the shapers of mass culture—first in novels, then in films, and finally in newspapers and magazines—altered the popular media's previously negative attitude toward drink. In the eyes of many young people, especially the increasing numbers who populated colleges and universities, Prohibition was transformed from progressive reform to an emblem of a suffocating status quo.[35] The intransigence of the dominant wing of the ASL, which insisted on zero tolerance in law enforcement, gave substance to this perception and, in addition, aligned the league with the Ku Klux Klan and other forces promoting intolerance.[36] Thus, the work of attracting new drinkers to alcohol, which had been laid down by the dying liquor industry, was taken up by new hands.

One group of new drinkers—or newly public drinkers—whose emergence in that role was particularly surprising to contemporary observers was women. Such surprise, however, was a product of the prior invisibility of women's domestic consumption: women had in fact never been as abstemious as the Woman's Christian Temperance Union's activism had made them appear.[37] Women's new willingness to drink in public—or at least in the semipublic atmosphere of the speakeasy—owed much to Prohibition's achievement, the death of the saloon, whose masculine culture no longer governed norms of public drinking. The saloon's demise also made it possible for women to band together to oppose Prohibition, as hundreds of thousands did in the Women's Organization for National Prohibition Reform (WONPR).[38]

Public drinking by women and college youth and wet attitudes disseminated by cultural media pushed along a process that social scientists call the "normalization of drinking"—that is, the breakdown of cultural proscriptions against liquor. Normalization, part of the long history of decay in Victorian social mores, began before the Prohibition Era and did not fully bear fruit until long afterward, but the process gained impetus from both the achievements and the failures of National Prohibition.[39]

Other unintended and unexpected consequences of Prohibition included flourishing criminal activity centered on smuggling and bootlegging and the consequent clogging of the courts with drink-related prosecutions.[40] Prohibition also forced federal courts to take on the role of overseer of government regulatory agencies, and the zeal of government agents stimulated new concern for individual rights as opposed to the power of the state.[41] The bans on liquor importation and exportation crippled American ocean liners in the competition for transatlantic passenger service, thus contributing to the ongoing decline of the US merchant marine, and created an irritant in diplomatic relations with Great Britain and Canada.[42] Contrary to politicians' hopes that the Eighteenth Amendment would finally take the liquor issue out of politics, Prohibition continued to boil the political waters even in the presidential seas, helping to carry Herbert Hoover first across the finish line in 1928 and to sink him 4 years later.[43]

Why Repeal?

All prohibitions are coercive, but their effects can vary across populations and banned articles. We have no estimates of the size of the drinking population on the eve of National Prohibition (or on the eve of wartime prohibition, which preceded it by several months), but because of the phenomenon of "drinking drys" it was probably larger than the total of votes cast in referenda against state prohibition measures, and many of the larger states did not even hold such referenda. So Prohibition's implicit goal of teetotalism meant changing the drinking behavior of a substantial number of Americans, possibly a majority.

Because the Volstead Act was drafted only after ratification of the Eighteenth Amendment was completed, neither the congressmen and state legislators who approved submission and ratification, nor the voters who elected them, knew what kind of prohibition they were voting for.[44] The absolutism of the act's definition of intoxicating liquors made national alcohol prohibition a stringent ban, and the gap between what voters thought they were voting for and what they got made this sweeping interdict appear undemocratic. Nevertheless, support for prohibition in post-ratification state referenda and the boost given to Herbert Hoover's 1928 campaign by his dry stance indicate continued electoral approval of Prohibition before the stock-market crash of 1929.

Historians agree that enforcement of the Volstead Act constituted National Prohibition's Achilles' heel. A fatal flaw resided in the amendment's second clause, which mandated "concurrent power" to enforce Prohibition by the federal government and the states. ASL strategists expected that the states' existing criminal-justice machinery would carry out the lion's share of the work of enforcement. Consequently, the league did not insist on creating adequate forces or funding for federal enforcement, thereby avoiding conflict with Southern officials determined to protect states' rights. The concurrent-power provision, however, allowed states to minimize their often politically divisive enforcement activity, and the state prohibition statutes gave wets an obvious target, because repeal of a state law was easier than repeal of a federal law or constitutional amendment, and repeal's success would leave enforcement in the crippled hands of the federal government.[45] Even if enforcement is regarded as a failure, however, it does not follow that such a lapse undermined political support for Prohibition. Depending on the number of drinking drys, the failure of enforcement could have produced the opposite effect, by allowing voters to gain access to alcohol themselves while voting to deny it to others.

Two other possible reasons also fall short of explaining Repeal. The leading antiprohibitionist organization throughout the 1920s was the Association Against the Prohibition Amendment (AAPA), which drew its support mainly from conservative businessmen, who objected to the increased power given to the federal government by National Prohibition. Their well-funded arguments, however, fell on deaf ears among the voters throughout the era, most tellingly in the presidential election of 1928. Both the AAPA and the more widely supported WONPR also focused attention on the lawlessness that Prohibition allegedly fostered. This argument, too, gained little traction in the electoral politics of the 1920s. When American voters changed their minds about Prohibition, the AAPA and WONPR, together with other repeal organizations, played a key role in focusing and channeling sentiment through an innovative path to Repeal, the use of specially elected state conventions.[46] But they did not create that sentiment.

> Thus, the arguments for Repeal that seemed to have greatest resonance with voters in 1932 and 1933 centered not on indulgence but on economic recovery. Repeal, it was argued, would replace the tax revenues foregone under Prohibition, thereby allowing governments to provide relief to suffering families.

Finally, historians are fond of invoking widespread cultural change to explain the failure of National Prohibition. Decaying Victorian social mores allowed the normalization of drinking, which was given a significant boost by the cultural trendsetters of the Jazz Age. In such an atmosphere, Prohibition could not survive.[47] But it did. At the height of the Jazz Age, American voters in a hard-fought contest elected a staunch upholder of Prohibition in Herbert Hoover over Al Smith, an avowed foe of the Eighteenth Amendment. Repeal took place, not in the free-flowing good times of the Jazz Age, but rather in the austere gloom 4 years into America's worst economic depression.

Thus, the arguments for Repeal that seemed to have greatest resonance with voters in 1932 and 1933 centered not on indulgence but on economic recovery. Repeal, it was argued, would replace the tax revenues foregone under Prohibition, thereby allowing governments to provide relief to suffering families.[48] It would put unemployed workers back to work. Prohibitionists had long encouraged voters to believe in a link between Prohibition and prosperity, and after the onset of the Depression they abundantly reaped what they had sown.[49] Voters who had ignored claims that Prohibition excessively centralized power, failed to stop drinking, and fostered crime when they elected the dry Hoover now voted for the wet Franklin Roosevelt. They then turned out to elect delegates pledged to Repeal in the whirlwind series of state conventions that ratified the Twenty-First Amendment, Thus, it was not the stringent nature of National Prohibition, which set a goal that was probably impossible to reach and that thereby foredoomed enforcement, that played the leading role in discrediting alcohol prohibition. Instead, an abrupt and radical shift in context killed Prohibition.

Legacies of Prohibition

The legacies of National Prohibition are too numerous to discuss in detail; besides, so many of them live on today and continue to affect Americans' everyday lives that it is even difficult to realize that they are Prohibition's byproducts. I will briefly mention the principal ones, in ascending order from shortest-lived to longest. The shortest-lived child of Prohibition actually survived to adulthood. This was the change in drinking patterns that depressed the level of consumption compared with the pre-Prohibition years. Straitened family finances during the Depression of course kept the annual per capita consumption rate low, hovering around 1.5 US gallons. The true results of Prohibition's success in socializing Americans in temperate habits became apparent during World War II, when the federal government turned a more cordial face toward the liquor industry than it had during World War I, and they became even more evident during the prosperous years that followed.[50] Although annual consumption rose, to about 2 gallons per capita in the 1950s and 2.4 gallons in the 1960s, it did not surpass the pre-Prohibition peak until the early 1970s.[51]

The death rate from liver cirrhosis followed a corresponding pattern.[52] In 1939, 42% of respondents told pollsters that they did not use alcohol at all. If that figure reflected stability in the proportionate size of the non-drinking population since the pre-Prohibition years, and if new cohorts—youths and women—had begun drinking during Prohibition, then the numbers of new drinkers had been offset by Prohibition's socializing effect. By 1960, the proportion of abstainers had fallen only to 38%.[53]

The Prohibition Era was unkind to habitual drunkards, not because their supply was cut off, but because it was not. Those who wanted liquor badly enough could still find it. But those who recognized their drinking as destructive were not so lucky in finding help. The inebriety asylums had closed, and the self-help societies had withered away. In 1935, these conditions gave birth to a new self-help group, Alcoholics Anonymous (AA), and the approach taken by these innovative reformers, while drawing from the old self-help tradition, was profoundly influenced by the experience of Prohibition.

AA rejected the prohibitionists' claim that anyone could become a slave to alcohol, the fundamental assumption behind the sweeping approach of the Volstead Act. There were several reasons for this decision, but one of the primary ones was a perception that Prohibition had failed and a belief that battles already lost should not be refought. Instead, AA drew a rigid line between normal drinkers, who could keep their consumption within the limits of moderation, and compulsive drinkers, who could not. Thus was born the disease concept of alcoholism. Although the concept's principal aim was to encourage sympathy for alcoholics, its result was to open the door to drinking by everyone else.[54] Influenced by Repeal to reject temperance ideology, medical researchers held the door open by denying previously accepted links between drinking and disease.[55]

Another force energized by Prohibition also promoted drinking: the liquor industry's fear that Prohibition might return. Those fears were not unjustified, because during the late 1930s two fifths of Americans surveyed still supported national Prohibition.[56] Brewers and distillers trod carefully, to be sure, attempting to surround liquor with an aura of "glamour, wealth, and sophistication," rather than evoke the rough culture of the saloon. To target women, whom the industry perceived as the largest group of abstainers, liquor ads customarily placed drinking in a domestic context giving hostesses a central role in dispensing their products.[57] Too much can easily be made of the "cocktail culture" of the 1940s and 1950s, because the drinking population grew only slightly and per capita consumption rose only gradually during those years. The most significant result of the industry's campaign was to lay the foundation for a substantial increase in drinking during the 1960s and 1970s.

By the end of the 20th century, two thirds of the alcohol consumed by Americans was drunk in the home or at private parties.[58] In other words, the model of drinking within a framework of domestic sociability, which had been shaped by women, had largely superseded the style of public drinking men had created in their saloons and clubs.[59] Prohibition helped to bring about this major change in American drinking patterns by killing the saloon, but it also had an indirect influence in the same direction, by way of the state. When Prohibition ended, and experiments in economic regulation—including regulation of alcohol—under the National Recovery Administration were declared unconstitutional, the federal government banished public health concerns from its alcohol policy, which thereafter revolved around economic considerations.[60]

Some states retained their prohibition laws—the last repeal occurring only in 1966—but most created pervasive systems of liquor control that affected drinking in every aspect.[61] Licensing was generally taken out of the hands of localities and put under the control of state administrative bodies, in an attempt to replace the impassioned struggles that had heated local politics since the 19th century with the cool, impersonal processes of bureaucracy. Licensing policy favored outlets selling for off-premise consumption, a category that eventually included grocery stores. With the invention of the aluminum beer can and the spread of home refrigeration after the 1930s, the way was cleared for the home to become the prime drinking site.

Lessons for Other Drug Prohibitions

Perhaps the most powerful legacy of National Prohibition is the widely held belief that it did not work. I agree with other historians who have argued that this belief is false: Prohibition did work in lowering per capita consumption. The lowered level of consumption during the quarter century following Repeal, together with the large minority of abstainers, suggests that Prohibition did socialize or maintain a significant portion of the population in temperate or abstemious habits.[62] That is, it was partly successful as a public health innovation. Its political failure is attributable more to a changing context than to characteristics of the innovation itself.

Today, it is easy to say that the goal of total prohibition was impossible and the means therefore were unnecessarily severe—that, for example, National Prohibition could have survived had the drys been willing to compromise by permitting beer and light wine[63]—but from the perspective of 1913 the rejection of alternate modes of liquor control makes more sense. Furthermore, American voters continued to support Prohibition politically even in its stringent form, at least in national politics, until their economy crashed and forcefully turned their concerns in other directions. Nevertheless, the possibility remains that in 1933 a less restrictive form of Prohibition could have satisfied the economic concerns that drove Repeal while still controlling the use of alcohol in its most dangerous forms.

Scholars have readied no consensus on the implications of National Prohibition for other forms of prohibition, and public discourse in the United States mirrors our collective ambivalence.[64] Arguments that assume that Prohibition was a failure have been deployed most effectively against laws prohibiting tobacco and guns, but they have been ignored by those waging the war on other drugs since the 1980s, which is directed toward the same teetotal goal as National Prohibition.[65] Simplistic assumptions about government's ability to legislate morals, whether pro or con, find no support in the historical record. As historian Ian Tyrell writes, "each drug subject to restrictions needs to be carefully investigated in terms of its conditions of production, its value to an illicit trade, the ability to conceal the substance, and its effects on both the individual and society at large."[66] From a historical perspective, no prediction is certain, and no path is forever barred—not even the return of alcohol prohibition in some form. Historical context matters.

References

1. Esa Österberg, "Finland," in *Alcohol and Temperance in Modern History: An International Encyclopedia*, vol 1, ed. Jack S. Blocker Jr, David M. Fahey, and Ian R. Tyrrell (Santa Barbara, Calif: ABC-Clio, 2003). 240–243: Sturla Nordlund, "Norway," in *Alcohol and Temperance in Modern History*, vol 2, 458–463: William Lahey, "Provincial Prohibition (Canada), in *Alcohol and Temperance in Modern History*, vol 2, 496–499: Daniel J. Malleck, "Federal Prohibition (Canada)," in *Alcohol and Temperance in Modern History*, vol 1, 229: Laura L. Phillips, *Bolsheviks and the Bottle: Drink and Worker Culture in St. Petersburg. 1900–1920* (Dekalb: Northern Illinois University Press, 2000).

2. Thomas R. Pegram, *Battling Demon Rum: The Struggle for a Dry America. 1800–1933* (Chicago: Ivan R. Dee, 1998): Jack S. Blocker Jr, *American Temperance Movements: Cycles of Reform* (Boston: Twayne, 1989), 106–129: W. J. Rorabaugh, "Reexamining the Prohibition Amendment," *Yale Journal of Law and the Humanities* 8 (1996): 285–294; Ian Tyrrell, "The US Prohibition Experiment: Myths, History and Implications," *Addiction* 92 (1997): 1405–1409.

3. Ian R. Tyrrell, *Sobering Up: From Temperance to Prohibition in Antebellum America. 1800–1860* (Westport, Conn: Greenwood Press, 1979), 89–90 and passim: Jack S. Blocker Jr, *Retreat from Reform the Prohibition Movement in the United States, 1890–1913* (Westport, Conn: Greenwood Press, 1976), 83; Blocker, *American Temperance Movements*, 24–25; Edward J. Wheeler, *Prohibition: The Principle, the Policy, and the Party* (New York: Funk & Wagnalls, 1889), 39–49, 57–66.

4. Blocker, *American Temperance Movements*, 21–27, 69–70; Tyrrell, *Sobering Up*, 135–145, 227–245; K. Austin Kerr, *Organized for Prohibition: A New History of the Anti-Saloon League* (New Haven, Conn: Yale University Press, 1985), 35–138; Anne-Marie E. Szymanski, *Pathways to Prohibition: Radicals, Moderates, and Social Movement Outcomes* (Durham, NC: Duke University Press, 2003); Sarah W. Tracy, *Alcoholism in America: From Reconstruction to Prohibition* (Baltimore, Md: Johns Hopkins University Press, 2005).

5. Joan L. Silverman, "I'll Never Touch Another Drop": *Images of Alcohol and Temperance in American Popular Culture, 1874–1919* [PhD dissertation] (New York: New York University, 1979), 338–340, and "The Birth of a Nation: Prohibition Propaganda," *Southern Quarterly* 19 (1981): 23–30.

6. James H. Timberlake, *Prohibition and the Progressive Movement, 1900–1920* (Cambridge. Mass: Harvard University Press, 1963). 39–66, Denise Herd, "Ideology, History and Changing Models of Liver Cirrhosis Epidemiology," *British Journal of Addiction* 87 (1992): 1113–1126; Brian S. Katcher, "The Post-Repeal Eclipse in Knowledge About the Harmful Effects of Alcohol," *Addiction* 88 (June 1993): 729–744.

7. Harry Gene Levine, "The Discovery of Addiction: Changing Conceptions of Habitual Drunkenness in America," *Journal of Studies on Alcohol* 39 (January 1978): 161–162.

8. Jonathan Zimmerman, *Distilling Democracy: Alcohol Education in America's Public Schools, 1880–1925* (Lawrence: University Press of Kansas, 1999).

9. Catherine Gilbert Murdock, *Domesticating Drink: Women, Men, and Alcohol in America, 1870–1940* (Baltimore: Johns Hopkins University Press, 1998). For studies of saloon culture, see Madelon Powers, *Faces Along the Bar: Lore and Order in the Workingman's Saloon, 1870–1920* (Chicago: University of Chicago Press, 1998); Craig Heron, *Booze: A Distilled History* (Toronto: Between the Lines, 2003), 105–121; Perry Duis, *The Saloon: Public Drinking in Chicago and Boston, 1880–1920* (Urbana: University of Illinois Press, 1983), 172–197; Elaine Frantz Parsons, *Manhood Lost: Fallen Drunkards and Redeeming Women in the 19th-century United States* (Baltimore: Johns Hopkins University Press, 2003).

10. Local option, through which many areas in states lacking prohibition statutes were rendered "dry," of course affected only the sale of liquor within the local jurisdiction; it could not, nor did it attempt to, prevent local drinkers from importing alcohol from wet areas, either by bringing it themselves or through mail order. Pegram, *Battling Demon Rum*, 141–142.

11. Richard F. Hamm, *Shaping the Eighteenth Amendment: Temperance Reform, Legal Culture, and the Polity, 1880–1920* (Chapel Hill: University of North Carolina Press, 1995), 56–91, 212–226.

12. Szymanski, *Pathways to Prohibition*, 100–121, 131–140.

13. Jack S. Blocker Jr, "Consumption and Availability of Alcoholic Beverages in the United States, 1863–1920," *Contemporary Drug Problems* 21(1994): 631–666.

14. Ibid.

15. David E. Kyvig, *Explicit and Authentic Acts: Amending the US Constitution, 1776–1995* (Lawrence: University Press of Kansas, 1996), 216–218. Creation of a national income tax also provided an alternative source of revenue for the federal government, thereby freeing Congress from reliance on liquor excise taxes. Donald J. Boudreaux and A. C. Pritchard, "The Price of Prohibition," *Arizona Law Review* 10 (1994): 1–10.

16. Kerr, *Organized for Prohibition*, 139–147.

17. Blocker, *Retreat From Reform*, 228; Kerr, *Organized for Prohibition*, 140–141; Thomas R. Pegram, "Prohibition," in *The American Congress: The Building of Democracy*, ed. Julian E. Zelizer (Boston: Houghton Mifflin, 2004), 411–427.

18. National Institute for Alcohol Abuse and Alcoholism (NIAAA), "Apparent per Capita Ethanol Consumption for the United States, 1850–2000," available at www.niaaa .nih.gov/databases/consum01.htm, accessed August 2004; Blocker, "Consumption and Availability," 652. All statistics

given in this article for per capita consumption are for US gallons of ethanol per capita of population 15 years of age and older prior to 1970 and population 14 years of age and older thereafter.

19. Angela K. Dills and Jeffrey A. Miron, "Alcohol Prohibition and Cirrhosis," *American Law and Economics Review* 6 (2004): 285–318, esp. Figure 3; E. M. Jellinek, "Recent Trends in Alcoholism and in Alcohol Consumption," *Quarterly Journal of Studies on Alcohol*, 8 (1947): 40.

20. Blocker, *American Temperance Movements*, 117.

21. Timberlake, *Prohibition and the Progressive Movement*.

22. Robert G. LaForge, *Misplaced Priorities: A History of Federal Alcohol Regulation and Public Health Policy* [PhD dissertation] (Baltimore: Johns Hopkins University, 1987), 56.

23. Kerr, *Organized for Prohibition*, 181–184.

24. Szymanski, *Pathways to Prohibition*, LaForge, *Misplaced Priorities*; Kerr, *Organized for Prohibition*, 181–184.

25. Pegram, *Battling Demon Rum*, 144–147.

26. Blocker, *American Temperance Movements*, 118; Kyvig, *Explicit and Authentic Acts*, 224.

27. *Statistical Abstract of the United States: 1928* (Washington, DC: US Bureau of the Census, 1928), 767.

28. *Statistics Concerning Intoxicating Liquors* (Washington, DC: Bureau of Industrial Alcohol, US Treasury Department, 1930), 3, 60, 64, 72.

29. William H. Mulligan Jr, "Coors, Adolph, Brewing Company," in *Alcohol and Temperance in Modern History*, vol 1, 174; Mulligan, "Miller Brewing Company," in *Alcohol and Temperance in Modern History*, vol 2. 418; Amy Mittelman, "Anheuser-Busch," in *Alcohol and Temperance in Modern History*, vol 1, 43–45.

30. Even the death of slavery, although it put an end to the domestic slave trade, did not hinder cotton culture.

31. Pegram, *Battling Demon Rum*, 149.

32. Jeffrey A. Miron and Jeffrey Zwiebel, "Alcohol Consumption During Prohibition," *American Economic Review* 81 (1991): 242–247; Dills and Miron, "Alcohol Prohibition and Cirrhosis"; NIAAA, "Apparent per Capita Ethanol Consumption." The figure is for 1935.

33. John R. Meers, "The California Wine and Grape Industry and Prohibition," *California Historical Society Quarterly* 46 (1967): 19–32.

34. Norman H. Clark, *Deliver Us from Evil: An Interpretation of American Prohibition* (New York: W. W. Norton, 1976), 143–146; Powers, *Faces Along the Bar*, 234–236; Duis, *The Saloon* 274–303; Pegram, *Battling Demon Rum*, 163.

35. Robin Room, "'A Reverence for Strong Drink': The Lost Generation and the Elevation of Alcohol in American Culture," *Journal of Studies on Alcohol* 45 (1984): 540–546; John C. Burnham, *Bad Habits: Drinking, Smoking, Taking Drugs, Gambling, Sexual Misbehavior, and Swearing in American History* (New York: New York University Press, 1993), 34–38; Paula Fass, *The Damned and the Beautiful: American Youth in the 1920's* (New York: Oxford University Press, 1977); Murdock, *Domesticating Drink*, 93–94.

36. Thomas R. Pegram, "Kluxing the Eighteenth Amendment: The Anti-Saloon League, the Ku Klux Klan, and the Fate of Prohibition in the 1920s," in *American Public Life and the Historical Imagination*, ed. Wendy Gamber, Michael Grossberg, and Hendrik Hartog (Notre Dame, Ind: University of Notre Dame Press, 2003), 240–261.

37. Murdock, *Domesticating Drink*.

38. Ibid, 134–158; Kenneth D. Rose, *American Women and the Repeal of Prohibition* (New York: New York University Press, 1996).

39. Burnham, *Bad Habits*, 34–49; Room, "A Reverence for Strong Drink": Room, "The Movies and the Wettening of America: The Media as Amplifiers of Cultural Change," *British Journal of Addiction* 83 (1988): 11–18; David E. Kyvig, *Repealing National Prohibition* (Chicago: University of Chicago Press, 1979), 28–29.

40. Andrew Sinclair, *Prohibition: The Era of Excess* (New York: Harper & Row, 1962), 211–212, 220–230; Kyvig, *Repealing National Inhibition*, 30.

41. Paul L. Murphy, "Societal Morality and Individual Freedom," in *Law, Alcohol, and Order: Perspectives on National Prohibition*, ed. David E. Kyvig (Westport, Conn: Greenwood Press, 1985), 67–80; Rayman L. Solomon, "Regulating the Regulators: Prohibition Enforcement in the Seventh Circuit," in *Law, Alcohol, and Order*, 81–96.

42. Lawrence Spinelli, *Dry Diplomacy: The United States, Great Britain, and Prohibition* (Wilmington, Del: Scholarly Resources, 1989).

43. Kyvig, *Repealing National Prohibition*, 147–168; Alan P. Grimes, *Democracy and the Amendments to the Constitution* (Lexington, Mass: Lexington Books, 1978), 109–112.

44. Kerr, *Organized for Prohibition*, 222.

45. Hamm, *Shaping the Eighteenth Amendment*, 266–269; Pegram, *Battling Demon Rum*, 156–160.

46. Kyvig, *Repealing National Prohibition*.

47. Kerr, *Organized for Prohibition*, 279; Hamm, *Shaping the Eighteenth Amendment*, 269; Pegram, *Battling Demon Rum*, 175–176.

48. Boudreaux and Pritchard, "Price of Prohibition," 5–10.

49. Sinclair, *Prohibition*, 387–399.

50. Jay L. Rubin, "The Wet War: American Liquor Control, 1941–1945," in *Alcohol, Reform and Society: The Liquor Issue in Social Context*, ed. Jack S. Blocker Jr (Westport, Conn: Greenwood Press, 1979), 235–258.

51. NIAAA, "Apparent per Capita Ethanol Consumption."

52. Dills and Miron, "Alcohol Prohibition and Cirrhosis," Figure 3.

53. Blocker, *American Temperance Movements*, 138. The United States continues to be distinguished among societies where temperance ideology was once influential by its high proportion of abstainers. Michael H. Hilton, "Trends in US Drinking Patterns: Further Evidence From the Past 20 Years," *British Journal of Addiction* 83 (1988): 269–278; Klaus Mäkelä, Robin Room, Eric Single, Pekka Sulkunen, and Brendan Walsh, *A Comparative Study of Alcohol Control*, vol 1 of Alcohol, Society, and the State (Toronto: Addiction Research Foundation, 1981), 21–24.

54. Ernest Kurtz, *Not-God: A History of Alcoholics Anonymous*, rev ed (Center City, Minn: Hazelden, 1991); Bruce H. Johnson, *The Alcoholism Movement in America: A Study in Cultural Innovation* [PhD dissertation] (University of Illinois at Urbana-Champaign, 1973); Blocker, *American Temperance Movements*, 139–154.

55. Herd, "Ideology, History and Changing Models of Liver Cirrhosis Epidemiology"; Katcher, "Post-Repeal Eclipse in Knowledge"; Philip J. Pauly, "How Did the Effects of Alcohol on Reproduction Become Scientifically Uninteresting?" *Journal of the History of Biology* 29 (1996): 1–28.

56. Blocker, *American Temperance Movements*, 136.

57. Cheryl Krasnick Warsh, "Smoke and Mirrors: Gender Representation in North American Tobacco and Alcohol Advertisements Before 1950," *Histoire sociale/Social History* 31 (1998): 183–222 (quote from p. 220); Lori Rotskoff, *Love on the Rocks: Men, Women, and Alcohol in Post-World War II America* (Chapel Hill: University of North Carolina Press, 2002), 194–210; Burnham, *Bad Habits*, 47.

58. Stephen R Byers, "Home, as Drinking Site," in *Alcohol and Temperance in Modern History*, vol 1, 296.

59. Murdock, *Domesticating Drink*.

60. LaForge, *Misplaced Priorities*.

61. Harry Gene Levine, "The Birth of American Alcohol Control: Prohibition, the Power Elite, and the Problem of Lawlessness," *Contemporary Drug Problems* 12 (1985): 63–115; David Fogarty. "From Saloon to Supermarket: Packaged Beer and the Reshaping of the US Brewing Industry," *Contemporary Drug Problems* 12 (1985): 541–592.

62. John C. Burnham, "New Perspectives on the Prohibition 'Experiment' of the 1920's," *Journal of Social History* 2 (1968): 51–68; Clark, *Deliver Us From Evil*, 145–158; Kerr, *Organizing for Prohibition*. 276–277; Tyrrell, "US Prohibition Experiment," 1406.

63. Murdock, *Domesticating Drink*, 170.

64. Burnham, *Bad Habits*, 293–297; Jeffrey A. Miron, "An Economic Analysis of Alcohol Prohibition," *Journal of Drug Issues* 28 (1998): 741–762; Harry G. Levine and Craig Reinarman, "From Prohibition to Regulation: Lessons From Alcohol Policy to Drug Policy," *Milbank Quarterly* 69 (1991): 461–494.

65. James A. Morone, *Hellfire Nation: The Politics of Sin in American History* (New Haven, Conn: Yale University Press, 2003), 343.

66. Tyrrell, "US Prohibition Experiment" 1407; Robin Room, "Alcohol Control and Public Health," *Annual Review of Public Health* 5 (1984): 293–317.

Critical Thinking

1. Describe the evolution of prohibition in the U.S., and explain how it succeeded and failed.

2. How does the concept of prohibition apply today?

The author is with the Department of History, Huron University College, University of Western Ontario, London, Ontario.

Requests for reprints should be sent to **JACK S. BLOCKER,** Jr, PhD, Huron University College, 1349 Western Road, London. Ontario N6G 1H3 Canada (e–mail: jblocker@uwo.ca).

Acknowledgments—Tom Pegram and Ted Brown provided helpful comments on an earlier version of the article.

Tackling Top Teen Problem— Prescription Drugs

"Taking prescription drugs makes you feel 'chill'," a teenager recently told the Bulletin, "and nothing worries you."

GEORGE LAUBY AND KAMIE WHEELOCK

Many people ages 11 to 18 routinely take pills such as Vicodin, Percocet, Xanax, Klonopin, Adderal, Concerta, Ritalin or generic knockoffs of the same.

The illegal use of prescription drugs looms larger than problem drinking or marijuana use, North Platte High School Principal Jim Whitney said.

The drugs are stolen from medicine cabinets, parents' or grandparents' medicine cabinets, or from a friend's house, or even bought off the Internet.

Drugs are passed to friends, either for free or for money. Some pills are reportedly taken by the handful at so-called "pharma parties" where pills are reportedly dumped in a bowl for anyone and everyone, and chased down with beers.

"You are just messed up," a student said of the effects. "You don't even want to move. You just want to lay there and stare off into space."

"Prescription drug abuse has been around in different forms for a long time," Whitney said, "but in the last year and a half it has probably become more popular than alcohol."

In a 2007 Lincoln County survey, 12–14 percent of high school students said they had abused prescription drugs. The same survey found more than 3 percent of sixth graders abused the drugs, and more than 5 percent of eighth graders.

The number who get caught is much lower. Only 12 students have been caught with illegal prescription drugs this year at the high school, Whitney said. Nearly all of them were suspended.

Kids steal drugs not just to chill, but to sell. Many pills bring from $2–5 each. Oxycontin can bring $40 each, according to a high school user who asked to remain anonymous.

"Have you ever attended a pharma or pill party?" we asked the student.

"I wouldn't call them pill parties," she said, "but at pretty much any party there's someone who has pills, or is on pills. Recently a couple of people had some Adderal and we were snorting it. Adderal is popular because it makes it so you can drink more and you can stay up all night long."

Adderal is an amphetamine usually prescribed to treat attention deficit hyperactivity.

Taking the Call

The growing problem prompted a group of North Platte residents to fight back. Listeners are hearing hundreds of radio announcements on virtually every North Platte radio station, alerting the public to the problem.

The group has distributed thousands of pamphlets, bundles of posters and dozens of banners.

They have set a day—April 25—aside to collect prescription drugs, including syringes and over-the-counter drugs. They will set up a drive-up drop point at the high school.

The drugs will ultimately be incinerated.

They have lined up a team of powerful speakers who will talk about the danger, the self-destruction that comes with drug abuse.

The group of residents joined together during the Leadership Lincoln County program, wherein 20 people spend a year learning about major businesses and public services so they can get good things done.

In one part of the leadership program, the 20 split into groups of 5–6 people. Each group was challenged to develop a public project that will continue into the future.

The group–Wendy Thompson, Wanda Cooper, Sandy Ross, Bob Lantis, Patrick O'Neil and Connie Cook— kicked around ideas. After a visit with law enforcement officials they agreed to tackle the prescription drug problem at the urging of Capt. Jim Parish of the Nebraska State Patrol.

"The more we learned, the more we got involved," said Cook, a driving force in the project. "The information was riveting— and motivating. We learned about some kids at high school who got in trouble. Their parents were completely shocked. We were shocked. We had no idea."

"Now, we're passionate to do something constructive," Cook said. "It's amazing; every day we learn more and more."

"Have you taken other drugs?" the Bulletin asked another student.

"Yeah. I smoke weed like every day and used ecstasy once and I dabbled in coke for a couple of months last year and still do it every once in awhile," he said.

"I tried meth twice, but it made me crazy. I don't want to ever do very much of it; it's bad stuff. I've done mushrooms a couple times too, and of course alcohol is a drug too."

"I'm out of my alcoholic phase but I still drink on the weekends," he said. "I won't buy any drug except weed or alcohol but if someone's offering, I'll do pretty much anything. I'll never do heroin though, but I want to try acid in a few years just to see what it's like."

"Do a lot of your friends take pills?"

"Yeah, pretty much all of them. I have five friends that always have them. They take them pretty much every day."

"What do they think of it?"

"It's not considered a bad thing to do. Pills are the equivalent of smoking weed for people who can't smoke because they are on probation or just don't like pot. Like, the preppy kids do it because their parents would know if they smoked pot because they'd smell it. But most parents have no idea that their kids are getting messed up on pills."

Leadership Is Learning

The leadership group recently dropped posters and flyers at all of Lincoln County's schools, plus Stapleton.

At North Platte's middle schools, they asked the principals if they have caught kids using prescription drugs.

"They told us, 'As far as catching them, no, we've not caught them yet, but we know there are kids here who are stealing drugs so they can sell them to other kids," Cook said.

"We want this information out to the public," she said. "We know there is a need to educate those who are all the way from 101 years old to 10 years old. They need to know it's happening and how bad it is for kids, and the environment."

Cook said kids don't understand the dangers.

"What do you take the most?" we asked a North Platte high school student.

"I started out taking Xanax because I got as many as I wanted, for free. Then I had some Percocet. I loved those but they're too addictive to take for a long time. Most people take pain pills (Vicodin/Percocet), anxiety pills (Xanax/Klonopin), or attention deficit disorder pills (Adderal/Concerta/Ritalin)."

"How much would a kid spend on drugs in an average week?"

"People always gave them to me for free, but the average pill popper could probably spend $50–100 a week. The preppies can spend a lot from their lunch-gas-pocket money."

Harm to Creatures Large and Small

Even when the drugs are thrown away, they are usually flushed down the toilet.

Even when drugs are taken properly, traces enter the waste stream that eventually empties into nature, according to the Environmental Protection Agency.

The EPA is becoming more concerned. A study in Boulder, Colo. found female sucker fish outnumber males 5 to 1, and 50 percent of the males have female sex indicators, apparently from estrogen traces from pills for women.

Near Dallas, tiny amounts of Prozac have been found in the livers and brain cells of channel catfish and crappie.

Lots of Help

As part of the leadership project, Cook addressed the Lincoln County noon Rotary in mid-March. She cited national reports that the use of Oxycontin increased by 30 percent in one year—2007—among high school seniors. And she said one out of 10 high school seniors that year used Vicodin illegally.

Eighty-one percent of teens who abuse prescription or over-the-counter drugs combine them with alcohol, the national study said.

Hospital emergency room visits involving such drugs increased 21 percent in 2008. Nearly half of those visits were from patients 12 to 20 years old.

The number of teens going into drug treatment has increased 300 percent in the last 10 years.

As Cook painted the alarming picture of abuse and incapacitation, community members offered to help. So far, 24 individuals and businesses have stepped up to sponsor the local education and collection effort.

"The support is overwhelming," Cook said.

The Language of Pharming

Big boys, cotton, kicker–Various slang for prescription pain relievers.

Chill pills, french fries, tranqs–Various slang for prescription sedatives and tranquilizers.

Pharming (pronounced "farming")–From the word pharmaceutical. It means kids getting high by raiding their parents' medicine cabinets for prescription drugs.

Pharm parties–Parties where teens bring prescription drugs from home, mix them together into a big bowl (see 'trail mix'), and grab a handful. Not surprisingly, pharm parties are usually arranged while parents are out.

Pilz (pronounced pills)–A popular term used to describe prescription medications. Can also include over-the-counter medications.

Recipe–Prescription drugs mixed with alcoholic or other beverages.

Trail mix–A mixture of various prescription drugs, usually served in a big bag or bowl at pharm parties.

"We heard you got into serious medical trouble once from taking too many drugs. Why didn't that stop you from taking more?" we asked a student.

"Well, I know I won't ever take that many again, and it did stop me for the most part. I was getting messed up every day. After that I didn't touch a pill for months. I switched to coke for a couple months, then pot when the person that always gave me coke got sent to rehab."

Featured Speaker—Former Abuser

Former Husker football All-American Jason Peter will speak to the public at the end of the drug collection day, April 25.

Peter, one of the nation's best defensive linemen in 1997, graduated from Nebraska and went to the NFL, where he earned $6.5 million from the Carolina Panthers. But he blew most of the money on illegal drugs, taking up to 80 pain killers a day.

Jason Peter's life finally crashed. A series of injuries took him off the NFL roster.

He managed to clean up and wrote a book, "Heros of the Underground" and now hosts an ESPN talk show from his hometown of Lincoln. He spends his spare time traveling, talking about the dangers of drug abuse.

"Prescription drugs are a lot more addictive than people realize," another North Platte student told the Bulletin.

"You can get into big-time trouble," he said. "Possession of a controlled substance is a felony. They can even charge you for each pill in your possession. If they think

you're selling them you get possession of a controlled substance with intent to distribute, which is prison time."

National Obsession

"Our national pastime—self-destruction," writer Jerry Stahl said in a review of Jason Peter's book.

"We are a nation obsessed with pharmaceuticals," Cook said as she addressed the Rotary. "We spend vast sums to manage our health, and we pop pills to address every conceivable symptom. In this nation, we abuse prescription drugs . . . daily."

Persons 65 and older take one-third of all prescribed medications even though they comprise 13 percent of the population, Cook said. Older patients are more likely to have multiple prescriptions, which can lead to unintentional misuse, more drugs stored in medicine cabinets for kids to steal.

The leadership group advises to keep medicine containers closed, even locked. Keep a record of prescriptions and the amount on hand. Reinforce a message of caution and restraint to your children. Start early, long before adolescence. Build a solid foundation for resisting temptations and outside influences.

North Platte Therapist: Most Clients Abuse Prescriptions

Young people steal grandma's pills and distribute them at school. Senior citizens falsify prescriptions for more pain medication. Babysitters take pills from cabinets.

An Ohio real estate agent lost her license for pilfering pills from bathrooms at open houses.

The appeal is obvious—the drugs can be legally obtained, the stigma of going to a street pusher can be avoided, and the price isn't steep.

There are an estimated 800,000 web sites which sell prescription drugs on the Internet and will ship them to households no questions asked.

Today, about one-third of all U.S. drug abuse is prescription drug abuse.

Approximately 1.9 million persons age 12 or older have used Oxycontin (pain reliever, like morphine) nonmedically at least once in their lifetime, according to Columbia University's National Center on Addiction and Substance Abuse.

Vicki Dugger, a therapist with New Beginnings Therapy Associates in North Platte, said about 75 percent of the patients she treats admitted abusing prescription drugs.

Dugger said many more people are aware of it today than in the 1980s and 1990s. Still, much more awareness is needed.

"There's a misconception that abusing prescription medication is not harmful," Dugger said. "The fact is, it can have deadly results."

Dugger said. kids have died after attending pharming parties. She has some tips for parents to help keep their teenagers safe:

- Consider your own drug behavior and the message you are sending.
- Do a drug inventory. Forgotten or expired prescriptions or leftover over-the-counter meds could be appealing to kids, so get rid of them. Put new drugs away.
- Reach out and have a discussion. Dugger said research showed that kids who learn a lot about drug risks from their parents are up to half as likely to use drugs as kids who haven't had that conversation from mom and dad.
- Look on the computer. Try conducting your own web search to see how easily one can buy prescription meds without a prescription.
- Watch for warning signs. These may include unexplained disappearance of meds from medicine cabinets, declining grades, loss of interest in activities, changes in friends and behaviors, disrupted sleeping or eating patterns and more.

Dugger said she recently had a mother of a teen ask her about all the Musinex boxes around her house.

Musinex is a medication that is used for temporary relief of coughs caused by certain respiratory tract infections but teens have been known to abuse it by taking more than the recommended amounts to get high.

Dugger said she advised the mother to have a conversation with her teen immediately.

Critical Thinking

1. Do you see an abuse of prescription drugs among your friends or fellow classmates? How will you know when abuse exists?

2. What, in your opinion, needs to take place in the wider society to lessen dependency and prevent the abuse of prescription drugs?

The entire Bulletin staff contributed to this report. It was first published April 1 in the Bulletin print edition.

Smoking, Drugs, Obesity Top Health Concerns for Kids

It's only natural for adults to worry about children's health and well-being at school, on the roads and even online.

But adults' No. 1 health concern for children and adolescents in the United States? It's smoking, according to new results from the University of Michigan C.S. Mott Children's Hospital National Poll on Children's Health. Drug abuse ranked No. 2.

The poll, which asked adults to rate 17 different health problems for children living in their communities, also found that childhood obesity now ranks among the public's top three concerns for children's health, ahead of alcohol abuse and teen pregnancy.

Also making the public's overall list of top 10 health concerns for kids: Driving accidents, Internet safety, school violence, sexually transmitted infections, and abuse and neglect. The child health issues that didn't make the top 10 list, but were still rated as "big problems" by 6 to 18 percent of adults: Psychological stress, depression, eating disorders, suicide, autism, childhood cancer and food contamination.

"We found that major race/ethnicity groups differ when it comes to the top three health concerns for children as well. While white adults list smoking, drug abuse and alcohol abuse at their top three concerns, black adults rate teen pregnancy, smoking and drug abuse, and Hispanic adults rank smoking, drug abuse and childhood obesity as the three major health problems for children," says Matthew M. Davis, MD, MAPP, director of the National Poll on Children's Health, part of the U-M Department of Pediatrics and Communicable Diseases and the Child Health Evaluation and Research (CHEAR) Unit in the U-M Division of General Pediatrics.

To rank the public's top health concerns for children, the National Poll on Children's Health, in collaboration with Knowledge Networks, Inc., conducted a national online survey in March 2007. The survey, administered to a random sample of 2,076 adults who are a part of Knowledge Network's online KnowledgePanelSM, revealed the top 10 out of 17 health concerns for children in the U.S.

Top 10 Overall Health Concerns for Children in the U.S.

1. Smoking. Forty percent of adults rate smoking as their top health concern for children. Among black adults, smoking ranks No. 2. Forty-five percent of black adults, however, rate smoking as a big problem.

2. Drug abuse. Adults are more likely to rate drug abuse as a concern based on their children's emotional health. Those who report their child's emotional health as "good," "fair" or "poor" are more likely to view drug abuse as a major health problem for children compared with parents who rate their child's emotional health as "excellent" or "very good."

3. Childhood obesity. According to poll results, adults with higher education are more likely to rate childhood obesity as their No. 1 health issue for children than adults with high school education or less. In fact, 40 percent of adults with a college degree view obesity as a top concern, while those with less than a high school education rate it as their No. 10 concern, with 25 percent reporting it as a top concern. The National Poll on Children's Health also found Hispanic adults are more likely to report obesity as a problem, with 42 percent viewing it as a major problem, compared with only 31 percent of white adults and 36 percent of black adults. "These differences somewhat reflect the higher prevalence of obesity among black and Hispanic youth compared with white youth," notes Davis.

4. Alcohol abuse. "Households with lower incomes less than $30,000 per year are significantly more likely to rate alcohol abuse as a problem than families with higher annual incomes," says Davis. "We also found that alcohol abuse by teens was a bigger concern in households with a single or divorced parent, compared with households with married parents."

5. Motor vehicle accidents. Driving accidents involving teenagers are a universal concern across all socioeconomic groups studied, says Davis.

6. Teen pregnancy. Black adults rate teen pregnancy as the No. 1 health problem for youth, with 51 percent reporting it's a major health concern compared with only 25 percent of white adults. "This difference echoes differences in rates of teen pregnancy by race/ethnicity, which have declined among all teens over the past decade, but remain two times higher among blacks than whites," says Davis.

7. Internet safety. "Internet safety is a relatively new health concern in relation to other health issues," says Davis. "Women and black adults are more likely to report it as a major concern." Thirty-two percent of women and

21 percent of men report they are concerned about Internet safety, while 37 percent of black adults and 25 percent of white adults say it is a big problem.

8. School violence. "School violence didn't rate as high as driving accidents and alcohol use. Yet it still is in the top 10, and that speaks to the current level of concern in the U.S. about this problem," says Davis. "We measured school violence concerns before the recent tragedy at Virginia Tech, so it is likely that it may rank higher today than it did just a few weeks ago." Davis also notes that black adults are more than twice as likely as white adults to report school violence as a big problem, ranking it their No. 4 health concern. It also was viewed as a bigger health problem among lower income households.

9. Sexually transmitted infections. Sexually transmitted infections among youth are considered to be a bigger problem by black adults and Hispanics, with 40 percent of black adults and 34 percent of Hispanics adults viewing it as a big problem, compared with only 20 percent of white adults. Households with lower incomes also rate sexually transmitted infections as a greater health concern for children.

10. Abuse and neglect. About 22 percent of survey respondents view abuse and neglect as a health concern for children. "Similar to other health issues in the poll, more black respondents feel abuse and neglect is a big health concern than among Hispanic and white respondents," says Davis.

Ratings for the top 10 list did not differ between adults who have children in their households, and those who do not. Overall, higher proportions of blacks and Hispanic adults rated all 17 concerns as "big problems" compared with white adults.

"This poll provides us with a detailed picture of what the public views as some of the biggest health concerns for children and adolescents today," says Davis, associate professor of general pediatrics and internal medicine at the U-M Medical School, and associate professor of public policy at the Gerald R. Ford School of Public Policy. "It also suggests that the government may want to target more investment toward issues such as teen smoking, drug abuse and childhood obesity, in a way that reflects the fact that the public is currently prioritizing these problems as even bigger than other issues on the list."

About the National Poll on Children's Health

The C.S. Mott Children's Hospital National Poll on Children's Health is funded by the Department of Pediatrics and Communicable Diseases at the U-M Health System. As part of the U-M Division of General Pediatric Child Health Evaluation and Research (CHEAR) Unit, the National Poll on Children's Health is designed to measure major health care issues and trends for U.S. children. For a copy of the reports from National Poll on Children's Health, visit www.chear.umich.edu. For regular podcasts of polling results, go to www.med.umich.edu/podcast.

About Knowledge Networks

Knowledge Networks delivers quality and service to guide leaders in business, government and academia uniquely bringing scientifically valid research to the online space through its probability-based, online KnowledgePanelSM. The company delivers unique study design, science, analysis, and panel maintenance, along with a commitment to close collaboration at every stage of the research process. KN leverages its expertise in brands, media, advertising, and public policy issues to provide insights that speak directly to clients' most important concerns. For more information about Knowledge Networks, visit www.knowledgenetworks.com.

Critical Thinking

1. How would you rank the top 10 health concerns in the U.S. among children? What influences your ranking?

2. Do you see a decrease in smoking among children? What, according to you, is primarily responsible for their taking up the habit of smoking, or any other bad health habit or behavior?

From *Medical News Today*, May 6, 2007. Copyright © 2007 by Medical News Today. Reprinted by permission.

San Diego State U. Defends Its Role in Federal Drug Sting

Sara Lipka

Drugs are common on college campuses. Federal stings are not.

But when a freshman at San Diego State University died of a cocaine overdose last May, the campus police chief decided to pursue a full-scale investigation. In December he summoned undercover agents from the federal Drug Enforcement Administration to pose as students and roam the campus in search of illegal drugs.

This month San Diego County's district attorney disclosed the yearlong investigation—Operation Sudden Fall—and its outcome: 125 arrests, including 95 students. Law-enforcement officers seized $100,000 in drugs, $60,000 in cash, and four guns. University officials suspended six fraternities, as well as 33 students charged with felonies, and congratulated themselves.

"Drug use is a concern on virtually every campus in our country," the president, Stephen L. Weber, said in a written statement the day the arrests were announced. "SDSU has taken this action to confront it directly."

But such a sweeping drug investigation raises high-stakes questions. When should a university punish instead of educate? Does inviting undercover federal agents onto a campus strain an administration's relationship with its students? Will trying to solve a problem make an institution notorious for having it?

San Diego State officials have no regrets. "It's not just that we were looking at a problem of degree and seeing more drug usage than previously," Mr. Weber said in an interview with *The Chronicle*. "We're talking about what is at least now alleged to be drug trafficking on campus, things like loaded shotguns and semiautomatic weapons. . . . That's serious business."

James R. Kitchen, vice president for student affairs, said the university had two options: "We could either close our eyes to it or make a bold move."

Covert Investigation

When Shirley J. Poliakoff died of a drug overdose in May 2007, San Diego State police suspected that the freshman's source was on the 35,000-student campus. The chief, John Browning, told the administration that he would investigate.

"He was seeing a pattern in drug activity that concerned him and that led him to think that it wasn't just business as usual," Mr. Weber says of Mr. Browning, who declined to be interviewed for this article.

Officers discovered sophisticated drug trafficking and sales, says Jack Beresford, a university spokesman. In December, without telling the president, Mr. Browning brought in federal drug agents, a rare move in higher education. (In 1991 the Drug Enforcement Administration led a huge raid at the University of Virginia, and a spokeswoman for the agency could not recall another similar case.)

On April 21, two months after a student at a nearby college had died of a drug overdose at a San Diego State fraternity house, Mr. Browning told the president that the investigation was coming to a head and informed him that federal agents had been on the campus. Mr. Weber supported the chief's decision to involve them.

"In taking these things seriously," Mr. Weber says, "you run beyond the resources of the university itself." San Diego State's police department has about 30 officers, who are too recognizable to go undercover. Also, experts point out, campus police often lack experience in complex drug stings.

Some students and professors at San Diego State have complained that federal agents arrived on the campus without the president's consent, but Mr. Weber dismisses that concern. "We have a chief of police who's a law-enforcement professional, whose judgment I trust," he says. Strict confidentiality, he adds, was necessary to protect the investigation—and the officers involved.

On April 28, Mr. Weber learned that several arrests were planned for May 6. He then tipped off Charles B. Reed, chancellor of the California State University system, and Mr. Kitchen in student affairs.

Mr. Kitchen understood the late notice. Had too many people known in advance, he says, someone may have—intentionally or not—spread the word. He waited a few days to tell his staff members to prepare letters of suspension and eviction from university housing. Law-enforcement authorities did not release the students' names until May 6.

The university suspended the 33 students charged with felonies, who it says were "arrested as part of the special operation." Many others in the district attorney's tally of 95 were charged with possession of marijuana.

Susan Henry, a health educator at San Diego State, first heard about the sting from students. She typically fights drug use with prevention programs, but given the presence of trafficking on the campus, she says, a criminal investigation was necessary. "Education alone doesn't work," she says.

'Zero Tolerance'

Generations of students have tried to get away with illegal activities on college campuses. Often they do, says Max Bromley, an associate professor of criminology at the University of South Florida.

"It's always a balance between how strict are you going to be versus how far are you going to let things go," says Mr. Bromley, who served as a campus police officer for more than two decades.

Sometimes firm enforcement is impractical, he says: "If you tried to bust everyone for having a drink at a football game, you'd load the jails for the weekend."

But over the years, injuries, deaths, and concerns about liability have driven colleges to take tougher stances. "There comes a time," Mr. Bromley says, "that there will be a zero-tolerance approach."

Some students and their families have applauded San Diego State's crackdown. "I am grateful that they took this head-on and did something about it, instead of hoping that the problem went away," says Jack D. Klunder, a member of the university's parent-advisory board.

The problem was bigger than the two deaths, says Wendy Fry, a senior. Administrators had to take action, she says: "I'm proud that they did."

But many students are upset, says Ms. Fry, who has covered the case for the campus newspaper. Some accuse the district attorney of playing up the case, touting the 95 arrests when just a fraction were for dealing drugs. Others, says Ms. Fry, "feel betrayed by having the feds come onto campus and infiltrate their fraternities."

A faculty member who spoke on the condition of anonymity had a similar concern. "We know what happens when federal agents are authorized to come in," the professor says. "The original impetus is all about law and order, and ultimately . . . they may be coming in to investigate or squelch political dissent."

But university officials say this case was about one thing.

"If the health and safety of your students is your top priority, then you cannot weigh that priority against your reputation," says Mr. Weber, the president. "At the end of the day, it is more important that the university do what's right and let its reputation sort itself out."

Critical Thinking

1. What do you think should be the role played in your school regarding drug abuse and enforcement?
2. Do you think the "zero tolerence" policy works? What would be your approach to drug policy?

Reflections on 40 Years of Ethnographic Drug Abuse Research: Implications for the Future

Robert Carlson et al.

Introduction

This paper focuses on past, present, and potential future contributions of ethnographic research to describing and understanding ìstreet culturesî of drug use and the implications these have for informing various interventions. The first section provides an overview of ethnography and drug abuse research. This is followed by a historical perspective on the ethnography of street cultures. Next, the significance of ethnographic drug abuse research is highlighted, with a focus on its methodology. Ethnographic contributions to the development, implementation, and evaluation of interventions are discussed, including ethical issues. Subsequently, the interdisciplinary nature of ethnographic drug abuse research is described. Methodological challenges emerged over time as the definition of street cultures and drug trends shifted. These are illustrated with examples, including the use of prescription drugs, new heroin users, and rural drug and methamphetamine use. The final sections focus on career opportunities for ethnographers and opportunities and barriers for the future. We address training needs for interdisciplinary inquiry, the potential role of ethnographers in prevention and treatment research, and the link to studies on the brain and genetics. The future of ethnographic research on drug use will be influenced by the funding structure. We conclude with a summary of reflections on the past and aspirations for the future.

Ethnographic research is known for its ability to explore cultures, including more hidden cultures, such as the "street cultures" of drug users that are the focus of this paper. A common definition of "culture" is the shared beliefs, values, attitudes, and behaviors among members of a group. Using this definition, culture provides a sense of identity and meaning, the structure that guides how individuals are expected to behave and the ways in which individuals and those around them interpret experiences. Ethnographic researchers recognize the importance of examining the processes associated with the "transmission" of culture and its ever-shifting understanding among group members. In other words, culture to ethnographers does not constitute a fixed set of behavioral traits, as it is understood to be flexible, inventive, process-focused, and contested within contexts of social interaction and relative to ongoing historic trends and in terms of wider social structures. Through this lens on culture, ethnographic research allows for gaining insights into the perspective of drug users themselves, including the meanings attached to specific actions and the ways in which behaviors are impacted both by the immediate social context and the larger structural framework that shapes their world and experiences. Ethnographic findings provide an evidence-based foundation for the development of targeted prevention and intervention programs. Ethnographic data collection methods include participant observation, visual ethnography, in-depth interviewing, focus groups, and systematic data collection strategies, such as free listing, pile sorting, and keeping diaries. Findings are presented in narrative format, often revealing the detailed and contextualized realities behind the numbers presented in quantitative research.

In this paper, we specifically focus on ethnographic research that addresses "street cultures," namely cultural patterns found in the public domain and often played out on urban street corners or at similar venues. Street cultures provide a dynamic and fluid set of informal rules guiding individual behaviors and social interactions as well as models for interpretation for those who are part of the street scene. For example, street cultures offer meaningful frameworks for behavior such as heroin addicts hustling on a street corner, crack cocaine users "hitting a pipe" while hiding in the bushes, marijuana smokers walking through the park, or MDMA/ecstasy users dancing and waving colored glow sticks at a rave. Acquiring an understanding of drug use culture requires building trust with those being studied and subsequently gaming access to more hidden users as well as the social settings in which drugs are acquired and consumed and where related activities unfold (e.g., shooting galleries, crack houses, encampments, clubs, and private parties). Also of concern in the study of street culture are patterns of social life and cultural expression in other settings frequented by street drug users, such as shelters, syringe exchange programs, and soup kitchens. Ethnographic research on street cultures results in an emphasis on those drug users to be found in public urban settings, whereas inquiries among more hidden drug users, such as professionals, the middle-class, and suburban residents, as well as rural drug users, are less common. In addition, most ethnographic focus has been on the consumers of illicit drugs rather than on the suppliers.

Historical Context

Major changes regarding the use of alcohol and drugs occurred in the United States at the end of the 19th and the beginning of the 20th centuries. Up until then, drug use was either largely ignored by public officials or at least roughly tolerated. However, the prohibition movement resulted in a characterization of alcohol use as immoral and destructive of the social fabric of families and communities. The subsequent Volstead Act in 1919 prohibited the possession of alcohol. Prior to this act, state legislations already accomplished the same goal. The approach shifted somewhat in the direction of a medical and disease orientation to drug users with the establishment of the two Federal narcotics hospitals and treatment units in Lexington, Kentucky, and Fort Worth, Texas, in the late 1930s. Rather than portraying addicts as criminals, they were more compassionately portrayed as suffering from a treatable disease. Up until that time, addicts were generally viewed as "sick" individuals by psychologists and "deviants" by sociologists. The "disease" model predominates even today through the portrayal of alcohol and other substance abuse largely as a disease of the brain or a genetic disorder. At the same time, the criminalization perspective continues to remain prominent and to dominate social policy (Musto, 1973).

As Western society developed its perspective on drug use, the understandings of the users themselves remained largely unexplored. Among the earliest works to consider the insider's point of view were the autobiographies by Claude Brown (1965), Piri Thomas (1967), Iceberg Slim (1969), and William Burroughs (1953). Beginning in the 1950s, such writings attested to the central importance of heroin addiction in the life of urban America and in ethnic ghettos. Concurrently, a number of ethnographers (among them, Preble & Casey [1969], Feldman [1968], Fiddle [1967], Finestine [1964], Hughes [1977], Siegal [Siegal, 1978; Siegal & Inciardi, 1982], and Sutter [1966]) presented addiction as a viable and purposeful lifestyle. Rather than characterizing drug users as pathetic, anomic, and isolated individuals, they were instead identified as members of a highly sophisticated and complicated subculture that revolved around the use of heroin, sometimes combined with other drugs. The drug lifestyle provided a meaningful self-identity as a street addict. The subculture had its own set of norms and values, prescribing behavior and language (even poetry), and provided a hierarchical social structure (Preble & Casey, 1969). The perspective of "addiction as a lifestyle" continued to be developed, often in book-length treatises that covered drugs such as heroin, cocaine, methamphetamine, and ecstasy. These monographs, by ethnographic authors like Adler (1993), Agar

(1973), Biernacki (1986), Bourgois (2003), Hoffer (2006), Inciardi (1986), Murphy (Murphy and Rosenbaum, 1999), Page (Page, Gonzalez, McCoy, & McBride, 1981), Rosenbaum (1981), Singer (2006a), Stephens (1991), Sterk (1999), Waldorf (1973), and Zinberg (1979) expanded our knowledge on a wide range of topics, including gender differences, drug user heterogeneity, survival strategies, and health issues.

Drug Trends and Ethnographic Research Shifts

Stephens (1991) was among the first to point out the importance of substance, set, and setting when studying drug use. Epidemiological drug trends show the dominance of certain substances on the U.S. drug market over time, often by population group and geographic region. Heroin and hallucinogens were popular in the 1960s and 1970s; crack cocaine moved to the forefront during the 1980s; subsequently, in the late 1980s throughout the 1990s, so-called "club drugs," such as MDMA/ecstasy, ketamine, and methamphetamine, gained a presence (Carlson et al., 2004). In recent years, illicit use of pharmaceutical analgesics and tranquilizers has become increasingly common. At the same time, "old drugs," like PCP, have returned, and poly-drug use has become the norm. Ethnographic studies of drug users often are in the vanguard of identifying and describing changes in the drug markets as well as in associated use patterns, such as the shift among powder cocaine users to crack, among crack smokers to liquefied crack injection, among amphetamine users to heroin injection, and among heroin injectors to snorting or smoking and vice versa.

Often, shifts in available drugs and changes in route of administration have involved new groups of users. For example, ethnographic research has made major contributions to understanding new heroin users whose White, middle-class background, intranasal route of use, and settings of use differ significantly from those of poor, inner-city, heroin injectors (Agar & Reisinger, 1999). As such, ethnographic research can serve as an early detection mechanism for anticipating and evaluating epidemiologic changes in drug use/misuse trends. Ethnographic researchers can play a vital role in informing experts of such changes, including those in public health, drug abuse treatment, social and health services in general, and public policy (Singer, 2006b). Singer and his colleagues have tracked the return of PCP and the emergence of methamphetamine in Hartford and used findings to inform the local public health and drug abuse treatment systems. Carlson and his colleagues operate the Ohio Substance Abuse Monitoring Network, a statewide epidemiological surveillance system based on qualitative data collected from active drug users (Daniulaityte, Carlson and Kenne, 2006; Siegal, Carlson, Kenne, Starr, & Stephens, 2000). Ethnographic researchers also have contributed to postmarketing surveillance of the abuse of buprenorphine (Suboxone® Subutex®) prescribed for opioid dependence. The Community Epidemiology Working Group of the National Institute on Drug Abuse (NIDA) has expanded its emphasis from merely relying on epidemiological indicators to including ethnographic ones.

Despite the growing knowledge about drug use, many questions remain. For example, is the lifestyle of the "new" heroin users similar to that of the heroin users studied in the 1960s and 1970s? To what extent are methamphetamine users in urban and rural areas similar or different? More recently, ethnographic drug abuse researchers have expanded investigations beyond urban settings to rural areas. Carlson and his team in Ohio (Draus & Carlson, 2006; Sexton, Carlson, Leukefeld, & Booth, 2008), Trotter, Price, and colleagues in Arizona, Dew, Elifson and their team in Georgia, Gorman in Missouri, and others have alerted us to the problems of substance use in rural areas and the emerging rural subcultures of methamphetamine use. One of the strengths of ethnographic drug research is its ability to detect the early use of a new drug and its spread among users. This capacity, when combined with the methodology's focus on culture, permits insights not possible with other approaches.

Significance of Ethnographic Drug Research: Methodological Perspective

In contrast with inquiries into substance use, abuse, and addiction by scientists in fields such as psychology and psychiatry, ethnographic researchers endeavor to present an accurate and detailed description of how people who use drugs view their drug use and related behaviors, their lives in general, and their place in the world. Ethnographic researchers contend that such an understanding can help inform the strategies that can be used to motivate behavioral change, including prevention of drug use, risk reduction, and abstinence from drug use. Whereas many drug abuse treatment and related health services label users based on their "primary" drug of use, ethnographic research has shown the importance of recognizing that most individuals use multiple substances and readily mix legal and illegal drugs to achieve particular desired effects or because of fluctuations in availability. Sterk et al., (2008) not only explored poly-drug use in-depth, but they also identified several patterns, such as simultaneous or sequential poly-drug use.

Without question, ethnographic researchers believe the perspective of the users themselves to be at least as salient as understanding drug use as a "brain disease" or the outcome of a genetic vulnerability. Ethnographers have also emphasized the importance of the social relations and networks that form among drug users as factors that influence drug use patterns, HIV risk, and barriers to changing behaviors. Work by Trotter (Trotter, Bowen, & Potter, 1995) and Weeks (Weeks et al., 2002), for example, has helped rethink older understandings of drug users as marginalized social isolates. Ethnographic contributions to the development, implementation, and evaluation of various interventions have become increasingly recognized. Central among these have been ethnographic studies focusing on preventing and/or reducing risk behaviors associated with the transmission of HIV and other blood-borne pathogens and those with a focus on drug abuse treatment. Ethnographic researchers have described the complex ways in which political economy and disadvantage influence drug using behavior as well as risk for HIV transmission. More recently, Sterk, Elifson, and Theall (2007) explored the link between individual risk-taking and community social capital, and Singer (2007) has provided an extensive analysis of the role of legal and illegal drugs in the maintenance of structures of social inequality.

Beyond methodological issues, ethnographic inquiries of drug use raise important issues in research ethics. Ethnographers conduct their research on the "home turf" of their study participants, develop close relations with key informants, gain access to intimate details of participants' lives, and tend to be more self-revealing than other types of behavioral researchers and certainly more so than clinical or laboratory researchers. As a result, the opportunities for moral uncertainty and potential ethical violation are multiple. NIDA published a monograph in 1999 with findings from a workshop on ethical issues in illicit drug research called Toward the Establishment of Ethical Guidelines (Singer et al., 1999). Recently, Fisher and Singer (Fisher, Oransky, Mahadevan, Singer, Mirhej, & Hodge, 2008) conducted a NIDA-funded study of drug user attitudes and experiences with issues of consent, coercion, therapeutic misunderstanding, and related ethical topics.

Interdisciplinary Nature of Ethnographic Drug Abuse Research

In the late 1980s, the emergence of the HIV epidemic among injection drug users renewed scientific interest in ethnographic research. Through NIDA's National AIDS Demonstration Research Projects (NADR) and the subsequent Cooperative Agreement for AIDS prevention (COOP), ethnographic researchers demonstrated their unique value in understanding and preventing HIV risk behaviors. Carlson made an early ethnographic contribution on needle sharing (Carlson, 1996), and Clatts, Page, and Koester (Clatts, Heimer, 1999; Inciardi & Page, 1991; Koester, Booth & Wiebel, 1990; Koester, Glanz, & Baron, 2005; Needle et al., 1998; Page, 1990) studied needle and drug sharing and the impact of the local context, including paraphernalia laws, on injection-related risk. Subsequently, ethnographic researchers have made important contributions to understanding HIV risk related to non-injection drug use and sexual behaviors related to drug use.

The AIDS epidemic also required ethnographic researchers to be engaged in the ethnographic multi/interdisciplinary studies. In the NADR and COOP projects, researchers' findings on the users' perspective were used to design survey instruments, including the wording of questions and answer categories, the development of hypotheses, and the content and format of interventions to ensure cultural sensitivity. Significant interdisciplinary contributions by ethnographers in the context of the AIDS epidemic also include the merging of ethnography and epidemiology, such as the NIDA monograph edited by Marshall, Singer, and Clatts (1999). The challenges of HIV/AIDS have also resulted in collaborations between ethnographic researchers and, among others, laboratory scientists, infectious disease researchers, virologists, ethicists, lawyers, and economists (Clatts et al., 1999). At the community level, numerous ethnographers were involved in the national Rapid Assessment, Response, and Evaluation project that used ethnographic methods to empower local communities with the information needed to address local barriers to risk reduction among drug users and other populations as documented in a volume edited by Bowser, Quimbey, and Singer (2007). Similarly, a number of ethnographers have contributed to the assessment of syringe exchange as a structural intervention for limiting the spread of HIV/AIDS.

The National Institutes of Health (NIH) Roadmap provides new opportunities for ethnographic researchers to engage in interdisciplinary and multidisciplinary teams focused on promoting the application of new knowledge to the development of new prevention strategies, diagnostics, and treatments, and, ultimately, to the transfer of these innovations to health care providers and the public. Ethnographic researchers bring the skills and knowledge that will enable them to contribute to the development of new prevention strategies, to assist in getting people to understand new diagnostics and treatments, and to transfer research findings into everyday practice. As Carlson (2006) argues, the implementation of any novel intervention, biomedical or behavioral, involves complex political, economic, sociocultural, and behavioral processes that require an insider's perspective. Understanding how people representing various subcultures respond to the adoption of new forms of intervention raises critical research questions that ethnographers are well suited to help answer. Past experience tempers this enthusiasm somewhat, however. Ethnographers wonder why their potential contributions have not been fully explored, for example, in NIDA's Clinical Trials Network. Indeed, as Michael Agar (2006)—a founding figure in drug ethnography—has recently argued, the long history of ethnographic findings on what drug users actually do and believe has largely been ignored by policy makers who are focused on promoting a seemingly never-ending war on drugs. Addiction and recovery involve complex transformation in lifestyle, including associated neurochemical, social, and psychological processes; individual risk factors, such as genetic vulnerability or mental illness; social and cultural factors; as well as the larger social structural contexts. Providing field-based understandings and helping to integrate such diverse perspectives exemplifies some of what ethnographers can contribute.

Career Opportunities for Future Ethnographic Drug Abuse Researchers

Interdisciplinary Scholarship

While in the past ethnographic researchers often "fell into" careers in drug research, recent research by Singer, Page, and Houle (in press) suggests that people are increasingly choosing this career track and that they do not feel marginalized within the field. This suggests that useful and productive career opportunities lie ahead for the next generation of ethnographic drug researchers. However, these opportunities require them to be open to multi-level and cross-disciplinary scholarship. This includes having a background in ethnographic, qualitative, and quantitative research methods, a willingness to collaborate with other social and behavioral scientists, having colleagues in the biomedical sciences, knowing policy makers, and knowing service providers. Academic training is typically organized within disciplinary boundaries, creating barriers to experiences that prepare researchers for interdisciplinary inquiry. Tension can arise easily within the social and behavioral sciences (e.g., anthropology, economics, psychology, and sociology) as well as across broader fields, such as between the social sciences and the humanities, natural sciences, and the professional schools that prepare people in law, business, or the health sciences field because of different disciplinary languages, ways of thinking about problems, and methods of conducting research. Ethnographic researchers need to work with institutions of higher education to allow for appropriate training of the next generation.

Prevention Research

Thus far, ethnographic work on ways to prevent drug addiction has been limited. Understanding the economic role of drugs in a community, the positive and negative ways in which the immediate community views users, the impact of drug users' social networks on drug use, and the reasons why users may give up life as a drug user by resurrecting previous salient roles, all may lead to developing meaningful prevention programs. As Rosenbaum (1981) has shown, knowing how to use, support, and empower the very central role of being a "mother" to prevent a woman from becoming a drug user could derive directly from ethnographic studies. Other ethnographic researchers, such as Biernacki (1986), presented mechanisms by which individuals have reduced or stopped using drugs without relying on formal drug treatment. Likewise, Zinberg (1984) has outlined the "rituals" by which significant numbers of individuals can limit their use of narcotics to recreational use that does not progress to addiction. The potential role of ethnographic contributions to prevention of drug and alcohol abuse remains a wide-open opportunity.

The Brain and Genetics

Potential ethnographic contributions also exist in collaborations with those who study the brain and addiction. As Alan Leshner, past Director of NIDA, explained, sociocultural factors and behavior cannot be ignored in neurobiological research. To date, few linkages have been developed between neuroscientists and ethnographic drug researchers. Similarly, collaboration between genetic and ethnographic drug researchers is limited as well. As the field of genetics advances and continues to identify genetic markers for drug use and abuse, ethnographic researchers can provide insights into environmental cues that may trigger such vulnerabilities. The inductive approach characteristic of ethnographic studies complements the deductive models of inquiry developed by natural and biomedical scientists.

Concluding Comments

When reflecting on the past 40 years of ethnographic research on drug use, we realize the importance of considering the perspective of drug users themselves as well as the role of culture and the larger political economic factors. Whereas initially much of the scholarship was published in single-authored ethnographic monographs, publications in peer-reviewed journals and with multiple authors—often representing a wide range of disciplines—have become more common. Ethnographic drug research has and continues to make important contributions to understanding and improving public health.

A number of barriers to ethnographic research exist, however, including those caused by disciplinary-bound training. Interdisciplinary training is needed that permits communication across fields of study. In addition, scientists in other fields need to recognize ethnographic contributions more fully. As these contributions in the drug use field increase in number, this is likely to occur. We need to avoid "ethnographic shortcuts," such as tacking on a few focus groups to a quantitative study or adding some open-ended questions to a survey instrument. These do not constitute ethnographic research, which requires participation and immersion in the life worlds of the group being studied. Even open-ended interviews conducted in a research institution cannot take the place of ethnographic immersion and observation in natural settings that are not under the control of researchers.

Funding for ethnographic drug research needs to be considered as well. Grant reviewers often are socialized to look for hypotheses to be tested, appropriate measures, sample composition, and statistical power analysis for sample size calculations. Ethnographic studies are unlikely to include any of these. Reviewers need to be made aware of the unique nature of ethnographic research, and the NIH guide on such proposals should be brought to their attention. Distributing the pamphlet developed by the Office of Behavioral Social Sciences Research entitled Qualitative Methods in Health Research: Opportunities and Considerations in Application and Review (Office of Behavioral and Social Science Research, 2001) to reviewers would help to achieve this goal. In addition, a funding structure is needed that facilitates time-sensitive funding for early detection of emerging drug trends as well as for multi site and longitudinal ethnographic studies.

References

Adler, P. 1993 Wheeling and dealing. An ethnography of an upper-level drug dealing and smuggling community. New York: Columbia University Press,

Agar, M.H. 1973 Ripping and running. New York: Academic Press.

Agar, M.H. 2006 Dope double agent. The naked emperor on drugs. Mornsville, NC: Lulu Press.

Agar, M.H., & Reisinger, H. 1999 Numbers and patterns: Heroin indicators and what they represent. Human Organization, 58, 365–374.

Biernacki, P. 1986 Pathways from heroin addiction: Recovery without treatment. Philadelphia: Temple University Press.

Boeri, M., Sterk, C., Bahora, M. & Elifson, K. 2008 Poly-drug use among ecstasy users: Separate, synergistic, and indiscriminate patterns. Journal of Drug Issues, 38(2), 517–542.

Bourgois, P. 2003 In search for respect. Selling crack in el barrio. 2nd ed. Cambridge: Cambridge University Press.

Bowser, B., Quimby, E., & Singer, M., (Eds.) 2007 Communities assessing their AIDS epidemics: Results of the rapid. Assessment of HIV/AIDS in eleven U.S. cities. Lanham, Maryland: Lexington Books.

Brown, C. 1965 Manchild in the promised land. New York: New York American Library.

Burroughs, W. 1953 Junkie. New York: Ace Books.

Carlson, R.G. 1996 The political economy of AIDS among drug users in the United States: Beyond blaming the victim or powerful others. American Anthropologist, 98, 266–278.

Carlson, R.G. 2000 Shooting galleries, dope houses, and "doctors": Examining the social ecology of HIV risk behaviors among drug injectors in Dayton, Ohio. Human Organization, 59, 325–333.

Carlson, R.G. 2006 Ethnography and applied substance misuse research: Anthropological and cross-cultural factors. In W.R. Miller & K.M. Carroll (Eds.), Rethinking substance abuse: What the science shows, and what we should do about it (pp. 201–219). New York: The Guilford Press.

Carlson, R.G., McCaughan, J.A., Falck, R.S., Wang, J., Siegal, H.A., & Daniulaityte, R. 2004 Perceived adverse consequences associated with MDMA/ecstasy use among young polydrug users in Ohio: Implications for intervention. International Journal of Drug Policy, 15, 265–274.

Clatts, M.C., Heimer, R., Abdala, N., Goldsamt, L.A., Southeran, J.L., Anderson, K.T., Gallo, T.M., Hoffer, L., Luciano, P.A., & Kyriakides, T. 1999 HIV-1 transmission in injection paraphernalia: Heating drug solutions may inactivate HIV-1. The Journal of Acquired Immune Deficiency Syndromes, 22, 194–199.

Clatts, M.C., Heimer, R., Sotheran, J.L., & Goldsamt, L.A. 1999 Interdisciplinary research on the transmission of blood-borne pathogens in drug injection practices: Applications of ethnography in epidemiology and public health. In P.L. Marshall, M. Singer, & M.C. Clatts (Eds.), Integrating cultural, observational, and epidemiological approaches in the prevention of drug abuse and HIV/AIDS (pp. 74–93). Bethesda, MD: National Institute on Drug Abuse.

Daniulaityte, R., Carlson, R.G., & Kenne, D. 2006 Initiation to pharmaceutical opioids and patterns of misuse: Preliminary qualitative findings obtained by the Ohio Substance Abuse Monitoring Network. Journal of Drug Issues, 36, 787–788.

Draus, P., & Carlson, R. 2006 Needles in the haystacks: The social context of initiation to heroin injection in rural Ohio. Substance Use & Misuse, 41, 1111–1124.

Feldman, H. 1968 Ideological supports to becoming and remaining a heroin addict. Journal of Health and Social Behavior, 9, 131–139.

Fiddle, S. 1967 Portrait from a shooting gallery. New York: Harper and Row.

Finestine, H. 1964 Cats, kicks, and color. In H. Becker (Ed.), The Otherside. New York: Free Press.

Fisher, C., Oransky, M., Mahadevan, M., Singer, M., Mirhej, G., & Hodge, G.D. 2008 Marginalized populations and drug addiction research: Realism, mistrust, and misconception. IRB Journal, 30(3);1–9.

Hoffer, L. 2006 Junkie business." The evolution and operation of a heroin dealing network." Belmont, CA: Thomas.

Hughes, P.H. 1977 Behind the wall of respect. Chicago: University of Chicago Press.

Inciardi, J. 1986 The war on drugs: Heroin, cocaine, crime, and public policy. Mountain View, California: Mayfield Publishing Co.

Inciardi, J.A., & Page, J.B. 1991 Drug sharing among intravenous drug users. AIDS, 5, 772–773.

Koester, S., Booth, R., & Wiebel, W. 1990 The risk of HIV transmission from sharing water, drug mixing containers and cotton filters among IV drug users. International Journal of Drug Policy, 1, 28–30.

Koester, S., Glanz, J., & Baron, A. 2005 Drug sharing among heroin networks: Implications for HIV and hepatitis B and C prevention. AIDS and Behavior, 9, 27–39.

Marshall, P., Singer, M. & Clatts, M. (Eds.) 1999 Integrating cultural observational, and epidemiological approaches in the prevention of drug abuse and HIV/AIDS. Rockville, MD: National Institute on Drug Abuse.

Murphy, S. & Rosenbaum, M. 1999 Pregnant women on drugs. New Burnswick: Rutgers University Press.

Musto, D.F. 1973 The American disease. New Haven, CT: Yale University Press.

Needle, R., Coyle, S., Cesari, H., Trotter, R., Clatts, M.C., & Koester, S. 1998 HIV risk behaviors associated with the injection process: Multiperson use of drug injection equipment & paraphernalia in injection drug user networks. Substance Use & Misuse, 33, 2403–2423.

Office of Behavioral and Social Sciences Research. 2001 Qualitative methods in health research: Opportunities and considerations in application and review. (NIH Publication No. 02-5040). Washington, DC: National Institutes of Health.

Page, J. B. 1990 Shooting scenarios and risk of HIV 1 infection. American Behavioral Scientist, 33, 478–490.

Page, J.B., Gonzalez, D., McCoy, C., & McBride, D. 1981 The Ethnography of Cuban drug use. Report submitted to the National Institute on Drug Abuse in fulfillment of Grant No. 1 -R01-DA-02320-02. 1981.

Page, J.B. & Singer, M. in press The ethnography of drug use. New Brunswick: Rutgers University Press.

Preble, E., & Casey, J.J. 1969 Taking care of business: The heroin user's life on the street. International Journal of the Addictions, 4(1), 1–24.

Rosenbaum, M. 1981 Women on heroin. New Brunswick, NJ: Rutgers University Press.

Sexton, R., Carlson, R., Leukefeld, C., & Booth, B. 2008 Trajectories of methamphetamine use in the rural south: A longitudinal qualitative study. Human Organization, 67, 181–193.

Siegal, H.A. 1978 Outposts of the forgotten. New Brunswick, NJ: Transaction Books.

Siegal, H.A., Carlson, R.G., Kenne, D., Starr, S., & Stephens, R. 2000 The Ohio Substance Abuse Monitoring Network: Constructing and operating a statewide epidemiologic intelligence system. American Journal of Public Health, 90, 1835–1837.

Siegal, H.A. & Inciardi, J. 1982 The demise of skid row. Society, 19, 39–45.

Singer, M. 2006a The face of social suffering: The life history of a street drug addict. Long Grove, IL: Waveland Press.

Singer, M. 2006b Something dangerous. Emergent and changing illicit drug use and community health. Prospect Heights, IL: Waveland Press.

Singer, M. 2007 Drugging the poor: Legal and illegal drug industries and the structuring of social inequality. Prospect Heights, IL: Waveland Press.

Singer, M., Marshall, P., Trotter, R., Schensul, J., Weeks, M., Simmons, J. & Radda, R. 1999 Ethics, ethnography, drug use and AIDS: dilemmas and standards in federally funded research. Integrating cultural, observational, and epidemiological approaches in the prevention of drug abuse and HIV/AIDS. P. Marshall, M. Singer, & M. Clatts, (Eds.), pp. 198–222. Bethesda, MD: National Institute on Drug Abuse.

Slim, I. 1969 Pimp. The story of my life. Los Angeles, CA: Holloway.

Stephens, R.C. 1991 The street addict role: A theory of heroin addiction. New York: State University of New York Press.

Sterk, C. 1999 Fast lives: Women who use crack cocaine. Philadelphia: Temple University Press.

Sterk, C., Elifson, K., & Theall, K. 2007 Individual action and community context: The health intervention project. American Journal of Preventive Medicine, 32(6), S177–S181.

Sutter, A. 1966 The world of the righteous dope fiend. Issues in Criminology, 2(2); 177–222.

Thomas, P. 1967 Down these mean streets. New York: Alfred A. Knopf, Inc.

Trotter, R., Bowen, A., & Potter, J. 1995 Network models for HIV outreach and prevention programs for drug users. NIDA research monograph, 151, 144–180.

Waldorf, D. 1973 Careers in dope. Englewood Cliffs: Prentice-Hall.

Weeks, M., Clair, S., Borgatti, S., Radda, K., & Schensul, J. 2002 Social networks of drug users in high-risk sites: Finding the connections. AIDS and Behavior, 6, 193–206.

Zinberg, N. 1984 Drug, set and setting: The basis for controlled intoxicant use. New Haven, CT: Yale University Press.

Critical Thinking

1. How is ethnographic research useful?

2. How could we take the information gathered and apply it to treatment and prevention programs?

3. Are there ethical implications for both the study participants and researchers? If so, explain what they are and how they affect the participants/researchers?

4. Describe what you see in the future regarding ethnographic research.

ROBERT G. CARLSON is Director of the Center for Interventions, Treatment and Addictions Research and Professor in the Department of Community Health, Wright State University Boonschoft School of Medicine. MERRILL SINGER, PhD, is a Senior Research Fellow at the Center for Health, Intervention and Prevention and Professor of Anthropology at the University of Connecticut. RICHARD C. STEPHENS, PhD, is currently Interim Director of the Institute for Health and Social Policy at The University of Akron. He is Professor Emeritus of Sociology and former Director of the Institute.

Article 6. Reflections on 40 Years of Ethnographic Drug Abuse Research: Implications for the Future

CLAIRE E. STERK, PHD, is Charles Howard Candler Professor in Public Health at Emory University and Senior Vice Provost for Academic Affairs. She specializes in ethnographic and mixed-methods research and prevention interventions with a focus on drug use, health, crime, and intergenerational dynamics.

Acknowledgments—We wish to honor the late Harvey A. Siegal, a leader in ethnographic drug research and role model to many of us. A previous version of this paper was presented at the conference entitled, "Reflections on 40 Years of Drug Abuse Research," held in Key Largo, Florida, May 15–17, 2006.

Mexico Drug Cartels Extend Reach in U.S.

CAROL CRATTY

The availability of illegal drugs is increasing in the United States—fueled largely by expanding activity from Mexican drug cartels—and abuse of controlled prescription drugs is getting worse, according to the National Drug Threat Assessment 2010 report, released Thursday.

"The trafficking and abuse of drugs affects everyone," said Michael T. Walther, director of the Justice Department's National Drug Intelligence Center, which produced the report. "The economic cost alone is estimated at nearly $215 billion annually."

The Mexican cartels, the report says, are "the single greatest drug trafficking threat to the United States." The Mexican organizations have operations in every region of the United States and are expanding into more rural and suburban areas.

They've also stepped up cooperation with U.S. street and prison gangs for distribution.

With drug violence on a frightening rise along the Mexican border, the assessment found greater levels of heroin, marijuana, and methamphetamine flowing across the border than ever before—and predicts more to come.

That increased traffic, the report suggests, is partly to blame for a rise in the purity of heroin and a drop in its price, along with an increase in overdoses and overdose deaths. Government officials, in fact, estimate that heroin production in Mexico jumped from 17 metric tons in 2007 to 38 tons in 2008.

The report's authors credited the Mexican government with moving to ban the importation of certain chemicals used to produce methamphetamine, but notes the cartels have found substitutes.

Earlier this week, Secretary of State Hillary Clinton traveled to Mexico with other high-level administration officials to discuss the Merida Initiative, a multi year, $1.4 billion project aimed at helping Mexico combat organized crime. Clinton said the initiative would emphasize social and economic development in addition to security.

Mexican police announced on Thursday, the arrest of a suspected drug kingpin they believe is a major supplier of heroin to the United States.

Jose Antonio Medina Reguin, known as the "King of Heroin" or "Don Pepe," is suspected of smuggling up to 200 kilograms (441 pounds) of heroin into the United States each month, netting him up to $12 million monthly, federal police said at a news conference.

Illegal drugs are crossing America's other large border as well, the report says. Asian criminal organizations manufacture the drug MDMA, more commonly known as ecstasy, in Canada and smuggle it into the United States.

MDMA is also smuggled into the United States over the southwest border via commercial air, the report said, and its distributors are finding more users in the African–American and Hispanic communities.

Cocaine, on the other hand, remains in short supply in the United States, a trend that began in 2007.

Officials attribute that to decreased cocaine production in Colombia, a high number of cocaine seizures and a high worldwide demand, especially in European countries.

While the use and abuse of illegal drugs is of great concern, the abuse of prescription drugs is rapidly becoming more alarming, said the report, which also said that more state and local law enforcement groups identify prescription drug abuse as their top worry.

Increased abuse of prescription opioids such as morphine, codeine, and methadone sparked a 98 percent rise in overdose deaths between 2002 and 2006, the report said.

"The 2010 National Drug Threat Assessment highlights diversion and abuse of prescription drugs as a serious and increasing problem," said Gil Kerlikowske, the director of the National Drug Control Policy.

Kerlikowske said the Obama administration has "developed a plan to curb prescription drug abuse, which includes expanding prescription drug monitoring programs and educating healthcare providers and patients about the danger of abusing prescription drugs."

"This report presents a comprehensive analysis of the drug threat to our nation and will be valuable in helping direct our fight against drug trafficking and abuse," said Attorney General Eric Holder.

Critical Thinking

1. Explain the social repercussions regarding the increasing availability and abuse of illegal and prescription drugs in the United States.

2. Is there is relationship between the increase in illegal drugs available in the United States and rising prescription abuse trends?

A Pill Problem

Prescription drug abuse is the fastest growing form of substance abuse.

KARMEN HANSON

The figure is startling: A 96.6 percent increase in drug-related deaths in a five-year period.

What's most shocking is that the drugs involved are not cocaine or heroin or even methamphetamine. They are prescription drugs—medication prescribed every day by doctors, mostly for pain.

"The prescription drug problem is a crisis that is steadily worsening," says Dr. Len Paulozzi, a medical epidemiologist with the Centers for Disease Control and Prevention. "The vast majority of unintentional drug overdose deaths are not the result of toddlers getting into medicines or the elderly mixing up their pills. Our scientific evidence suggests that these deaths are related to the increasing use of prescription drugs, especially opioid painkillers, among people during the working years of life."

"The prescription drug problem is a crisis that is steadily worsening."

—Dr. Len Paulozzi, Centers for Disease Control and Prevention

Opioid analgesic painkillers, one of the largest growing segments of prescription drugs, are medications such as Oxy-Contin, Darvon and Vicodin. They include ingredients such as oxycodone, hydrocodone, fentanyl and propoxyphene. More than 201 million prescriptions were written in 2007 for products that have a potential for abuse—opioid analgesics, methylphenidates and amphetamines—according to Verispan, a prescription information database.

It was a CDC study that found the 96.6 percent increase in prescription opioid analgesic-related deaths in 28 metropolitan areas from 1997 to 2002. During the same period, deaths from cocaine overdoses increased 12.9 percent, and deaths from heroin or morphine decreased 2.7 percent.

The problem is growing faster than previously estimated. Some 4.7 million people used various prescription drugs—pain relievers, sedatives and stimulants—nonmedically for the first time in 2008, according to the National Survey on Drug Use and Health.

As Paulozzi points out, "drug overdoses are now the second leading cause of unintentional injury death in the United States, exceeded only by motor vehicle fatalities."

People who initially take prescriptions for legitimate pain relief may go on to abuse these drugs for a recreational high. Others are abusing prescription drugs from the beginning as an alternative to illegal drugs.

State legislators are hoping to reverse this growing trend. In 2009, at least 11 state legislatures enacted Drug Abuse Awareness months, regulated pain clinics, and created prescription drug monitoring programs and unused prescription drug disposal programs to help prevent fraud and abuse and to rehabilitate current abusers.

Going after the Supply

The problem is widespread across the country, hitting every type of community. It began to increase after doctors started treating chronic pain with new, stronger medications in the 1990s. While thousands of people use these products legitimately every day, they may become addicted if the drugs are not used as prescribed.

More than half the nonmedical users of prescription pain relievers get them from a friend or relative for free, according to the national drug survey. The majority of those people had obtained the drugs from one doctor. Fewer than 10 percent bought the pain relievers from a friend or relative.

In Iowa, the Division of Narcotics Enforcement opened 243 percent more pharmaceutical abuse cases and seized 412 percent more prescription drugs in 2009 than in 2008. And the Statewide Poison Control Center reported a 1,225 percent increase since 2002 in calls about suspected hydrocodone and oxycodone overdoses.

To combat such increases, Iowa launched the first statewide prescription and over-the-counter drug abuse awareness campaign, called Take a Dose of Truth. A website features information for teens, parents, older adults and professionals on recognizing, educating and treating prescription drug abuse.

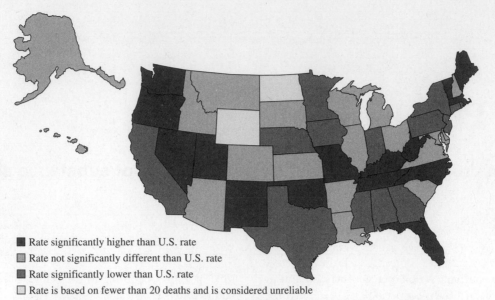

■ Rate significantly higher than U.S. rate

■ Rate not significantly different than U.S. rate

■ Rate significantly lower than U.S. rate

□ Rate is based on fewer than 20 deaths and is considered unreliable

Drug Deaths. Age-adjusted death rates involving opioid analgesics varied more than eightfold among states in 2006.

Florida's "Pill Mills"

In some states, such as Florida, pain clinics are popping up everywhere, including in shopping centers. In fact, Florida has one of the highest concentrations of pain clinics in the country. Doctors in Broward County, for example, handed out more than 6.5 million oxycodone pills, and 45 south Florida doctors gave out nearly 9 million oxycodone pills in the second half of 2008, according to an interim report of the Broward County Grand Jury.

Florida's numbers are potentially larger than nearby states because it does not have a prescription drug monitoring program. Pill seekers from across state lines may prey on neighboring states that do not track who is filling prescriptions for products prone to abuse and recreational use.

John Burke, president of the National Association of Drug Diversion Investigators, says he saw the problem play out before when Kentucky had a prescription drug monitoring program, and Ohio did not.

"Scores of folks from the Bluegrass State came into Ohio to obtain their medication at our pharmacies. Only after Ohio put their [program] in place did the influx of Kentucky illegal drug-seekers subside."

"Unfortunately this same situation exists today in Florida," he says. "The migration of Ohio drug diverters to Florida to obtain prescriptions for oxycodone is partly fueled by the fact that no [monitoring program] exists yet in Florida."

Florida legislators are considering bills to better regulate pain clinics and ensure legitimate medical need. For example, Senator Dan Gelber is sponsoring legislation that would require private pain management clinics to be registered with the department of health.

"Last year's effort to stem the tide of 'pill mills' didn't preclude felons from owning and operating pain-management clinics. This industry has attracted far too many bad apples, and this loophole needs to be closed," says Gelber. "This new provision is just common sense. The public expects, and the state should guarantee, that we do not allow convicted felons to be in the business of providing powerful narcotics to people who need legitimate pain management."

A House bill proposed by Representative Joseph Abruzzo would allow only licensed physicians to own and operate the pain clinics. "This is a national issue, as law enforcement agencies across the country are finding pill bottles with Broward or Palm Beach county addresses on them," Abruzzo says. "We need to make sure that the people who own and operate these clinics are licensed medical professionals."

> **"This is a national issue. We need to make sure that the people who own and operate these clinics are licensed medical professionals."**
>
> —Joseph Abruzzo, Florida Representative

Another House bill from Representative John Legg would limit pain prescriptions to a 72-hour supply. This effectively would eliminate abusive pain clinics, Legg says, that we make money from volume dispensing, not physician visits or prescribing. Patients requiring more than a 72-hour dose would have to go to a licensed pharmacy to fill their prescriptions, instead of getting the drugs directly from their doctor's office or a questionable pill mill.

Texas lawmakers recently passed legislation to regulate pill mills because of concerns similar to those in Florida.

"The legitimate practice of pain management clinics has a valuable role in the state," says Representative Mike Hamilton, one supporter of the new law. "However, some pain management clinics work as an illegal drug diversion, causing great harm to many families and communities. We have seen an increase in the demand of controlled substances throughout the state, and part of the problem is the proliferation of these pill mills."

Role for Doctors and Pharmacists

Physicians and pharmacists play pivotal roles in curbing abuse. They are expected to identify and care for patients who are dependent on or addicted to prescription medicines and to help prevent prescription drug abuse. It is often difficult, however, to determine if a patient is one of the 70 million Americans who experience pain every day or among the 10 percent who struggle with addiction.

Physicians, including most in primary care and emergency medicine, are often trained to recognize drug-seeking behavior and how to thwart drug abuse. They may also rely on validated questionnaires or interview instruments to recognize uncontrolled pain, and have recently begun using clinician-patient agreements defining the expectations and responsibilities of patients receiving addictive substances. Doctors also can refer to prescription drug monitoring programs for more information about a patient's history with controlled substances.

These approaches, however, can increase time-consuming paperwork. And even the well-trained and methodical physician can fall victim to dishonest patients.

Pharmacists are responsible for ensuring that patients get the most benefit from their medications. They can also be part of the first line of defense in recognizing prescription drug abuse. By monitoring prescriptions for falsification or alterations and being aware of potential "doctor shopping"—patients who obtain multiple prescriptions from different doctors—pharmacists play a valuable role in prevention. They are trained to detect suspicious behaviors, including fraudulent prescriptions.

About half the states require security features such as watermarks on prescription pads to help prevent fraud. Pharmacy and insurance company computer systems may also issue a warning if patients are taking too many controlled substances or refilling their prescriptions too quickly.

State and local pharmacy associations have historically relied on "phone trees" to contact each other when a physician reports a stolen prescription pad or a customer attempts to pass a fraudulent prescription. Greater use of electronic health records, electronic prescribing and the exchange of information may help prevent drug abuse and diversion.

"The best way for a pharmacist to balance the risks of drug abuse and undertreatment is to have a relationship with the patient and the physician," says Dr. John O'Brien of the College of Notre Dame of Maryland School of Pharmacy. "A pharmacist-physician conversation can identify more information helpful in preventing a chronic pain sufferer from being branded an addict, and also identify a patient in need of assistance with addiction or dependency."

Critical Thinking

1. Why is prescription drug abuse seemingly such a large issue? How has it become that way?

2. Are there social media that might influence the prescription drug crises? How?

KARMEN HANSON covers prescription drug issues for NCSL.

UNIT 2

Understanding How Drugs Work—Use, Dependency, and Addiction

Unit Selections

Learning Outcomes

After reading this unit, you should be able to:

• Explain why some people become dependent on certain drugs far sooner than other people.

• Describe how is it possible to predict one's own liability for becoming drug dependent.

• Discuss how it is possible for a person to say that he or she intends to be only a recreational user of drugs like cocaine or methamphetamine.

• Determine that of all of the influences that combine to create one's liability for addiction, which ones do you believe to be the most significant?

Student Website

www.mhhe.com/cls

Internet References

AddictionSearch.com
www.addictionsearch.com

Addiction Treatment Forum
www.atforum.com

APA Help Center from the American Psychological Association
www.apahelpcenter.org/articles/article.php?id=45

British Broadcasting Company Understanding Drugs
www.bbc.co.uk/health/conditions/mental_health
drugs_use.shtml

Centre for Addiction and Mental Health (CAMH)
www.camh.net

Dealing with Addictions
http://kidshealth.org/teen/your_mind/problems/addictions.html

Drugs and the Body: How Drugs Work
www.doitnow.org/pdfs/223.pdf

The National Center on Addiction and Substance Abuse at Columbia University
www.casacolumbia.org

National Institute on Drug Abuse (NIDA)
www.nida.nih.gov

Public Agenda
www.publicagenda.org

Understanding Addiction—Regret, Addiction and Death
http://teenadvice.about.com/library/weekly/aa011501a.htm

National Alcoholism Drug Information Center
http://addictioncareoptions.com

Understanding how drugs act upon the human mind and body is a critical component to the resolution of issues concerning drug use and abuse. An understanding of basic pharmacology is requisite for informed discussion on practically every drug-related issue and controversy. One does not have to look far to find misinformed debate, much of which surrounds the basic lack of knowledge of how drugs work. Different drugs produce different bodily effects and consequences. All psychoactive drugs influence the central nervous system, which, in turn, sits at the center of how we physiologically and psychologically interpret and react to the world around us. Some drugs, such as methamphetamine and LSD, have great, immediate influence on the nervous system, while others, such as tobacco and marijuana, elicit less-pronounced reactions. Almost all psychoactive drugs have their effects on the body, which are mitigated by the dosage level of the drug taken, the manner in which it is ingested, and the physiological and emotional state of the user. Cocaine smoked in the form of crack versus snorted as powder produces profoundly different physical and emotional effects on the user. However, even though illegal drugs often provide the most sensational perspective from which to view these relationships, the abuse of prescription drugs is being reported as an exploding new component of the addiction problem. Currently, the non-medical use of painrelievers such as oxycodone and hydrocodone is continuing at alarming rates. This trend has been increasing steadily since 1994, and it currently competes with methamphetamine abuse as the most alarming national trend of drug abuse. Currently, more than 5 million Americans use prescription pain medications for non-medical reasons.

Molecular properties of certain drugs allow them to imitate and artificially reproduce certain naturally occurring brain chemicals that provide the basis for the drug's influence. The continued use of certain drugs and their repeated alteration of the body's biochemical structure provide one explanation for the physiological consequences of drug use. The human brain is the quintessential master pharmacist and repeatedly altering its chemical functions by drug use is risky. Doing such things may produce profound implications for becoming addicted. For example, heroin use replicates the natural brain chemical endorphin, which supports the body's biochemical defense to pain and stress. The continued use of heroin is believed to deplete natural endorphins, causing the nervous system to produce a painful physical and emotional reaction when heroin is withdrawn. Subsequently, one significant motivation for continued use is realized. A word of caution is in order, however, when proceeding through the various explanations for what drugs do and why they do it. Many people, because of an emotional and/or political relationship to the world of drugs, assert a subjective predisposition when interpreting certain drugs' effects and consequences. One person is an alcoholic while another is a social drinker. People often argue, rationalize, and explain the perceived nature of drugs' effects based upon an extremely superficial understanding of diverse pharmacological properties of different drugs. A detached and scientifically sophisticated awareness of drug pharmacology may help strengthen the platform from which to interpret the various consequences of

drug use. Drug addiction results as a continuum comprised of experimentation, recreational use, regular use, and abuse. The process is influenced by a plethora of physiological, psychological, and environmental factors. Although some still argue that drug dependence is largely a matter of individual behavior—something to be chosen or rejected—most experts agree that new scientific discoveries clearly define the roots of addiction to live within molecular levels of the brain. Powerful drugs, upon repeated administration, easily compromise the brain's ability to make decisions about its best interests.

One theory used to describe specific drugs as more addictive or less addictive explains a process referred to as "reinforcement." Simply explained, reinforcement is a form of psychological conditioning that results from a drug's influence on a person's brain. Reinforcement is the term used to describe a person's behavior that expresses the uncontrollable need to repeatedly introduce the drug to the body. Powerful drugs such as the stimulant cocaine and the depressant oxycodone influence the brain's reward pathway and promote behavior in which drug seeking is recognized by the brain as actions necessary for survival. Persons addicted to drugs known to be strongly reinforcing typically report that they care more about getting the drug than about anything else—even in the face of self-destruction.

Drug addiction and the rate at which it occurs must compete with certain physiological and psychological, as well as environmental variables that are unique to individuals. A drug user with a greater number of biological markers, known to be associated with drug addiction, such as mental illness, alcoholism, and poor physical health, may encourage drug dependency sooner than a person with fewer biological markers. Similarly, a person's positive environmental associations, or "natural reinforcers," such as a strong family structure, and healthy personal and professional relationships may not only make experimentation unappealing, it may delay a user's developing drug addiction. Subsequently, one's liability for drug addiction is closely associated with genetics, environment, and the use of psychoactive drugs. Understanding the concept of addiction requires an awareness of these factors. For many people, drug addiction and the reasons that contribute to it are murky concepts.

The articles in Unit 2 illustrate some of the current research and viewpoints on the ways that drugs act upon the human body. New science is suggesting that a new era has begun relative to understanding drugs and their pharmacological influence on the human body. This new science is critical to understanding the assorted consequences of drug use and abuse. Science has taken us closer to understanding that acute drug use changes brain function profoundly, and that these changes may remain with the user long after the drug has left the system. New research investigating the liabilities produced by adolescents smoking tobacco suggests that even small amounts produce a remarkable susceptibility for addiction. Subsequently, many new issues have emerged for drug- and health-related public policy. Increasingly, drug abuse competes with other social maladies as public enemy number one. Further, the need for a combined biological, behavioral, and social response to this problem becomes more evident. Many healthcare professionals and healthcare educators, in addition to those from other diverse backgrounds, argue that research dollars spent on drug abuse and addiction should approach that spent on heart disease, cancer, and AIDS. The articles in Unit 2 provide examples of how some new discoveries have influenced our thinking about addiction. They also provide examples of how, even in light of new knowledge, breaking addictions is so very hard to do.

Drug Addiction and Its Effects

Many people do not understand why individuals become addicted to drugs or how drugs change the brain to foster compulsive drug abuse. They mistakenly view drug abuse and addiction as strictly a social problem and may characterize those who take drugs as morally weak. One very common belief is that drug abusers should be able to just stop taking drugs if they are only willing to change their behavior. What people often underestimate is the complexity of drug addiction—that it is a disease that impacts the brain and because of that, stopping drug abuse is not simply a matter of willpower. Through scientific advances we now know much more about how exactly drugs work in the brain, and we also know that drug addiction can be successfully treated to help people stop abusing drugs and resume their productive lives.

What Is Drug Addiction?

Addiction is a chronic, often relapsing brain disease that causes compulsive drug seeking and use despite harmful consequences to the individual that is addicted and to those around them. Drug addiction is a brain disease because the abuse of drugs leads to changes in the structure and function of the brain. Although it is true that for most people the initial decision to take drugs is voluntary, over time the changes in the brain caused by repeated drug abuse can affect a person's self control and ability to make sound decisions, and at the same time send intense impulses to take drugs.

It is because of these changes in the brain that it is so challenging for a person who is addicted to stop abusing drugs. Fortunately, there are treatments that help people to counteract addiction's powerful disruptive effects and regain control. Research shows that combining addiction treatment medications, if available, with behavioral therapy is the best way to ensure success for most patients. Treatment approaches that are tailored to each patient's drug abuse patterns and any co-occurring medical, psychiatric, and social problems can lead to sustained recovery and a life without drug abuse.

Similar to other chronic, relapsing diseases, such as diabetes, asthma, or heart disease, drug addiction can be managed successfully. And, as with other chronic diseases, it is not uncommon for a person to relapse and begin abusing drugs again. Relapse, however, does not signal failure—rather, it indicates that treatment should be reinstated, adjusted, or that alternate treatment is needed to help the individual regain control and recover.

What Happens to Your Brain When You Take Drugs?

Drugs are chemicals that tap into the brain's communication system and disrupt the way nerve cells normally send, receive, and process information. There are at least two ways that drugs are able to do this: (1) by imitating the brain's natural chemical messengers, and/or (2) by overstimulating the "reward circuit" of the brain.

Some drugs, such as marijuana and heroin, have a similar structure to chemical messengers, called neurotransmitters, which are naturally produced by the brain. Because of this similarity, these drugs are able to "fool" the brain's receptors and activate nerve cells to send abnormal messages.

Other drugs, such as cocaine or methamphetamine, can cause the nerve cells to release abnormally large amounts of natural neurotransmitters, or prevent the normal recycling of these brain chemicals, which is needed to shut off the signal between neurons. This disruption produces a greatly amplified message that ultimately disrupts normal communication patterns.

Nearly all drugs, directly or indirectly, target the brain's reward system by flooding the circuit with dopamine. Dopamine is a neurotransmitter present in regions of the brain that control movement, emotion, motivation, and feelings of pleasure. The overstimulation of this system, which normally responds to natural behaviors that are linked to survival (eating, spending time with loved ones, etc.), produces euphoric effects in response to the drugs. This reaction sets in motion a pattern that "teaches" people to repeat the behavior of abusing drugs.

As a person continues to abuse drugs, the brain adapts to the overwhelming surges in dopamine by producing less dopamine or by reducing the number of dopamine receptors in the reward circuit. As a result, dopamine's impact on the reward circuit is lessened, reducing the abuser's ability to enjoy the drugs and the things that previously brought pleasure. This decrease compels those addicted to drugs to keep abusing drugs in order to attempt to bring their dopamine function back to normal. And, they may now require larger amounts of the drug than they first did to achieve the dopamine high—an effect known as tolerance.

Long-term abuse causes changes in other brain chemical systems and circuits as well. Glutamate is a neurotransmitter that influences the reward circuit and the ability to learn. When the optimal concentration of glutamate is altered by drug abuse, the brain attempts to compensate, which can impair cognitive function. Drugs of abuse facilitate nonconscious (conditioned) learning, which leads the user to experience uncontrollable cravings when they see a place or person they associate with the drug experience, even when the drug itself is not available. Brain imaging studies of drug-addicted individuals show changes in areas of the brain that are critical to judgment, decisionmaking, learning and memory, and behavior control. Together, these changes can drive an abuser to seek out and take drugs compulsively despite adverse consequences—in other words, to become addicted to drugs.

Why Do Some People Become Addicted, While Others Do Not?

No single factor can predict whether or not a person will become addicted to drugs. Risk for addiction is influenced by a person's biology, social environment, and age or stage of development. The more risk factors an individual has, the greater the chance that taking drugs can lead to addiction. For example:

- **Biology.** The genes that people are born with—in combination with environmental influences—account for about half of their addiction vulnerability. Additionally, gender, ethnicity, and the presence of other mental disorders may influence risk for drug abuse and addiction.
- **Environment.** A person's environment includes many different influences—from family and friends to socioeconomic status and quality of life in general. Factors such as peer pressure, physical and sexual abuse, stress, and parental involvement can greatly influence the course of drug abuse and addiction in a person's life.

- **Development.** Genetic and environmental factors interact with critical developmental stages in a person's life to affect addiction vulnerability, and adolescents experience a double challenge. Although taking drugs at any age can lead to addiction, the earlier that drug use begins, the more likely it is to progress to more serious abuse. And because adolescents' brains are still developing in the areas that govern decisionmaking, judgment, and self-control, they are especially prone to risk-taking behaviors, including trying drugs of abuse.

Prevention Is the Key

Drug addiction is a preventable disease. Results from NIDA-funded research have shown that prevention programs that involve the family, schools, communities, and the media are effective in reducing drug abuse. Although many events and cultural factors affect drug abuse trends, when youths perceive drug abuse as harmful, they reduce their drug taking. It is necessary, therefore, to help youth and the general public to understand the risks of drug abuse and for teachers, parents, and healthcare professionals to keep sending the message that drug addiction can be prevented if a person never abuses drugs.

Critical Thinking

1. Drug addiction carries with it a stigma, and is often not thought of as a disease. Explain the reason behind this.
2. If drug addiction is a preventable disease, what do you think the future of drug abuse will look like?

Family History of Alcohol Abuse Associated with Problematic Drinking among College Students

Joseph W. LaBrie et al.

1. Introduction

Risky drinking among college students is of particular concern for university administrators and health professionals. Researchers have attempted to isolate correlates of risky drinking. A family history of alcohol abuse (FH+) is a well-documented risk factor for heavy alcohol use and alcohol-related problems (Chalder, Elgar, & Bennett, 2006; Cotton, 1979; Hussong, Curran, & Chassin, 1998; Kuntsche Rehm, & Gmel, 2004; Pullen, 1994; Turnbull, 1994; Warner, White, & Johnson., 2007). About 20% of college students are FH+ (Perkins, 2002) and the college environment may be more harmful for those students predisposed to alcohol problems. A few studies have revealed considerably higher rates of alcohol use (Kushner & Sher, 1993; LaBrie, Kenney, Lac, & Migliuri, 2009; Pullen, 1994) and alcohol-related problems (Leeman, Fenton, & Volpicelli, 2007) among FH+ compared with FH– college students. In contrast, other studies have found no relationship between family history and problematic alcohol use among college students (Engs, 1990; MacDonald, Fleming, & Barry, 1991; Harrell, Slane, & Klump, 2009). Further, there have been conflicting results on the role gender plays among FH+ college students. Some have found FH+ males to be more susceptible to risky drinking and consequences than FH+ females (e.g. Andersson, Johnsson, Berglund, & Öjehagen, 2007; Jackson, Sher, Gotham, & Wood, 2001; Sher, Walitzer, Wood, & Brent, 1991), while Hartford, Parker and Grant (1992) found no such gender difference. Inconsistencies in existing research highlight the need to explicate how family history status may impact drinking behaviors and problems in collegiate populations.

Alcohol expectancies, the specific beliefs about the behavioral, emotional, and cognitive effects of alcohol (Leigh, 1987), are a potential psychosocial motivator of risky drinking. Stronger positive alcohol expectancies are associated with problem drinking (e.g. Anderson, Schweinsburg, Paulus, Brown, & Tapert, 2005; Brown, Goldman, & Christiansen, 1985).

Alcohol-outcome expectancies result from both personal experience with alcohol and from mirroring drinking behavior of individuals (Lundahl et al, 1997), and have thus been shown to differ by family history status in that FH+ individuals have endorsed stronger alcohol-related expectancies, particularly overall positive expectancies (Morean et al, 2009; Pastor & Evans, 2003). Further, FH+ individuals with stronger overall positive expectancies are most likely to experience alcohol-related problems (Conway, Swendsen, & Merikangas, 2003; VanVoorst & Quirk, 2003).

Much of the previous research on family history of alcohol abuse has focused on COAs (children of alcohols) during adolescence (Barnow, Schuckit, Lucht, John, & Freyberger, 2002; Brown, Creamer, & Stetson, 1987; Chalder et al., 2006; Nash, McQueen, & Bray, 2005; Sher et al., 1991) and middle–late adulthood (Beaudoin, Murray, Bond, & Barnes, 1997; Cloninger, Sigvardsson, & Bohman, 1996; Curran et al., 1999). Moreover, family history studies involving college students have suffered from various limitations, such as a relatively small sample size (e.g., Leeman et al., 2007; Pullen, 1994), single-sex samples (e.g. LaBrie et al., 2009; Harrell et al., 2009), or first-year student samples (e.g. Andersson et al., 2007, Gotham, Sher, & Wood, 2003; Jackson et al., 2001). The present study broadens previous research by offering unique insight into family history of alcohol abuse, alcohol-related behaviors and problems, and further examines the moderating effect of gender in family history status on alcohol consumption, alcohol expectancies, and alcohol-related consequences among a large, multisite, ethnically diverse sample of male and female college students.

2. Methods
2.1 Participants

Participants were recruited from two west-coast universities, a large, public institution with 30,000 undergraduates and a mid-sized private institution with approximately 5500 undergraduates. Of a randomly selected pool of 7000 students, 3753 (53.6%) consented to participate. Representative of the makeup of the corresponding institutions, participants' mean age was 19.88 ($SD = 1.36$) and the majority of the participants were female (61%). The sample consisted of 18.9% first-year students, 24.5% sophomores, 27.4% juniors, and 29.2% seniors. Racial representation was as follows: 57.4% Caucasian, 18.7% Asian, 10.7% Multiracial, 3.2% African American, and 10.0% reported other racial/ethnic groups. On average, participants consumed 6.04 ($SD = 8.58$) drinks over 1.59 ($SD = 1.53$) drinking days per week. Among the 67.5% of students who drank, they consumed an average of 8.94 ($SD = 9.11$) drinks per week and averaged 2.36 ($SD = 1.30$) drinking days.

2.2. Design and Procedure

At the start of the fall semester, 7000 students (3500 from each campus), received letters inviting them to participate in a study about alcohol use and perceptions of college-student drinking. The students were directed to a link for an online survey. After students clicked on the link and entered their individual pin, they were presented with a local IRB-approved consent form. Participants then completed a 20 min survey, for which they received a $20 compensation.

2.3 Measures

2.3.1. Demographics

Participants indicated their gender, age, most recent GPA, and race.

2.3.2. Family History

Participants indicated whether they had a biological relative that "has or has had a significant drinking problem—one that should or did lead to treatment." This measure was previously developed and successfully used by Miller & Marlatt (1984).

2.3.3. Alcohol Consumption

The Daily Drinking Questionnaire (DDQ: Collins, parks, & Marlan, 1985; Kivlahan, Marlatt, Fromme, & Coppel, 1990) asked students to report, from the past 30 days, the typical number of drinks they consumed each day of the week. Responses were summed to form a total drinks per week variable used in this analysis.

2.3.4. Negative Consequences

The 25-item Rutgers Alcohol Problem Index (RAPI, White & Labouvie, 1989) ($\alpha = .925$) assessed alcohol-related consequences. Using a 0 (*never*) to 4 (*more than 10 times*) scale, participants indicated how many times in the past three months they had experienced each stated circumstance (e.g., "Caused shame or embarrassment to someone," "Passed out or fainted suddenly," or "Felt that you had a problem with school.").

2.3.5. Alcohol Expectancies and Evaluations

The Comprehensive Effects of Alcohol (CEOA; Fromme, Stroot, & Kaplan, 1993) is a two-part questionnaire consisting of 76 items. In Part 1, representing items tapping expectancies, participants indicated expectations concerning how he or she may act or feel under the influence of alcohol (e.g., "I would enjoy sex more," "I would act sociable"; 1 = "disagree" 4 = "agree"). In Part 2, representing evaluations, participants subjectively evaluated the effects of alcohol with the same 38 items as Part 1 of the questionnaire (e.g., "Enjoying sex more," "Feeling sociable"; 1 = "bad" 3 = "neutral" 5 = "good"). Each of the expectancies and evaluations components may be further divided into positive factors (sociability, tension reduction, liquid courage, and sexuality) and negative factors (cognitive behavioral impairment, risk and aggression, and self-perception).

3. Results

A family history of alcohol abuse was reported by 35.0% of the total sample, and FH+ participants were more likely to have drank in the past year than their FH− peers (81% vs. 74%; $\chi^2 = 9.63$, $p < .001$). Independent sample t-tests, separately conducted for males and females, revealed several systematic differences between FH+ and FH− respondents (Table 1). Among males, FH+ respondents averaged significantly higher than their FH− counterparts on drinks per week, negative consequences, overall positive expectancies, positive expectancies concerned with tension reduction and liquid courage, as well as positive evaluations concerned with tension reduction. Among females, FH+ respondents reported significantly higher drinks per week, negative consequences, overall positive expectancies, as well as positive expectancies concerned with sociability, tension reduction, and sexuality in comparison to the FH− participants. Typically, FH+ females reported negative evaluations (risk and aggression, and self-perception) to be worse than did FH− females.

Additional analyses show that, among males, FH+ participants drank 45.7% more drinks per week and experienced 43.6% more negative consequences than those classified as FH−. Among females, however, FH+ individuals consumed 14.4% more drinks and experienced 23.6% more negative consequences than their FH− counterparts. Such results, taken together, suggest that a family history of alcohol abuse may adversely impact males more than females in the college environment.

An ANCOVA model, controlling for age, GPA, race, overall positive and negative expectancies, and overall positive and negative evaluations, was performed to predict drinks per week. Family history status (FH+ or FH−) and respondent gender (male or female) served as the independent factors. After ruling out the statistical contribution of the covariates, main effects were found for both family history and gender, and their interaction also emerged (Table 2). This statistical interaction, presented in Figure 1, revealed that the difference between FH+ and FH− on drinking was more pronounced in males than females, and that FH+ males were especially vulnerable to higher levels of alcohol consumption.

A second ANCOVA model was conducted to predict alcohol negative consequences. Age, GPA, race, and drinks per week were entered as covariates, and family history and gender served

Table 1 Mean Difference on Drinking Variable by Family History, for Males and Females.

Measure	Males					Females				
	FH+ (n = 435)		FH– (n = 1008)			FH+ (n = 875)		FH– (n = 1420)		
	M	(SD)	M	(SD)	t-test	M	(SD)	M	(SD)	t-test
Drinks per week	10.75	(12.83)	7.38	(10.43)	5.21***	4.94	(6.04)	4.32	(5.68)	2.48*
Negative consequences	6.72	(9.10)	4.68	(8.77)	5.21***	4.55	(6.64)	3.68	(6.03)	3.11**
Overall positive expectancies	2.55	(0.55)	2.47	(0.58)	2.16*	2.42	(0.58)	2.35	(0.59)	2.73**
Sociability	2.94	(0.68)	2.88	(0.70)	1.50	2.96	(0.73)	2.87	(0.73)	2.74**
Tension reduction	2.63	(0.71)	2.53	(0.74)	2.39*	2.32	(0.72)	2.24	(0.72)	2.53*
Liquid courage	2.48	(0.69)	2.39	(0.72)	2.14*	2.29	(0.71)	2.25	(0.73)	1.18
Sexuality	2.13	(0.73)	2.09	(0.73)	0.93	2.12	(0.76)	2.05	(0.75)	2.11*
Overall negative expectancies	2.28	(0.52)	2.28	(0.59)	0.07	2.20	(0.56)	2.20	(0.58)	0.21
Cognitive behavioral imp.	2.64	(0.60)	2.63	(0.65)	0.32	2.64	(0.65)	2.62	(0.68)	0.73
Risk and aggression	2.31	(0.71)	2.26	(0.73)	1.21	2.10	(0.74)	2.11	(0.74)	–0.40
Self-perception	1.89	(0.64)	1.95	(0.72)	–1.34	1.87	(0.69)	1.87	(0.69)	0.25
Overall positive evaluations	3.48	(0.84)	3.40	(0.83)	1.75	3.18	(0.85)	3.19	(0.86)	–0.39
Sociability	3.84	(0.93)	3.80	(0.92)	0.85	3.66	(0.94)	3.65	(0.95)	0.27
Tension reduction	3.82	(1.00)	3.67	(0.97)	2.55*	3.41	(0.99)	3.40	(1.00)	0.26
Liquid courage	2.95	(0.91)	2.90	(0.90)	0.98	2.72	(0.90)	2.79	(0.91)	–1.79
Sexuality	3.32	(1.07)	3.21	(1.02)	1.69	2.92	(1.08)	2.92	(1.05)	–0.20
Overall negative evaluations	1.89	(0.57)	1.92	(0.62)	–0.89	1.68	(0.50)	1.76	(0.55)	–3.45***
Cognitive behavioral imp.	1.82	(0.64)	1.82	(0.68)	0.04	1.62	(0.56)	1.63	(0.58)	–0.19
Risk and aggression	2.13	(0.83)	2.15	(0.84)	–0.39	1.92	(0.76)	2.07	(0.81)	–4.25***
Self-perception	1.71	(0.64)	1.79	(0.71)	–1.85	1.49	(0.55)	1.58	(0.61)	–3.49***

*p<.05. **p<.01. ***p<.001.

as the independent variables. After the variance attributed to the covariates were accounted for in the model, family history remained statistically significant, but no gender main effect or interaction was discovered (Table 2).

4. Discussion

The present investigation uses a large multisite sample and corroborates extant literature by identifying family history as a significant risk factor for alcohol misuse and related consequences among male and female college students (Kushner & Sher, 1993; Leeman et al., 2007; LaBrie et al., 2009; Pullen, 1994). More specifically, this study extends previous research by finding that, whether attributable to genetics or environmental upbringing, familial ties to alcoholism were considerably more hazardous for males than females in regard to excessive alcohol consumption. Compared to FH– same-sex peers, FH+ males drank 41% more drinks per week and FH+ females drank 14% more drinks per week. Notably, results covaried out other important predictors

of drinking (e.g. age, GPA, race) to better assess how FH status and gender may be related to drinking in college, over and above such variables. By highlighting family history positive college students' heightened susceptibility to risky drinking and consequences, and male FH+ students' enhanced risk for alcohol misuse, the current results may help college personnel identify and target prevention efforts to at-risk students. Preventative interventions taking place early in college with FH+ students might help them better understand their heightened alcohol-related vulnerabilities and provide them with tools and motivation to reduce potential harm.

In addition, findings both confirm and extend relevant research examining the role that alcohol expectancies play in FH+ college students' alcohol behaviors and outcomes. Not only did students reporting familial alcohol abuse endorse significantly greater overall positive expectancies than same-sex FH– counterparts, but FH+ female respondents evaluated the negative effects of alcohol to be substantially "more bad" than FH– females. This paradoxical finding, in which women exposed to familial alcohol

Table 2 ANCOVA Models Predicting Drinks Per Week and Negative Consequences.

Variable	df	MS	F test
DV: drinks per week			
Covariates			
Age	1	137.51	2.29
GPA	1	209.84	3.49
Race	1	5207.62	86.57***
Overall positive expectancies	1	10,846.35	108.31***
Overall negative expectancies	1	6536.75	108.67***
Overall positive evaluations	1	6.15	0.10
Overall negative evaluations	1	2833.10	47.10***
Family history	1	1032.70	17.17***
Gender	1	8485.34	141.06***
Family history × gender	1	1025.75	17.05***
DV: negative consequences			
Covariates			
Age	1	95.33	2.34
GPA	1	452.91	11.09***
Race	1	423.66	10.39**
Drinks per week	1	43,439.92	1063.97***
Family history	1	460.67	11.28
Gender	1	130.98	3.21
Family history × gender	1	2.71	0.07

Note: race (1 = Caucasian, 0 = non-Caucasian).
* $p < .05$. ** $p < .01$. *** $p < .001$.

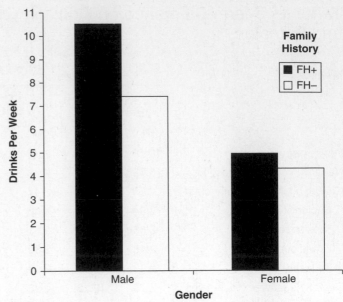

Figure 1 Family history status × gender interaction on drinks per week.

abuse judged alcohol's negative evaluations to be worse, yet were more likely to agree that drinking personally yielded positive effects (i.e., expectancies) may suggest that FH+ women may not equate their own drinking with that of alcoholic family members and thus may feel immune to the negative evaluations they themselves associate with alcohol. More concerning, however, is the possibility that these findings may be indicative of cognitive dissonance, whereby highly endorsed positive expectancies contribute to continued drinking, often heavy drinking, in students even though they have been exposed to, and thus recognize, the negative aspects of drinking. By rationalizing alcohol misuse through heightened expectancies, FH+ college females may be able to reduce dissonance and fulfill strong, possibly genetically predisposed desires to imbibe. Regardless, FH+ students' apparent awareness of the negative effects of alcohol use through their own familial experience may be a promising avenue for intervening. Intervention with these students should allow them to reflect on and be mindful of their experiences with these negative effects, thereby building motivation to avoid these same consequences while challenging positive alcohol expectancies.

The present findings are limited in that they do not account for environmental risk factors known to co-occur with FH+ status (e.g., histories of physical or sexual abuse or attraction to high-risk student groups) and that may confound the relationship between FH+ status and both alcohol expectancies and misuse. Future studies assessing such risk factors may be warranted. Another limitation of the current study is the use of one, nonspecific classification of FH+ status. Future research may benefit from distinguishing first, second, and third degree affiliation to alcohol abuse (e.g. parent vs. grandparent or aunt/uncle), gender of the relative with alcohol problems (e.g. mother vs. father), or familial history density (i.e., whether an individual has more than one family member with an alcohol problem). A more defined classification of FH status may also reveal environmental risk factors; for instance, the extent to which residential exposure to alcoholism may heighten risk.

The current study reveals that FH+ students make up a substantial percentage (35%) of the college population and that these students are at increased risk for problematic drinking and consequences as compared to their FH− peers. Despite this and previous research in concert with the current findings, preventative interventions targeting FH+ students are lacking. Both researchers and college health personnel may wish to invest resources in targeting these individuals.

References

Anderson, K. G., Schweinsburg, A., Paulus, M., Brown, S. A., & Tapert, S. (2005). Examining personality and alcohol expectancies using functional magnetic resonance imaging (fMRI) with adolescents. *Journal of Studies on Alcohol, 66,* 323–331.

Article 10. Family History of Alcohol Abuse Associated with Problematic Drinking among College Students

Andersson, C., Johnsson, K., Berglund, M., & Öjehagen, A. (2007). Alcohol involvement in Swedish university freshmen related to gender, age, serious relationship and family history of alcohol problems. *Alcohol and Alcoholism, 42*(5), 448–455.

Barnow, S., Schuckit, M., Lucht, M., John, U., & Freyberger, H. J. (2002). The importance of positive family history of alcoholism, parental rejection and emotional warmth, behavioral problems and peer substance use for alcohol problems in teenagers: a path analysis. *Journal of Studies on Alcohol, 63,* 305–315.

Beaudoin, C. M., Murray, R. P., Bond, J., Jr., & Barnes, G. E. (1997). Personality characteristics of depressed or alcoholic adult children of alcoholics. *Personality and Individual Differences, 23,* 559–567.

Brown, S. A., Creamer, V. A., & Stetson, B. A. (1987). Adolescent alcohol expectancies in relation to personal and parental drinking patterns. *Journal of Abnormal Psychology, 96,* 117–121.

Brown, S., Goldman, M., & Christiansen, B. (1985). Do alcohol expectancies mediate drinking patterns of adults? *Journal of Consulting and Clinical Psychology, 53*(4), 512–519.

Chalder, M., Elgar, F. J., & Bennett, P. (2006). Drinking and motivations to drink among adolescent children of parents with alcohol problems. *Alcohol & Alcoholism, 41*(1), 107–113.

Cloninger, C. R., Sigvardsson, S., & Bohman, M. (1996). Type I and Type II Alcoholism: an update. *Alcohol Health and Research World, 20,* 18–23.

Collins, R. L., Parks, G. A., & Marlett, A. (1985). Social determinants of alcohol consumption: the effects of social interaction and model status on self-administration of alcohol. *Journal of Consulting and Clinical Psychology, 53*(2), 189–200.

Conway, K. P., Swendsen, J. D., & Merikangas, K. R. (2003). Alcohol expectancies, alcohol consumption, and problem drinking. *The moderating role of family history. Addictive Behaviors, 28,* 823–836.

Cotton, N. S. (1979). The familial incidence of alcoholism: a review. *Journal of Studies on Alcohol, 40*(1), 89–116.

Curran, G. M., Stoltenberg, S. F., Hill, E. M., Mudd, S. A., Blow, F. C., & Zucker, R. A. (1999). Gender differences in the relationship among SES, family history of alcohol disorders and alcohol dependence. *Journal of Studies on Alcohol, 60,* 825–832.

Engs, R. (1990). Family background of alcohol abuse and its relationship to alcohol consumption among college students: an unexpected finding. *Journal of Studies on Alcohol, 51*(6), 542–547.

Fromme, K., Stroot, E., & Kaplan, D. (1993). Comprehensive effects of alcohol: development and psychometric assessment of a new expectancy questionnaire. *Psychological Assessment, 5*(1), 19–26.

Gotham, H. J., Sher, K. J., & Wood, P. K. (2003). Alcohol involvement and development task completion during young adulthood. *Journal of Studies on Alcohol, 64,* 32–42.

Harford, T., Parker, D., & Grant, B. (1992). Family history, alcohol use and dependence symptoms among young adults in the United States. *Alcoholism: Clinical and Experimental Research, 16*(6), 1042–1046.

Harrell, Z., Slane, J., & Klump, K. (2009). Predictors of alcohol problems in college women: the role of depressive symptoms, disordered eating, and family history of alcoholism. *Addictive Behaviors, 34*(3), 252–257.

Hussong, A. M., Curran, P. J., & Chassin, L. (1998). Pathways of risk for accelterated heavy alcohol use among adolescent children of alcohol parents. *Journal of Abnormal Child Psychology, 26*(6), 453.

Kivlahan, D. R., Marlatt, G. A., Fromme, K., & Coppel, D. B. (1990). Secondary prevention with college drinkers: evaluation of an alcohol skills training program. *Journal of Consulting and Clinical Psychology, 58,* 805–810.

Kuntsche, E., Rehm, J., & Gmel, G. (2004). Characteristics of binge drinkers in Europe. *Social Science & Medicine, 59,* 113–127.

Kushner, M. G., & Sher, K. J. (1993). Comorbidity of alcohol and anxiety disorders among college students: effects of gender and family history of alcoholism. *Addictive Behaviors, 18,* 543–552.

Jackson, K. M., Sher, K. J., Gotham, H. J., & Wood, P. K. (2001). Transition into and out of large-effect drinking in young adulthood. *Journal of Abnormal Psychology, 110*(3), 378–391.

LaBrie, J. W., Kenney, S. R., Lac, A., & Migliuri, S. M. (2009). Differential drinking patterns of family history positive and family history negative first semester college females. *Addictive Behaviors, 34,* 190–196.

Leeman, R., Fenton, M., & Volpicelli, J. (2007). Impaired control and undergraduate problem drinking. *Alcohol & Alcoholism, 42*(1), 42–48.

Leigh, B. C. (1987). Evaluations of alcohol expectancies: do they add to prediction of drinking patterns? *Psychology of Addictive Behaviors, 1*(3), 135–139.

Lundahl, L., Davis, T., Adesso, V., & Lukas, S. (1997). Alcohol expectancies: effects of gender, age, and family history of alcoholism. *Addictive Behaviors, 22*(1), 115–125.

MacDonald, R., Fleming, M., & Barry, K. (1991). Risk factors associated with alcohol abuse in college students. *American Journal of Drug and Alcohol Abuse, 17*(4), 439–449.

Miller, W. R., & Marlatt, G. A. (1984). Brief drinking profile. Odessa, FL: Psychological Assessment Resources.

Morean, M. E., Corbin, W. R., Sinha, R., & O'Malley, S. S. (2009). Parental history of anxiety and alcohol-use disorders and alcohol expectancies as predictors of alcohol-related problems. *Journal of Studies on Alcohol and Drugs, 70,* 227–236.

Nash, S. G., McQueen, A., & Bray, J. H. (2005). Pathways to adolescent alcohol use: family environment, peer influence, and parental expectations. *Journal of Adolescent Health, 37,* 19–28.

Pastor, A. D., & Evans, S. M. (2003). Alcohol outcome expectancies and risk for alcohol use problems in women with and without a family history of alcoholism. *Drug and Alcohol Dependence, 70,* 201–214.

Perkins, H. W. (2002). Surveying the damage: a review of research on consequences of alcohol misuse in college populations. *Journal of Studies on Alcohol, 14,* 91–100.

Pullen, L. M. (1994). The relationship among alcohol abuse in college students and selected psychological/demographic variables. *Journal of Alcohol and Drug Education, 40*(1), 36–50.

Sher, K. J., Walitzer, K. S., Wood, P. K., & Brent, E. E. (1991). Characteristics of children of alcoholics: putative risk factors, substance use and abuse, and psychopathology. *Journal of Abnormal Psychology, 100,* 427–448.

Turnbull, J. E. (1994). Early background variables as predictors of adult alcohol problems in women. *International Journal of the Addictions, 29,* 707–728.

VanVoorst, W. A., & Quirk, S. W. (2003). Are relations between parental history of alcohol problems and changes in drinking moderated by positive expectancies? *Alcoholism: Clinical and Experimental Research, 26,* 25–30.

White, H., & Labouvie, E. (1989). Towards the assessment of adolescent problem drinking. *Journal of Studies on Alcohol, 50*(1), 30–37.

Warner, L. A., White, H. R., & Johnson, V. (2007). Alcohol initiation experiences and family history of alcoholism as predictors of problem-drinking trajectories. *Journal of Studies on Alcohol and Drugs, 68,* 56–65.

Critical Thinking

1. Explain why FH+ women may experience cognitive dissonance regarding their own use of alcohol?

2. Would having this information available influence college student's behavior?

Acknowledgment—Support for this research was provided by National Institute of Alcohol Abuse and Alcoholism grant R01-AA012547.

Biological Perspectives-Antimethamphetamine Antibodies: A New Concept for Treating Methamphetamine Users

CYNTHIA JANE ANDERSON, SN, KATHLEEN GILCHRIST, PhD, RN, AND NORMAN L. KELTNER, EdD, APRN

"Honestly, there's nothing I miss about being a tweaker."
—Former methamphetamine user

Crystal, speed, ice, crank, railes, smack, hydro, go fast, chalk, white cross, the hard, Tina; these are just some of the street names for an incredibly addicting and nearly ubiquitous drug: methamphetamine (KCI The Anti-Methamphetamine Site, 2008). In 2006, an estimated 731,000 people in the United States over the age of 12 years were using methamphetamines, and 1.9 million people 12 years of age and older had abused the drug at least once in the year preceding the survey (National Institute on Drug Abuse, 2008). Because of this widespread use and the serious social implications, methamphetamine has been receiving national attention in recent years with vigorous advertising campaigns to combat its allure and abuse (U.S. Department of Justice Drug Enforcement Administration [DEA], 2007).

A national initiative in 2005, called The Combat Methamphetamine Epidemic Act, made it illegal to sell some of the over-the-counter ingredients used to make methamphetamine (e.g., pseudoephedrine, ephedrine, and phenylpropanolamine; DEA, 2007). Equally important to preventing the production and use of methamphetamine is understanding the process of recovery from this addiction. This article begins with a review of pathophysiological issues that nurses should consider when working with methamphetamine-addicted individuals.

Amphetamines were synthetically developed in 1887 and have been used to treat conditions such as attention-deficit/hyperactivity disorder, narcolepsy, obesity, and even as an adjunct to psychotherapy. Amphetamines can be snorted, swallowed in pill form, injected, or smoked (Townsend, 2006).

Methamphetamine is, of course, an amphetamine—actually amphetamine with a methyl group [CH_3] attached. McCance and Grey (2008) defined the different levels of methamphetamine use as low intensity, high intensity, and tweaking (frantic, compulsive behavior related to methamphetamine use).

Methamphetamines are indirect-acting sympathomimetics. These indirect mechanisms include an increase in presynaptic norepinephrine release and inhibition of norepinephrine reuptake. These actions produce increased levels of norepinephrine in the synaptic cleft, resulting in an overall overstimulation of postsynaptic neurons. Decreased levels of norepinephrine have been linked with depression, so the flood of norepinephrine in the synaptic space may add to the euphoria that amphetamines produce. Interestingly, most methamphetamine users never recapture the level of intensity of the euphoria experienced during their first high; yet they may seek it continually (Keltner & Pugh, 2007). Methamphetamine side effects include tachycardia, restlessness, agitation, insomnia, palpitations, hypertension, and weight loss (Sugerman, 2008).

Keltner and Pugh (2007) also note that amphetamines produce a profound effect on the "pleasure pathways" in the brain by enhancing dopamine production. Much in the same way as norepinephrine stimulation, amphetamines block dopamine reuptake, increasing release while decreasing enzymatic breakdown by monoamine oxidase (Seeley, Stephens, & Tate, 2006). It is believed that these effects on the dopamine system are what contribute to the addicting nature of this drug. However, increased brain dopamine is also posited to explain schizophrenia. Amphetamine-induced psychosis is a diagnosis given when methamphetamine users present in a state, albeit temporary (Cho, 1990), that is almost indistinguishable from paranoid schizophrenia.

Too little dopamine, in contrast, is associated with extrapyramidal symptoms (EPS) including akathisia, akinesia, dystonia, and abnormal posturing (Melega et al., 1997). EPS have been observed during an acute withdrawal from methamphetamine when dopamine levels suddenly drop (Rawson, Gonzales, & Brethen, 2002). Rawson and associates (2002) noted that after withdrawal from methamphetamine and the subsequent depletion of the pleasure hormone dopamine, users experienced a very intense craving for the drug, including prolonged anhedonia and dysphoria. They surmise that the intensity of the craving is directly related to the increased amount of dopamine in the brain during methamphetamine use (Rawson et al., 2002).

Are There Irreversible Neurological Changes Related to Methamphetamine Abuse?

Numerous studies have documented the plasticity of the brain and its ability to rebound from neurotransmitter depletion and structural insults, even after long-term methamphetamine use (Clemens, Cornish, Hunt, & McGregor, 2007; Hanson et al., 2009; Melega et al., 1997; O'Shea, Granados, Esteban, Colado, & Green, 1998; Segal, Kuczenski, O'Neil, Melega, & Cho, 2003). Clemens and associates (2007) found, however, that even though the brain's neurochemistry rebounds after prolonged methamphetamine use, lasting social deficits remained. "Such results indicate that while a sustained pattern of moderate [methamphetamine] use may not lead to long-term monoamine depletion, negative behavioral effects may persist, especially those related to social behavior" (Clemens et al., 2007, p. 189). Conversely, these same scientists found that repeat administration of methamphetamine across a 4-month time span resulted in a lasting depletion of norepinephrine and serotonin levels in the prefrontal brain cortex. This could account for persistent dysphoria after drug withdrawal. According to this study, long-lasting depletions were more likely a consequence of binge dosing (Clemens et al., 2007).

Animal Studies

Melega and associates (1997), using positron emission tomography, studied vervet monkeys to measure recovery from methamphetamine use. Results indicated depleted levels of dopamine at 3–4 weeks post-methamphetamine injection, but that neurochemical recovery was recognizable at 10–12 weeks postinjection. Their study demonstrated that toxicity was reversible due to "endogenous restorative mechanisms of the striatal dopamine system" (Melega et al., 1997, p. 118).

Hanson and colleagues (2009) found that rats initially exposed to a neurotoxic methamphetamine-binge injection followed by a second methamphetamine-binge injection actually became resistant to further negative effects on dopamine transporter receptors. It is these transporters that pump dopamine back into the presynaptic neuron (Erickson, Eiden, & Hoffman, 1992; Weihe & Eiden, 2000). It is also the receptor site where methamphetamine is said to primarily work and would thereby indicate dopamine terminal function (Hanson et al., 2009; Segal et al., 2003). Hanson and colleagues (2009) concluded that although initial binge doses produced neurotoxic effects lasting about 14 days, repeat binge doses thereafter did not produce additional harm to dopamine transporters' function.

Other researchers have argued that despite high doses of methamphetamine leading to neuronal damage/death, neuronal regrowth and recovery of normal functioning is possible. Segal and colleagues (2003) found that injecting rats gradually with methamphetamine before initiating a binge dose decreased, if not eliminated, nerve terminal damage reported in other research. Essentially, they demonstrated that the brain gradually adjusted to toxic effects; hence, later binge doses produced no lasting damage. To confirm this statement, they cited the brain's ability to begin neuronal sprouting after withdrawal from methamphetamine use (Segal et al., 2003).

In light of these opposing studies (Clemens et al., 2007; Hanson et al., 2009; Melega et al., 1997; O'Shea et al., 1998; Segal et al., 2003), it is crucial for researchers to work toward definitive answers to the question: Are there irreversible neurobiological changes related to methamphetamine? Once this question is answered, this information can be used to inform treatment for methamphetamine addiction.

Antimethamphetamine Antibodies

Potential biologically based approaches for treating methamphetamine intoxication include immunotherapy, which involves the production of antimethamphetamine antibodies (mAbs) that bind to methamphetamine and subsequently prevent its effects on the brain (Byrnes-Blake et al., 2003; Danger et al., 2006; Kosten & Owens, 2005; Laurenzana et al., 2003; McMillan et al., 2004). In their 2006 study, Danger and colleagues created monoclonal antibodies that bound methamphetamine, thereby ridding it from the brain and circulation. Kosten and Owens (2005) noted that research exists for the effectiveness of mAbs to protect against methamphetamine intoxication, but that the metabolites of methamphetamine, such as amphetamine, have a different biophysical profile and require a different antibody to prevent additional intoxication.

Similarly, Byrnes-Blake and associates (2003) proposed that if antimethamphetamine immunotherapy had cross-specificity with amphetamines or if a pharmaceutical containing both antimethamphetamine and antiamphetamine monoclonal antibodies were developed, it would allow greater therapeutic responsiveness in treatment for methamphetamine intoxication.

McMillan and colleagues (2004) and Laurenzana and associates (2003) demonstrated that methamphetamine bound to mAbs could not be metabolized and, therefore, only circulating free methamphetamine would be converted to its amphetamine metabolite, hence a decrease in overall amphetamine metabolite production. Whereas Laurenzana and associates (2003) observed that mAbs did not prevent the initial distribution of methamphetamine to the brain, they did note that mAbs decreased the effects of methamphetamine stimulation and prevented some neurotoxic effects. They acknowledged that the decreased levels of both methamphetamine and amphetamine were hard to attribute to one sole source, and that further investigative research was warranted to draw conclusions regarding the efficacy of mAbs in reducing methamphetamine and its metabolically active metabolites.

In another study, McMillan and colleagues (2004) found that mAbs have a higher effectiveness when used during bouts of an acute methamphetamine overdose. Since methamphetamine would be evenly distributed in the user's plasma, an intravenous administration of mAbs could then effectively bind and neutralize methamphetamine's effects. These researchers believe that mAbs disrupt the equilibrium of methamphetamine between circulating plasma and the brain, creating a concentration gradient that moves methamphetamine molecules from the brain into the plasma, achieving a homeostatic balance. Consequently, an opportunity for additional mAbs to bind to more methamphetamine molecules develops, successfully decreasing methamphetamine's effects on the user. Unfortunately, prophylactic immunization of individuals to combat drug self-administration would be much more difficult, due to the insidious nature of methamphetamine once in the blood stream. Intravenous methamphetamine rapidly distributes itself in bolus form into supple tissues, such as the brain. Because of this, mAbs distributed throughout the entire body from an inoculation would not have time to bind and deactivate methamphetamine administered in bolus form before it affected the brain. This reality allows for the intoxicating and indulging effects desired by the methamphetamine user (McMillan et al., 2004).

Kosten and Owens (2005) agreed, postulating that immunoglobulin therapy needs to begin as a "therapeutic vaccine" used to treat methamphetamine-intoxicated patients and withdrawing methamphetamine users, rather than being implemented as a "prophylactic vaccine" used to ward off the potential of drug addiction (Kosten & Owens, 2005). They listed different routes in which mAbs can be administered: patient-controlled (similar to insulin), orally, intranasally, or as a sustained-release injection for periods of peak vulnerability. McMillan and colleagues (2004) validated this finding, demonstrating that mAbs are most effective during acute intoxication, decreasing self-administration for a short time rather than long-term preventative effects. Promisingly, Kosten and Owens (2005) foresaw potential for immunoglobulin therapy becoming prophylactic, being used in populations like adolescent methamphetamine users who are on a course toward methamphetamine addiction.

What Are the Nursing Implications for Methamphetamine Treatment?

Research suggests that mAbs could easily be administered in an emergency room during an acute methamphetamine intoxication episode to aide in methamphetamine withdrawal treatment (Danger et al., 2006; Kosten & Owens, 2005; McMillan et al., 2004). MAbs have been created for and shown to decrease the effects of methamphetamine on the brain by effectively binding

to methamphetamine in the plasma to neutralize its intoxicating effects (Byrnes-Blake et al., 2003; Danger et al., 2006; Kosten & Owens, 2005; Laurenzana et al., 2003; McMillan et al., 2004). Additional research proposed that because of the long half-life of immunoglobulins, an mAb could possibly protect methamphetamine patients from relapsing for up to a few weeks (Kosten & Owens, 2005). Antibody research has only just begun with rats and needs to be refined and replicated in double-blind studies before being implemented in human trials; but its potential appears superior to some of the traditional pharmaceuticals used to treat methamphetamine addiction.

As with any new potential treatment, challenges will exist in using mAbs. For example, methamphetamine abuse has physiological, psychological, emotional, and social components, which affect the allure of this addiction. Legal questions and implications will exist in using this drug with patients who are addicted to methamphetamines. For example, under what criteria may nurses administer mAbs when patients are admitted to the emergency room with different levels of methamphetamine addiction? Under what conditions may patients displaying different levels of addiction (e.g., low, high intensity, and tweaking) refuse mAbs, especially when they are experiencing intoxicating and indulging effects of methamphetamine abuse? What side effects do nurses need to monitor patients for when they administer mAbs?

In conclusion, if mAbs prove to be useful to patients who wish to break their addictions, programs that provide resources to address physiological, psychological, emotional, and social components of using methamphetamines need to be developed and strengthened. For example, social networks that will support patients to avoid situations that encourage the use of methamphetamines are needed. Patient education programs that will assist patients to evaluate how they deal with stressful situations and develop more effective coping skills to address common everyday problems are needed. As with most treatment approaches that rely heavily on patient education, nurses can be pivotal to the success of methamphetamine treatment.

References

Byrnes-Blake, K. A., Laurenzana, E. M., Carroll, F. I., Abraham, P., Gentry, W. B., Landes, R. D., & Owens, S. M. (2003). Pharmacodynamic mechanisms of monoclonal antibody-based antagonism of (+)-methamphetamine in rats. *European Journal of Pharmacology, 461,* 119–128. doi:10.1016/S0014-2999(03)01313-X

Cho, A. K. (1990). Ice: A new dosage form of an old drug. *Science, 249,* 631–634. doi: 10.1126/science.249.4969.631

Clemens, K. J., Cornish, J. L., Hunt, G. E., & McGregor, I. S. (2007). Repeated weekly exposure to MDMA, methamphetamine or their combination: Long-term behavioural and neurochemical effects in rats. *Drug and Alcohol Dependence, 86,* 183–190. doi:10.1016/j.drugalcdep.2006.06.004

Danger, Y., Gadjou, C., Devys, A., Galons, H., Blanchard, D., & Follea, G. (2006). Development of murine monoclonal antibodies to methamphetamine and methamphetamine analogues. *Journal of Immunological Methods, 309,* 1–10. doi:10.1016/j.jim.2005.10.017

Erickson, J. D., Eiden, L. E., & Hoffman, B. J. (1992). Expression cloning of a reserpine-sensitive vesicular monoamine transporter. *Proceedings of the National Academy of Science of the United States of America, 89,* 10993–10997.

Hanson, J. E., Birdsall, E., Seferian, K. S., Crosby, M. A., Keefe, K. A., Gibb, J. W., et al. (2009). Methamphetamine-induced dopaminergic deficits and refractoriness to subsequent treatment. *European Journal of Pharmacology, 607,* 68–73. doi:10.1016/j.ejphar. 2009.01.037

Keltner, N. L., & Pugh, G. I. (2007). Substance-related disorders. In N.L. Keltner, L. H. Schwecke, & C. E. Bostrom (Eds.), *Psychiatric nursing* (pp. 493–534). St. Louis, MO: Mosby Elsevier.

KCI The Anti-Methamphetamine Site. (2008). Slang, jargon, and nicknames for crystal methamphetamine/methamphetamine. Retrieved from www.kci.org/methamphetamine_info/slang_names.htm

Kosten, T., & Owens, S. M. (2005). Immunotherapy for the treatment of drug abuse. *Pharmacology & Therapeutics, 108,* 76–85. doi:10.1016/j.pharmthera.2005.06.009

Laurenzana, E. M., Byrnes-Blake, K. A., Milesi-Halle, A., Gentry, W. B., Williams, D. K., & Owens, S. M. (2003). Use of anti-(+)-methamphetamine monoclonal antibody to significantly alter (+)-methamphetamine and (+)-amphetamine disposition in rats. *Drug Metabolism and Disposition, 31,* 1320–1326. doi:10.1124/dmd.31.11.1320

Melega, W. P., Raleigh, M. J., Stout, D. B., Lacan, G., Huang, S.-C., & Phelps, M. E. (1997). Recovery of striatal dopamine function after acute amphetamine-and methamphetamine-induced neurotoxicity in the vervet monkey. *Brain Research, 766,* 113–120. doi:10.1016/S0006-8993(97)00548-9

McCance, K. L., & Grey, T. C. (2008). Altered cellular and tissue biology. In S. E. Huether, K. L. McCance, V. L. Brashers, & N. S. Rote (Eds.), *Understanding pathophysiology* (pp. 62–98). St. Louis, MO: Mosby Elsevier.

McMillan, D. E., Hardwick, W. C., Li, M., Gunnell, M. G., Carroll, F. I., Abraham, P., et al. (2004). Effects of murine-derived anti-methamphetamine monoclonal antibodies on (+)-methamphetamine self-administration in the rat. *Journal of Pharmacology and Experimental Therapeutics, 309,* 1248–1255. doi:10.1124/jpet.103.061762

National Institute on Drug Abuse. (2008). NIDA infofacts: Methamphetamine. Retrieved from www.nida.nih.gov/Infofacts/methamphetamine.html

O'Shea, E., Granados, R., Esteban, B., Colado, M. I., & Green, A. R. (1998). The relationship between the degree of neurodegeneration of rat brain 5-HT nerve terminals and the dose and frequency of administration of MDMA ("ecstasy"). *Neuropharmacology, 37,* 919–926. doi:10.1016/S0028-3908(98)00029-X

Rawson, R. A., Gonzales, R., & Brethen, M. A. (2002). Treatment of methamphetamine use disorders: An update. *Journal of Substance Abuse Treatment, 23,* 145–150.

Seeley, R. R., Stephens, T. D., & Tate, P. (2006). *Anatomy and physiology.* New York: McGraw Hill.

Segal, D. S., Kuczenski, R., O'Neil, M. L., Melega, W. P., & Cho, A. K. (2003). Escalating dose methamphetamine pretreatment alters the behavioral and neurochemical profiles associated with exposure to a high-dose methamphetamine binge. *Neuropyschopharmacology, 28,* 1730–1740. doi:10.1038/sj.npp.1300247

Sugerman, R. A. (2008). Structure and function of the neurologic system. In S. E. Huether, K. L. McCance, V. L. Brashers, & N. S. Rote (Eds.), *Understanding pathophysiology* (pp. 273–304). St. Louis, MO: Mosby Elsevier.

Townsend, M. C. (2006). *Psychiatric mental health nursing: Concepts of care in evidence-based practice.* Philadelphia, PA: FA Davis Company.

U.S. Department of Justice Drug Enforcement Administration (DEA). (2007). The combat methamphetamine act of 2005. Retrieved from www.deadiversion.usdoj.gov/methamphetamine/q_a.htm

Weihe, E., & Eiden, L. E. (2000). Chemical neuroanatomy of the vesicular amine transporters. *The Federation of American Societies for Experimental Biology Journal, 14,* 2435–2449

Critical Thinking

1. How effective would mAbs be in a treatment center and why?

2. Should we require young meth abusers to use the immunoglobulin in therapy in an effort to prevent them from becoming lifetime meth addicts?

3. If this is effective at diminishing acute intoxication, shouldn't we make it available to doctors and nurses to use?

Cynthia Jane Anderson, SN, is a senior nursing student at California State University at Bakersfield (CSUB), Bakersfield, CA, USA; **Kathleen Gilchrist,** PhD, RN, is Professor of Nursing, CSUB, Bakersfield, CA, USA; and **Norman L. Keltner,** EdD, APRN is former Chair, Department of Nursing, CSUB, Bakersfield, CA, USA.

From *Perspectives in Psychiatric Care,* April 2010, pp. 163–167. Copyright © 2010 by Nursecom, Inc. Reprinted by permission via Rightslink.

Medical Marijuana and the Mind

More is Known about the Psychiatric Risks than the Benefits

The movement to legalize marijuana for medical use in the United States has renewed discussion about how this drug affects the brain, and whether it might be useful in treating psychiatric disorders.

Unfortunately, most of the research on marijuana is based on people who smoked the drug for recreational rather than medical purposes. A review by researchers in Canada (where medical marijuana is legal) identified only 31 studies (23 randomized controlled trials and 8 observational studies) specifically focused on medical benefits of the drug.

A separate review by the American Medical Association (AMA) also concluded that the research base remains sparse. This was one reason that the AMA recently urged the federal government to reconsider its classification of marijuana as a Schedule 1 controlled substance (prohibiting both medical and recreational use), so that researchers could more easily conduct clinical trials.

Consensus exists that marijuana may be helpful in treating certain carefully defined medical conditions. In its comprehensive 1999 review, for example, the Institute of Medicine (IOM) concluded that marijuana may be modestly effective for pain relief (particularly nerve pain), appetite stimulation for people with AIDS wasting syndrome, and control of chemotherapy-related nausea and vomiting.

Given the availability of FDA-approved medications for these conditions, however, the IOM advised that marijuana be considered as a treatment only when patients don't get enough relief from currently available drugs. Additional research since then has confirmed the IOM's core findings and recommendations.

Although anecdotal reports abound, few randomized controlled studies support the use of medical marijuana for psychiatric conditions. The meager evidence for benefits must be weighed against the much better documented risks, particularly for young people who use marijuana.

Challenges in Drug Delivery

Marijuana is derived from the hemp plant, *Cannabis*. Although marijuana contains more than 400 chemicals, researchers best understand the actions of two: THC (delta-9-tetrahydrocannabinol) and cannabidiol.

THC is the chemical in marijuana primarily responsible for its effects on the central nervous system. It stimulates cannabinoid receptors in the brain, triggering other chemical reactions that underlie marijuana's psychological and physical effects—both good and bad.

Less is known about cannabidiol, although the research suggests that it interacts with THC to produce sedation. It may independently have anti-inflammatory, neuroprotective, or antipsychotic effects, although the research is too preliminary to be applied clinically.

Drug delivery remains a major challenge for medical marijuana. The FDA has approved two pills containing synthetic THC. Dronabinol (Marinol) combines synthetic THC with sesame oil. Most of the active ingredient is metabolized during digestion, so that only 10% to 20% of the original dose reaches the bloodstream. Nabilone (Cesamet) uses a slightly different preparation of synthetic THC that is absorbed more completely into the bloodstream. Among the concerns about both of these drugs, however, are that they do not work rapidly, and the amount of medication that reaches the bloodstream varies from person to person.

Another medication under investigation in the United States (and already approved for sale in Canada) combines THC and cannabidiol. In Canada, it is marketed as Sativex. This drug is sometimes referred to as "liquid cannabis" because it is sprayed under the tongue or elsewhere in the mouth, using a small handheld device. However, it takes time to notice any effects,

Key Points

- Medical marijuana may be an option for treating certain conditions, such as nerve pain or chemotherapy-related nausea.
- There is not enough evidence to recommend medical marijuana as a treatment for any psychiatric disorder.
- The psychiatric risks are well documented, and include addiction, anxiety, and psychosis.

as the drug has to be absorbed through tissues lining the mouth before it can reach the bloodstream.

Inhalation is the fastest way to deliver THC to the bloodstream, which is why patients may prefer smoking an herbal preparation. But while this method of drug delivery works fast, smoking marijuana exposes the lungs to multiple chemicals and poses many of the same respiratory health risks as smoking cigarettes. Limited research suggests that vaporizers may reduce the amount of harmful chemicals delivered to the lungs during inhalation.

More Psychiatric Risk than Benefit

Part of the reason marijuana works to relieve pain and quell nausea is that, in some people, it reduces anxiety, improves mood, and acts as a sedative. But so far the few studies evaluating the use of marijuana as a treatment for psychiatric disorders are inconclusive, partly because this drug may have contradictory effects in the brain depending on the dose of the drug and inborn genetic vulnerability.

Much more is known about the psychiatric risks of marijuana (whether used for recreational or medical purposes) than its benefits.

Addiction

Observational studies suggest that one in nine people who smokes marijuana regularly becomes dependent on it. Research both in animals and in people provides evidence that marijuana is an addictive substance, especially when used for prolonged periods.

Addiction specialists note with concern that THC concentration has been increasing in the herbal form of marijuana. In the United States, THC concentrations in marijuana sold on the street used to range from 1 to 4% of the total product; by 2003, average THC concentration had risen to 7%. Similar trends are reported in Europe. This increased potency might also accelerate development of dependence.

Less conclusive is the notion that marijuana is a "gateway drug" that leads people to experiment with "hard" drugs such as cocaine. The research is conflicting.

Anxiety

Although many recreational users say that smoking marijuana calms them down, for others it has the opposite effect. In fact, the most commonly reported side effects of smoking marijuana are intense anxiety and panic attacks. Studies report that about 20–30% of recreational users experience such problems after smoking marijuana. The people most vulnerable are those who have never used marijuana before.

Dose of THC also matters. At low doses, THC can be sedating. At higher doses, however, this substance can induce intense episodes of anxiety.

It is not yet known whether marijuana increases the risk of developing a persistent anxiety disorder. Observational studies have produced conflicting findings. Studies of recreational users suggest that many suffer from anxiety, and it is difficult to know what underlies this association. Possibilities include selection bias (e.g., that anxious people are more likely to use marijuana), a rebound phenomenon (e.g., that marijuana smokers feel worse when withdrawing from the substance), and other reasons (e.g., genetic vulnerability).

Mood Disorders

Little controlled research has been done about how marijuana use affects patients with bipolar disorder. Many patients with bipolar disorder use marijuana, and the drug appears to induce manic episodes and increases rapid cycling between manic and depressive moods. But it is not yet clear whether people who use marijuana are at increased risk of developing bipolar disorder.

The small amount of research available on depression is also muddied. In line with what studies report about anxiety, many marijuana users describe an improvement in mood. Animal studies have suggested that components of marijuana may have antidepressant effects. Yet several observational studies have suggested that daily marijuana use may, in some users, actually increase symptoms of depression or promote the development of this disorder.

For example, an Australian study that followed the outcomes of 1,601 students found that those who used marijuana at least once a week at ages 14 or 15 were twice as likely to develop depression seven years later as those who never smoked the substance—even after adjusting for other factors. Young women who smoked marijuana daily were five times as likely to develop depression seven years later as their nonsmoking peers. Although such studies do not prove cause and effect, the dose-outcomes relationship is particularly worrisome.

Psychosis

Marijuana exacerbates psychotic symptoms and worsens outcomes in patients already diagnosed with schizophrenia or other psychotic disorders. Several large observational studies also strongly suggest that using marijuana—particularly in the early teenage years—can increase risk of developing psychosis.

An often-cited study of more than 50,000 young Swedish soldiers, for example, found that those who had smoked marijuana at least once were more than twice as likely to develop schizophrenia as those who had not smoked marijuana. The heaviest users (who said they had used the drug more than 50 times) were six times as likely to develop schizophrenia as the nonsmokers.

Until recently, the consensus view was that this reflected selection bias: Individuals who were already vulnerable to developing psychosis or in the early stages (the prodrome) might be more likely to smoke marijuana to quell voices and disturbing thoughts. But further analyses of the Swedish study, and other observational studies, have found that marijuana use increases the risk of psychosis, even after adjusting for possible confounding factors.

Although cause and effect are hard to prove, evidence is accumulating that early or heavy marijuana use might not only trigger psychosis in people who are already vulnerable, but might also cause psychosis in some people who might not otherwise have developed it.

Certainly genetic profile mediates the effect of marijuana. People born with a variation of the gene COMT are more vulnerable to developing psychosis, for example. Because there is as yet no reliable way for clinicians to identify vulnerable young people in advance, however, it is safest to restrict use of medical marijuana to adults.

Other Effects

A review of side effects caused by medical marijuana found that most were mild. When compared with controls, people who used medical marijuana were more likely to develop pneumonia and other respiratory problems, and experience vomiting, and diarrhea.

There's no question that recreational use of marijuana produces short-term problems with thinking, working memory, and executive function (the ability to focus and integrate different types of information). Although little research exists on medical marijuana, anecdotal reports indicate that some patients take the drug at night to avoid these types of problems.

The real debate is about whether long-term use of marijuana (either for medical or recreational purposes) produces persistent cognitive problems. Although early studies of recreational users reported such difficulties, the studies had key design problems. Typically, they compared long-term marijuana smokers with people who had never used the drug, for example, without controlling for baseline characteristics (such as education or cognitive functioning) that might determine who continues to smoke the drug and who might be most at risk for thinking and memory problems later on.

Recent studies suggest that although overall cognitive ability remains intact, long-term use of marijuana may cause subtle but lasting impairments in executive function. There is no consensus, however, about whether this affects real-world functioning.

Additional research, focused on the benefits and consequences of medical marijuana use for specific disorders, may help to clarify some issues. In the meantime, there is not enough evidence to recommend marijuana as a medical treatment for any psychiatric disorder.

References

Crippa JA, et al. "Cannabis and Anxiety: A Critical Review of the Evidence," *Human Psychopharmacology* (Oct. 2009): Vol. 24, No. 7, pp. 515–23.

Grinspoon L, et al. *Marijuana: The Forbidden Medicine* (Yale University, 1997).

Iversen LL. *The Science of Marijuana, Second Edition* (Oxford University Press, 2008).

Wang T, et al. "Adverse Effects of Medical Cannabinoids: A Systematic Review," *Canadian Medical Association Journal* (June 17, 2008): Vol. 178, No. 13, pp. 1669–78.

Critical Thinking

1. According to the research, do the benefits of medical marijuana outweigh the consequences?

2. What is the proper arena for us to study the effects of medical marijuana? Why?

Scripps Research Team Finds Stress Hormone Key to Alcohol Dependence

The Findings Suggest Development of Drug Treatment for Substance Abuse

M. ROBERTO

La Jolla, CA—January 25, 2010—A team of scientists from The Scripps Research Institute has found that a specific stress hormone, the corticotropin-releasing factor (CRF), is key to the development and maintenance of alcohol dependence in animal models. Chemically blocking the stress factor also blocked the signs and symptoms of addiction, suggesting a potentially promising area for future drug development.

The article, the culmination of more than six years of research, will appear in an upcoming print edition of the journal *Biological Psychiatry*.

"I'm excited about this study," said Associate Professor Marisa Roberto, who led the research. "It represents an important step in understanding how the brain changes when it moves from a normal to an alcohol-dependent state."

The new study not only confirms the central role of CRF in alcohol addiction using a variety of different methods but also shows that in rats the hormone can be blocked on a long-term basis to alleviate the symptoms of alcohol dependence.

Previous research had implicated CRF in alcohol dependence, but had shown the effectiveness of blocking CRF only in acute single doses of an antagonist (a substance that interferes the physiological action of another). The current study used three different types of CRF antagonists, all of which showed an anti-alcohol effect via the CRF system. In addition, the chronic administration of the antagonist for 23 days blocked the increased drinking associated with alcohol dependence.

Out of Control

Alcoholism, a chronic disease characterized by compulsive use of alcohol and loss of control over alcohol intake, is devastating both to individuals and their families and to society in general. About a third of the approximately 40,000 traffic fatalities every year involve drunk drivers, and direct and indirect public health costs are estimated to be in the hundreds of billions of dollars yearly.

"Research to understand alcoholism is important for society," said Roberto, a 2010 recipient of the prestigious Presidential Early Career Award for Scientists and Engineers. "Our study explored what we call in the field 'the dark side' of alcohol addiction. That's the compulsion to drink, not because it is pleasurable—which has been the focus of much previous research—but because it relieves the anxiety generated by abstinence and the stressful effects of withdrawal."

CRF is a natural substance involved in the body's stress response. Originally found only in the area of the brain known as the hypothalamus, it has now been localized in other brain regions, including the pituitary, where it stimulates the secretion of corticotropin and other biologically active substances, and the amygdala, an area that has been implicated in the elevated anxiety, withdrawal, and excessive drinking associated with alcohol dependence.

To confirm the role of CRF in the central amygdala for alcohol dependence, the research team used a multidisciplinary approach that included electrophysiological methods not previously applied to this problem.

The results from these cellular studies showed that CRF increased the strength of inhibitory synapses (junctions between two nerve cells) in neurons in a manner similar to alcohol. This change occurred through the increased release of the neurotransmitter GABA, which plays an important role in regulating neuronal excitability.

Blocking the Stress Response

Next, the team explored if the effects of CRF could be blocked through the administration of CRF antagonists. To do this, the scientists tested three different CRF1 antagonists (called antalarmin, NIH-3, and R121919) against alcohol in brain slices and injected R121919 for 23-days into the brains of rats that were exposed to conditions that would normally produce a dependence on alcohol.

Remarkably, the behavior of the "alcohol-dependent" rats receiving one of the CRF antagonists (R121919) mimicked their non-addicted ("naive") counterparts. Instead of seeking out large amounts of alcohol like untreated alcohol-dependent rats, both the treated rats and their non-addicted brethren self-administered alcohol in only moderate amounts.

"This critical observation suggests that increased activation of CRF systems mediates the excessive drinking associated with development of dependence," said Roberto. "In other words, blocking CRF with prolonged CRF1 antagonist administration may prevent excessive alcohol consumption under a variety of behavioral and physiological conditions."

Importantly, in the study, the rats did not exhibit tolerance to the suppressive effects of R121919 on alcohol drinking. In fact, they may have become even more sensitive to its effects over time—a good sign for the efficacy of this type of compound as it might be used repeatedly in a clinical setting.

The scientists' cellular studies also supported the promising effects of CRF1 antagonists. All of the CRF antagonists decreased basal GABAergic responses and abolished alcohol effects. Alcohol-dependent rats exhibited heightened sensitivity to CRF and the CRF1 antagonists on GABA release in the central amygdala region of the brain. CRF1 antagonist administration into the central amygdala reversed dependence-related elevations in extracellular GABA and blocked alcohol-induced increases in extracellular GABA in both dependent and naive rats. The levels of CRF and CRF1 mRNA in the central amygdala of dependent rats were also elevated.

Roberto notes that another intriguing aspect of the work is that it provides a possible physiological link between stress-related behaviors, emotional disorders (i.e. stress disorders, anxiety, depression), and the development of alcohol dependence.

In addition to Roberto, the paper, "CRF-induced Amygdala GABA Release Plays a Key Role in Alcohol Dependence," was co-authored by Maureen T. Cruz, Nicholas W. Gilpin, Valentina Sabino, Paul Schweitzer, Michal Bajo, Pietro Cottone, Samuel G. Madamba, David G. Stouffer, Eric P. Zorrilla, George F. Koob, George R. Siggins, and Loren H. Parsons, all of Scripps Research. For more information, see *Biological Psychiatry.* www.ncbi.nlm.nih.gov/pubmed/20060104?log$=activity

This research was supported by the National Institutes of Health's National Institute on Alcohol Abuse and Alcoholism (NIAAA) and National Institute on Drug Abuse (NIDA), as well as the Pearson Center for Alcoholism and Addiction Research and the Harold L. Dorris Neurological Research Institute, both at Scripps Research.

About the Scripps Research Institute

The Scripps Research Institute is one of the world's largest independent, non-profit biomedical research organizations, at the forefront of basic biomedical science that seeks to comprehend the most fundamental processes of life. Scripps Research is internationally recognized for its discoveries in immunology, molecular and cellular biology, chemistry, neurosciences, autoimmune, cardiovascular, and infectious diseases, and synthetic vaccine development. Established in its current configuration in 1961, it employs approximately 3,000 scientists, postdoctoral fellows, scientific and other technicians, doctoral degree graduate students, and administrative and technical support personnel. Scripps Research is headquartered in La Jolla, California. It also includes Scripps Florida, whose researchers focus on basic biomedical science, drug discovery, and technology development. Scripps Florida is located in Jupiter, Florida.

Critical Thinking

1. Could this hormone be used to replace current alcohol-addiction treatments such as antabuse, etc.? Why?

2. What are the ethical considerations with this treatment?

The Genetics of Alcohol and Other Drug Dependence

Danielle M. Dick and Arpana Agrawal

This article explores the hypothesis that certain genetic factors increase a person's risk of both alcohol abuse and dependence and other drug abuse and dependence. It first reviews the evidence suggesting that certain genetic factors contribute to the development of alcohol and other drug (AOD) use disorders, as well as to the development of a variety of forms of externalizing psychopathology—that is, psychiatric disorders characterized by disinhibited behavior, such as antisocial personality disorder, attention deficit/hyperactivity disorder, and conduct disorder. After summarizing the difficulties associated with, and recent progress made in, the identification of specific genes associated with AOD dependence, the article then discusses evidence that implicates several genes in a person's risk for dependence on both alcohol and illicit drugs.

Genetic Epidemiology of AOD Dependence

Alcohol dependence frequently co-occurs with dependence on illicit drugs (Hasin et al. 2007). Both alcohol use disorders (i.e., alcohol abuse and alcohol dependence) and drug use disorders (drug abuse and drug dependence) are influenced by several factors. For example, family, twin, and adoption studies have convincingly demonstrated that genes contribute to the development of alcohol dependence, with heritability estimates ranging from 50 to 60 percent for both men and women (McGue 1999). Dependence on illicit drugs only more recently has been investigated in twin samples, but several studies now suggest that illicit drug abuse and dependence also are under significant genetic influence. In these studies of adult samples, heritability estimates ranged from 45 to 79 percent (for reviews, see Agrawal and Lynskey 2006; etc. Kendler et al. 2003a; Tsuang et al. 2001).

Twin studies also can be used to assess the extent to which the co-occurrence of disorders is influenced by genetic and/or environmental factors. Thus, a finding that the correlation between alcohol dependence in twin 1 and drug dependence in twin 2 is higher for identical (i.e., monozygotic) twins, who share 100 percent of their genes, than for fraternal (i.e., dizygotic) twins, who share on average only 50 percent of their genes, indicates that shared genes influence the risk of both alcohol and drug dependence. The twin studies conducted to date support the role of such shared genetic factors. For example, in the largest twin study of the factors underlying psychiatric disorders, Kendler and colleagues (2003b) analyzed data from the Virginia Twin Registry and found that a common genetic factor contributed to the total variance in alcohol dependence, illicit drug abuse and dependence, conduct disorder, and adult antisocial behavior. This pattern also has been identified in several other independent twin studies (Krueger et al. 2002; Young et al. 2000). Taken together, these findings suggest that a significant portion of the genetic influence on alcohol dependence and drug dependence is through a general predisposition toward externalizing disorders, which may manifest in different ways (e.g., different forms of AOD dependence and/or antisocial behavior) (see Figure). However, some evidence also suggests that disorder-specific genetic influences contribute to AOD dependence (Kendler et al. 2003b). These specific influences likely reflect the actions of genes that are involved in the metabolism of individual drugs.

The idea that alcohol and drug dependence share a genetic liability with each other, as well as with other forms of externalizing psychopathology, is further supported by electrophysiological studies recording the brain's electrical activity. These studies, which are conducted using electrodes placed on the person's scalp, provide a noninvasive, sensitive method of measuring brain function in humans. They generate a predictable pattern in the height (i.e., amplitude) and rate (i.e., frequency) of brain waves that can show characteristic abnormalities in people with certain types of brain dysfunction. For example, electrophysiological abnormalities have been observed in people with a variety of externalizing disorders as well as in unaffected children of these people. These findings suggest that electrophysiological measurements can be used as markers of a genetic vulnerability to externalizing disorders.

One commonly measured electrophysiological characteristic is the so-called P3 component of an event-related potential—that is, a spike in brain activity that occurs about 300 milliseconds after a person is exposed to a sudden stimulus (e.g., a sound or light). Researchers have observed that the amplitude of the P3 component is reduced in alcohol-dependent people and their children, suggesting that this abnormality is a marker for a genetic predisposition to alcohol dependence (Porjesz et al. 1995). However, the abnormal P3 response is not specific to alcohol dependence but appears to be associated with a variety of disinhibitory disorders, including other forms of drug dependence, childhood externalizing disorders, and adult antisocial personality disorder, again suggesting a shared underlying predisposition to multiple forms of AOD dependence and other externalizing problems (Hicks et al. 2007).[1]

Interestingly, electrophysiological abnormalities are most pronounced in alcohol-dependent people who also have a diagnosis of illicit drug abuse or dependence (Malone et al. 2001). This observation is consistent with data from twin and family studies suggesting that co-morbid dependence on alcohol and another drug represents a more severe disorder with higher heritability than dependence on one drug alone (Johnson et al. 1996; Pickens et al. 1995). This conclusion also appears to be supported by new studies exploring the roles of specific genes, which are discussed later in this article.

Identifying Specific Genes Related to AOD Dependence

With robust evidence indicating that genes influence both alcohol dependence and dependence on illicit drugs, efforts now are underway to identify specific genes involved in the development of these disorders. This identification, however, is complicated by many factors. For example, numerous genes are thought to contribute to a person's susceptibility to alcohol and/or drug dependence, and affected people may carry different combinations of those genes. Additionally, environmental influences have an impact on substance use, as does gene–environment interaction (Heath et al. 2002). Finally, the manifestation of AOD dependence varies greatly among affected people, for example, with respect to age of onset of problems, types of symptoms exhibited (i.e., symptomatic profile), substance use history, and presence of co-morbid disorders.

Despite the complications mentioned above, the rapid growth in research technologies for gene identification in recent years has led to a concomitant increase in exciting results. After suffering many disappointments in early attempts to identify genes involved in complex behavioral outcomes (i.e., phenotypes), researchers now are frequently succeeding in identifying genes that help determine a variety of clinical phenotypes. These advances have been made possible by several factors. First, advances in technologies to identify a person's genetic makeup (i.e., genotyping technology) have dramatically lowered the cost of genotyping, allowing for high-throughput analyses of the entire genome. Second, the completion of several large-scale research endeavors, such as the Human Genome Project, the International HapMap Project,[2] and other government and privately funded efforts,

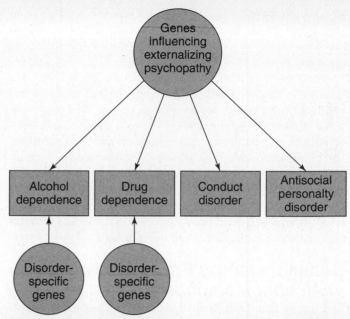

Figure Schematic representation of a model to illustrate the influence of genetic factors on the development of alcohol dependence, dependence on other drugs, and other externalizing disorders (e.g., conduct disorder or antisocial personality disorder). Some of the proposed genetic factors are thought to have a general influence on all types of externalizing conditions, whereas others are thought to have a disorder-specific influence.

have made a wealth of information on variations in the human genome publicly available. Third, these developments have been complemented by advances in the statistical analysis of genetic data.

Several large collaborative projects that strive to identify genes involved in AOD dependence currently are underway. The first large-scale project aimed at identifying genes contributing to alcohol dependence was the National Institute on Alcohol Abuse and Alcoholism (NIAAA)-sponsored Collaborative Study on the Genetics of Alcoholism (COGA), which was initiated in 1989. This study, which involves collaboration of investigators at several sites in the United States, examines families with several alcohol-dependent members who were recruited from treatment centers across the United States. This study has been joined by several other gene identification studies focusing on families affected with alcohol dependence, including the following:

- A sample of Southwestern American Indians (Long et al. 1998);
- The Irish Affected Sib Pair Study of Alcohol Dependence (Prescott et al. 2005a);
- A population of Mission Indians (Ehlers et al. 2004);
- A sample of densely affected families collected in the Pittsburgh area (Hill et al. 2004); and
- An ongoing data collection from alcohol-dependent individuals in Australia.

Importantly, most of these projects include comprehensive psychiatric interviews that focus not only on alcohol use and alcohol use disorders but which also allow researchers to collect information about other drug use and dependence. This comprehensive approach permits researchers to address questions about the nature of genetic influences on AOD dependence, as discussed below.

More recently, additional studies have been initiated that specifically seek to identify genes contributing to various forms of illicit drug dependence as well as general drug use problems (for more information, see www.nida.nih.gov/about/organization/Genetics/consortium/index.html). Through these combined approaches, researchers should be able to identify both genes with drug-specific effects and genes with more general effects on drug use. The following sections focus on several groups of genes that have been identified by these research efforts and which have been implicated in affecting risk for dependence on both alcohol and illicit drugs.

Genes Encoding Proteins Involved in Alcohol Metabolism

The genes that have been associated with alcohol dependence most consistently are those encoding the enzymes that metabolize alcohol (chemically known as ethanol). The main pathway of alcohol metabolism involves two steps. In the first step, ethanol is converted into the toxic intermediate acetaldehyde; this step is mediated by the alcohol dehydrogenase (ADH) enzymes. In a second step, the acetaldehyde is further broken down into acetate and water by the actions of aldehyde dehydrogenase (ALDH) enzymes. The genes that encode the ADH and ALDH enzymes exist in several variants (i.e., alleles) that are characterized by variations (i.e., polymorphisms) in the sequence of the DNA building blocks. One important group of ADH enzymes are the ADH class I isozymes ADH1A, ADH1B, and ADH1C. For both the genes encoding ADH1B and those encoding ADH1C, several alleles resulting in altered proteins have been identified, and the proteins encoded by some of these alleles exhibit particularly high enzymatic activity in laboratory experiments (i.e., in vitro) (Edenberg 2007). This suggests that in people carrying these alleles, ethanol is more rapidly converted to acetaldehyde.[3] Several studies have reported lower frequencies of both the *ADH1B*2* and *ADH1C*1* alleles, which encode some of the more active proteins, among alcoholics than among non-alcoholics in a variety of East Asian populations (e.g., Shen et al. 1997) and, more recently, in European populations (Neumark et al. 1998; Whitfield et al. 1998).

In addition, genome-wide screens to identify genes linked to alcoholism and alcohol-related traits have been conducted in three independent samples consisting largely of people of European descent—the COGA study (Saccone et al. 2000), the Irish Affected Sib Pair Study of Alcohol Dependence (Prescott et al. 2005*a*), and an Australian sample (Birley et al. 2005). These studies have found evidence that a region on chromosome 4 containing the ADH gene cluster shows linkage to the phenotypes studied. This cluster contains, in addition to the genes encoding ADH class I isozymes, the genes *ADH4, ADH5, ADH6,* and *ADH7,* which encode other ADH enzymes. Polymorphisms exist for each of these genes, some of which also have been associated with alcohol dependence (Edenberg et al. 2006; Luo et al. 2006*a,b;* Prescott et al. 2005*b*).

Interestingly, the effects of these genes do not appear to be limited to alcohol dependence. One study compared the frequency of alleles that differed in only one DNA building block (i.e., single nucleotide polymorphisms [SNPs]) throughout the genome between people with histories of illicit drug use and/or dependence and unrelated control participants. This study detected a significant difference for a SNP located near the ADH gene cluster (Uhl et al. 2001). More recent evidence suggests that genetic variants in the *ADH1A, ADH1B, ADH1C, ADH5, ADH6,* and *ADH7* genes are associated with illicit drug dependence and that this association is not purely attributable to co-morbid alcohol dependence (Luo et al. 2007). The mechanism by which these genes may affect risk for illicit drug dependence is not entirely clear. However, other observations[4] also indicate that enzymes involved in alcohol metabolism may contribute to illicit drug dependence via pathways that currently are unknown but independent of alcohol metabolism (Luo et al. 2007).

Genes Encoding Proteins Involved in Neurotransmission

AODs exert their behavioral effects in part by altering the transmission of signals among nerve cells (i.e., neurons) in the brain. This transmission is mediated by chemical messengers (i.e., neurotransmitters) that are released by the signal-emitting neuron and bind to specific proteins (i.e., receptors) on the signal-receiving neuron. AODs influence the activities of several neurotransmitter systems, including those involving the neurotransmitters γ-aminobutyric acid (GABA), dopamine, and acetylcholine, as well as naturally produced compounds that structurally resemble opioids and cannabinoids. Accordingly, certain genes encoding components of these neurotransmitter systems may contribute to the risk of both alcohol dependence and illicit drug dependence.

Genes Encoding the GABA$_A$ Receptor

GABA is the major inhibitory neurotransmitter in the human central nervous system—that is, it affects neurons in a way that reduces their activity. Several lines of evidence suggest that GABA is involved in many of the behavioral effects of alcohol, including motor incoordination, anxiety reduction (i.e., anxiolysis), sedation, withdrawal signs, and preference for alcohol (Grobin et al. 1998). GABA interacts with several receptors, and much of the research on alcohol's interactions with the GABA system has focused on the GABA$_A$ receptor. This receptor also is the site of action for several medications that frequently are misused and have high addictive potential, such as benzodiazepines, barbiturates, opiates, α-hydroxybutyrates, and other sedative–hypnotic compounds. Accordingly, this receptor likely is involved in dependence on these drugs as well (Orser 2006).

The GABA$_A$ receptor is composed of five subunits that are encoded by numerous genes, most of which are located in clusters. Thus, chromosome 4 contains a cluster comprising the genes *GABRA2, GABRA4, GABRB1,* and *GABRG1;* chromosome 5 contains *GABRA1, GABRA6, GABRB2,* and *GABRG2;* and chromosome 15 contains *GABRA5, GABRB3,* and *GABRG3* (see www.ncbi.nlm.nih.gov/sites/entrez?db=gene).

Interest in the GABA$_A$ receptor genes on chromosome 4 grew when this region consistently was identified in genome-wide scans looking for linkage with alcohol dependence (Long et al. 1998; Williams et al. 1999). Subsequently, COGA investigators systematically evaluated short DNA segments of known location (i.e., genetic markers) that were situated in the GABA$_A$ receptor gene cluster on chromosome 4. These studies found that a significant association existed between multiple SNPs in the *GABRA2* gene and alcohol dependence (Edenberg et al. 2004). This association has been replicated in multiple independent samples (Covault et al. 2004; Fehr et al. 2006; Lappalainen et al. 2005; Soyka 2007). In addition, the same SNPs in the *GABRA2* gene have been shown to be associated with drug dependence in both adults and adolescents (Dick et al. 2006*a*), as well as with the use of multiple drugs in another independent sample (Drgon et al. 2006).

Variations in the *GABRA2* gene are associated not only with AOD dependence but also with certain electrophysiological characteristics (i.e., endophenotypes) in the COGA sample (Edenberg et al. 2004). As reviewed above, these electrophysiological characteristics are not unique to alcohol dependence but also are found in individuals with other forms of externalizing psychopathology. This association supports the hypothesis that the *GABRA2* gene generally is involved in AOD use and/or externalizing problems. Interestingly, subsequent analyses investigating the role of *GABRA2* in drug dependence (Agrawal et al. 2006) found that the association with *GABRA2* was strongest in people with co-morbid AOD dependence, with no evidence of association in people who were only alcohol dependent. This observation supports the assertion that co-morbid AOD dependence may represent a more severe, genetically influenced form of the disorder.

Several other GABA$_A$ receptor genes have yielded more modest evidence of association with different aspects of AOD dependence. Thus, *GABRB3* (Noble et al. 1998) and *GABRG3* (Dick et al. 2004) are modestly associated with alcohol dependence, *GABRA1* (Dick et al. 2006*b*) is associated with alcohol-related phenotypes (e.g., history of alcohol-induced blackouts and age at first drunkenness), and *GABRG2* (Loh et al. 2007) is associated with aspects of drug dependence. These findings await confirmation in independent samples.

Genes Involved in the Cholinergic System

The cholinergic system includes neurons that either release the neurotransmitter acetylcholine or respond to it. Acetylcholine generally has excitatory effects in the human central nervous system—that is, it affects neurons in a way that enhances their activity. It is thought to be involved in such processes as arousal, reward, learning, and short-term memory. One of the receptors through which acetylcholine acts is encoded by a gene called *CHRM2*. In the COGA sample, linkage was observed between a region on chromosome 7 that contains the *CHRM2* gene and alcohol dependence, and subsequent experiments confirmed that an association existed between alcohol dependence and the *CHRM2* gene (Wang et al. 2004). This association has been replicated in a large independent study (Luo et al. 2005) that also found evidence that the gene was associated with drug dependence.

As with the *GABRA2* gene described above, the association between *CHRM2* and alcohol dependence in the COGA sample was strongest in people who had co-morbid AOD dependence (Dick et al. 2007). Additional analyses in the COGA sample have suggested that *CHRM2* is associated with a generally increased risk of externalizing disorders, including symptoms of alcohol dependence and drug dependence (Dick et al. 2008). This potential role of *CHRM2* in contributing to the general liability of AOD use and externalizing disorders is further supported by findings that *CHRM2*, like *GABRA2*, also is associated with certain electrophysiological endophenotypes (Jones et al. 2004).

Genes Involved in the Endogenous Opioid System

Endogenous opioids are small molecules naturally produced in the body that have similar effects as the opiates (e.g., morphine and heroin) and which, among other functions, modulate the actions of other neurotransmitters. The endogenous opioid system has been implicated in contributing to the reinforcing effects of several drugs of abuse, including alcohol, opiates, and cocaine. This is supported by the finding that the medication naltrexone, which prevents the normal actions of endogenous opioids (i.e., is an opioid antagonist), is useful in the treatment of alcohol dependence and can reduce the number of drinking days, amount of alcohol consumed, and risk of relapse.

Research on the role of the endogenous opioids in AOD dependence has centered mainly on a gene called *OPRM1*, which encodes one type of opioid receptor (i.e., the μ-opioid receptor), although the results so far have been equivocal. This gene contains a polymorphism resulting in a different protein product (i.e., a non-synonymous polymorphism) that in one study was found to bind one of the endogenous opioids (i.e., β-endorphin) three times as strongly as the main variant of the gene (Bond et al. 1998); other studies, however, could not confirm this finding (Befort et al. 2001; Beyer et al. 2004).

Laboratory studies have suggested that *OPRM1* is associated with sensitivity to the effects of alcohol (Ray and Hutchison 2004). In addition, several studies have reported evidence of an association between *OPRM1* and drug dependence (e.g., Bart et al. 2005). Other studies, however, have failed to find such an association (e.g., Bergen et al. 1997), and a combined analysis of several studies (i.e., a meta-analysis) concluded that no association exists between the most commonly studied *OPRM1* polymorphism and drug dependence (Arias et al. 2006). However, this finding does not preclude the possibility that other genetic variants in *OPRM1* and/or other genes related to the endogenous opioid system are involved in risk for drug dependence. For example, a recent study determining the genotypes of multiple genetic variants across the gene uncovered evidence of association with *OPRM1* and AOD dependence (Zhang et al. 2006).

Researchers also have investigated genetic variations in other opioid receptors and other components of the endogenous opioid system; however, the results have been mixed. One study

(Zhang et al. 2007) found modest support that the genes *OPRK1* and *OPRD1*—which encode the κ- and δ-opioid receptors, respectively—are associated with some aspects of drug dependence. Other researchers (Xuei et al. 2007) reported evidence that the genes *PDYN, PENK,* and *POMC*—which encode small molecules (i.e., peptides) that also bind to opioid receptors—may be associated with various aspects of drug dependence.

Genes Involved in the Endogenous Cannabinoid System

Endogenous cannabinoids are compounds naturally produced in the body that have a similar structure to the psychoactive compounds found in the cannabis plant and which bind cannabinoid receptors. The endogenous cannabinoid system is thought to regulate brain circuits using the neurotransmitter dopamine, which likely helps mediate the rewarding experiences associated with addictive substances. The main cannabinoid receptor in the brain is called CB1 and is encoded by the *CNR1* gene, which is located on chromosome 6. This gene is an excellent candidate gene for being associated with AOD dependence because the receptor encoded by this gene is crucial for generating the rewarding effects of the compound responsible for the psychoactive effects associated with cannabis use (i.e., Δ9-tetrahydrocannabinol). However, the findings regarding the association between *CNR1* and AOD dependence to date have been equivocal, with some studies producing positive results (e.g., Zhang et al. 2004) and others producing negative results (e.g., Herman et al. 2006). Most recently, Hopfer and colleagues (2006) found that a SNP in the *CNR1* gene was associated with cannabis dependence symptoms. Moreover, this SNP was part of several sets of multiple alleles that are transmitted jointly (i.e., haplotypes), some of which are associated with developing fewer dependence symptoms, whereas others are associated with an increased risk for cannabis dependence. Finally, a recent case–control study found that multiple genetic variants in *CNR1* were significantly associated with alcohol dependence and/or drug dependence (Zuo et al. 2007).

Conclusions

For both alcohol dependence and drug dependence, considerable evidence suggests that genetic factors influence the risk of these disorders, with heritability estimates of 50 percent and higher. Moreover, twin studies and studies of electrophysiological characteristics indicate that the risk of developing AOD dependence, as well as other disinhibitory disorders (e.g., antisocial behavior), is determined at least in part by shared genetic factors. These observations suggest that some of a person's liability for AOD dependence will result from a general externalizing factor and some will result from genetic factors that are more disorder specific.

Several genes have been identified that confer risk to AOD dependence. Some of these genes—such as *GABRA2* and *CHRM2*—apparently act through a general externalizing phenotype. For other genes that appear to confer risk of AOD dependence—such as genes involved in alcohol metabolism and in the endogenous opioid and cannabinoid systems—however, the pathways through which they affect risk remain to be elucidated. Most of the genes reviewed in this article originally were found to be associated with alcohol dependence and only subsequently was their association with risk for dependence on other illicit drugs discovered as well. Furthermore, studies that primarily aim to identify genes involved in dependence on certain types of drugs may identify different variants affecting risk, underscoring the challenge of understanding genetic susceptibility to different classes of drugs.

This review does not exhaustively cover all genes that to date have been implicated in alcohol and illicit drug dependence. For example, several genes encoding receptors for the neurotransmitter dopamine have been suggested to determine at least in part a person's susceptibility to various forms of drug dependence. In particular, the *DRD2* gene has been associated with alcohol dependence (Blum et al. 1990) and, more broadly, with various forms of addiction (Blum et al. 1996). This association remains controversial, however, and more recent studies suggest that the observed association actually may not involve variants in the *DRD2* gene but variants in a neighboring gene called *ANKK1* (Dick et al. 2007b). Studies to identify candidate genes that influence dependence on illicit drugs, but not on alcohol, are particularly challenging because of the high co-morbidity between alcohol dependence and dependence on illicit drugs. Therefore, meaningful studies require large sample sizes to include enough drug-dependent people with no prior history of alcohol dependence.

The increasingly rapid pace of genetic discovery also has resulted in the identification of several genes encoding other types of proteins that appear to be associated with alcohol use and/or dependence. These include, for example, two genes encoding taste receptors (i.e., the *TAS2R16* gene [Hinrichs et al. 2006] and the *TAS2R38* gene [Wang et al. 2007]) and a human gene labeled *ZNF699* (Riley et al. 2006) that is related to a gene previously identified in the fruit fly *Drosophila* as contributing to the development of tolerance to alcohol in the flies. Future research will be necessary to elucidate the pathways by which these genes influence alcohol dependence and/or whether they are more broadly involved in other forms of drug dependence.

Notes

1. Abnormalities in the P3 response also have been associated with risk for other psychiatric disorders, such as schizophrenia (van der Stelt et al. 2004).

2. The International HapMap Project is a multicountry effort to identify and catalog genetic similarities and differences in human beings by comparing the genetic sequences of different individuals in order to identify chromosomal regions where genetic variants are shared. Using the information obtained in the HapMap Project, researchers will be able to find genes that affect health, disease, and individual responses to medications and environmental factors.

3. Rapid acetaldehyde production can lead to acetaldehyde accumulation in the body, which results in highly unpleasant effects, such as nausea, flushing, and rapid heartbeat, that may deter people from drinking more alcohol.

4. For example, the medication disulfiram, which inhibits another enzyme involved in alcohol metabolism called aldehyde dehydrogenase 2 (ALDH2) and is used for treatment of alcoholism, has demonstrated a treatment effect in cocaine dependence (Luo et al. 2007).

5. The SNP was not located in one of those gene regions that encode the actual receptor (i.e., in an exon) but in a region that is part of the gene but is eliminated during the process of converting the genetic information into a protein product (i.e., in an intron).

Critical Thinking

1. Why are electrophysiological abnormalities most pronounced in alcohol-dependent people who also have a diagnosis of illicit drug abuse or dependence?

2. What are risk factors for for cannabis dependence? Explain.

DANIELLE M. DICK, PhD, is an assistant professor of psychiatry, psychology, and human genetics at the Virginia Institute for Psychiatric and Behavioral Genetics, Virginia Commonwealth University, Richmond, Virginia. **ARPANA AGRAWAL,** PhD, is a research assistant professor in the Department of Psychiatry, Washington University, St. Louis, Missouri.

Acknowledgments—Danielle M. Dick is supported by NIAAA grant AA–15416 and Arpana Agrawal is supported by National Institute on Drug Abuse (NIDA) grant DA–023668. The COGA project is supported by grant U10–AA–08401 from NIAAA and NIDA.

Role of Cannabis and Endocannabinoids in the Genesis of Schizophrenia

EMILIO FERNANDEZ-ESPEJO ET AL.

Introduction

Cannabis sativa contains several addictive cannabinoid substances such as $(-)$-Δ^9-tetrahydrocannabinol (Δ-9-THC) and $(-)$-Δ^8-tetrahydrocannabinol, and these exogenous cannabinoid substances influence the central nervous system through the endocannabinoid receptors. Cannabis, as a drug of abuse, induces changes in the nervous system which ultimately lead to dependence. Brain chemistry is modified after the action of repeated cannabis, and the drug could induce psychotic symptoms (among others), in a similar fashion to other drugs such as psychostimulants. However, the link between cannabis and schizophrenic psychosis is a matter of controversy. Some authors defend that there is an independent nosological entity or "cannabis psychosis," as it is the case with "amphetamine psychosis" (Thacore and Sukhla 1976; Núñez and Gurpegui 2002). Other authors reject the existence of a nosological entity (Thornicroft 1990; Hall 1998), and they postulate that cannabis influences the development of schizophrenic psychosis, or it is a risk factor involved in the likelihood to suffer from schizophrenia. However, it is important to bear in mind that cannabis use was noted to be as high as 43% of patients who had schizophrenia (Bersani et al. 2002) and in 51% of patients with first-episode schizophrenia (Barnett et al. 2007). The greatest risk of onset of cannabis use is in the age range 15–20 years that coincides with the onset of schizophrenia (Grant et al. 2008).

Interestingly, acute intoxication with cannabis leads to a syndrome with similar characteristics to a psychotic state: confusion, depersonalization, paranoid delusions, hallucinations, blunted affect, anxiety, and agitation (D'Souza et al. 2004; Favrat et al. 2005). However, this acute episode is transient and wears off once the main psychoactive component of cannabis, Δ-9-THC, is eliminated from the blood. A similar syndrome takes place in schizophrenic patients where intravenous Δ-9-THC induces an increase of positive and negative schizophrenic symptoms (D'Souza et al. 2005). Chronic abuse seems not to be accompanied by such a bizarre state, and it has been suggested that frequent users of cannabis develop tolerance to these effects of cannabinoids (D'Souza et al. 2008a). It is hence important to differentiate chronic versus acute effects of cannabis/cannabinoids, and this review deals with neurobiological, neurophysiological, and epidemiological data supporting a role for cannabis/cannabinoids in schizophrenia (the so-called cannabinoid hypothesis of schizophrenia), including a review of animal experimental studies on the topic. Neurobiological studies reveal that cannabis and endocannabinoids can dysregulate neurotransmitter systems involved in the pathophysiology of schizophrenia, such as the dopaminergic and glutamatergic systems, but also indicate that some endocannabinoids can act as

"protective" compounds against the disorder. These are the two sides of cannabinoid effects on psychosis, at present known as the "ups and downs" theory of endocannabinoids in disease (Di Marzo 2008). This fact is linked to the pleiotropic nature of cannabinoids, and it is well known that the cannabinoid system is affected in more than just one way by a given pathological stimulus (Di Marzo 2008). In this context, the presence of a polymorphism (G allele) of the cannabinoid gene CNR1 has been associated with a better therapeutic effect of antipsychotics (Hamdani et al. 2008); and cannabis use in schizophrenics have been interpreted as "self-medication," at least at the beginning of the syndrome. However, epidemiological studies further support a link between cannabis abuse and schizophrenia, and they indicate that cannabis abuse is a risk factor in people with special vulnerability to schizophrenic psychosis; it influences the course of schizophrenia, or it can affect normal brain development during adolescence, increasing the risk for psychosis in adulthood (Verdoux and Tournier 2004; Stefanis et al. 2004). Experimental animal studies support that adolescence is a critical period, and drug contact during this period is a risk factor for suffering psychotic symptoms in the adulthood.

Cannabis and the Endocannabinoid System

From a neurobiological point of view, it is important to note that the relationship between cannabis/cannabinoids and schizophrenia has two aspects (Müller-Vahl and Emrich 2008), which could be defined as endogenous and exogenous. The endogenous aspect is based on the endogenous cannabinoid system whose dysregulation could be a factor influencing the onset of schizophrenic psychosis per se or could indirectly modify other neurotransmitter systems either leading to schizophrenia or worsening it. The exogenous side refers to cannabis abuse as a risk factor that could alter the endocannabinoid system or other neurotransmitter systems, hence facilitating the onset of schizophrenia or aggravating its time course. It is crucial to understand how the endogenous cannabinoid system can be altered in schizophrenia or can affect those well-known disturbances of neural systems such as the dopamine and glutamate ones that have been associated to schizophrenia by many authors; in other words, it is necessary to integrate the "cannabinoid hypothesis" of schizophrenia in the "dopaminergic and glutamatergic hypotheses" of schizophrenia.

The endogenous cannabinoid system is aubiquitous lipid signaling system which appeared early in evolution and which has important regulatory functions throughout the body in all vertebrates. The endogenous cannabinoid system was discovered thanks to the identification of the first receptor for the main psychoactive constituent of *Cannabis sativa* preparations, Δ-9-THC (Gaoni and Mechoulam 1964). This receptor termed cannabinoid CB_1 receptor (Devane et al. 1988; Herkenham et al. 1991) was rapidly cloned (Matsuda et al. 1990) and extensive structure–activity research led to the development of synthetic compounds with high potency and stereoselectivity (Howlett et al. 1990). The discovery of the cannabinoid receptor and the availability of very selective and potent cannabinomimetics led to the rapid identification of a family of lipid transmitters that serve as natural ligands for the cannabinoid CB_1 receptor: arachidonoylethanolamide, named anandamide from the Sanskrit "internal bliss" (Devane et al. 1992), and 2-arachidonoylglycerol (Mechoulam et al. 1995; Sugiura et al. 1995). The pharmacological properties of the endocannabinoids were found to be very similar to those of synthetic cannabinomimetics (Piomelli et al. 2000; Rodríguez de Fonseca et al. 2001).

Two major cannabinoid receptors have been cloned, both of which belong to the superfamily of G protein-coupled receptors. The first receptor described was named the CB_1 receptor and it is mainly located in the terminals of nerve cells (central and peripheral neurons and glial cells), the reproductive system (i.e., testicles), some glandular systems, and the microcirculation (Howlett et al. 1990). A remarkable characteristic of the CB_1 receptors is their very high expression in the brain. The CB_1 receptor is the most abundant G protein-coupled receptor with densities 10 to 50 times above those of classical transmitters such as dopamine or opioid receptors (Howlett et al. 1990; Herkenham et al. 1991). The CB_2 cannabinoid receptor was found initially in multiple lymphoid organs with the highest expression detected in B lymphocytes, medium expression in monocytes and polymorphonuclear neutrophils, and the lowest expression in T lymphocytes, although subsequent studies also identified it in microglial cells (Galiègue et al. 1995; Munro et al. 1993; Piomelli 2003). Recent reports place the cannabinoid CB_2 receptor in neuronal nets of the brain stem and the cerebellum (Onaivi 2006; Suarez et al. 2008), although its role in neurotransmission remains obscure.

Endocannabinoids are released upon demand after cellular depolarization or receptor stimulation in a calcium-dependent manner. Once produced, they act in cannabinoid receptors located in cells surrounding the site of production. This property indicates that endocannabinoids are local mediators similar to the autacoids (i.e., prostaglandins). In the central nervous system, the highly organized distribution of endocannabinoid signaling elements in GABAergic and glutamatergic synapses and their preservation of this distribution throughout evolution suggest a pivotal role in synaptic transmission. Because of the inhibitory effects on adenylyl cyclase, the activation of K^+ currents and the inhibition of Ca^{2+} entry into cells, the net effect of cannabinoid CB_1 receptor stimulation is a local hyperpolarization that leads to the general inhibitory effects described. If endocannabinoids act postsynaptically, they will counteract excitatory inputs entering the postsynaptic cells. This mechanism has been proposed for postsynaptic interactions with dopaminergic transmission (Felder et al. 1998; Giuffrida et al. 2004; Rodríguez de Fonseca et al. 1998). Despite its importance, this effect is secondary to the important presynaptic actions whose existence is supported by two facts: (a) the concentration of cannabinoid CB_1 receptors in presynaptic terminals and (b) the well-documented inhibitory effects of cannabinoid CB_1 receptor agonists on the release of GABA, glutamate, acetylcholine, and noradrenaline (Piomelli 2003; Schlicker and Kathmann 2001). This inhibitory effect has also been demonstrated for neuropeptides such as corticotrophin-releasing factor and cholecystokinin (Beinfeld and Connolly 2001; Rodríguez de Fonseca et al. 1997). Presynaptic inhibition of neurotransmitter release is associated with the inhibitory action

of endocannabinoids on Ca^{2+} presynaptic calcium channels through the activation of CB_1 receptors. Presynaptic inhibition of transmitter release by endocannabinoids may adopt two different forms of short-term synaptic plasticity, depending on the involvement of GABA or glutamate transmission, respectively: depolarization-induced suppression of inhibition (DSI) and depolarization-induced suppression of excitation (DSE) (Diana and Marty 2004; Wilson and Nicoll 2002). Both forms of synaptic plasticity involve the initial activation of a postsynaptic large projecting neuron (pyramidal or Purkinje cells) that sends a retrograde messenger to a presynaptic GABA terminal (DSI) or a presynaptic glutamate terminal (DSE), inducing a transient suppression of either the presynaptic inhibitory or the presynaptic excitatory input. The contribution of endocannabinoids to these forms of short-term synaptic plasticity has been described in the hippocampus and the cerebellum (Diana and Marty 2004; Wilson et al. 2001; Wilson and Nicoll 2001). The role of endocannabinoid-induced DSI or DSE seems to be the coordination of neural networks within the hippocampus and cerebellum that are involved in relevant physiological processes, such as memory or motor coordination.

Overall, endocannabinoids act as local messengers that adjust synaptic weight and contribute significantly to the elimination of information flow through specific synapses in a wide range of time frames. The fact that cannabinoid receptor stimulation has a major impact on second messengers involved not only in synaptic remodeling (Derkinderen et al. 1996; Piomelli 2003) but also in neuronal differentiation (Rueda et al. 2002) and neuronal survival (Marsicano et al. 2003), indicates that this signaling system is a major homeostatic mechanism that guarantees a fine adjustment of information processing in the brain and provides counter-regulatory mechanisms aimed at preserving the structure and function of major brain circuits. Both processes are relevant for homeostatic behavior, such as motivated behavior (motor learning, feeding, reproduction, relaxation, and sleep), and emotions, as well as for cognition, since learning and memory require dynamic functional and morphological changes in brain circuits. An experimental confirmation of this hypothetical role of the endogenous cannabinoid system was the demonstration of its role in the control of the extinction of aversive memories (Marsicano et al. 2002).

Disturbances of the Endocannabinoid System in Schizophrenia

Preclinical Studies: Alternations in Endocannabinoid Signaling in Animal Models of Schizophrenia

It is evident that psychosis is difficult to study from an experimental point of view in laboratory animals, since cognitive deficits are crucial in human schizophrenia. However, certain "psychotic-like" alterations have an animal correlate, and their study is considered as acceptable. For instance, prepulse inhibition (PPI) is a phenomenon wherein the startle response is reduced when the startling stimulus is preceded by a low-intensity prepulse (Graham 1975; Hoffman and Ison 1980; Geyer et al. 2001). It represents a normal sensorimotor gating response that is typically impaired in schizophrenic patients (Geyer et al. 2001). In rats and mice, PPI is selectively disrupted (decreased PPI) by dopamine agonists such as apomorphine, serotonergic compounds acting at the $5-HT_{2A}$ serotonin receptor, as well as psychotomimetics (Mansbach et al. 1988; Ralph-Williams et al. 2001, 2002; Ouagazzal et al. 2001; Geyer et al. 2002). Disruption of PPI is attenuated by antipsychotic drugs; hence, it is considered as a valid predictor of "psychosis-like" drug properties in animal models (Geyer et al. 2001; Ouagazzal et al. 2001). Contradictory results have been reported regarding cannabinoid effects on PPI. Some authors have observed that CB_1 receptor agonists such as WIN55,212-2, AM404, or CP55,940 disrupt the PPI (Mansbach et al. 1996; Schneider and Koch 2002), but others have not seen changes (Stanley-Cary et al. 2002; Bortolato et al. 2006). The indirect agonist, AM404, that increases the availability of the endocannabinoids 2-AG and anandamide in the biophase also disrupts the PPI in Swiss mice (Fernández-Espejo and Galán-Rodríguez 2004), although this finding has not been corroborated by others (Bortolato et al. 2006). On the other hand, Ballmaier et al. (2007) report that the CB_1 antagonists SR141716A and AM251 act as antipsychotic compounds in rats reversing phencyclidine- and dizocilpine-induced disruption of PPI. It has been proposed that PPI changes in rodents may be masked by decreased startle response amplitudes (Martin et al. 2003) or that the use of ethanol as solvent can induce false results because ethanol has significant effects on PPI performance on its own (Stanley-Cary et al. 2002). Contradictory results on PPI seem to be more related to rearing condition or age of the animals, pointing to an individual susceptibility based on these factors. Thus, chronic Δ-9-THC does not affect adult rats reared in groups, but it disrupts PPI whether rats have been kept isolated to each other upon weaning (Malone and Taylor 2006). The cannabinoid WIN55,212-2 disrupts PPI in prepubertal rats but not in adult animals, and this disruption is selectively reversed with haloperidol (Schneider and Koch 2003).

Auditory-evoked potential can be recorded during sensory gating tests in laboratory animals. Sensory gating has been demonstrated to be impaired in schizophrenic humans as explained and, by using auditory-evoked electroencephalography responses, a positive wave occurring 50 ms (P50) following the auditory stimulus is the most widely used auditory-evoked response to assess gating in humans (Adler et al. 1982; Cadenhead et al. 2000). Studies using the auditory conditioning–testing paradigm in rats have shown gating of a negative auditory-evoked potential recorded from implanted skull electrodes and from the CA3 region of the hippocampus around 40 ms after an auditory stimulus (Adler et al. 1986). This wave, known as N40, is considered a homolog to the P50 wave recorded in humans (Adler et al. 1986). The cannabinoid agonist WIN55,212-2 disrupts auditory gating in rats, in the hippocampus (CA3, dentate gyrus) and the medial prefrontal cortex (mPFC), and this disruption is prevented by the CB_1 antagonist SR141716A (Dissanayake et al. 2008; Zachariou et al. 2008). The CB_1 agonist CP-55940 has been reported not only to impair PPI in rats but also auditory gating and neuronal synchrony in limbic areas such as the hippocampus and entorhinal cortex, as evaluated through theta field potential oscillations (Hajós et al. 2008). It seems clear that, at least in rats, cannabinoid agonists impair auditory gating function in the limbic circuitry, supporting a connection between cannabis abuse and schizophrenia as evaluated through this animal model.

Another "psychotic-like" test is based on the induction of disorganized behavior in rodents (oral stereotypies) by psychotomimetic drugs and its attenuation with antipsychotics. These responses are considered to be a consequence of the hyperdopaminergic activity induced by the drug. These types of stereotypies are also observed in psychotic humans, and they are exacerbated with dopaminergic agonists and attenuated by antipsychotics, being considered as a "psychotic-like" sign in animal models of psychosis (Giuliani and Ferrari 1997). In this respect, Δ-9-THC has been reported to potentiate the stereotyped behavior in rats after amphetamine (Gorriti et al. 1999). Figure 1 depicts two examples on the role of the endogenous cannabinoid system as a potential modulator of disorganized behavior. Moreno et al. (2005) reported that chronic treatment with HU-210, a potent THC-like cannabinoid agonist, resulted in an exacerbation to

dopamine D_2-mediated disorganized behaviors. This was observed after the induction of CB_1 receptor desensitization with HU-210 and was evident after a washout period of the drug, when a substantial CB_1 downregulation is present. These results support the idea that cannabinoid CB_1 receptors serves as a brake for disorganized behavior mediated by dopaminergic transmission overactivity. Removal of this brake by desensitizing cannabinoid CB_1 receptor sensitizes to dopamine-mediated behavioral disorganization. This was further confirmed by Ferrer et al. (2007) in a simple experiment: acute blockade of central CB_1 receptors with a selective cannabinoid CB_1 receptor antagonist led to potentiation of dopamine D_1 and D_2 receptor-mediated induction of stereotypies. Additionally, Beltramo et al. (2000) have observed that dopamine D_2 receptor-mediated head stereotypies are reversed by AM404 (10 mg/kg), an indirect cannabinoid agonist. This AM404-induced effect is inhibited by pretreatment with the selective CB_1 receptor antagonist SR141716A, confirming the participation of cannabinoid receptors in these effects. Overall, these results show two important sides: while the endogeneous cannabinoid system is protective against behavioral disorganization, its dowregulation may result in a sensitization to psychosis-like states.

Animal research also indicates that neuregulin 1 (Nrg1), a gene from chromosome 8p, seems to be a susceptibility gene for schizophrenia (Stefansson et al. 2002; Karl et al. 2007). Mutant mice heterozygous for the transmembrane domain of Nrg1 (Nrg1 HET mice) exhibit a schizophrenia-related behavioral phenotype (Stefansson et al. 2002; Karl et al. 2007). Boucher et al. (2007a, b) have studied the relationship between neuregulin, schizophrenia, and cannabinoids in mice. Nrg1 HET mice are more sensitive to the acute effects of Δ-9-THC in an array of different behaviors including those that model symptoms of schizophrenia. It appears that variation in the schizophrenia-related neuregulin 1 gene alters the sensitivity to the behavioral effects of cannabinoids. It is worth noting that neurodevelopmental alterations take place in neuregulin 1 mutant mice. Nrg1 is a ligand for ErbB receptor tyrosine kinases which, when stimulated, may affect schizophrenia-related neurodevelopmental processes such as myclination, axon guidance, neuronal migration, and glial differentiation (Falls 2003). Neurodevelopmental alterations linked to cannabis abuse have been associated with schizophrenia in humans (see the "Clinical studies" section).

There is indeed preclinical evidence indicating that chronic administration of cannabinoid agonists during the periadolescent period causes diverse persistent behavioral alterations in adulthood. For instance, chronic administration of the cannabinoid receptor agonist CP 55,940 (CP) from PND 35 to PND 45 in rats resulted in marked sex-dependent alterations in motor and exploratory activity (Biscaia et al. 2003) and a 21-day treatment with the same drug in 30-day-old rats resulted in long-term increased anxiety and a lasting impairment of working memory (O'Shea et al. 2004). Interestingly, these later behavioral changes were observed in adolescent but not adult drug-treated rats. In another study, chronic pubertal treatment with another cannabinoid agonist, WIN 55,212-2 (WIN), resulted in impaired memory in adulthood as well as in a disrupted PPI of the acoustic startle response and lower breakpoints in a progressive ratio operant behavior task (Schneider and Koch 2003). Since PPI deficits, object recognition memory impairments, and anhedonia/avolition are among the endophenotypes of schizophrenia, the authors of this study proposed chronic cannabinoid administration during pubertal development as a neurodevelopmental animal model for some aspects of the etiology of schizophrenia. In line with the study by O'Shea et al. (2004), these authors also showed that chronic treatment with WIN during adulthood did not lead to changes in any of the behaviors tested (Schneider and Koch 2003). Thus, the early adolescent

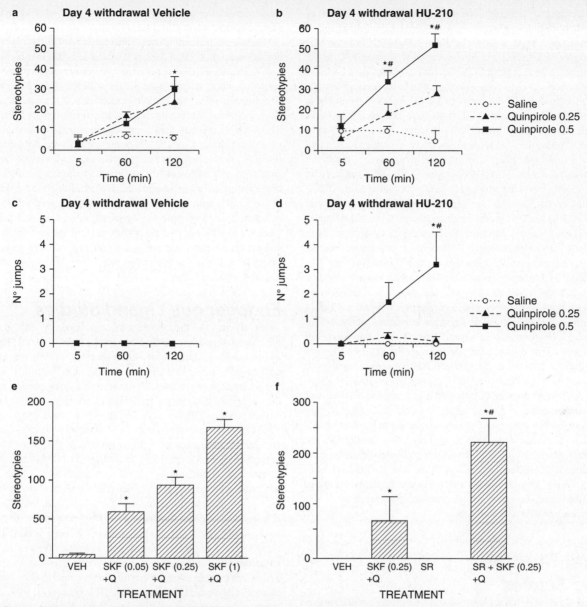

Figure 1 Desensitization (**a—d**) or blockade (**e, f**) of cannabinoid receptors increases dopamine-mediated disorganized behaviors and panic-like escape reactions. Stereotyped activity (**a, b**) and jumping escape behavior (**c, d**) (during 5-min scoring periods over a 125-min session) exhibited in an observation box after administration of dopamine D_2 agonist quinpirole (saline, 0.25, 0.5 mg/kg) at day 4 of withdrawal from chronic HU-210 (20 μg/kg, 14 days, i.p.) or vehicle treatment. Treatment effect, *$p < 0.05$ versus acute saline administration in same chronic treatment; interaction chronic treatment $\times$ acute administration $\times$ time effect, #$p < 0.05$ versus control group. Simultaneous administration of a fixed dose of the dopamine D_2 receptor agonist quinpirole (*Q*, 025 mg/kg) with increasing doses of the dopamine D_1 agonist SKF 38393 (*SKF*, 0.05, 0.25, and 1 mg/kg) produced disorganized behavior, as reflected in the increasing stereotyped activity (**e**). Blockade of cannabinoid CB_1 receptors with SR141716A (*SR*, 1 mg/kg) markedly enhanced the response to quinpirole (0.25 mg/kg) plus SKF (0.25 mg/kg), increasing the stereotyped behavior (**f**). *$p < 0.01$, different doses versus vehicletreated animals; #$p < 0.01$, SR + SKF + Q versus SKF + Q. All data are presented as the means $\pm$ standard error of the mean of 8–10 determinations per group, Newman—Keul's test (modified from Moreno et al. 2005 and Ferrer et al. 2007)

period appears to have a unique vulnerability to at least some of the adverse effects of cannabis. On the other hand, in a recent study by O'Shea et al. (2006), it was found that chronic exposure to the cannabinoid agonist CP during perinatal, adolescent, or early adulthood induced similar long-term memory impairments and increased anxiety in male rats. To explain the different results with respect to their previous study performed in female rats (O'Shea et al. 2004, see above), they claimed that adult males might be more vulnerable than adult females to some of the detrimental effects of cannabinoids,

such as cognitive disturbances. It would be very interesting to directly address possible sexual dimorphisms regarding increased risk to show schizophrenic-like symptoms in adolescent animals exposed to cannabinoids. Moreover, the effect of sex should be more carefully considered in epidemiological studies.

The three-hit model of schizophrenia proposes the following sequence: Genetic and early environmental factors disrupt central nervous system development and together act as a vulnerability factor that produces a long-term susceptibility to an additional adverse event (usually around puberty) that then precipitates the onset of schizophrenic symptoms (Maynard et al. 2001; Ellenbroek 2003). Based on this concept, Schneider and Koch (2005, 2007) have analyzed the effects of neonatal excitotoxic lesions of the mPFC and a chronic pubertal treatment with WIN on various forms of social and nonsocial behaviors. Their results indicated that behavioral deviations induced by neonatal mPFC lesions can be exacerbated by pubertal chronic cannabinoid treatment, leading to long-lasting impairments of mnemonic short-term information processing and reduced interest for social interaction. Inadequate social behavior and cognitive impairments are among the symptoms of schizophrenia (Robertson et al. 2006). In particular, object recognition memory is impaired in schizophrenic patients (Heckers et al. 2000; Doniger et al. 2002). Thus, animal models such as the one proposed by Schneider and Koch (2005, 2006) may be useful in elucidating the mechanisms by which adolescent cannabis exposure triggers psychotic symptoms in vulnerable individuals. With respect to possible neurochemical correlates of long-term effects of adolescent cannabis exposure, the PPI deficit induced by chronic peripubertal WIN treatment observed in the study by Schneider and Koch (2003, see above) was reversed by acute administration of the dopamine antagonist haloperidol 85 days after the chronic treatment, which suggests persistent alterations in the dopaminergic system (Schneider and Koch 2003). A more recent study has examined the effects of repeated cannabinoid administration on mesoaccumbens dopaminergic neuronal functions and responses to drugs of abuse. Animals were pretreated during adolescence or adulthood, for 3 days, with WIN or vehicle and allowed a 2-week interval. In WIN-administered rats, dopaminergic neurons were significantly less responsive to the stimulating action of the cannabinoid, regardless of the age of pretreatment. However, in the adolescent group, but not in the adult group, long-lasting cross-tolerance developed to morphine, cocaine, and amphetamine (Pistis et al. 2004). Thus, cannabis exposure at a young age may induce long-term neuronal adaptations in the mesolimbic dopaminergic system and hence affect the responses to both natural rewards and drugs of abuse.

Clinical Studies
Genetic Studies
Several genetic alterations have been linked to a higher predisposition to suffer from schizophrenia after cannabis abuse. Thus, the gene codifying the enzyme catechol-O-methyl-transferase (COMT), which is involved in dopamine degradation, shows a functional polymorphism (Vall58Met) with two variants (G and A) that induce a single amino acid change in the protein (valine or methionine, respectively). Those individuals with the G variant (Val/Val genotype) or Val/Met heterozygotes have a greater likelihood to suffer from psychotic disorder after cannabis abuse (Caspi et al. 2005). These two COMT isoforms degrade dopamine at a higher rate than the Met/Met homozygotes, and dopamine dysregulation is related to schizophrenia.

Genetic alterations affecting the CNR1 gene which codes for the cannabinoid CB_1 receptor could also be related to schizophrenia. Ujike et al. (2002) reported that hebephrenic schizophrenia could be linked to a nine-time repetition of the triplet AAT in the 3' region of the codifying exon of the gene. Recently, Chavarría-Siles et al. (2008) have confirmed that hebephrenic schizophrenia is associated with the CNR1 gene and present a type of symptomatology that resembles cannabinoid-induced psychosis. It, therefore, seems that the CNR1 gene and its molecular expression could be linked to a special predisposition to suffer from this type of schizophrenia. However, alterations in the CNR1 gene leading to an increased risk for schizophrenia is substantiated in a small number of human studies, and alternative

possibilities have not been ruled out (i.e., other consequences of the mutated gene).

On the other hand, polymorphisms in the CNR1 gene can also be associated to protection for psychosis or to better therapeutic outcome. Ujike et al. (2002) also report that 17-time repetition of the AAT triplet confers protection against the disorder, although this hypothesis cannot be validated using epidemiological evidence because of the possible changes in other brain systems that might result from such a mutation. The CNR1 gene has also been associated to the therapeutic effects of antipsychotics. A 1359G/A polymorphism of the CNR1 gene (G allele) is associated to a better pharmacological response to atypical antipsychotics with a clear dose effect of the G allele in a population of French schizophrenic patients (Hamdani et al. 2008). The G allele of the CNR1 gene polymorphisms could be a psychopharmacogenetic rather than a vulnerability factor regarding schizophrenia and its treatment. In conclusion, genetic studies confirm the two sides of the coin: some polymorphisms are associated to higher risk for schizophrenia, and others are associated to protection against the disorder or better response to antipsychotic therapy.

Endogenous Ligand Studies
An involvement of the endogenous cannabinoid system in schizophrenia is also supported by findings in the cerebrospinal fluid (CSF) in patients with schizophrenia. Leweke et al. (1999) reported that the endocannabinoids anandamide (AEA) and palmitoylethanolamide (PEA) are elevated in the CSF of untreated schizophrenic patients, and they proposed a relationship between the onset of schizophrenia and altered AEA and PEA levels. Levels of 2-arachidonylglycerol (2-AG) were not observed to be affected because they were below detection. Di Marzo's group reported that anandamide levels are also enhanced in the blood of patients with schizophrenia (De Marchi et al. 2003).

However, Giuffrida et al. (2004), while confirming these findings, observed that typical antipsychotic treatment reversed CSF AEA excess, in contrast to treatment with atypical antipsychotics. In accordance, they suggest that anandamide hyperactivity is not involved in the onset of psychosis, but it seems to be a homeostatic mechanism tending to reduce hyperdopaminergia. Typical antipsychotics antagonize D_2, dopamine receptors, while atypical compounds possess a wider receptorial spectrum, acting upon other receptors such as serotonergic 5-HT2A and 5-HT2C receptors. It is known that D_2 stimulation increases AEA release that otherwise reduces dopamine release through a feedback mechanism, hence inhibition of AEA augmentation after typical antipsychotics relieving schizophrenia would indicate that hyperanandamidergia is a compensatory homeostatic mechanism tending to reduce excessive dopaminergic stimulation. In fact, there is a clear negative correlation between psychotic symptoms and CSF AEA levels (Giuffrida et al. 2004).

In another study, Leweke et al. (2007) examined whether cannabis use alters serum and CSF anandamide levels in first-episode antipsychotic-naïve schizophrenic humans. In patients with low-frequency cannabis use, CSF AEA levels were more than tenfold higher than in high-frequency users. They propose that frequent cannabis exposure may down-regulate anandamide signaling in the CNS of patients with schizophrenia, and this fact could increase the risk for new psychotic episodes.

CB_1 Receptor Studies in Postmortem
Three independent research groups have performed post-mortem evaluations of CB_1 receptors densities in the brain of schizophrenic patients. Dean et al. (2001) reported upregulation of CB_1 receptors in the dorsolateral prefrontal cortex by using autoradiography and in situ binding with the radioligand [³H]CP-55940, a nonselective cannabinoid agonist. The prefrontal cortex belongs to the dopaminergic

mesocorticolimbic system, and it is involved in attentional and cognitive processes. Zavitsanou et al. (2004), by using the more selective radioligand [³H]SR141716A, found that there is an upregulation of around 64% in density of CB$_1$ receptors in the anterior cingulate cortex, a cortical area intimately connected with the prefrontal cortex. Finally, Mewell et al. (2006) detected an increase in the density of receptors in the posterior cingulate cortex, another region of the cingulate cortex involved in cognition. In this context, the cingulate cortex is a site of integration of information sources that include cognitive, emotional, and interoceptive signals, and it is considered as divided into four regions with different roles in the processing of emotional information (the four-region model; Vogt 2005), these regions being activated in important cognitive processes such as fear, sadness, self-awareness, normal social cognition, and decision-making (Gallagher et al. 2003; Wicker et al. 2003; Vogt 2005). The prefrontal cortex is also known to participate in negative aspects of schizophrenia such as anhedonia, poor thinking, apathy, blunted social interaction, and amotivation; hence, all data point to a possible role of CB$_1$ receptor changes in these areas in the symptomatology of schizophrenia. These studies have been criticized due to the low number of studied patients and the possible interference of the antipsychotic medication, but they point to an intrinsic disturbance of the endocannabinoid system in frontal and cingulate areas in schizophrenia.

Cannabis Abuse, Schizophrenia, and Brain Morphology

As already mentioned, the greatest risk of onset of cannabis use is in the age range 15–20 years that coincides with the onset of schizophrenia (Grant et al. 2008). It is possible that cannabis may affect neurodevelopmental processes, such as synaptic plasticity, thought to be impaired in schizophrenia (Feinberg 1982; Keshavan et al. 1994): Exogenous cannabinoids could alter endogenous cannabinoid-mediated synaptic plasticity, affecting brain maturation in adolescence (Robbe et al. 2003). Magnetic resonance imaging studies in cannabis users without schizophrenia have revealed reductions of gray matter density (Matochik et al. 2005). However, this reduction was not found by Block et al. (2000), but they did find that cannabis users have lower ventricular CSF volume compared with nonusers. A recent study by Bangalore et al. (2008) indicates that cannabis-using patients with first-episode schizophrenia have more prominent gray matter density and volume reduction in the right posterior cingulate cortex compared to patients not using cannabis or healthy subjects. Rais et al. (2008) confirmed that first-episode schizophrenia patients who use cannabis show a more pronounced brain volume reduction over a 5-year follow-up than patients with schizophrenia who do not use cannabis. However, brain volume reduction has not been found by other authors (Cahn et al. 2004) by using magnetic resonance acquisition and processing procedures. It is also important to note that antipsychotic use has been shown to affect brain structure in patients with first-episode psychosis (Lieberman et al. 2005) and causes volume changes in the caudate nucleus (Scheepers et al. 2001), and this factor is a confounding variable in many studies. To sum up, contradictory results have been reported regarding the association between cannabis-induced neuroplastic changes and first episode of schizophrenia.

Cannabis Abuse, Schizophrenia, and Neurodevelopment During Adolescence

According to the Feinberg hypothesis (Feinberg 1982, 1987), a substantial reorganization of cortical connections, involving a programmed synaptic pruning, takes place during adolescence in humans. An excessive pruning of the prefrontal corticocortical and corticosubcortical synapses, perhaps involving the excitatory glutamatergic inputs to pyramidal neurons, may underlie schizophrenia. A reciprocal failure of pruning in certain subcortical structures, such as the lenticular nuclei, may also occur. Several developmental trajectories, related to early brain insults as well as genetic factors affecting postnatal neurodevelopment, could lead to the illness (Spear 2000; Adriani and Laviola 2004; Marek and Merchant 2005). The high rates of cannabis use among adolescents and young adults (Hall and Degenhardt 2007; United Nations Office on Drugs and Crime, http://www.unodc.org/unodc/index.html; The European Monitoring Centre for Drugs and Drug Addiction (EMCDDA), http://www.emcdda.europa.eu/) makes it pertinent to investigate the short-term and long-term consequences of cannabis use during this critical period of development. Indeed, the research of the last decade has provided substantial evidence indicating that cannabis use in adolescence increases the likelihood of experiencing symptoms of schizophrenia in adulthood (Andreasson et al. 1987; Arseneault et al. 2002; Stefanis et al. 2004). This association has very important consequences in terms of risk-reduction strategies, which would contribute to prevention and early implementation of therapeutic programs (De Irala et al. 2005; Verdoux et al. 2005; Miettunen et al. 2008). The evidence pertaining to cannabis use and occurrence of psychotic or affective mental health outcomes has been recently reviewed by Moore et al. (2007). The authors found that there was an increased risk of any psychotic outcome in individuals who had ever used cannabis (pooled adjusted odds ratio = 1.41, 95% confidence interval [95%CI] = 1.20–1.65). Findings were consistent with a dose—response effect with greater risk in people who used cannabis most frequently (odds ratio = 2.09, 95% CI = 1.54–2.84) and suggested that cannabis increases the risk of psychotic outcomes, independent of confounding and transient intoxication effects.

It is as yet unclear what the causal relationship between cannabis use during adolescence and the development of schizophrenia in adulthood is. It is also important to note that the conclusion that early chronic cannabinoid use is detrimental to those at risk for schizophrenia as adults is based largely on animal data. The ultimate proof of a causal relationship between cannabis use and psychotic illness later in life would come from studies in which healthy young people were exposed to Δ-9-THC and followed up until adulthood. Obviously, for practical and ethical reasons, such an approach is impossible. In fact, among many other important health risks, it is well known that cannabis induces harmful effects on cognitive function (Nordentoft and Hjorthøj 2007; Solowij and Michie 2007; Solowij et al. 2002). On the other hand, such studies can be performed in animals under well-controlled conditions. Hence, such animal models can shed light on the underlying neurobiological mechanisms and the relationship between cannabis use and schizophrenia, as detailed in a previous section of this review. As discussed in previous sections of this review, a dysregulation of the endocannabinoid system may be implicated in the pathogenesis of schizophrenia. The peripubertal period appears to be critical for the development of cannabinoid CB$_1$ receptors and endocannabinoid levels (Rodriguez de Fonseca et al. 1993; Wenger et al. 2002). Therefore, it is conceivable that chronic interference by cannabis with the developing endocannabinoid system during this critical time interval leads to severe and persistent functional impairments (Schneider and Koch 2007) that might reflect, at least in part, psychosis-related symptoms.

The association between neuregulin 1 and neurodevelopment alterations is also of interest. Human and animal research indicates that neuregulin 1 (Nrg1), a gene from chromosome 8p, seems to be a susceptibility gene for schizophrenia (Stefansson et al. 2002; Karl et al. 2007, Walss-Bass et al. 2006a, b). Walss-Bass et al. have identified a missense mutation (Val to Leu) in exon 11, which codes for the transmembrane region of the neuregulin 1 protein, and this mutation is associated with psychosis ($p = 0.0049$) and schizophrenia ($p = 0.0191$). As explained, Nrg1 is a ligand for ErbB tyrosine kinase receptor which may affect schizophrenia-related neurodevelopmental processes such as myelination, axon guidance, neuronal migration, and glial differentiation after stimulation (Falls 2003). The variation in the schizophrenia-related neuregulin 1 gene alters the sensitivity to the behavioral effects of cannabinoids.

Modulation of Endocannabinoid Signaling by Antipsychotics

Haloperidol medication is known to worsen the cognitive effects of Δ-9-THC in schizophrenics, indicating that there is a cross-talk between the cannabinoid and dopaminergic systems in schizophrenic patients (D'Souza et al. 2008b). On the other hand, cannabis-induced psychosis is responsive to treatment with antipsychotic drugs (Berk et al. 1999), further suggesting that the endocannabinoid system is involved in psychosis or the therapeutic effects of antipsychotics. The atypical antipsychotic drug clozapine decreases the use of cannabis in patients with schizophrenia (Drake et al. 2000). In this context, Sundram et al. (2005) have reported that, by using in situ radioligand binding and quantitative autoradiography with the selective cannabinoid CB_1 receptor agonist $(-)$-cis-3-[2-hydroxy-4-(1,1-dimethylheptyl)phenyl]-trans-4-(3-hydroxypropyl)cyclohexanol (side chain-2,3,4(N)-3H) ([^{3}H] CP 55940) to measure the density of the CB_1 receptor in the frontal cortex, hippocampus, nucleus accumbens, and striatum, the antipsychotic clozapine significantly decreased [^{3}H] CP 55940 binding in the nucleus accumbens compared with vehicle. This effect is not observed with haloperidol, chlorpromazine, or olanzapine; hence, this effect of clozapine is a mechanism that makes it uniquely effective in schizophrenia and comorbid cannabis use. Antipsychotics also influence the density of the CB_1 receptor and the actions of Δ-9-THC. Thus, Wiley et al. (2008) report that subchronic treatment with haloperidol and clozapine decreases CB_1 receptor-mediated G protein activity in specific forebrain regions in adult female rats without affecting CB_1 receptor densities. In vivo, subchronic treatment with clozapine, but not haloperidol, attenuates Δ-9-THC-induced suppression of activity in adult females. In contrast, antipsychotic treatment did not change CB_1 receptor-mediated G protein activation in any brain region in adult male rats and in adolescents of either sex. In vivo, haloperidol, but not clozapine, enhanced Δ-9-THC-mediated suppression of activity and hypothermia in adult male rats, whereas neither antipsychotic affected Δ-9-THC-induced in vivo effects in adolescent rats. These findings suggest that modulation of the endocannabinoid system might contribute in a sex- and age-selective manner to differences in motor side effects of clozapine versus haloperidol.

Finally, it is worth mentioning that typical antipsychotic treatment reverses CSF excess of the endocannabinoid anandamide in schizophrenics, in contrast to treatment with atypical antipsychotics (Giuffrida et al. 2004). Since haloperidol medication worsens the cognitive effects of Δ-9-THC in schizophrenics, this later fact is in contrast with the proposed homeostatic protective role of anandamide excess in schizophrenics (Giuffrida et al. 2004).

Neurobiological Integration of Cannabinoid Dysregulation with Current Theories of Schizophrenia

Schizophrenic symptoms are attributed, among other mechanisms, to a hyperdopaminergic state in the mesolimbic system (the ventral striatum as the main region) together with a hypodopaminergic tone in

the mesocortical system, the prefrontal cortex being the main region (Grace 1991; Moore et al. 1999). Schizophrenia has consistently been related to increased dopamine function in the striatum (Seeman and Lee 1975; Angrist and Van Kammen 1984), possibly caused by a disinhibition of striatal dopamine transmission (Laruelle et al. 1996). Biochemical information confirms that neural dopaminergic systems are altered in schizophrenia because striatal D_2 receptors are upregulated in schizophrenic brains (Hirvonen et al. 2005) and the dopamine transporter DAT is downregulated in the prefrontal cortex, a homeostatic response suggestive of reduced dopamine release in the biophase (Sekine et al. 2003). The dopaminergic hypothesis of schizophrenia is strongly supported by the fact that the most effective antipsychotics are antidopaminergic compounds, mostly acting upon D_2 receptors.

Exogenous or endogenous cannabinoids could participate in the dysregulation of the mesocorticolimbic dopaminergic activity in schizophrenia (Gardner and Vorel 1998) because the endocannabinoid system is a feedback mechanism negatively regulating dopamine release (Rodríguez de Fonseca et al. 1998). Exogenous administration of cannabinoid agonists enhances activity of dopamine neurons located in the ventral tegmental area (VTA; French et al. 1997), leading to augmentation of dopamine release in the ventral striatum or nucleus accumbens (Gardner et al. 1988). Although stimulation of CB_1 autoreceptors is known to reduce dopamine release (Beltramo et al. 2000; Wilson and Nicoll 2002), systemic administration of CB_1 agonists enhances dopamine release. This is due to the inhibitory effects of CB_1 agonists on GABAergic interneurons in the VTA, which leads to a disinhibition of VTA neurons (see Figure 2). Recently, Bossong et al. (2009) have demonstrated that Δ-9-THC induces dopamine release in the human striatum. Using the dopamine D_2/D_3 tracer [^{11}C] raclopride and positron emission tomography, they demonstrate that Δ-9-THC inhalation reduces [^{11}C]raclopride binding in the ventral striatum and the precommissural dorsal putamen, which is consistent with an increase in dopamine levels in these regions.

It can be speculated that dysregulation of the endocannabinoid system in the VTA or excessive stimulation of CB_1 receptors (for instance, after prolonged abuse of Δ-9-THC) could be linked to schizophrenia through a facilitation of dopamine release in the mesolimbic system, a dysregulation of dopaminergic activity or a desensitization of limbic CB_1 receptors (Pertwee 2005). At a molecular level, both dopamine D_2 and cannabinoid CB_1 receptor stimulation induces a decrease in cAMP content in limbic regions such as the nucleus accumbens. When dopamine activity is enhanced (as it is the case in schizophrenia), heterologous sensitization develops: D_2 receptor stimulation enhances cAMP levels instead. CB_1 stimulation opposes D_2-mediated cAMP augmentation (Jarrahian et al. 2004), a fact that could help explain why anandamide is enhanced in schizophrenics' CSF. However, prolonged endocannabinoid action (or Δ-9-THC abuse) would desensitize CB_1 receptors which would no longer oppose D_2-mediated effects, facilitating hyperdopaminergic effects and surely aggravating the course of schizophrenic psychosis. In this context, as already mentioned, cannabis abuse is also known to reduce CSF hyperanandamidergia, indicating that cannabis abuse would antagonize the "protective" role attributed to anandamide (Leweke et al. 2007). The neurophysiological integration of the endocannabinoid system with the dopaminergic hypothesis of schizophrenia is also favored by the fact that there is augmentation of CB_1 receptor density in the prefrontal cortex of schizophrenics (Dean et al. 2001). Logically, upregulation of cannabinoid receptors and a higher endocannabinoid tone would reduce dopamine release at a presynaptic level, which could help explain hypodopaminergic activity in the prefrontal cortex.

Another interesting phenomenon observed in schizophrenics who do not consume cannabis is the reduction in striatal DAT expression, as measured through [^{3}H]mazindol binding, while these levels are normal

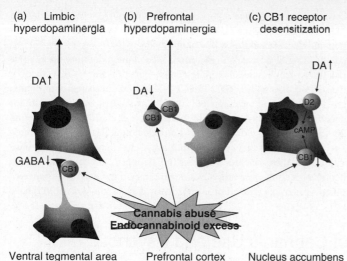

Figure 2 Cannabis abuse/endocannabinoid excess, and the dopaminergic system in schizophrenia. Cannabis abuse, mostly its active component Δ-9-THC (or endogenous cannabinoid excess), acts upon CB_1 receptors inducing (a) limbic dopaminergic hyperactivity (through inhibition of GABA neurons of the VTA), (b) prefrontal dopaminergic hypoactivity (CB_1 receptors density is enhanced in the prefrontal cortex of schizophrenics, and stimulation of CB_1 receptors reduces tonic dopamine release), and (c) desensitizes CB_1 receptors (i.e., in the nucleus accumbens) thereby blocking antagonistic properties between CB_1 and D_2 dopamine receptors (leading to upregulation of cAMP, as detected in schizophrenics). *DA* dopamine, *GABA* gammaminobutyric acid, *CB_1* cannabinoid receptor type 1, *D_2* dopamine receptor type 2

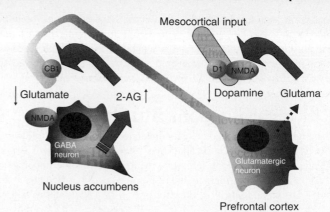

Figure 3 Endocannabinoids, the NDMA glutamatergic system, and schizophrenia. In schizophrenic brains, medium spiny GABA neurons located in the nucleus accumbens would have an enhanced endocannabinoid tone (mostly affecting 2-AG release and its biophase levels). Enhanced 2-AG diminishes corticostriatal glutamatergic release through presynaptic CB_1 receptors. In parallel, a reduced glutamate release in the prefrontal cortex would in turn reduce dopamine release from mesocortical terminals (prefrontal dopaminergic hypoactivity). *GABA* gamma-aminobutyric acid, *CB_1* cannabinoid receptor type 1, *D_1* dopamine receptor type 1, *NMDA* N-methyl-D-aspartate receptor

in patients who are also cannabis abusers (Dean et al. 2003). This effect would point to a modulation of DAT levels after repeated Δ-9-THC which could counteract limbic hyperdopaminergia, suggesting a potentially "self-medication" role for Δ-9-THC. However, it is also evident that with repeated Δ-9-THC consumption and the subsequent desensitization of the CB_1 receptors, the "self-medication" effect would likely wear off.

The *N*-methyl-D-aspartate (NMDA) receptor hypothesis of schizophrenia states that there is an impairment of the glutamatergic neurotransmission in limbic and cortical regions and reduced activity of NDMA receptors is a central factor. This hypothesis helps explain why NMDA receptor antagonist such as phencyclidine and ketamine induce psychotic symptoms (Javitt and Zukin 1991), acting as hallucinogenic drugs. With regard to the endocannabinoid system, 2-AG, unlike anandamide, is especially involved in glutamatergic neurotransmission, and this endocannabinoid negatively modulates glutamate release acting through presynaptic CB_1 receptors (Katona et al. 2006). It is worth noting that data supporting an interaction between endocannabinoids and glutamate underlying schizophrenia are only preclinical, and there is so far no clinical evidence. The endocannabinoid 2-AG is known to reduce glutamate release in several neuronal areas related to schizophrenia such as the hippocampus (Fujiwara and Egashira 2004), prefrontal cortex (Auclair et al. 2000), nucleus accumbens (Robbe et al. 2001), and amygdala (Azad et al. 2003). Glutamate and NMDA receptor hypoactivity in the prefrontal cortex is also important for understanding some changes in dopamine neurotransmission because reduced glutamate release in the prefrontal cortex is accompanied by reduced dopamine release as well (see Figure 3). Taken all together,

these data are in accordance with the proposed hypodopaminergic state in the prefrontal cortex in schizophrenia.

Experimentally, it is known that glutamate release in the striatum or accumbens induces the postsynaptic production and release of 2-AG through the activation of mGluR5 receptors. The endocannabinoid 2-AG acts through CB_1 autoreceptors by blocking glutamate release (Katona et al. 2006). It is of interest that the antipsychotic effects of the cannabinoid antagonist rimonabant in animal models are due to changes in glutamatergic transmission in the nucleus accumbens, without dopaminergic participation (Soria et al. 2005), suggesting an important role for the interaction of endocannabinoids and glutamate in this nucleus in psychotic effects. Recently, it has been reported that there is a functional interaction between 2-AG and AEA in striatal areas because AEA downregulates the other endocannabinoids (Maccarrone et al. 2008), even though effects can also be synergic, and the picture is far from being fully understood (Di Marzo and Maccarrone 2008). It is interesting to note that neuregulin 1 mutant mice display a hypofunctional glutamatergic system with a deficit in NMDA receptor expression (Stefansson et al. 2002; Karl et al. 2007). In addition, stimulation of tyrosine kinase ErbB receptor affects glutamate transmission, which is in line with the NMDA hypothesis of schizophrenia.

At a clinical level, it is possible that there are local changes of 2-AG in striatal areas. However, Leweke et al. (2007) reported that, in patients with high-frequency cannabis use, CSF AEA levels were more than tenfold lower than in patients with low-frequency use. Taken together, these facts allow us to propose a hypothesis based on an opposing role for 2-AG and AEA in schizophrenia, a hypothesis that needs to be tested with clinical studies. Thus, a possible dysregulation of both endocannabinoids could affect glutamate release in limbic and cortical areas, and the 2-AG/AEA ratio in these areas could be important for predicting whether or not there is a special risk for psychosis. To sum up, chronic exposure to cannabinoids or dysregulation of the endocannabinoid system could alter dopamine and glutamate systems in such a way that a "cannabinoid hypothesis" can be integrated in the neurobiological hypotheses of schizophrenia. However, it is important to note that cannabinoid function affects multiple systems in the brain and other neurotransmitter systems could be involved or neurobiological compensatory processes could also occur.

Epidemiological Studies

The emergence of psychotic symptoms have been reported following chronic cannabis use (Castle and Ames 1996; Hall and Solowij 1997), the age of first use being important, which confirms the importance of adolescence as a critical period (Zammit et al. 2002; Henquet et al. 2005). The initial study by Andreasson et al. (1987) postulated a relation between cannabis use and the development of schizophrenic syndrome. They studied the association between the level of cannabis consumption and development of schizophrenic during a 15-year follow-up in a cohort of 45,570 Swedish conscripts. They concluded that the relative risk for schizophrenia among high consumers of cannabis (use on more than 50 occasions) was 6.0 (95%CI = 4.0–8.9) compared with nonusers. Other authors have carried out similar studies leading to similar conclusions (Zammit et al. 2002; Arseneault et al. 2002; van Os et al. 2002), as summarized in Table 1. Ferdinand et al. (2005) carried out a 14-year follow-up study of 1,580 initially 4- to 16-year-old Dutch individuals and they concluded that the link between cannabis use and psychotic symptoms is specific, not depending on the earlier presence of other types of psychopathology. Recently, Fergusson et al. (2005) have

Table 1 Summary of Prospective Studies of Cannabis Use and Psychotic Symptoms

Study	Sample	Assessment	Outcome Measure	Cannabis use Criteria	Association between Cannabis and Psychosis (95%CI)
Andreasson et al. (1987)	45,570 male Swedish military conscripts aged 18 to 21	At 15 year follow-up	Clinical diagnosis of schizophrenia	Structural interview	Relative risk 6 (4.0 to 8.9)
Tien and Anthony (1990)	4,994 adult household residents		Diagnostic interview	Self-report (daily use)	Odds ratio 2.62
Arseneault et al. (2002)	759 members of New Zealand birth cohort	At age 26	DMS-IV criteria for schizophreniform disorder	Cannabis use (three times or more)	Cannabis users by age 15; odds ratio 1.95 (0.76 to 5.01)
van Os et al. (2002)	4,104 participants in Dutch general population study	Assessed three times over 4 years	BPRS (>1 positive rating on psychotic symptom items)	Cannabis use derived from Composite International Diagnostic Interview (CIDI)	Odds ratio 6.81 (1.79 to 25.92)
Zammit et al. (2002)	50,087 Swedish subjects	>97% population aged 18 to 20	Admissions to hospital for ICD-8/9 schizophrenia and other psychoses	Structure interview	Odds ratio 1.3 (1.1 to 1.5) in cannabis only users; odds ratio for using cannabis >50 times was 6.7 (2.1 to 21.7)
Caspi et al. (2005)	803 members of New Zealand birth cohort	At age 26	DMS-IV criteria for schizophreniform disorder	Self-report	Participants with Val/Val variant of COMT gene; odds ratio 10.9 (2.2 to 54.1)
Henquet et al. (2005)	2,437 German participants aged 14 to 24	At baseline and 4-year followup	One or two psychotic outcomes	L-section of M-CIDI	Odds ratio 2.23 (1.30 to 3.84)
Ferdinand et al. (2005)	1,580 Dutch individuals	At 14-year follow-up (initially 4- to 16-year-old subjects)	Psychotic symptoms were assessed with the CIDI	CIDI	Odds ratio 2.81 (1.79 to 4.43)
Fergusson et al. (2005)	1,055 members of New Zealand birth cohort	At age 25	No. of psychotic symptoms in past month	Cannabis dependence	Daily cannabis users; incident rate ratio 1.77 (1.28 to 2.44)

Despite considerable variation in how cannabis exposure and psychosis were elicited or defined, there is a notable consistency in unadjusted odds ratio across the population groups studied. This table suggests that cannabis abuse is a risk factor, increasing the chance for developing schizophrenia or a schizophrenic-like psychotic illness by approximately threefold studied 1,055 members of New Zealand birth cohort during 4 years and they found that the relative risk for schizophrenic psychosis in cannabis abusers is 2.23 and rates of psychotic symptoms were between 1.6 and 1.8 times higher ($p < 0.001$) than nonusers of cannabis. Moreover, cannabis is associated with an increased risk of developing schizophrenia in a dose-dependent fashion (Zammit et al. 2002; Henquet et al. 2005). This association between cannabis and schizophrenia is not explained by use of other psychoactive drugs. In the studies by Zammit et al. (2002), Arseneault et al. (2002), van Os et al. (2002), and Fergusson et al. (2005), the effects of the use of other drugs (cocaine, amphetamine, alcohol, and nicotine) have also been evaluated, and the odds ratios remain being significant after controlling for this confounding factor (Smit et al. 2004). Semple et al. (2005) reviewed all previous epidemiological studies and conclude that cannabis is a risk factor for psychosis and psychotic symptoms, independent of the presence of other factors (i.e., genetic factors). More recent studies have been carried out in different countries: Stefanis et al. (2004) in Greece shows that cannabis use is also an important risk factor for the negative dimensions of schizophrenia; Rössler et al. (2007) in Switzerland found significant relationships between cannabis use in adolescence and the nuclear syndrome of schizophrenia. The latest one is carried out in Trinidad and Tobago by Konings et al. (2008) with similar results concerning the importance of the age of beginning. In a recent meta-analysis, Moore et al. (2007) concluded that cannabis use increases the risk for psychosis, independent of the presence of several confounding factors, and the presence of an alteration in COMT is just representative for a small group of persons.

On the other hand, some epidemiological studies are in disagreement with the hypothesis of a causal relationship between cannabis abuse and schizophrenic psychosis. Macleod et al. (2004) think that the relationship is confounded by many uncontrolled factors. A major disagreement is that the prevalence of schizophrenia remains stable, despite the increased amount of cannabis abuse worldwide. However, at a local level, Boydell et al. (2006) and Ajdacic-Gross et al. (2007) have found an increase in the prevalence of schizophrenia, related with the increase of cannabis abuse in South London and Switzerland, respectively.

Some authors consider cannabis-induced psychosis as a first step towards schizophrenia (Hart 1978). A recent study by Arendt et al. (2005) has shown that, in a sample of subjects with a diagnosis of cannabis-induced psychosis, close to 50% of them developed a schizophrenia spectrum disorder in a 3-year follow-up study; and male gender and early beginning of cannabis use appeared to be additional risk factors. Personality traits also seem to influence the onset of schizophrenia. Núñez and Gurpegui (2002) report that the risk of schizophrenia is higher in subjects with antisocial personality traits and prolonged cannabis abuse with respect to subjects with different personality traits. Schneier and Siris (1987) propose that there is a clear association between the emergence of psychotic symptoms and personality alterations in cannabis abusers. Mendhiratta et al. (1988) reported that neuroticism as evaluated through the Minnesota Multiphasic Personality Inventory test is more intense in subjects with toxic psychosis, and Negrete (1983) reported similar results.

Few studies have tried to discern the role of genetic factors in the relative risk for schizophrenia. McGuire et al. (1993) found a high percentage of relative risk among those cannabis abusers suffering from psychosis. Varma and Sharma (1993) found that 30% among siblings of schizophrenic patients use cannabis. A recent genetic study found that the link between cannabis and psychosis is stronger in those who have the Val/Val variant of the COMT gene (Caspi et al. 2005) with odds ratio being high (10.9, from 2.2 to 54.1). This enzyme is quite important in the regulation of dopamine levels since it mediates dopamine degradation, and dopamine is known to be involved in schizophrenia. This fact indicates that a genetic enzymatic alteration is able to enhance the risk for developing schizophrenia in susceptible cannabis users.

Conclusions

Available epidemiological and neurobiological data suggest that cannabis abuse is a risk factor for psychosis in genetically predisposed people, may lead to a worse outcome of the disease, or it can affect normal brain development during adolescence, increasing the risk for schizophrenia in adulthood. Regarding genetic predisposition, alterations affecting the CNR1 gene which codes for the cannabinoid CB_1 receptor could be related to schizophrenia, although this is substantiated in a small number of human studies, and a missense mutation in the gene which codes for the transmembrane region of the neuregulin 1 protein is also associated with schizophrenia and alters the sensitivity to the behavioral effects of cannabinoids. The endogenous cannabinoid system is altered in schizophrenia (i.e., increased density of cannabinoid CB_1 receptor binding in corticolimbic regions, enhanced anandamide levels in the CSF), and dysregulation of this system (that could be induced by exogenous cannabis) can interact with neurotransmitter systems in such a way that a "cannabinoid hypothesis" can be integrated in the neurobiological hypotheses of schizophrenia (dopamine and glutamate ones). Finally, there is also evidence that some genetic alterations of the CNR1 gene can act as protectant against schizophrenia rather than as a risk factor or they can be a psychopharmacogenetic rather than a vulnerability factor.

References

Adler LE, Pachtman E, Franks RD, Pecevich M, Waldo MC, Freedman R (1982) Neurophysiological evidence for a defect in neuronal mechanismsinvolved in sensory gating in schizophrenia. Biol Psychiatry 17(6):639–654

Adler LE, Rose G, Freedman R (1986) Neurophysiological studies of sensory gating in rats: effects of amphetamine, phencyclidine, and haloperidol. Biol Psychiatry 21(8–9):787–798

Adriani W, Laviola G (2004) Windows of vulnerability to psychopathology and therapeutic strategy in the adolescent rodent model. Behav Pharmacol 15:341–352

Ajdacic-Gross V, Lauber C, Warnke I, Haker H, Murray RM, Rössler W (2007) Changing incidence of psychotic disorders among the young in Zurich. Schizophr Res 95(1–3):9–18

Andreasson S, Allebeck P, Engstrom A, Rydberg U (1987) Cannabis and schizophrenia. A longitudinal study of Swedish conscripts. Lancet 2:1483–1486

Angrist B, Van Kammen DP (1984) CNS stimulants as tools in the study of schizophrenia. Trends Neurosci 7:388–390

Arendt M, Rosenberg R, Foldager L, Perto G, Munk-Jørgensen P (2005) Cannabis-induced psychosis and subsequent schizophrenia-spectrum disorders: follow-up study of 535 incident cases. Br J Psychiatry 187:510–515

Arseneault L, Cannon M, Poulton R, Murray R, Caspi A, Moffitt TE (2002) Cannabis use in adolescence and risk for adult psychosis: longitudinal prospective study. BMJ 325:1212–1213

Auclair N, Otani S, Soubrie P, Crepel F (2000) Cannabinoids modulate synaptic strength and plasticity at glutamatergic synapses of rat prefrontal cortex pyramidal neurons. J Neurophysiol 83:3287–3293

Azad SC, Eder M, Marsicano G, Lutz B, Zieglansberger W, Rammes G (2003) Activation of the cannabinoid receptor type 1 decreases glutamatergic and GABAergic synaptic transmission in the lateral amygdala of the mouse. Learn Mem 10:116–128

Ballmaier M, Bortolato M, Rizzetti C et al (2007) Cannabinoid receptor antagonists counteract sensorimotor gating deficits in the phencyclidine model of psychosis. Neuropsychopharmacology 32(10):2098–2107

Bangalore SS, Prasad KM, Montrose DM, Goradia DD, Diwadkar VA, Keshavan MS (2008) Cannabis use and brain structural alterations in first episode schizophrenia—a region of interest, voxel based morphometric study. Schizophr Res 99(1–3):1–6

Barnett JH, Werners U, Secher SM et al (2007) Substance use in a population-based clinic sample of people with first-episode psychosis. Br J Psychiatry 190:515–520

Beinfeld MC, Connolly K (2001) Activation of CB1 cannabinoid receptors in rat hippocampal slices inhibits potassium-evoked cholecystokinin release, a possible mechanism contributing to the spatial memory defects produced by cannabinoids. Neurosci Lett 301:69–71

Beltramo M, Rodriguez de Fonseca F, Navarro M et al (2000) Reversal of dopamine D_2 receptor responses by an anandamide transport inhibitor. J Neurosci 20:3401–3407

Berk M, Brook S, Trandafir AI (1999) A comparison of olanzapine with haloperidol in cannabis-induced psychotic disorder: a double-blind randomized controlled trial. Int Clin Psychopharmacol 14(3):177–180

Bersani G, Orlandi V, Kotzalidis GD, Pancheri P (2002) Cannabis and schizophrenia: impact on onset, course, psychopathology and outcomes. Eur Arch Psychiatry Clin Neurosci 252(2):86–92

Biscaia M, Marín S, Fernández B, Marco E, Rubio M, Guaza C, Ambrosio E, Viveros MP (2003) Chronic treatment with CP 55, 940 during the periadolescent period differentially affects the behavioural responses of male and female rats in the adulthood. Psychopharmacology 170:301–308

Block RI, O'Leary DS, Ehrhardt JC, Augustinack JC, Ghoneim MM, Arndt S, Hall JA (2000) Effects of frequent marijuana use on brain tissue volume and composition. NeuroReport 11 (3):491–496

Bortolato M, Campolongo P, Mangieri RA et al (2006) Anxiolytic-like properties of the anandamide transport inhibitor AM404. Neuropsychopharmacology 31:2652–2659

Bossong MG, van Berckel BN, Boellaard R, Zuurman L, Schuit RC, Windhorst AD, van Gerven JM, Ramsey NF, Lammertsma AA, Kahn RS (2009) Delta 9-tetrahydrocannabinol induces dopamine release in the human striatum. Neuropsychopharmacology 34 (3):759–766

Boucher AA, Arnold JC, Duffy L, Schofield PR, Micheau J, Karl T (2007a) Heterozygous neuregulin 1 mice are more sensitive to the behavioural effects of Delta9-tetrahydrocannabinol. Psychopharmacology (Berl) 192(3):325–336

Boucher AA, Hunt GE, Karl T, Micheau J, McGregor IS, Arnold JC (2007b) Heterozygous neuregulin 1 mice display greater baseline and Delta(9)-tetrahydrocannabinol-induced c-Fos expression. Neuroscience 149(4):861–870

Boydell J, Van Os J, Caspi A, Kennedy N, Giouroukou E, Fearon P, Farrell M, Murray RM (2006) Trends in cannabis use prior to first presentation with schizophrenia, in South-East London between 1965 and 1999. Psychol Med 36(10):1441–1446

Cadenhead KS, Light GA, Geyer MA, Braff DL (2000) Sensory gating deficits assessed by the P50 event-related potential in subjects with schizotypal personality disorder. Am J Psychiatry 157(1):55–59

Cahn W, Hulshoff Pol HE, Caspers E, van Haren NE, Schnack HG, Kahn RS (2004) Cannabis and brain morphology in recent-onset schizophrenia. Schizophr Res 67(2–3):305–307

Caspi A, Moffitt TE. Cannon M et al (2005) Moderation of the effect of adolescent-onset cannabis use on adult psychosis by a functional polymorphism in the catechol-O-methyltransferase gene: longitudinal evidence of a gene x environment interaction. Biol Psychiatry 57:1117–1127

Castle DJ, Ames FR (1996) Cannabis and the brain. Aust N Z J Psychiatry 30(2):179–183

Chavarría-Siles I, Contreras-Rojas J, Hare E, Walss-Bass C, Quezada P, Dassori A, Contreras S, Medina R, Ramirez M, Salazar R, Raventos H, Escamilla MA (2008) Cannabinoid receptor 1 gene (CNR1) and susceptibility to a quantitative phenotype for hebephrenic schizophrenia. Am J Med Genet B Neuropsychiatr Genet 147(3):279–284

De Irala J, Ruiz-Canela M, Martinez-González MA (2005) Causal relationship between cannabis use and psychotic symptoms or depression. Should we wait and see? A public health perspective. Med Sci Monit 11:RA355–RA358

De Marchi N, De Petrocellis L, Orlando P, Daniele F, Fezza F, Di Marzo V (2003) Endocannabinoid signalling in the blood of patients with schizophrenia. Lipids Health Dis 19:5

Dean B, Sundram S, Bradbury R, Scarr E, Copolov D (2001) Studies on [^{3}H]CP-55490 binding in the human central nervous system: regional specific changes in density of cannabinoid-1 receptors associated with schizophrenia and cannabis use. Neuroscience 103:9–15

Dean B, Bradbury R, Copolov DL (2003) Cannabis-sensitive dopaminergic markers in postmortem central nervous system: changes in schizophrenia. Biol Psychiatry 53:585–592

Derkinderen P, Toutant M, Burgaya F, Lebert M, Siciliano JC, Defranciscis V, Gelman M, Girault JA (1996) Regulation of a neuronal form of focal adhesion kinase by anandamide. Science 273:1719–1722

Devane WA, Dysarz FA, Johnson MR, Melvin LS, Howlett AC (1988) Determination and characterization of cannabinoid receptor in rat brain. Mol Pharmacol 34:605–613

Devane WA, Hanus L, Breuer A, Pertwee RG, Stevenson LA, Griffin G, Gibson D, Mandelbaum A, Etinge A, Mechoulam R (1992) Isolation and structure of a brain constituent that binds to the cannabinoid receptor. Science 258:1946–1949

Di Marzo V (2008) Targeting the endocannabinoid system: to enhance or reduce? Nat Rev Drug Discov 7:438–455

Di Marzo V, Maccarrone M (2008) FAAH and anandamide: is 2-AG really the odd one out? Trends Neurosci 29:229–233

Diana MA, Marty A (2004) Endocannabinoid-mediated short-term synaptic plasticity: depolarization-induced suppression of inhibition (DSI) and depolarization-induced suppression of excitation (DSE). Br J Pharmacol 142:9–19

Dissanayake DW, Zachariou M, Marsden CA, Mason R (2008) Auditory gating in rat hippocampus and medial prefrontal cortex: effect of the cannabinoid agonist WIN55,212-2. Neuropharmacology 55(8):1397–1404

Doniger GM, Foxe JJ, Murray MM, Higgins BA, Javitt DC (2002) Impaired visual object recognition and dorsal/ventral stream interaction in schizophrenia. Arch Gen Psychiatry 59:1011–1020

Drake RE, Xie H, McHugo GJ, Green AI (2000) The effects of clozapine on alcohol and drug use disorders among patients with schizophrenia. Schizophr Bull 26(2):441–449

D'Souza DC, Perry E, MacDougall L et al (2004) The psychomimetic effects of intravenous delta9-tetrahydrocannabinol in healthy individuals: implications for psychosis. Neuropsychopharmacology 29:1558–1572

D'Souza DC, Abi-Saab WM, Madonick S, Forselius-Bielen K, Doersch A, Braley G, Gueroguieva R, Cooper TB, Krystal JH (2005) Delta-9-tetrahydrocannabinol effects in schizophrenia: implications for cognition, psychosis, and addiction. Biol Psychiatry 57(6):594–608

D'Souza DC, Ranganathan M, Braley G, Gueorguieva R, Zimolo Z, Cooper T, Perry E, Krystal J (2008a) Blunted psychotomimetic and amnestic effects of delta-9-tetrahydrocannabinol in frequent users of cannabis. Neuropsychopharmacology 33(10):2505–2516

D'Souza DC, Braley G, Blaise R, Vendetti M, Oliver S, Pittman B, Ranganathan M, Bhakta S, Zimolo Z, Cooper T, Perry E (2008b) Effects of haloperidol on the behavioral, subjective, cognitive, motor, and neuroendocrine effects of Delta-9-tetrahydrocannabinol in humans. Psychopharmacology (Berl) 198(4):587–603

Ellenbroek BA (2003) Animal models in the genomic era: possibilities and limitations with special emphasis on schizophrenia. Behav Pharmacol 14:409–417

Falls DL (2003) Neuregulins: functions, forms, and signaling strategies. Exp Cell Res 284(1):14–30

Favrat B, Ménétrey A, Augsburger M, Rothuizen LE, Appenzeller M, Buclin T, Pin M, Mangin P, Giroud C (2005) Two cases of "cannabis acute psychosis" following the administration of oral cannabis. BMC Psychiatry 5:17

Feinberg I (1982) Schizophrenia: caused by a fault in programmed synaptic elimination during adolescence? J Psychiatr Res 17(4):319–334

Feinberg I (1987) Adolescence and mental illness. Science 236 (4801):507–508

Felder CC, Joyce KE, Briley EM, Glass M, Mackie KP, Fahey KJ, Cullinan GJ, Hunden DC, Johnson DW, Chaney MO, Koppel GA, Brownstein M (1998) LY320135, a novel cannabinoid CB1 receptor antagonist, unmasks coupling of the CB1 receptor to stimulation of cAMP accumulation. J Pharmacol Exp Ther 284:291–297

Ferdinand RF, Sondeijker F, van der Ende J, Selten JP, Huizink A, Verhulst FC (2005) Cannabis use predicts future psychotic symptoms, and vice versa. Addiction 100(5):612–618

Fergusson DM, Horwood LJ, Ridder EM (2005) Tests of causal linkages between cannabis use and psychotic symptoms. Addiction 100(3):354–366

Fernandez-Espejo E, Galan-Rodriguez B (2004) Sensorimotor gating in mice is disrupted after AM404, an anandamide reuptake and degradation inhibitor. Psychopharmacology 175:220–224

Ferrer B, Gorriti MA, Palomino A, Gornemann I, de Diego Y, Bermudez-Silva FJ, Bilbao A, Fernandez-Espejo E, Moratalla R, Navarro M, Rodriguez de Fonseca F (2007) Cannabinoid CB1 receptor antagonism markedly increases dopamine receptor-mediated stereotypies. Eur J Pharmacol 559:180–183

French ED, Dillon K, Wu X (1997) Cannabinoids excite dopamine neurons in the ventral tegmental area and substantia nigra. NeuroReport 8:649–652

Fujiwara M, Egashira N (2004) New perspectives in the studies on endocannabinoid and cannabis: abnormal behaviors associate with CB_1 cannabinoid receptor and development of therapeutic application. J Pharmacol Sci 96:326–366

Galiègue S, Mary S, Marchand J, Dussossoy D, Carrière D, Carayon P, Bouaboula M, Shire D, Le Fur G, Casellas P (1995) Expression of central and peripheral cannabinoid receptors in human immune tissues and leukocyte subpopulations. Eur J Biochem 232:54–61

Gallagher HL, Happé F, Brunswick N, Fletcher PC, Frith U, Frith CD (2003) Reading the mind in cartoons and stories: an fMRI study of 'theory of mind' in verbal and nonverbal tasks. Neuropsychologia 38(1):11–21

Gaoni Y, Mechoulam R (1964) Isolation, structure and partial synthesis of an active constituent of hashish. J Am Chem Soc 86:1646–1647

Gardner EL, Vorel RH (1998) Cannabinoid transmission and reward-related events. Neurobiol Dis 5:502–533

Gardner EL, Paredes W, Smith D et al (1988) Facilitation of brain stimulation reward by d9-tetrahydrocannabinol. Psychopharmacology 341:39–44

Geyer MA, Krebs-Thomson K, Braff DL, Swerdlow NR (2001) Pharmacological studies of prepulse inhibition models of sensorimotor gating deficits in schizophrenia: a decade of review. Psychopharmacology 156:117–154

Geyer MA, McIlwain KL, Paylor R (2002) Mouse genetic models for prepulse inhibition: an early review. Mol Psychiatry 7:1039–1053

Giuffrida A, Leweke FM, Gerth CW et al (2004) Cerebrospinal anandamide levels are elevated in acute schizophrenia and are inversely correlated with psychotic symptoms. Neuropsycho-pharmacology 29:2108–2114

Giuliani D, Ferrari F (1997) Involvement of dopamine receptors in the antipsychotic profile of (–) eticlopride. Physiol Behav 61(4):563–567

Gorriti MA, Rodriguez de Fonseca F, Navarro M, Palomo T (1999) Chronic (–)-delta9-tetrahydrocannabinol treatment induces sensitization to the psychomotor effects of amphetamine in rats. Eur J Pharmacol 365:133–142

Grace AA (1991) Phasic versus tonic dopamine release and the modulation of dopamine system responsivity: a hypothesis for the etiology of schizophrenia. Neuroscience 41:1–24

Graham FK (1975) The more or less startling effects of weak prestimuli. Psychophysiology 12:238–248

Grant BF, Chou SP, Goldstein RB et al (2008) Prevalence, correlates, disability, and comorbidity of DSM-IV borderline personality disorder: results from the Wave 2 National Epidemiologic Survey on Alcohol and Related Conditions. J Clin Psychiatry 69(4):533–545

Hajós M, Hoffmann WE, Kocsis B (2008) Activation of cannabinoid-1 receptors disrupts sensory gating and neuronal oscillation: relevance to schizophrenia. Biol Psychiatry 63(11):1075–1083

Hall WD (1998) Cannabis use and psychosis. Drug Alcohol Rev 17:433–444

Hall W, Degenhardt L (2007) Prevalence and correlates of cannabis use in developed and developing countries. Curr Opin Psychiatr 20:393–397

Hall W, Solowij N (1997) Long-term cannabis use and mental health. Br J Psychiatry 171:107–108

Hamdani N, Tabeze JP, Ramoz N, Ades J, Hamon M, Sarfati Y, Boni C, Gorwood P (2008) The CNR1 gene as a pharmacogenetic factor for antipsychotics rather than a susceptibility gene for schizophrenia. Eur Neuropsychopharmacol 18(1):34–40

Hart WG (1978) Reply to a case report by Ian Sale and Henry Kristall-March issue. Aust N Z J Psychiatry 12(2):136–137

Heckers S, Curran T, Goff D, Rauch SL, Fischman AJ, Alpert NM, Schacter DL (2000) Abnormalities in the thalamus and prefrontal cortex during episodic object recognition in schizophrenia. Biol Psychiatry 48:651–657

Henquet C, Krabbendam L, Spauwen J, Kaplan C, Lieb R, Wittchen HU, van Os J (2005) Prospective cohort study of cannabis use, predisposition for psychosis, and psychotic symptoms in young people. BMJ 330(7481):11

Herkenham M, Lynn AB, Johnson MR, Melvin LS, de Costa BR, Rice KC (1991) Characterization and localization of cannabinoid receptors in rat brain: a quantitative in vitro autoradiographic study. J Neurosci 11:563–583

Hirvonen J, Van Erp TG, Huttunen J et al (2005) Increased caudate dopamine D_2 receptor availability as a genetic marker for schizophrenia. Arch Gen Psychiatry 62(4): 371–378

Hoffman HS, Ison JR (1980) Reflex modification in the domain of startle: I. Some empirical findings and their implications for how the nervous system processes sensory input. Psychol Rev 87:175–189

Howlett AC, Bidaut-Russell M, Devane WA, Melvin LS, Johnson MR, Herkenham M (1990) The cannabinoid receptor: biochemical, anatomical and behavioral characterization. Trends Neurosci 13:420–423

Jarrahian A, Watts VJ, Barker E (2004) D_2 dopamine receptors modulate $G\alpha$-subunit coupling of the CB_1 cannabinoid receptor. J Pharmacol Exp Ther 308:880–886

Javitt DC, Zukin SR (1991) Recent advances in the phencyclidine model of schizophrenia. Am J Psychiatry 148:1301–1308

Karl T, Duffy L, Scimone A, Harvey RP, Schofield PR (2007) Altered motor activity, exploration and anxiety in heterozygous neuregulin 1 mutant mice: implications for understanding schizophrenia. Genes Brain Behav 6(7):677–687

Katona I, Uran GM, Wallace M, Ledent C, Jung KM, Piomelli D, Mackie K, Freund TF (2006) Molecular composition of the endocannabinoid system at glutamatergic synapses. J Neurosci 26:5628–5637

Keshavan MS, Anderson S, Pettegrew JW (1994) Is schizophrenia due to excessive synaptic pruning in the prefrontal cortex? The Feinberg hypothesis revisited. J Psychiatr Res 28(3):239–265

Konings M, Henquet C, Maharajh HD, Hutchinson G, Van Os J (2008) Early exposure to cannabis and risk for psychosis in young adolescents in Trinidad. Acta Psychiatr Scand 118(3):209–213

Laruelle M, Abi-Dargham A, van Dyck CH et al (1996) Single photon emission computerized tomography imaging of amphetamine-induced dopamine release in drug-free schizophrenic subjects. Proc Natl Acad Sci U S A 93(17):9235–9240

Leweke FM, Giuffrida A, Wurster U, Emrich HM, Piomelli D (1999) Elevated endogenous cannabinoids in schizophrenia. NeuroReport 10:1665–1669

Leweke FM, Giuffrida A, Koethe D et al (2007) Anandamide levels in cerebrospinal fluid of first-episode schizophrenic patients: impact of cannabis use. Schizophr Res 94:29–36

Lieberman JA, Tollefson GD, Charles C, Zipursky R, Sharma T, Kahn RS, Keefe RS, Green AI, Gur RE, McEvoy, J, Perkins D, Hamer RM, Gu H, Tohen M, HGDH Study Group (2005) Antipsychotic drug effects on brain morphology in first-episode psychosis. Arch Gen Psychiatry 62(4):361–370

Maccarrone M, Rossi S, Bari M, De Chiara V, Fezza F, Musella A, Gasperi V, Prosperetti C, Bernardi G, Finazzi-Agrò A, Cravatt BF, Centonze D (2008) Anandamide inhibits metabolism and physiological actions of 2-arachidonoylglycerol in the striatum. Nat Neurosci 11(2):152–159

Macleod J, Oakes R, Copello A, Crome I, Egger M, Hickman M, Oppenkowski T, Stokes-Lampard H, Davey Smith G (2004) Psychological and social sequelae of cannabis and other illicit drug use by young people: a systematic review of longitudinal, general population studies. Lancet 363(9421):1579–1588

Malone DT, Taylor DA (2006) The effect of Delta9-tetrahydrocannabinol on sensorimotor gating in socially isolated rats. Behav Brain Res 166(1):101–109

Mansbach RS, Geyer MA, Braff DL (1988) Dopaminergic stimulation disrupts sensorimotor gating in the rat. Psychopharmacology 94:507–514

Mansbach RS, Rovetti CC, Winston EN, Lowe JA (1996) Effects of the cannabinoid CB_1 receptor antagonist SR141716A on the behavior of pigeons and rats. Psychopharmacology 124:315–322

Marek G, Merchant K (2005) Developing therapeutics for schizophrenia and other psychotic disorders. NeuroRx 2:579–589

Marsicano G, Wotjak CT, Azad SC, Rammes G, Cascio MG, Hermann H, Tang J, Hofmann C, Zieglgansberger W, Di Marzo V, Lutz B (2002) The endogenous cannabinoid system controls extinction of aversive memories. Nature 418:530–534

Marsicano G, Goodenough S, Monory K et al (2003) CB1 cannabinoid receptors and on-demand defense against excitotoxicity. Science 302:84–88

Martin RS, Secchi RL, Sung E et al (2003) Effects of cannabinoid receptor ligands on psychosis-relevant behavior models in the rat. Psychopharmacology 165:128–135

Matochik JA, Eldreth DA, Cadet JL, Bolla KI (2005) Altered brain tissue composition in heavy marijuana users. Drug Alcohol Depend 77(1):23–30

Matsuda LA, Lolait SJ, Brownstein MJ, Young AC, Bonner TI (1990) Structure of a cannabinoid receptor and functional expression of the cloned cDNA. Nature 346:561–564

Maynard TM, Sikich L, Lieberman JA, LaMantia AS (2001) Neural development, cell-cell signaling, and the "two-hit" hypothesis of schizophrenia. Schizophr Bull 27:457–476

McGuire P, Jones P, Murray R (1993) Psychiatric symptoms in cannabis users. Br J Psychiatry 163:698

Mechoulam R, Ben-Shabat S, Hanus L, Ligumsky M, Kaminski NE, Schatz AR, Gopher A, Almog S, Martin BR, Compton DR, Pertwee RG, Griffin G, Bayewitch M, Barg J, Vogel Z (1995) Identification of an endogenous 2-monoglyceride, present in canine gut, that binds to cannabinoid receptors. Biochem Pharmacol 50:83–90

Mendhiratta SS, Varma VK, Dang R, Malhotra AK, Das K, Nehra R (1988) Cannabis and cognitive functions: a re-evaluation study. Br J Addict 83(7):749–753

Mewell KA, Deng C, Huang XF (2006) Increased cannabinoid receptor density in the posterior cingulate cortex in schizophrenia. Exp Brain Res 172:550–560

Miettunen J, Törmänen S, Murray GK, Jones PB, Mäki P, Ebeling H, Moilanen I, Taanila A, Heinimaa M, Joukamaa M, Veijola J (2008) Association of cannabis use with prodromal symptoms of psychosis in adolescence. Br J Psychiatry 192:470–471

Moore H, West A, Grace AA (1999) The regulation of forebrain dopamine transmission: relevance to the pathophysiology and psychopathology of schizophrenia. Biol Psychiatry 46:40–55

Moore THM, Zammit S, Lingford-Hughes A, Barnes TRE, Jones PB, Burke M, Lewis G (2007) Cannabis use and risk of psychotic or affective mental health outcomes: a systematic review. Lancet 370:319–328

Moreno M, Lopez-Moreno JA, Rodríguez de Fonseca F, Navarro M (2005) Behavioural effects of quinpirole following withdrawal of chronic treatment with the CB1 agonist, HU-210, in rats. Behav Pharmacol 16:441–446

Müller-Vahl KR, Emrich HM (2008) Cannabis and schizophrenia: towards a cannabinoid hypothesis of schizophrenia. Expert Rev Neurother 8(7):1037–1048

Munro S, Thomas KL, Abu-Shaar M (1993) Molecular characterization of a peripheral receptor for cannabinoids. Nature 365:61–65

Negrete JC (1983) Effect of cannabis use on health. Acta Psiquiatr Psicol Am Lat 29(4):267–276

Nordentoft M, Hjorthøj C (2007) Cannabis use and risk of psychosis in later life. Lancet 370:293–294

Núñez LA, Gurpegui M (2002) Cannabis-induced psychosis: a cross-sectional comparison with acute schizophrenia. Acta Psychiatr Scand 105:151–157

Onaivi ES (2006) Neuropsychobiological evidence for the functional presence and expression of cannabinoid CB2 receptors in the brain. Neuropsychobiology 54(4):231–246

O'Shea M, Singh ME, McGregor IS, Mallet PE (2004) Chronic cannabinoid exposure produces lasting memory impairment and increased anxiety in adolescent but not adult rats. J Psychopharmacol 18:502–508

O'Shea M, McGregor IS, Mallet PE (2006) Repeated cannabinoid exposure during perinatal, adolescent or early adult ages produces similar long-lasting deficits in object recognition and reduced social interaction in rats. J Psychopharmacol 20: 611–621

Ouagazzal AM, Jenck F, Moreau JL (2001) Drug-induced potentiation of prepulse inhibition of acoustic startle in mice: a model for detecting antipsychotic activity? Psychopharmacology 156:273–283

Pertwee RG (2005) The therapeutic potential of drugs that target cannabinoid receptors or modulate the tissue levels or actions of endocannabinoids. AAPS J 7:E625–E654

Piomelli D (2003) The molecular logic of endocannabinoid signalling. Nat Rev Neurosci 4:873–884

Piomelli D, Giuffrida A, Calignano A, Rodriguez de Fonseca F (2000) The endocannabinoid system as a target for therapeutic drugs. Trends Pharmacol Sci 21:218–224

Pistis M, Perra S, Pillolla G, Melis M, Muntoni AL, Gessa GL (2004) Adolescent exposure to cannabinoids induces long-lasting changes in the response to drugs of abuse of rat midbrain dopamine neurons. Biol Psychiatry 56:86–94

Rais M, Cahn W, Van Haren N, Schnack H, Caspers E, Hulshoff Pol H, Kahn R (2008) Excessive brain volume loss over time in cannabis-using first-episode schizophrenia patients. Am J Psychiatry 165(4):490–496

Ralph-Williams RJ, Paulus MP, Geyer MA (2001) Strain-specific effects of amphetamine on prepulse inhibition and patterns of locomotor behavior in mice. J Pharmacol Exp Ther 298:148–155

Ralph-Williams RJ, Lehmann-Masten V, Otero-Corchon V, Low MJ, Geyer MA (2002) Differential effects of direct and indirect dopamine agonists on prepulse inhibition: a study in D1 and D2 receptor knock-out mice. J Neurosci 22:9604–9611

Robbe D, Alonso G, Duchamp F, Bockaert J, Manzoni OJ (2001) Localization and mechanisms of action of cannabinoid receptors at the glutamatergic synapses of the mouse nucleus accumbens. J Neurosci 21:109–116

Robbe D, Alonso G, Manzoni OJ (2003) Exogenous and endogenous cannabinoids control synaptic transmission in mice nucleus accumbens. Ann N Y Acad Sci 1003:212–225

Robertson GS, Hori SE, Powell KJ (2006) Schizophrenia: an integrative approach to modelling a complex disorder. J Psychiatry Neurosci 31:157–167

Rodriguez de Fonseca F, Ramos JA, Bonnin A, Fernandez-Ruiz JJ (1993) Presence of cannabinoid binding sites in the brain from early postnatal ages. NeuroReport 4:135–138

Rodriguez de Fonseca F, Carrera MR, Navarro M, Koob GF, Weiss F (1997) Activation of corticotropin-releasing factor in the limbic system during cannabinoid withdrawal. Science 276:2050–2054

Rodriguez de Fonseca F, Del Arco I, Martin-Calderon JL, Gorriti MA, Navarro M (1998) Role of the endogenous cannabinoid system in the regulation of motor activity. Neurobiol Dis 5:483–501

Rodriguez de Fonseca F, Navarro M, Gomez R, Escuredo L, Nava F, Fu J, Murillo-Rodriguez E, Giuffrida A, LoVerme J, Gaetani S, Kathuria S, Gall C, Piomelli D (2001) An anorexic lipid mediator regulated by feeding. Nature 414:209–212

Rössler W, Riecher-Rössler A, Angst J, Murray R, Gamma A, Eich D, van Os J, Gross VA (2007) Psychotic experiences in the general population: a twenty-year prospective community study. Schizophr Res 92(1–3):1–14

Rueda D, Navarro B, Martinez-Serrano A, Guzman M, Galve-Roperh I (2002) The endocannabinoid anandamide inhibits neuronal progenitor cell differentiation through attenuation of the Rap1/B-Raf/ERK pathway. J Biol Chem 277:46645–46650

Scheepers FE, Gispen de Wied CC, Hulshoff Pol HE, Kahn RS (2001) Effect of clozapine on caudate nucleus volume in relation to symptoms of schizophrenia. Am J Psychiatry 158(4):644–646

Schlieker E, Kathmann M (2001) Modulation of transmitter release via presynaptic cannabinoid receptor. Trends Pharmacol Sci 22:565–572

Schneider M, Koch M (2002) The cannabinoid agonist WIN 55,212-2 reduces sensorimotor gating and recognition memory in rats. Behav Pharmacol 13:29–37

Schneider M, Koch M (2003) Chronic pubertal, but not adult chronic cannabinoid treatment impairs sensorimotor gating, recognition memory, and the performance in a progressive ratio task in adult rats. Neuropsychopharmacology 28:1760–1769

Schneider M, Koch M (2005) Deficient social and play behavior in juvenile and adult rats after neonatal cortical lesion: effects of chronic pubertal cannabinoid treatment. Neuropsychopharmacology 30:944–957

Schneider M, Koch M (2007) The effect of chronic peripubertal cannabinoid treatment on deficient object recognition memory in rats after neonatal mPFC lesion. Eur Neuropsychopharmacol 17:180–186

Schneier FR, Siris SG (1987) A review of psychoactive substance use and abuse in schizophrenia. Patterns of drug choice. J Nerv Ment Dis 175(11):641–652

Seeman P, Lee T (1975) Antipsychotic drugs: direct correlation between clinical potency and presynaptic action on dopamine neurons. Science 188(4194):1217–1219

Sekine Y, Minabe Y, Ouchi Y et al (2003) Association of dopamine transporter loss in the orbitofrontal and dorsolateral prefrontal cortices with methamphetamine-related psychiatric symptoms. Am J Psychiatr 160(9):1699–1701

Semple DM, McIntosh AM, Lawrie SM (2005) Cannabis as a risk factor for psychosis: systematic review. J Psychopharmacol 19 (2):187–194

Smit F, Bolier L, Cuijpers P (2004) Cannabis use and the risk of later schizophrenia: a review. Addiction 99:425–430

Solowij N, Michie PT (2007) Cannabis and cognitive dysfunction: parallels with endophenotypes of schizophrenia? J Psychiatry Neurosci 32:30–52

Solowij N, Stephens RS, Roffman RA, Babor T, Kadden R, Miller M, Christiansen K, McRee B, Vendetti J, Marijuana Treatment Project Research Group (2002) Cognitive functioning of long-term heavy cannabis users seeking treatment. JAMA 287:1123–1131

Soria G, Mendizabal V, Touriño C et al (2005) Lack of CB$_1$ cannabinoid receptor impairs cocaine self-administration. Neuropsychopharmacology 30:1670–1680

Spear LP (2000) The adolescent brain and age-related behavioral manifestations. Neurosci Biobehav Rev 24:417–463

Stanley-Cary CC, Harris C, Martin-Iverson MT (2002) Differing effects of the cannabinoid agonist CP55, 940, in an alcohol or Tween 80 solvent, on prepulse inhibition of the acoustic startle reflex in the rat. Behav Pharmacol 13:15–28

Stefanis NC, Delespaul P, Henquet C, Bakoula C, Stefanis CN, Van Os J (2004) Early adolescent cannabis exposure and positive and negative dimensions of psychosis. Addiction 99:1333–1341

Stefansson H, Sigurdsson E, Steinthorsdottir V et al (2002) Neuregulin 1 and susceptibility to schizophrenia. Am J Hum Genet 71(4):877–892

Suárez J, Bermúdez-Silva FJ, Mackie K, Ledent C, Zimmer A, Cravatt BF, Rodriguez de Fonseca F (2008) Immunohistochemical description of the endogenous cannabinoid system in the rat cerebellum and functionally related nuclei. J Comp Neurol 509(4):400–421

Sugiura T, Kondo S, Sukagawa A, Nakane S, Shinoda A, Itoh K, Yamashita A, Waku K (1995) 2-Arachidonoylglycerol: a possible endogenous cannabinoid receptor ligand in brain. Biochem Biophys Res Commun 215:89–97

Sundram S, Copolov D, Dean B (2005) Clozapine decreases [3H] CP 55940 binding to the cannabinoid 1 receptor in the rat nucleus accumbens. Naunyn Schmiedebergs Arch Pharmacol 371(5):428–433

Thacore VR, Sukhla SRP (1976) Cannabis psychosis and paranoid schizophrenia. Arch Gen Psychiatry 33:383–386

Thornicroft G (1990) Cannabis and psychosis. Is there epidemiological evidence for an association? Br J Psychiatry 157:25–33

Tien AY, Anthony JC (1990) Epidemiological analysis of alcohol and drug use as risk factors for psychotic experiences. J Nerv Ment Dis 178(8):473–480

Ujike H, Takaki M, Nakata K et al (2002) CNR1, a central cannabinoid receptor gene, associated with susceptibility to hebephrenic schizophrenia. Mol Psychiatry 7:515–518

Van Os J, Bak M, Hanssen M, Bijl RV, de Graaf R, Verdoux H (2002) Cannabis use and psychosis: a longitudinal population-based study. Am J Epidemiol 156(4):319–327

Varma SL, Sharma I (1993) Psychiatric morbidity in the first-degree relatives of schizophrenic patients. Br J Psychiatry 162:672–678

Verdoux H, Tournier M (2004) Cannabis use and risk of psychosis: an etiological link? Epidemiol Psichiatr Soc 13(2):113–119

Verdoux H, Tournier M, Cougnard A (2005) Impact of substance use on the onset and course of early psychosis. Schizophr Res 79:69–75

Vogt BA (2005) Pain and emotion interactions in subregions of the cingulate gyrus. Nat Rev Neurosci 6:533–544

Walss-Bass C, Liu W, Lew DF et al (2006a) A novel missense mutation in the transmembrane domain of neuregulin 1 is associated with schizophrenia. Biol Psychiatry 60(6):548–553

Walss-Bass C, Raventos H, Montero AP, Armas R, Dassori A, Contreras S, Liu W, Medina R, Levinson DF, Pereira M, Leach RJ, Almasy L, Escamilla MA (2006b) Association analyses of the neuregulin 1 gene with schizophrenia and manic psychosis in a Hispanic population. Acta Psychiatr Scand 113(4):314–321

Wenger T, Gerendai I, Fezza F, Gonzalez S, Bisoqno T, Fernandez-Ruiz JJ, Di Marzo V (2002) The hypothalamic levels of the endocannabinoid, anandamide, peak immediately before the onset of puberty in female rats. Life Sci 70:1407–1414

Wicker B, Perrett DI, Baron-Cohen S, Decety J (2003) Being the target of another's emotion: a PET study. Neuropsychologia 41(2):139–146

Wiley JL, Kendler SH, Burston JJ, Howard DR, Selley DE, Sim-Selley LJ (2008) Antipsychotic-induced alterations in CB1 receptor-mediated G-protein signaling and in vivo pharmacology in rats. Neuropharmacology 55(7):1183–1190

Wilson RI, Nicoll RA (2001) Endogenous cannabinoids mediate retrograde signalling at hippocampal synapses. Nature 410:588–592

Wilson RI, Nicoll RA (2002) Endocannabinoid signaling in the brain. Science 296:678–682

Wilson RI, Kunos G, Nicoll RA (2001) Presynaptic specificity of endocannabinoid signaling in the hippocampus. Neuron 31:453–462

Zachariou M, Dissanayake DW, Coombes S, Owen MR, Mason R (2008) Sensory gating and its modulation by cannabinoids: electrophysiological, computational and mathematical analysis. Cogn Neurodyn 2(2):159–170

Zammit S, Allebeck P, Andreasson S, Lundberg I, Lewis G (2002) Self reported cannabis use as a risk factor for schizophrenia in Swedish conscripts of 1969: historical cohort study. BMJ 325 (7374):1199

Zavitsanou K, Garrick T, Huang XF (2004) Selective antagonist [^{3}H] SR141716A binding to cannabinoid CB$_1$ receptors is increased in the anterior cingulate cortex in schizophrenia. Prog Neuro-psychopharmacol Biol Psychiatry 28:355–360

Critical Thinking

1. If scientific studies are showing that cannabis use in adolescence increases changes of psychosis in adults, how can we continue to socially accept this as benign drug?

2. What is the difference between the endogenous and exogenous relationship between cannabis/endocannabinoids and schizophrenia, and why is it important to understand this?

3. Why do genetics factor into whether someone will or will not have a predisposition to drug addiction?

4. What are some implications of studies like this?

Acknowledgements—This study was supported by grants to EFE, MPV, and FRF from RED de Trastomos Adictivos (Instituto Carlos III, RD06/0001), to EFE from Delegacion del Gobierno para el Plan Nacional Sobre Drogas (3SI/05/4), and to MPV from MEC SAF2006-07523.

Movement Disorders and MDMA Abuse

JAMES ALLEN WILCOX, D O, PHD AND AIDEE HERRERA WILCOX, BA

3,4-Methylenedioxymethamphetamine (MDMA or Ecstasy) is a synthetic amphetamine analog. It is well known as a substance of abuse and carries the reputation of producing euphoria, mild hallucinatory effects, and a sense of emotional empathy. Although originally synthesized by Merk in 1914, the psychoactive properties of MDMA were not widely known until the late 1960s. By the year 2000 between 5 and 10% of American college students reported Ecstasy use (Strote, Lee & Wechsler 2002). It has been a popular party drug at "raves" and has also had a steady following in small group settings. Part of the rapid increase in use of this drug has been associated with its perceived safety (Strote, Lee & Wechsler 2002; Spruit 2001).

The method of action of MDMA is believed to be associated with its effect on the activity of serotonin and dopamine neurons in the cerebral cortex (Colado, O'Shea & Green 2003). It is thought that this unique combination of activity mediates most of the psychological effects of the drug. While contamination of any unregulated substance can occur, sampling studies have found that tablets of Ecstasy generally contain MDMA (Spruit 2001). This makes allegations of the effects of such tablets reasonably reliable for an illicit pharmaceutical.

Studies of MDMA's effects on brain tissue have found evidence of cellular damage related to chronic use (Semple et al. 1999). Some studies have detected axon degeneration in the substantia nigra, a part of the brain that controls movement, following MDMA use (Ricaurte, Yuan & McCann 2000; McKenna & Peroutka 1990). At this time, the literature reports five cases of Parkinson-like stiffness in chronic Ecstasy users (Suilleabhain & Giller 2003; Baggot, Mendelson & Jones 1999; Borg 1999; Mintzer, Hickenbottom & Gilman 1999; Sewell & Cozzi 1999), suggesting damage can occur in the substantia nigra of humans who use this drug. The same neural systems that control decreased movement are also involved in conditions of increased, purposeless movement such as dyskinesia (Suilleabhain & Giller 2003). We present two cases of young men who developed dyskinesia following chronic abuse of MDMA.

Mr. A is a 26-year-old single White male. He is a college graduate with a good job. He originally presented to the office with a complaint of anxiety related to constant involuntary movements. He had irregular movements of the shoulders, facial muscles, and tongue. He also had chronic spasms of the eyelids. These movements met the neurological description of dyskinesia. An Adult Involuntary Movements Scale (AIMS; Munetz & Benjamin 1988) was performed and found to have a score of 19, indicating a clinically significant level of involuntary movements.

The patient was checked for risk factors for dyskinesia. He had no previous exposure to neuroleptic medications. He had no personal history of streptococcal infection that could have caused Sydenham's chorea. His anti-streptolysin levels (ASO) were normal. He had no family history of chorea or dyskinesia. Genetic testing for Huntington's disease was negative as was laboratory testing for Wilson's disease. Mr. A had been remarkably healthy until the development of his involuntary movements. His history was, however, remarkable for substantial use of MDMA.

He related that he used Ecstasy about twice a week for three years. Mr. A stated that he would usually take 10–15 tablets of Ecstasy over a 24-hour period, staying up all night and falling asleep the next day. His pattern of use was unusual, due to the large number of tablets involved. His report of the Ecstasy experience was, however typical for euphoria, strong feelings of empathy, increased sexual desire, and subtle perceptual changes. He says that he took 20 to 30 tablets per week during the last three years of college and only stopped when he was hired into a job that required regular hours. Mr. A says that he developed twitching in his facial muscles during the second year of MDMA use, but ignored it. By the end of the third year, he had developed chorea-like motions of his shoulders and diaphragmatic twitching which caused hic-up phenomena when he attempted to speak. He has now been drug free for 18 months, but the twitching and jerking motions continue.

Mr. B is a 25-year-old single White male associate of Mr. A. He also presented to the clinic with involuntary movements of the facial muscles and shoulders. An AIMS rating on Mr. B was 17, a significant score. He was found to be free of any history of neuroleptic use, streptococcal infection or any laboratory values suggestive of Huntington's disease, Wilson's disease, or other risk factor suggestive of a movement disorder. He related that he bought Ecstasy from the same dealer as Mr. A and generally used 20 to 30 tablets per week over a period of three years. This quantity of tablets is an uncommonly large amount. He rapidly (over three weeks) developed jerking purposeless movements after three years of Ecstasy use and has subsequently been drug free. After one year of follow-up his involuntary motions continue.

Discussion

MDMA is a compound that has pronounced effects on human emotions and behavior. It has become very popular as a recreational drug. Scientific studies indicate that MDMA can be a neurotoxin in some animals (Ricaurte, Yuan & McCann 2000; McKenna & Peroutka 1990). Several case reports suggest that Ecstasy use causes Parkinsonian stiffness in some people. We believe that the cases presented in this article are the first reports of dyskinesia associated with Ecstasy abuse. These cases are of interest because the interaction between stiffness, dyskinesia, and damage to the basal ganglia of the brain is well documented. Although some evidence suggests MDMA as a primary neurotoxin, unregulated street drugs may have contaminants that can cause serious injury. We feel that our cases developed movement disorders from the use of what they believed to be Ecstasy. There is good reason for this suspicion. These men were unrelated and had negative risk factors for movement disorders. In fact, the only activity they had in common was that they obtained their recreational drugs from the same source. This leads to the conclusion that the dyskinesia seen in these two cases was either caused by prolonged abuse of MDMA or exposure to an unknown contaminant of the Ecstasy they used. We must emphasize that strong possibility of contamination seen in street drug use. Both of our subjects used large numbers of tablets to obtain MDMA-like results. They both bought their "MDMA" from the same illicit source. This calls to mind the inherent danger of using unregulated Pharmaceuticals and does imply that adulterants in the tablets marketed as MDMA may be serious risk factors for the development of dyskinesia. Being the first documented cases of such problems, this report is important in that it suggests that Ecstasy (or its contaminants) may produce neurotoxicity in ways not previously detected or discussed in the literature.

References

Baggot, M, Mendelson, J. & Jones, R. 1999. More about Parkinsonism after taking ecstasy [correspondence]. *New England Journal of Medicine* 341: 1400–1.

Borg, G. 1999. More about Parkinsonism after taking ecstasy [correspondence]. *New England Journal of Medicine* 341: 1400.

Colado, M.; O'Shea, E. & Green, A. 2003. Acute and long term effects of MDMA on cerebral dopamine biochemistry and function. *Psychopharmacology* 173: 249–63.

McKenna, D. & Peroutka, S. 1990. Neurochemistry and neurotoxicity of 3,4-methylenedioxymethamphetamine. *Journal of Neurochemistry* 54 (1): 14–22.

Mintzer, S.; Hickenbottom, S. &. Gilman, S. 1999. Parkinsonism after taking ecstasy. *New England Journal of Medicine* 340: 1443.

Munetz, M. & Benjamin, S. 1988. How to examine patients using the Abnormal Involuntary Movement Scale. *Hospital and Community Psychiatry* 39 (11): 1172–77.

Ricaurte, G.; Yuan, J. & McCann, U. 2000. 3, 4-Methylenedioxy methamphetamine (Ecstasy)-induced serotonin neurotoxicity: Studies in animals. *Neuropsychobiology* 42 (1): 5–10.

Semple, D.; Ebmeir, K.; Glabus, M.; O'Carroll, R. & Johnstone, E. 1999. Symptoms of MDMA abuse. *British Journal of Psychiatry* 175; 63–9.

Sewell, R. & Cozzi, N. 1999. More about Parkinsonism after taking ecstasy [correspondence]. *New England Journal of Medicine* 341: 1400.

Spruit, I., 2001. Monitoring synthetic drug markets, trends and public health. *Substance Use and Abuse* 36 (1–2): 23–47.

Strote, J.; Lee, J. & Wechsler, H. 2002. Increasing MDMA use among college students: results of a national survey. *Journal of Adolescent Health* 30 (1): 64–72.

Suilleabhain, P. & Giller, C. 2003. Rapidly progressive Parkinsonism in a self-reported user of ecstasy and other drugs. *Movement Disorders* 18(11): 1378–1400.

Critical Thinking

1. If these are the first reports of dyskinesia related to MDMA abuse, why would you expect to see more in the coming years?

2. What do you think may be causing this sudden side effect?

James Allen Wilcox, D O, PhD is a Professor of Clinical Psychiatry, University of Arizona, VAMC, Tucson, AZ. **Aidee Herrera Wilcox,** BA is a Research Assistant, University of Texas at El Paso, El Paso, TX. Please address correspondence and reprint requests to James Allen Wilcox, D.O., PhD., Professor of Clinical Psychiatry, University of Arizona, VAMC, 3601 South Sixth Avenue, Tucson, Arizona 85723. Phone: (520) 792-1450.

From *Journal of Psychoactive Drugs,* by James Allen Wilcox and Aidee Herrera Wicox. June 2009, pp. 203–204. Reproduced by permission of Taylor & Francis Group, LLC., www.taylorandfrancis.com

UNIT 3

The Major Drugs of Use and Abuse

Unit Selections

Learning Outcomes

After reading this unit, you should be able to:

• Explain why it is that some drugs have remained popular throughout history while others have not.

• Describe how the manner in which a drug is consumed changes or influences its effects on the user.

• Discuss the influences that help perpetuate the problem of binge drinking on college campuses.

• Discuss the methods the United States and its allies intend to employ to disrupt heroin production in Afghanistan and Colombia.

• List and discuss the distinct features associated with the spread of methamphetamine use across the United States.

Student Website
www.mhhe.com/cls

Internet References

National Institute on Drug Abuse
www.drugabuse.gov
Office of Applied Studies
www.oas.samhsa.gov
QuitNet
www.quitnet.org
The American Journal of Psychiatry
http://ajp.psychiatryonline.org/cgi/content/abstract/155/8/1016
Streetdrugs.org
www.streetdrugs.org

The following articles discuss those drugs that have evolved historically to become the most popular drugs of choice. Although pharmacological modifications emerge periodically to enhance or alter the effects produced by certain drugs or the manner in which various drugs are used, basic pharmacological properties of the drugs remain unchanged. Crack is still cocaine, ice is still methamphetamine, and black tar is still heroin. In addition, all tobacco products supply the drug nicotine, coffee and a plethora of energy drinks provide caffeine, and alcoholic beverages provide the drug ethyl alcohol. All these drugs influence the way we act, think, and feel about ourselves and the world around us. They also produce markedly different effects within the body and within the mind.

To understand why certain drugs remain popular over time, and why new drugs become popular, one must be knowledgeable about the effects produced by individual drugs. Why people use drugs is a bigger question than why people use tobacco. However, understanding why certain people use tobacco, or cocaine, or marijuana, or alcohol is one way to construct a framework from which to tackle the larger question of why people use drugs in general. One of the most complex relationships is the one between Americans and their use of alcohol. More than 76 million Americans have experienced alcoholism in their families.

The most recent surveys of alcohol use estimate that 127 million Americans currently use alcohol. The use of alcohol is a powerful influence that serves to shape our national consciousness about drugs. The relationship between the use of alcohol and tobacco, and alcohol and illicit drugs provides long-standing statistical relationships. The majority of Americans, however, believe that alcohol is used responsibly by most people who use it, even though approximately 10 percent of users are believed to be suffering from various stages of alcoholism.

Understanding why people initially turn to the non-medical use of drugs is a huge question that is debated and discussed in a voluminous body of literature. One important reason why the major drugs of use and abuse, such as alcohol, nicotine, cocaine, heroin, marijuana, amphetamines, and a variety of prescription, designer, over-the-counter, and herbal drugs, retain their popularity is because they produce certain physical and psychological effects that humans crave. They temporarily restrain our inhibitions; reduce our fears; alleviate mental and physical suffering; produce energy, confidence, and exhilaration; and allow us to relax. Tired, take a pill; have a headache, take a pill; need to lose weight, take a pill; need to increase athletic performance, the options seem almost limitless. There is a drug for everything. Some drugs even, albeit artificially, suggest a greater capacity to transcend, redefine, and seek out new levels of consciousness. And they do it upon demand. People initially use a specific drug, or class of drugs, to obtain the desirable effects historically associated with the use of that drug.

Heroin and opiate-related drugs such as Oxycontin and Vicodin produce, in most people, a euphoric, dreamy state of

© Mikael Karlsson

well-being. The abuse of these prescription painkillers is one of the fastest growing (and alarming) drug trends. Methamphetamine and related stimulant drugs produce euphoria, energy, confidence, and exhilaration. Alcohol produces a loss of inhibitions and a state of well-being. Nicotine and marijuana typically serve as relaxants. Ecstasy and other "club drugs" produce stimulant as well as relaxant effects. Various over-the-counter and herbal drugs attempt to replicate the effects of more potent and often prohibited or prescribed drugs. Although effects and side effects may vary from user to user, a general pattern of effects is predictable from most major drugs of use and their analogs. Varying the dosage and altering the manner of ingestion is one way to alter the drug's effects. Some drugs, such as LSD and certain types of designer drugs, produce effects on the user that are less predictable and more sensitive to variations in dosage level and to the user's physical and psychological makeup.

Although all major drugs of use and abuse have specific reinforcing properties perpetuating their continued use, they also produce undesirable side effects that regular drug users attempt to mitigate. Most often, users attempt to mitigate these effects with the use of other drugs. Cocaine, methamphetamine, heroin, and alcohol have long been used to mitigate each other's side effects. A good example is the classic "speedball" of heroin and cocaine. When they are combined, cocaine accelerates and intensifies the euphoric state of the heroin, while the heroin softens the comedown from cocaine. Add to this the almost limitless combinations of prescription drugs, mixed and traded at "pharming" parties, and an entirely new dimension for altering drugs' physiological effects emerges.

Additionally, other powerful influences on drug taking, such as advertising for alcohol, tobacco, and certain prescription drugs, significantly impact the public's drug-related consciousness. The alcohol industry, for example, dissects numerous layers of society to specifically market alcoholic beverages to subpopulations of Americans, including youth. The same influences exist with tobacco advertising. What is the message in Philip Morris's advertisements about its attempts to mitigate smoking by youth? Approximately 500 thousand Americans die each year from tobacco-related illness. Add to the mix advertising by prescription-drug companies for innumerable human maladies and one soon realizes the enormity of the association between business and drug taking. Subsequently, any discussion of major drugs could begin and end with alcohol, tobacco, and prescription drugs.

An Update on the Effects of Marijuana and Its Potential Medical Use

Forensic Focus

Sherwood O. Cole

Introduction

Marijuana is the most commonly used illicit drug in the United States (National Institute on Drug Abuse [NIDA], n.d.; Compton, Grant, Colliver, Glantz, & Stinson, 2004). The task of offering expert testimony on the clinical or psychological effects of the drug is particularly difficult. This is due to two primary factors: (1) the controversy related to classifying marijuana compared to other psychoactive drugs and (2) the widespread lack of a balanced perspective on the effects of marijuana.

Regarding the first factor, marijuana is not a simple drug (it contains over 200 compounds) and, unlike most psychoactive drugs, is hard to describe from a single perspective. Also, its effects are phase-dependent and, to a large degree, individualistic. Accordingly, rather than classifying marijuana among other psychoactive drugs, most authors prefer to treat it as a separate topic or issue (Ray & Ksir, 2004). Most certainly, marijuana is not a narcotic, as it is often incorrectly referred to by law-enforcement agencies and the legal system.

Regarding the second factor, the public is bombarded with culturally confusing messages about the risks and benefits of marijuana (Alexander, 2003). The public and some professionals view marijuana from two conflicting perspectives, resulting in a lack of a balanced (moderate) view of its action. Some view marijuana as a very dangerous drug while others see it as a harmless drug. Those viewing marijuana as a dangerous drug are supported by the federal government's prohibition of possession and use of the drug and by outdated and unproven horror stories about marijuana-related criminal acts (Ray & Ksir, 2004). Those viewing marijuana as a harmless drug base their opinions primarily on personal experiences with the drug and on the belief that the federal government has been lying and exaggerating the potential danger of marijuana.

In view of the above issues, there seems to be a specific need to provide updated data on marijuana for scientific accuracy and forensic credibility. Forensic science relies upon facts and scientific findings (not speculation or anecdotal information), and the value of forensic testimony is seriously compromised in those instances where such standards are not implemented.

This article attempts to present an updated picture of the effects, potential dangers, and possible beneficial uses of marijuana in hopes that it will provide a valuable database for scientific reporting in the context of expert forensic testimony. In order to assure that the picture of marijuana presented here is current, only recent studies are reviewed. While no attempt has been made to exhaust all available studies, a genuine attempt has been made to be representative and fair in reviewing such findings.

The Nature of Marijuana and Its Action

Marijuana (also referred to as cannabis in the literature) is a preparation of leafy material from the cannabis plant (Cannabis sativa). While herbal cannabis contains over 400 compounds, including over 60 cannabinoids, its most important and primary active ingredient is delta-9-tetrahydrocannabinol (THC) (Ashton, 2001). Cannabinoids are chemicals that are unique to the cannabis plant and are structurally related to THC. The main recreational purpose of marijuana is its euphoric effect or high, although the drug can also produce dysphoric reactions such as panic and anxiety (Ashton). The potency of marijuana varies depending upon the part of the plant used and the amount of resin present. The flowering top of the plant contains the most resin, with the leaves and fibrous stalk containing progressively less. While marijuana of past years may have been relatively harmless, experimentation and crossbreeding have resulted in an increase in the potency of the drug found on the market today (Compton et al., 2004; ElSohly, et al., 2000). Evidence obtained from confiscated marijuana suggests that its increase in potency nearly doubled during the period from the early 90s to the late 90s (ElSohly, et al.). There is also some suggestion that the increase in the potency of marijuana may contribute to the rising rate in abuse (Compton et al.).

The mechanism of action underlying cannabinoids has only recently been clarified (D'Souza & Kosten, 2001) and involves the identification of two receptor subtypes referred to as CB1 and CB2 (Ledent et al., 1999; Watson, Benson, & Joy, 2000). CB1 receptors are distributed throughout the central nervous system including the cerebral cortex, hippocampus, amygdala, basal ganglia, cerebellum, thalamus, and brainstem (Ashton, 2001) as well as some areas of the peripheral nervous system (Ledent et al.). The newly discovered endogenous cannabinoid anandamide is believed to be a critical pre-synaptic component of neurotransmitter systems related to CB1 subtype systems and involved in the central mediation of marijuana effects (Ashton). This conclusion finds support in studies where pretreatment with the CB1 antagonist SR 141716 blocked the effects of smoked marijuana on self-reports of acute intoxication (Huestis et al., 2001) as well as the effects of peripherally administered anandamide on induced overeating (Williams & Kirkham, 1999). In contrast to CB1 receptors, less is known about CB2 receptor types, although they are found mainly in immune cells. However, the role of cannaboids in the immune system is likely to be multifaceted and, at present, remains vague (Watson et al., 2000).

Marijuana Dependence, Withdrawal, and Treatment

While the latest edition of the American Psychiatric Association's Diagnostic and Statistical Manual of Mental Disorders recognizes marijuana dependence (2000), it is less certain about marijuana withdrawal symptoms and their clinical significance. However, evidence clearly suggests that individuals using marijuana can develop both dependence and withdrawal symptoms, although under a narrower range of conditions than with some other drugs (Watson et al., 2000; Johns, 2001). Such withdrawal symptoms include restlessness, insomnia, anxiety, increased aggression, anorexia, muscle tremors, and autonomic effects (Ashton, 2001). In heavy users of marijuana, these symptoms appear to be more pronounced during the initial

10 days of abstinence, but some symptoms may persist as long as 28 days (Kouri & Pope, 2000). The symptoms are similar in type and magnitude to those observed with nicotine withdrawal and less severe than those observed with alcohol or opiate withdrawal (Budney, Hughes, Moore, & Novy, 2001). While the development of tolerance to the drug may lead some marijuana users to escalate dosage, the presence of withdrawal symptoms encourages continued use of the drug.

While the treatment of marijuana dependence is still in its infancy, there appear to be some interesting prospects on the horizon. For one, there is some optimism about the potential therapeutic use of the CB1 antagonist SR 141716A (and possibly other similar antagonists) in the treatment of marijuana dependence, although caution is advised (D'Souza & Kosten, 2001). In contrast to chemical treatment, brief intervention programs that utilize multi-component therapy (motivational, cognitive, behavioral) appear to be more effective than single component therapy in treating cannabis-dependent adults (Babor, 2004). Additional intervention programs directed at curbing marijuana use/abuse include the use of targeted public service announcements with high-sensation-seeking adolescents (Palmgreen, Donohew, Lorch, Hoyle, & Stevenson, 2001) and family skill training to equip parents with drug information and coping strategies (Spoth, Redmond, & Shin, 2001).

One additional important finding of interest is the evidence from animal studies of an interconnected role of CBI and opiate receptors in brain areas and its potential importance to the mediation of addictive behavior (Ledent et al., 1999). The cross-sensitization observed between delta-9-THC and morphine, which was symmetrical, suggests that common neurobiological substrates may be involved in addiction to marijuana and opiates (Cadoni, Pisanu, Solinas, Acquas, & DiChiara, 2001). These homologies between cannabinoids and opiates, while not providing direct evidence for a causal relationship between cannabis and opiate use, are nonetheless consistent with this possibility (Parolaro & Rubino, 2002). The functional link in the mechanism of addictive action by both types of drugs may be through u-opiate receptor influence on mesolimbic dopamine systems (Manzanares et al., 1999; Rubino, Massi, Vigano, Fuzio, & Parolaro, 2000). While there may also be functional links between cannabinoid properties and other centrally acting drugs, these links are at present less clearly defined (Wiley & Martin, 2003).

Deleterious Effects of Marijuana

The areas reviewed here include (1) the effects of marijuana on cognitive performance; (2) the potential role of marijuana as a stepping-stone to "hard drug" use; and

(3) the relationship of marijuana use to the later development of psychotic illness. Following this, comments will be made regarding some additional marijuana effects of continued interest in the literature.

The effects of marijuana on cognitive performance. The impairment of cognitive performance by cannabis is generally well accepted in the literature. In some respects, this impairment is similar to that observed with alcohol and includes slow reaction time, lack of coordination, deficits in concentration, and impairment in performance of complex tasks (Ashton, 2001). However, two specific issues appear to be of primary interest in the context of such impairment: (1) the influence of amount of marijuana on cognitive impairment, and (2) the duration or sustaining power of the cognitive impairment produced by the drug.

Regarding the first of these issues, evidence clearly suggests that there is a direct relationship between the amount of marijuana use and the degree of cognitive impairment. For example, in studies where a large battery of neuropsychological tests wcrc employed, abstaining subjects with a history of heavy marijuana use performed significantly less well than controls or subjects with a history of moderate drug use (Bolla, Brown, Eldreth, Tate, & Cadet, 2002; Solowij et al., 2002). Interestingly, while heavy marijuana users differed from controls on the majority of tests administered in one study, the moderate drug users differed very little from controls (Solowij et al.). In general, while the impairment in cognitive functions resulting from marijuana use is moderate, it would appear to have the potential of impairing driving ability, operation of equipment, task proficiency, and daily functioning.

Regarding the duration or sustaining power of cognitive impairment resulting from marijuana use, results are less consistent. For example, some evidence suggests that the cognitive deficits associated with cannabis use may persist up to only 7 days after subjects last smoked the drug (Pope, Gruber, Hudson, Huestis, & Yurgelun-Todd, 2001), while other evidence suggests that such cognitive deficits may persist up to 28 days after abstinence from marijuana (Bolla et al., 2002). Such a difference in findings raises critical issues related to possible mechanisms by which the drug mediates such discrepancies. In the case of the short-term deficits, the effects may simply be associated with marijuana-induced agitation associated with withdrawal from the drug often lasting this long (Pope et al.). However, in the case of cognitive deficits persisting up to 28 days, such an explanation is inadequate. In this case, the deficits may be due to neurological changes in the previously mentioned cannabinoid receptor systems and the effect of marijuana on such systems over a longer period of time (Solowij et al., 2002).

In addition, marijuana-induced hypo-activity in the posterior cerebellum may play an immediate role in such a cognitive deficit, particularly in light of the role of this brain area in the sense of timing (Block et al., 2000a). The effects of marijuana on attention-related regional cerebral blood flow may also play some underlying role in such a cognitive deficit (Block et al., 2000b). However, the relevance of these changes in activity level and blood flow to the issue of duration of cognitive impairment remains unclear.

While the bulk of evidence strongly supports the findings of a cognitive impairment produced by marijuana, one study reported no evidence for cognitive decline between heavy, light, and non-users of cannabis (Lyketsos, Garrett, Liang, & Anthony, 1999). However, the failure to detect cognitive decline in this case may reflect insufficient heavy or chronic use of cannabis or the use of insensitive assessment instruments (Solowij et al., 2002).

The Potential Role of Marijuana as a Stepping Stone to "Hard Drugs"

Marijuana has long been referred to as a gateway drug, implying that its use serves as a stepping stone to the later use of other "hard drugs" (e.g., heroin, cocaine, hallucinogens, etc.). Such an assumption finds strong support in studies where both national diversity and differences in subsequent "hard drug" use have been investigated.

In one Australian twin study, twin pair members who had used cannabis by age 17 had higher additional drug-use rates than their twin siblings who had not used cannabis by age 17 (Lynskey et al., 2003). It is unlikely such differences were due to environmental factors since the twin pairs were raised in the same household. While the association between early marijuana use and later additional drug use did not differ significantly between monozygotic and dizygotic twins, the age of initiation of cannabis use (before age 17) was influenced by heritable factors (Lynskey et al.).

Additional non-twin studies conducted in New Zealand and the United States generally support the findings of the above study in that early cannabis use preceded the later use of other illicit drugs (Fergusson & Horwood, 2000; Wagner & Anthony, 2002; Merline, O'Malley, Schulenberg, Bachman, & Johnston, 2004). In one of these studies, subjects previously using cannabis on more than 50 occasions per year demonstrated hazards of subsequent illicit drug use that were 59 times higher than non-users (Fergusson & Hotwood). Another one of these studies also points out the persistence of such subsequent drug use; it was still rather prevalent among adults 35 years of age, although influenced by adult role and experiences

(Merline et al.). Not only does marijuana use increase the risk of subsequent illicit drug use, it also increases the risk of problems in general, which limits the individual's adjustment and performance (Brook, Balka, & Whiteman, 1999).

While there is little dispute over the influence of early marijuana use on subsequent "hard drug" use, one of the major focal points of recent studies has been on the possible mechanism mediating such a relationship. One author suggests that the relationship is due to the fact that initial cannabis use may encourage later broader experimentation, reduce perceived risk of using other drugs, and bring users into contact with other drugs (Lynskey et al., 2003). A similar view is the suggestion that the interconnection between early marijuana use and subsequent illicit drug use is due to drug exposure opportunities; i.e., marijuana users will increasingly be exposed to greater opportunities to experiment with other drugs (Wilcox, Wagner, & Anthony, 2002). While both of the above mechanisms have a ring of truth about them, one cannot rule out, in light of previous evidence of cross-sensitization of delta-9-tetrahydrocannabinol and morphine (Cadoni et al., 2001), the potential role of neurobiological substrates in such a relationship. Although such a mechanism may not mediate the relationship between early marijuana use and all types of subsequent "hard drug" use, it may serve some role in the subsequent use of opioids. It is also possible that the relationship between early marijuana use and subsequent illicit drug use is non-causal and reflects factors not yet adequately addressed by studies (Fergusson & Horwood, 2000).

The relationship of marijuana use to later development of psychotic illness. One of the most interesting and important areas of marijuana research in recent years is the relationship between early marijuana use and the subsequent development of mental illness. In general, recent evidence obtained from cross-sectional national studies supports the conclusion that the previous use of marijuana significantly increases the subsequent occurrence of schizophrenia (van Os et al., 2002; Arseneault, Cannon, Witton, & Murray, 2004; Veen et al., 2004) and major depression (Brook, Brook, Zhang, Cohen, & Whiteman, 2002). Overall, cannabis use appears to confer a two-fold risk of the later development of schizophrenia compared to that found in the general population (Arseneault et al.). Further evidence also suggests that, while gender and age may further influence the onset of the first psychotic episode, it is the use of cannabis itself that proves to be a much stronger predictor of the onset of the first psychotic episode (Veen et al., 2004). Parenthetically, it is of further interest to note that comorbidity (presence of additional mental illness) is also present in many adolescent substance users (including marijuana users) (Latimer, Stone, Voight, Winters, & August, 2002; Robbins et al., 2002). Such an overlap in adolescent predictors increases, markedly, the difficulty of defining the association between early marijuana use and

subsequent mental illness (McGee, Williams, Poulton, & Moffitt, 2000).

While the evidence for the previous use of marijuana increasing the subsequent development of mental illness is relatively strong, the mechanism underlying this linkage is a controversial and highly debated topic. Although it is fairly clear that the linkage between previous marijuana use and mental illness is not simply a fortuitous or temporal association, suggestions as to the causative factors that may contribute to it are diversified. For example, one author suggests that early cannabis use may trigger or exacerbate symptoms of mental illness in subjects who may already be at genetic risk for developing the mental illness (Veen et al., 2004). This view appears to have some credibility in light of the aforementioned evidence for a co-occurrence of drug use and mental illness in adolescents (Latimer et al., 2002; Robbins et al., 2002). However, the majority of evidence suggests that cannabis use demonstrates temporal priority in relationship to mental illness (precedes it) and can produce psychosis in individuals who have no history of mental illness (Johns, 2001; van Os et al., 2002). More realistically, it may be appropriate to suggest that cannabis use is likely to play a causal role with regard to psychosis, but that it is not a necessary or sufficient condition for schizophrenia (Arseneault et al., 2004). That is to say, cannabis use is a component cause, one part of a constellation of causes that leads to subsequent schizophrenia (Arseneault et al.). Additional evidence suggests that such a "component cause" explanation of the linkage between cannabis use and mental illness may not go far enough (Leweke, Giuffrida, Wurster, Emrich, & Piomelli, 1999). In this case, the level of endogenous cannabinoids in the cerebrospinal fluids of schizophrenics was significantly higher than in controls, suggesting that a type of "hyper-cannabinergic state" in the central nervous system may contribute to the pathogenesis of schizophrenia (Leweke et al.). However, the relatively small sample of subjects in this study (10 schizophrenic patients) somewhat restricts the generalities of the findings. It is quite apparent that the final word on the mechanism underlying the linkage between marijuana use and subsequent mental illness awaits further study.

Additional Miscellaneous Marijuana Effects

The harmful effects of marijuana on the respiratory and cardiovascular systems have long been recognized (National Institute on Drug Abuse, n.d.; Ashton, 2001). Like tobacco, marijuana smoke increases the risk of cancer and lung damage (Watson et al., 2000). This should not be surprising since marijuana contains most of the same chemical components (except nicotine) that are found in tobacco. Also, the smoking of marijuana causes changes in the cardiovascular system that are, in general, characteristic of stress (Ray & Ksir, 2004). Recent studies further emphasize the increased risk of cardiac problems associated with such changes. For example, evidence suggests that chronic abuse of marijuana may increase the risk of stroke in young men aged 18-30 years (Bulletin Board, 2002) and that such an increased risk remains well past the period of withdrawal symptoms caused by abstinence from the drug. Additional evidence suggests that, within 1 hour after smoking marijuana, the risk of myocardial infarction onset was elevated approximately 5 fold (Mittleman, Lewis, Maclure, Sherwood, & Muller, 2001). Fortunately, after 1 hour, the risk of such an effect decreases markedly. While the risk of myocardial infarction significantly increases after smoking marijuana, the risk is much less than that associated with cocaine use (Mittleman et al., 1999).

Another long-standing interest associated with marijuana use is the concept of "amotivational syndrome" (Ray & Ksir, 2004). This syndrome is generally described as a diminished motivation accompanied by a loss of energy and drive to work. Such characteristics can, undoubtedly, have an important impact on one's ability to learn, school performance, and general effectiveness in dealing with everyday problems. However, such a syndrome may represent nothing more than the ongoing intoxication in frequent marijuana users (Johns, 2001). This appears to be particularly plausible in light of the long half-life of marijuana in the body and the fact that daily smokers can be chronically intoxicated (Ray & Ksir, 2004).

Finally, the impairment of short-term memory (ability to easily recall information learned just seconds or minutes before) by marijuana remains one of the most consistent findings in the literature. Since CB 1 receptors are distributed in the hippocampus, interference with their function may play a role in such impairment by marijuana, possibly by disrupting the encoding process (Hampson & Deadwyler, 1999). As to whether such an impairment in short-term memory is more permanent or tends to diminish with the passage of time is debatable (Johns, 2001). In any event, such impairment in short-term memory has the potential for impacting cognitive performance as discussed previously.

The Potential Medical Use of Marijuana

One of the most hotly-debated issues in our society is the legalization of marijuana for medical purposes. In spite of the continued debate, the evidence for the medical benefits of the drug grows and presently includes, by conservative estimate, the following uses (Watson, ct al., 2000; Ray & Ksir, 2004):

1. Reduction of the fluid pressure in the eyes of glaucoma patients.

2. Reduction of severe nausea caused by certain drugs in the treatment of cancer.
3. Stimulation of appetite and reduction of pain associated with wasting syndrome in patients with cancer and AIDS.
4. As a possible anticonvulsant in the treatment of epilepsy.

While the potential medical benefits of marijuana are generally recognized, the legalization of the drug for such purposes has, nevertheless, been hampered by three critical issues:

1. Marijuana is labeled a Schedule I drug under the Controlled Substance Act of 1970, which implies it has no accepted medical use and has high abuse potential. Accordingly, it is not available by prescriptions written by physicians.
2. There is general fear by the public that the legalization of marijuana for medical purposes would open the door to a general increased availability and abuse of the drug in our society.
3. There may not be a necessity for legalizing marijuana for medical purposes since there are presently alternative drugs that are equally effective and available for treatment.

Each of these issues will be briefly discussed in order to disclose the nature and potential fallacy of the position. It is hoped that such a discussion will indicate that medical marijuana may have a future, albeit in a slightly different direction than it is presently going.

Regarding the labeling of marijuana as a Schedule I drug by the federal government (FDA) and its lack of availability by prescription, the issue is not black and white. The National Institute on Drug Abuse did provide medical-grade marijuana cigarettes to a few patients with FDA approval of a "compassionate use" protocol (Ray & Ksir, 2004). The labeling of the drug as Schedule I pertains to the plant (botanical product) or to synthetic equivalents of the plant, not to all drugs containing THC (The Science of Medical Marijuana, n.d.). For example, Marinol (dronabinol) is a synthesized drug in capsule form containing THC in sesame oil and is available by prescription under a Schedule II label (The Science of Medical Marijuana, n.d.). The factor limiting the prescribing of Marinol by physicians may simply be the lack of awareness of the drug's efficacy or the fact that a Schedule II label, while making the drug available, is still a restricted category. In any case, the future of Marinol and other potential cannabinoid medications would appear to be found in pure drugs delivered by some means other than smoking (Watson et al., 2000).

The most promising delivery system to date would appear to be some form of inhalation, owing to the rapid onset and potential for better titration by the patient (The Science of Medical Marijuana, n.d.). Ironically, the federal government's handling of the marijuana issue has been so poor that a growing number of states have passed ballot initiatives (e.g., California's Proposition 215) designed to allow individuals to grow their own marijuana (Nofziger, 1998). This has led to additional state and federal legal action that has only further delayed a solution to the medical-marijuana issue (Murphy, 2004; Ray & Ksir, 2004).

Regarding the issue of general fear by the public that the legalization of marijuana for medical purposes would encourage a general increase in the illicit use and abuse of the drug in society, the answer is not immediately clear. However, evidence available suggests that this is not the case. For example, a comparison of marijuana use practices in two cities that are very similar demographically but different in legal availability of marijuana for recreational use (San Francisco, California, and Amsterdam, Netherlands) indicated such practices do not differ in the two locations (Reinarman, Cohen, & Kaal, 2004). Since total removal of criminalization restraints (Amsterdam) does not appear to increase the abuse potential over that observed in the context of such restraints (San Francisco), the partial relaxing of drug-control standards in making medical marijuana available would not appear to exacerbate marijuana abuse problems.

Furthermore, a time-series analysis could be undertaken to determine whether society is consuming marijuana at higher rates or in greater quantities than it was prior to medical legalization (Yacoubian, 2001). Such results could be achieved by monitoring the use of marijuana with national data collection systems (e.g., The National House Survey on Drug Abuse, The Drug Abuse Warning Network, etc.). A further benefit of the relaxing of drug control standards in making medical marijuana available might possibly be the control in the spread of disease by clean needle programs and controlled environments for drug use.

Regarding the fact that the legalization of marijuana may not be necessary because there are alternative drugs that are equally effective and available for treatment, the statement may be partially true and partially false. In the case of some treatment contexts, additional available drugs may be better and safer than marijuana. This appears to be true in the case of the treatment of fluid pressure in the eyes of glaucoma patients with available prescription eye drops. The effect of marijuana, in this case, is short-lived and the doses so high that the modest benefits gained are outweighed by the side effects (Watson et al. 2000). Also, in the case of the possible use of marijuana as an anticonvulsant, the available drug Dilantin (phenytoin) may prove to be equally effective.

In other instances, medical marijuana may not necessarily be better than other legal drugs on the market, but simply an alternative choice in the array of available medications. If marijuana is chosen as an alternative medication to those legally available, it is important to keep in mind that smoked marijuana is a complex mixture of active and inactive ingredients (The Science of Medical Marijuana, n.d.). Accordingly, concerns arise about product consistency, potency of active ingredients, and contamination.

While the debate over medical marijuana continues, cannabinoids are being developed for therapeutic application beyond those previously mentioned here. One of the most important new applications of cannabinoids is their potential role in "neuroprotection," a role associated with their antioxidant action (The Science of Medical Marijuana, n.d.). However, the future of such medications would appear to be found in pure drugs (chemically defined), not with the use of the plant or smoked form of marijuana (Watson et al., 2000).

Summary and Concluding Comments

Marijuana is not a completely benign substance but, rather, is a powerful drug with a variety of effects. Accordingly, it is important to examine these effects in a fair and balanced manner. This article attempts to do this by, first of all, presenting a general review on the nature of marijuana, its mechanisms of action, and evidence for dependence. Following this, the adverse effects of the marijuana on cognitive performance, the drug's role as a "stepping stone" to hard drugs, its potential for contributing to the development of mental illness, and other effects are reviewed for the purpose of demonstrating the cost associated with the drug's use. While these adverse effects are real, they are well within the range of effects tolerated by other medications on the market (Watson et al., 2000). A counterbalance to the adverse effects of marijuana is the fact that the drug clearly has some therapeutic value, albeit in a somewhat different form than the smoked one. Undoubtedly, the future of the growing medical use of cannabinoids depends upon the development of pure drugs, where the consistency of content, purity, and potency of the product can be carefully controlled.

Such a balanced and up-to-date view on the effects of marijuana, as presented here, is particularly important in the context of the forensic need to assure the accuracy and reliability of expert testimony. Such accuracy and reliability of testimony would appear to be particularly critical in light of the United States Supreme Court's ruling in the Daubert decision (Daubert v. Merrell Dow, 1993). While previous evidence was admissible on the basis of its "general acceptance" in the scientific community, the Daubert decision established a new set of criteria for courts to determine the admissibility of evidence. An outline and discussion of these criteria are presented elsewhere (Bloomer & Hurwitz, 2002; Cole, 2003). One of these criteria, "the actual or potential rate of error in the expert's methodology," is particularly relevant to the present discussion. For example, any inaccuracy or deficiency in the assessment of marijuana effects can potentially increase the rate of error in the testimony offered by expert witnesses. Protective measures appear to be particularly relevant in the case of marijuana, where anecdotal information and unscientific assumptions about the drug are still prevalent in the public mindset.

While there has been considerable debate as to whether the Daubert decision has made it easier or more difficult to admit expert testimony (Joseph, Atkins, & Flaks, 2000), there is little doubt that the decision has provided useful and standardized rules for such admission. Contrary to the loose criteria for expert testimony in existence prior to the Daubert decision, testimony that is subjective and controversial is now more likely to be excluded as unreliable (Cole, 2003). Experts in the courtroom are expected to employ the same level of intellectual rigor that characterizes their practices.

Expert witnesses need to become more aware of the scientific basis of their evidence, and up-to-date data is critical to this process. The evidence presented here provides a solid and current database for such witnessing related to marijuana effects. Thorough preparation by a potential witness will increase his or her credibility and will allow the witness to speak with authority and effectiveness.

While serving as an expert witness on the effects of marijuana (or any other psychoactive drug) can be an exciting and challenging role, the changes that have taken place in court procedures suggest the need for better and more thorough preparation. In the final analysis, it is important to remember that the legal game is still an adversarial system of justice.

References

Alexander, D. (2003). A marijuana screening inventory (experimental version): Description and preliminary psychometric properties. The American Journal of Drug and Alcohol Abuse, 29, 619–646.

American Psychiatric Association. (2000). Diagnostic and Statistical Manual of Mental Disorders (text revision). Washington, DC: Author.

Arseneault, L., Cannon, M., Witton, J., & Murray, R. M. (2004). Causal association between cannabis and psychosis: Examination of the evidence. The British Journal of Psychiatry, 184, 110–117.

Ashton, C. H. (2001). Pharmacology and effects of cannabis: A brief review. The British Journal of Psychiatry, 178, 101–106.

Babor, T. F. (2004). Brief treatments for cannabis dependence: Findings from a randomized multisite trial. Journal of Consulting and Clinical Psychology, 72, 455–466.

Block, R. I., O'Leary, D. S., Hichwa, R. D., Augustinack, J. C., Ponto, L. L. B., Ghoneim, M. M., Arndt, S., Ehrhardt, J. C., Hurtig, R. R., Watkins, G. L., Hall, J. A., Nathan, P. E., & Andreasen, N. C. (2000a). Cerebellar hypoactivity in frequent marijuana users. Neuro Report, 11, 749–753.

Block, R. I., O'Leary, D. S., Augustinack, J. C., Ponto, L. L. B., Ghoneim, M. M., Hurtig, R. R., Hall, J. A., & Nathan, P. E. (2000b). Effects of frequent marijuana use on attention-related regional cerebral blood flow. Society for Neuroscience Abstract, 26, 2080.

Bloomer, R. H., & Hurwitz, B. (2002, September). So you're going to testify: What every young neuropsychologist should know about tests and the courts. Paper presented at the American College of Forensic Examiners Conference, Orlando, FL.

Bolla, K. I., Brown, K., Eldreth, D., Tate, K., & Cadet, J. L. (2002). Dose-related neurocognitive effects of marijuana use. Neurology, 59, 1337–1343.

Brook, J. S., Balka, E. B., & Whiteman, M. (1999). The risks for late adolescence of early adolescent marijuana use. American Journal of Public Health, 89, 1549–1554.

Brook, D. W., Brook, J. S., Zhang, C., Cohen, E, & Whiteman, M. (2002). Drug use and the risk of major depressive disorder, alcohol dependence, and substance use disorders. Archives of General Psychiatry, 59, 1039–1044.

Budney, A. J., Hughes, J. R., Moore, B. A., & Novy, P. L. (2001). Marijuana abstinence effects in marijuana smokers maintained in their home environment. Archives of General Psychiatry, 58, 917–924.

Bulletin Board (2002). Chronic marijuana abuse may increase risk of stroke. NIDA Notes, 17, 14–15.

Cadoni, C., Pisanu, A., Solinas, M., Acquas, E., & DiChiara, G. (2001). Behavioral sensitization after repeated exposure to A9-tetrahydrocannabinol and cross-sensitization with morphine. Psychopharmacology, 158, 259–266.

Cole, S. O. (2003). Comorbidity of mental illness and drug treatment requirements: Impact on forensic evidence. The Forensic Examiner, 12 (11 & 12), 28–34.

Compton, W. M., Grant, B. F., Colliver, J. D., Glantz, M. D., & Stinson, F. S. (2004). Prevalence of marijuana use disorders in the United States, 1991–1992 and 2001–2002. Journal of the American Medical Association, 291, 2114–2121.

Daubert v. Merrell Dow Pharmaceuticals, Inc. (1993). 113, S. Ct. 2786.

D'Souza, D. C., & Kosten, T. R. (2001). Cannabinoid antagonists: A treatment in search of an illness. Archives of General Psychiatry, 58, 330–331.

ElSohly, M. A., Ross, S. A., Mehmedic, Z., Arafat, R., Yi, B., & Banahan, B. F. (2000). Potency trends of A9-THC and other cannabinoids in confiscated marijuana from 1980–1997. Journal of Forensic Science, 45, 24–30.

Fergusson, D. M., & Horwood, L. J. (2000). Does cannabis use encourage other forms of illicit drug use? Addiction, 95, 505–520.

Hampson, R. E., & Deadwyler, S. A. (1999). Cannabinoids, hippocampal function and memory. Life Sciences, 65, 715–723.

Huestis, M. A., Gorelick, D. A., Heishman, S. J., Preston, K. L., Nelson, R. A., Moolchan, E. T., & Frank, R. A. (2001). Blockade of effects of smoked marijuana by the CB1-selective cannabinoid receptor antagonist SR 141716. Archives of General Psychiatry, 58, 322–328.

Johns, A. (2001). Psychiatric effects of cannabis. The British Journal of Psychiatry, 178, 116–122.

Joseph, G. W., Atkins, E. L., & Flaks, D. K. (2000). Admissibility of expert psychological testimony in the era of Daubert. The case of hedonic damages. American Journal of Forensic Psychology, 1 & 3–34.

Kouri, E. M., & Pope, H. G., Jr. (2000). Abstinence symptoms during withdrawal from chronic marijuana use. Experimental and Clinical Psychopharmacology, 8, 483–492.

Latimer, W. W., Stone, A. L., Voight, A., Winters, K. C., & August, G. J. (2002). Gender differences in psychiatric comorbidity among adolescents with substance use disorders. Experimental and Clinical Psychopharmacology, 10, 310–315.

Ledent, C., Valverde, O., Cossu, G., Petitet, E, Aubert, J-F, Beslot, E, Bohme, G. A., Imperato, A., Pedrazzini, T., Roques, B. E, Vassart, G., Fratta, W., & Parmentier, M. (1999). Unresponsiveness to cannabinoids and reduced addictive effects of opiates in CB1 receptor knockout mice. Science, 283, 401–404.

Leweke, F. M., Giuffrida, A., Wurster, U., Emrich, H. M., & Piomelli, D. (1999). Elevated endogenous cannabinoids in schizophrenia. NeuroReport, 10, 1665–1669.

Lyketsos, C. G., Garrett, E., Liang, K. Y., & Anthony, J. C. (1999). Cannabis use and cognitive decline in persons under 65 years of age. American Journal of Epidemiology, 149, 794–800.

Lynskey, M. T., Heath, A. C., Bucholz, K. K., Slutske, W. S., Madden, P. A. E, Nelson, E. C., Statham, D. J., & Martin, N. G. (2003). Escalation of drug use in early-onset cannabis users vs. co-twin controls. Journal of the American Medical Association, 289, 427–433.

Manzanares, J., Corchero, J., Romero, J., Fernandez-Ruiz, J. J., Ramos, J. A., & Fuentes, J. A. (1999). Pharmacological and biochemical interactions between opioids and cannabinoids. Trends in Pharmacological Science, 20, 287–294.

McGee, R., Williams, S., Poulton, R., & Moffitt, T. (2000). A longitudinal study of cannabis use and mental health from adolescence to early adulthood. Addiction, 95, 491–503.

Merline, A. C., O'Malley, P. M., Schulenberg, J. E., Bachman, J. G., & Johnston, L. D. (2004). Substance use among adults 35 years of age: Prevalence, adulthood predictors, and impact of adolescent substance use. American Journal of Public Health, 94, 96–102.

Mittleman, M. A., Mintzer, D., Maclure, M., Tofler, G. H., Sherwood, J. B., & Muller, J. E. (1999). Triggering of myocardial infarction by cocaine. Circulation, 99, 2737–2741.

Mittleman, M. A., Lewis, R. A., Maclure, M., Sherwood, J. B., & Muller, J. E. (2001). Triggering myocardial infarction by marijuana. Circulation, 103, 2805–2809.

Murphy, D. E. (2004, February 26). Court allows medical use of marijuana. New York Times.

National Institute on Drug Abuse. (n.d.). Info-Facts-marijuana. Retrieved March, 3, 2004 from www.nida.nih.gov

Nofziger, L. (1998). Forward in Marijuana Rx: The patients' fight for medicinal pot. New York: Thunder's Mouth Press.

Palmgreen, P., Donohew, L., Lorch, E. P., Hoyle, R.H., & Stevenson, M. T. (2001). Television campaigns and adolescent marijuana use: Tests of sensation seeking targeting. American Journal of Public Health, 91, 292–296.

Parolaro, D., & Rubino, T. (2002). Is cannabinoid transmission involved in rewarding properties of drugs of abuse? British Journal of Pharmacology, 136, 1083–1084.

Pope, H. G., Jr., Gruber, A. J., Hudson, J. I., Huestis, M. A., & Yurgelun-Todd, D. (2001). Neuropsychological performance in long-term cannabis users. Archives of General Psychiatry, 58, 909–915.

Ray, O., & Ksir, C. (2004). Drugs, society, and human behavior (10th ed.). New York: McGraw-Hill.

Reinarman, C., Cohen, P. D. A., & Kaal, H. L. (2004). The limited relevance of drug policy: Cannabis in Amsterdam and in San Francisco. American Journal of Public Health, 94, 836–842.

Robbins, M. S., Kumar, S., Walker-Barnes, C., Feaster, D. J., Briones, E., & Szapocznik, J. (2002). Ethnic differences in comorbidity among substance-abusing adolescents referred to outpatient therapy. Journal of the American Academy of Child and Adolescent Psychiatry, 41, 394–401.

Rubino, T., Massi, P., Vigano, D., Fuzio, D., & Parolaro, D. (2000). Long-term treatment with SR141716A, the CB1 receptor antagonist, influences morphine withdrawal syndrome. Life Sciences, 66, 2213–2219.

Solowij, N., Stephens, R. S., Roffman, R. A., Babor, T., Kadden, R., Miller, M., Christiansen, K., McRee, B., & Vendetti, J. (2002). Cognitive functioning of long-term heavy cannabis users seeking treatment. Journal of the American Medical Association, 287, 1123–1131.

Spoth, R. L., Redmond, C., & Shin, C. (2001). Randomized trial of brief family interventions for general populations: Adolescent substance use outcomes 4 years following baseline. Journal of Consulting and Clinical Psychology, 69, 627–642.

The Science of Medical Marijuana. (n.d.). Retrieved June 16, 2004, from http://www.medmjscience.org

van Os, J., Bak, M., Hanssen, M., Bijl, R. V., de Graaf, R., & Verdoux, H. (2002). Cannabis use and psychosis: A longitudinal population-based study. American Journal of Epidemiology, 156, 319–327.

Veen, N. D., Selten, J-P., van der Tweel, 1., Feller, W. G., Hock, H. W., & Kahn, R. S. (2004). Cannabis use and age at onset of schizophrenia. American Journal of Psychiatry, 161, 501–506.

Wagner, F. A., & Anthony, J. C. (2002). Into the world of illegal drug use: Exposure opportunity and other mechanisms linking the use of alcohol, tobacco, marijuana, and cocaine. American Journal of Epidemiology, 155, 918–925.

Watson, S. J., Benson, J. A., Jr., & Joy, J. E. (2000). Marijuana and medicine: Assessing the science base. Archives of General Psychiatry, 57, 547–552.

Wilcox, H. C., Wagner, F. A., & Anthony, J. C. (2002). Exposure opportunity as a mechanism linking youth marijuana use to hallucinogen use. Drug and Alcohol Dependence, 66, 127–135.

Wiley, J. L., & Martin, B. R. (2003). Cannabinoid pharmacological properties common to other centrally acting drugs. European Journal of Pharmacology, 471, 185–193.

Williams, C. M., & Kirkham, T. C. (1999). Anandamide induces overeating: Mediation by central cannabinoid (CB1) receptors. Psychopharmacology, 143, 315–317.

Yacoubian, G. S., Jr. (2001). Beyond the theoretical rhetoric: A proposal to study the consequences of drug legalization. Journal of Drug Education, 31, 319–328.

Sherwood O. Cole, PhD, Diplomate of the American Board Psychological Specialties.

Critical Thinking

1. What is your state's stand on medical marijuana? What do you think it should be?

2. Can you defend the belief that the pain management benefits associated with marijuana use outweigh the drug's harmful effects on the body?

Methamphetamines

MATT YORK

Sometimes called crank, ice, tina or crystal meth, methamphetamine is not new. For years, abuse has spread from rural areas of the West and South, slowly expanding to the Midwest and the East. Today meth abuse exists around the globe.

Even a quarter gram of meth can propel a user through a weekend devoid of sleep and food. Whether the drug is sniffed, smoked, swallowed, or injected, the body quickly absorbs it. Once meth reaches the circulatory system, it is a near instant flume ride to the central nervous system. It triggers the brain's neurotransmitters, particularly dopamine.

After meth triggers the release of neurotransmitters, it blocks their reuptake back into their storage pouches, much as cocaine and other stimulants. Unlike cocaine, however, meth also blocks the enzymes that help to break down invasive drugs, so the released chemicals float freely until they wear off. It remains active for 10 to 12 hours, compared with 45 minutes for cocaine.

The drug destroys the receptors and as a result may, over time, permanently reduce dopamine levels, sometimes leading to symptoms normally associated with Parkinson's disease like tremors and muscle twitches. As addiction deepens, meth wreaks havoc on the brain. In advanced cases of addiction, users can become psychotic with effects that mimic schizophrenia.

Meth increases the heart rate and blood pressure and can cause irreversible damage to blood vessels in the brain, which can lead to strokes. It can also cause arrhythmia and cardiovascular collapse, possibly leading to death. The drug has been known to compromise immune function and interfere with AIDS medications.

In the first effort to calculate the national price of meth abuse, a study said the addictive stimulant imposed costs of $23.4 billion in 2005. While the authors, from the RAND Corporation in Santa Monica, Calif., caution that many impacts were difficult to quantify, their study suggests that meth takes an economic toll nearly as great as heroin and possibly more.

Federal surveys suggest that the share of Americans using the drug in a given year has stabilized, at about 1% of the population over age 12, which is far higher than the rate for heroin but half the rate for cocaine. About 400,000 Americans are believed to be addicted to meth, but a rising number are smoking it rather than taking it orally or snorting it. Smoking brings a faster, jolting high, quicker addiction, and more ill effects.

Federal statistics show that the number of clandestine meth labs discovered in the United States rose by 14% in 2008, to 6,783, and has continued to increase, in part because of a crackdown on meth manufacturers in Mexico and in part because of the spread of a new, easier meth-making method known as "shake and bake."

Data on meth lab seizures suggest that there are tens of thousands of contaminated residences in the United States. Meth contamination can permeate drywall, carpets, insulation, and air ducts, causing respiratory ailments and other health problems.

Though the United States has made significant headway in the fight against small meth producers with tighter restrictions on the sales of the medications used in its production, enormous labs in Mexico and Asia continue to supply American users.

The meth epidemic is not just a scourge of the American heartland. It has a powerful foothold in Europe. The number of countries in Europe reporting seizures of methamphetamine more than doubled between 2000 and 2005, to 25 from 11, according to the United Nations Office on Drugs and Crime.

Drug experts say there is no methadone, no silver bullet, to treat methamphetamine addicts.

Critical Thinking

1. Despite meth's grave consequences, why is it still popular as a drug of abuse?

2. Law enforcement has spent an enormous amount of time and money combating the meth problem but it is not getting better. What else needs to be done? Can you provide examples?

Crystal Meth: The Dangers of Crystal Meth

With pharmacy's ability to control OTC sales of pseudoephedrine medicines under scrutiny, community pharmacist Bob Dunkley looks at the dangers posed by crystal **meth** and how the US dealt with the problem.

The discovery last year of crystal **meth** labs in the UK and the reports that the floors of the labs were coated with the empty packets of pseudoephedrine-containing medicines must give community pharmacists some pause for thought. If two labs have been discovered by the authorities—how many more are out there that have not been discovered?

The RPSGB[1] has produced Law and Ethics bulletins warning pharmacists of what can happen if they make injudicious sales of pseudoephedrine products, and now that we are in the middle of the cough and cold season an extra degree of vigilance is required.

It is important to reiterate the grave danger of crystal **meth.** One solution may lie with another part of the world that had a similar problem, but has adopted an approach that could be taken up in the UK.

Why Crystal **Meth?**

Crystal **meth** is a readily manufactured psychopharmacologic material that produces long lasting harm.[2,3] It hijacks the dopamine re-uptake protein in the brain and causes dopamine to act much longer than it should. In addition, methamphetamine re-enters the presynaptic neurone and causes an endless release of dopamine until the dopaminergic system "burns out".[3]

Why Dopamine?

Dopamine is the brain's pleasure principle—when you experience something pleasurable, dopamine is released, but shortly afterward various processes stop the dopamine acting, i.e. the dopamine re-uptake transporter.

Crystal **meth** takes over those processes, allowing dopamine a longer period of action and hence giving an intense high. As a result of excess dopamine stimulation, people exhibit symptoms of paranoia and violence, and this continues for some time after they stop taking crystal **meth.** The exact mechanism is beyond the scope of this article, but Stahl 2008 provides a good account of the mechanism with clear diagrams.

Therefore, a community where crystal **meth** is readily available is at grave danger from random acts of violence. And these acts can continue after all the crystal **meth** has been removed from the scene.

The Smurfing Technique

Pseudoephedrine is the lead compound for the production of crystal **meth,** and its sale can be controlled by community pharmacists. So why were so many packs of pseudoephedrine reportedly found at the crystal **meth** labs and does it cast doubt on the ability of pharmacists to control sales?

The more likely answer is that the gangs producing crystal **meth** use a technique called 'Smurfing'[4], whereby one pack of a pseudoephedrine—containing medicine is purchased by one person at a time—the little people: the Smurfs! Purchase enough small packs and you are in business to produce saleable crystal **meth** with its associated dangers.

The US Solution

The situation in the UK now is akin to the situation that the US found itself in a few years ago—pseudoephedrine could be bought in large quantities for crystal **meth** labs. But the communities in the US were not content to lie down and let it happen; they went on the offensive with an information program of what crystal **meth** would do if left unchecked. They mounted a public information campaign on crystal **meth** and the havoc it can wreak.[4] It is worth visiting the website of The Oregonian newspaper that deals with the crystal **meth** problem to see what can be done.[5,6]

Essentially, pressure was brought upon manufacturers to reformulate their medicines so that the product could not be converted into crystal **meth,** and so phenylephrine replaced pseudoephedrine. It has almost as good a decongestant action but, because it has a hydroxyl group on the benzene ring in a meta position to the propylamine chain, it is much harder, if not impossible, to convert to crystal **meth.**[4]

I have quoted extensively from The Oregonian newspaper because what has been done, in its communities could be done in the UK—they tackled the problem of crystal **meth** 'head on', and seem to be winning.

So, what is to be done here in the UK? If more crystal **meth** labs are discovered, then the MHRA will have no option but to remove pseudoephedrine-containing medicines from sale, depriving patients of a tried and trusted medicament. Some pseudoephedrine-containing products in the UK have been reformulated with phenylephrine, but until this happens for all products, we must all remain super vigilant.

References

1. RPSGB, www.rpsgb.org/pdfs/psephguide.pdf (accessed November H008).
2. Maldonado, R, (ed) Molecular biology of drug addiction, New York, Humana Press 2003.
3. Stahl, S M, Stahl's essential psychopharmacology 3rd edition, Cambridge University Press, 2008.
4. Bovett R, **Meth** lab eradication. www.globalmeth conference.com/prague-08/program.php (accessed November 2008).
5. The Oregonian, www.oregonlive.com/special/oregonian/meth/ (accessed November 2008).
6. The Oregonian, www.oregonlive.com/special/oregonian/meth/pdfs/1006meth_patent.pdf (accessed November 2008)

Critical Thinking

1. Can the U.S. response to combating meth work in the UK?
2. What could the UK do to stop meth before it becomes a major crisis?

Binge Drinking and Its Consequences Up Among American College Students

Scott Krueger, a freshman student at Massachusetts Institute of Technology (MIT), likely bore dreams of achieving academic glory and a long life of happiness and success. But those dreams were cut short when, in 1997, he died of alcohol poisoning with his blood–alcohol level at five times the drunken driving standards in that state. His fraternity brothers reported that he had multiple drinks within a short period of time—he was binge drinking.

However, Scott isn't the only college student who has met his demise through industrial-strength guzzling. In 1995, 318 people, ages 15–24, died from alcohol poisoning alone, many of them after a night binge at college. At the University of Virginia, a tradition called "Fourth-year Fifth," which has seniors drinking a fifth of hard liquor at the final game of the football season, has killed 18 students since 1990. The long-term risks of college drinking practices are just as sobering. As many as 300,000 of today's students will eventually die of alcohol-related causes such as drunk driving accidents, cirrhosis of the liver, heart disease, and various cancers.

But apparently the countless tragedies and alarming statistics have done nothing to curtail the habit. In fact, according to a new study from the U.S. National Institute on Alcohol Abuse and Alcoholism, binge drinking among American college students is on the rise; as is its consequences. From 1999 to 2005, the percentage of students aged 18 to 24 who said they had binged on alcohol in the last month rose from 41.7 percent to nearly 45 percent; drunk driving proportions among this group increased from 26.5 percent to almost 29 percent and the number of drinking-related deaths went from 1,440 in 1998 to 1,825 in 2005, an increase of 3 percent. But the greatest increase was seen in death from unintentional poisoning, which nearly tripled between 1998 and 2005.

But alcohol misuse among college students doesn't just affect the individual drinker; there are often consequences for other students, faculty members, the college, and the community as a whole. Consider these statistics:

- More than 696,000 students between the ages of 18 and 24 are assaulted by another student who has been drinking.
- More than 97,000 students between the ages of 18 and 24 are victims of alcohol-related sexual assault or date rape.
- 400,000 students between the ages of 18 and 24 had unprotected sex and more than 100,000 students between the ages of 18 and 24 report having been too intoxicated to know if they consented to having sex.
- About 11 percent of college student drinkers report that they have damaged property while under the influence of alcohol.
- More than 25 percent of administrators from schools with relatively low drinking levels and over 50 percent from schools with high drinking levels say their campuses have a "moderate" or "major" problem with alcohol-related property damage.

But many experts say the problem often begins before college. Recently, a study presented at the 2009 meeting of the Society for Prevention Research in Washington, D.C. revealed that the earlier alcohol is introduced to a child, the greater the likelihood that he or she will binge drink in college. Moreover, "the greater number of drinks that a parent set as a limit for the teens, the more often they drank and got drunk in college," said researcher Caitlin Abar of the Prevention Research and Methodology Center at Pennsylvania State University. On the other hand, whether the parents themselves drank appeared to have little effect on predicting their child's behaviors toward teen alcohol use.

In 31 states, parents can legally serve alcohol to their underage children. And though U.S. teenagers drink less often than adults, they tend to drink more at a time—five drinks in a sitting, on average—according to lead researcher Ralph Hingson, director of the institute's division of epidemiology and prevention research. "We as a society have a collective responsibility to try and change this culture of drinking at colleges and among young people," he said.

A growing number of colleges and universities are addressing campus drinking problems by providing prevention education; expanding counseling services; and offering more alternatives, such as alcohol-free parties. Hingson said that a number of these interventions have been shown to work, but that some colleges are not implementing them. "The challenge for us is to make sure colleges understand what things are working," he said. "We have to get them to expand screening and interventions to reach wider populations of students and work with communities."

Hingson says efforts similar to those used to reduce smoking are needed to deal with the drinking problem among our youth. "We as a society have a collective responsibility to try and change this culture of drinking at colleges and among young people." Dr. David L. Katz, director of the Prevention Research Center at Yale University School of Medicine, says for that to happen, society needs to take drinking among college students more seriously and the practice needs to be discouraged by those whose opinions matter the most—friends in their own peer group. "Options for bad judgment available to a college student are determined by society, and ours is decidedly ambivalent about alcohol," Katz said. "Drinking to excess is often given favorable treatment in the media, and in social groups."

At the same time, all of us must encourage college students to take personal responsibility for making healthy choices with the only lives they will ever have. Drinking to excess doesn't need to be a rite of passage and driving under the influence isn't a requirement for graduation.

Critical Thinking

1. Do wider social views toward college drinking influence it? Why?
2. What could colleges do to prevent students binge drinking?

Public Lands: Cartels Turn U.S. Forests into Marijuana Plantations Creating Toxic Mess

PHIL TAYLOR

Empty turtle shells, decaying skunk carcasses and a set of deer antlers lay strewn about an empty campsite in California's Sierra National Forest.

The butchered animals, as well as several five-pound propane canisters, camp stoves, and heaps of trash, were all that remained of the 69 marijuana plantations recently uncovered in Fresno County as part of operation "Save our Sierras."

The massive operation that began in February has already seized about 318,000 marijuana plants worth an estimated $1.1 billion, officials announced last week. In addition to 82 arrests, the multijurisdictional federal, state, and local operation netted 42 pounds of processed marijuana, more than $40,000 in cash, 25 weapons and three vehicles.

"Mexican drug trafficking organizations have been operating on public lands to cultivate marijuana, with serious consequences for the environment and public safety," said Gil Kerlikowske, chief of the White House's Office of National Drug Control Policy at a briefing on the investigation.

Subjects arrested were booked on charges of cultivation of marijuana, possession for sale, possession of a firearm during commission of a felony, and conspiracy.

The drug plantations are as much an environmental menace as they are a public safety threat.

Growers in Fresno County used a cocktail of pesticides and fertilizers many times stronger than what is used on residential lawns to cultivate their crop. "This stuff leaches out pretty quickly," said Shane Krogen, executive director of the High Sierra Volunteer Trail Crew in charge of helping clear the land of chemicals and trash so it can begin its slow restoration.

While the chemical pesticides kill insects and other organisms directly, fertilizer runoff contaminates local waterways and aids in the growth of algae and weeds. The vegetation in turn impedes water flows that are critical to frogs, toads, and salamanders in the Kings and San Joaquin rivers, Krogen said.

Northward-Shifting Operations

The Sierra operations are the latest in a growing number of illegal plantations run by foreign suppliers who have moved north of the U.S.–Mexico border where they are closer to U.S. drug markets. Of the 82 individuals arrested in the "Save our Sierras" sting, all but two were Mexican or some other foreign nationality.

Bankrolled by sophisticated drug cartels, suppliers are sidestepping border patrols to grow in relative obscurity on Forest Service, Bureau of Land Management and National Park Service lands across the West and even into the Southeast.

"It's easier to cross the border to grow marijuana on public lands than to grow it in Mexico and smuggle it across," Krogen said.

Earlier this month, $2.5 million worth of marijuana was seized from a sophisticated pot-growing operation in the mountains near Colorado's Cheesman Reservoir in the Pike National Forest. In early June, hikers in a remote area of southwest Idaho stumbled upon a marijuana crop that netted 12,545 marijuana plants with an estimated street value of $6.3 million.

"There is a growing issue of marijuana cultivation on public lands in the U.S., especially in California and Oregon, and it appears they have discovered southwestern Idaho," said BLM special agent in charge Loren Good.

Temperate climates on the West Coast have nurtured what has become a booming marijuana market. The number of marijuana plants confiscated by Forest Service officials has risen by an average of 51 percent in each of the past four years, reaching a high of 3.3 million plants in 2008.

The number of plants seized in California national forests alone has risen steadily from 569,000 in 2003 to 2.4 million in 2008.

"It's definitely a trend," said Keith McGrath, a law enforcement officer in BLM's Idaho office who was part of last month's raid in a far-flung desert canyon.

"We're seeing a shift to more organized grows and larger grows," McGrath said. "They're being set up and run through the cartels, and it's becoming a big chunk of our work load."

Strengthening Law Enforcement

Federal agencies are responding by beefing up law enforcement patrols and investing in technologies like helicopter surveillance and unmanned aerial drones to track down marijuana growers operating in California's lush woodlands.

Forest Service law enforcement staff was doubled from 14 to 28 agents in California between 2007 and 2008, said spokesman John Heil, resulting in the eradication of 3.1 million marijuana plants in the last fiscal year.

Congress is responding too, with a recent $3 million supplemental appropriation secured by Sen. Dianne Feinstein (D-Calif.) that allowed the Park Service to add 25 new law enforcement officers to its Pacific Region parks, said Ron Sundergill, regional director for the Washington, D.C.-based National Parks Conservation Association.

Sundergill applauded the land management agencies for increasing the pressure on illegal growers but said he fears such efforts are depleting agencies' already-thin budgets for things like interpretive services and ranger tours.

"Our parks shouldn't have to spend their limited resources fighting drug cartels when those resources could instead be used to educate and inspire our children—the future stewards of our national parks," Sundergill said.

More money is likely to be provided if Congress approves Interior's fiscal 2010 budget later this year. Feinstein, who chairs the subcommittee in charge of Interior Spending, said she was concerned over the increasing threat of drug cartels on public lands and would look to increase resources for enforcement.

Meanwhile, agency officials say they will remain vigilant in seeking out marijuana growers, even as they venture deeper into the nation's public lands network.

"As more pressure happens in California, they're going to start looking at Oregon, Nevada, and Idaho," said Krogen, of the High Sierra Volunteer Trail Crew. "Then they'll start looking at the Southeast too, closer to distribution."

Critical Thinking

1. How would you go about deterring the cartels from using public lands as their personal marijuana plantations?
2. Can you think of other ways in which we are affected by this type of behavior?

Pseudoephedrine Smurfing Fuels Surge in Large-Scale Methamphetamine Production in California

Preface

This Situation Report is in response to a request from the Office of National Drug Control Policy for information regarding pseudoephedrine smurfing in California. The National Drug Intelligence Center collected and analyzed data and reporting from 2007 through May 2009 related to methamphetamine production and pseudoephedrine smurfing. This report draws upon data from the National Seizure System (NSS) as well as information obtained through interviews with federal, state, and local law enforcement officers.

Executive Summary

Pseudoephedrine smurfing* has become increasingly organized and widespread in California, particularly since 2007, fueling an increase in the number of large-scale methamphetamine laboratories in the state.[1] Among the increased number of large-scale laboratories are those operated by Mexican criminal groups that have relocated to California from Mexico since 2007. Mexican criminal groups and some independent operators are increasingly acquiring bulk quantities of pseudoephedrine through smurfing. Despite strong efforts by law enforcement to curtail smurfing, there is no indication that this practice will decline in the near term. In fact, pseudoephedrine acquired through smurfing in California in 2009 was sent in bulk to methamphetamine producers in Mexico, an indication that some criminal groups in Mexico still find it easier to acquire pseudoephedrine through smurfing in California than from other sources.

Discussion

Pseudoephedrine smurfing increased significantly in California in 2008 and early 2009. The incidence of individuals and criminal groups organizing pseudoephedrine smurfing operations that supply pseudoephedrine to California-based methamphetamine producers has increased throughout California. These smurfing operations began to gain prominence in late 2007, when pseudoephedrine availability and methamphetamine production decreased in Mexico. For instance, in October 2007, a Fresno County investigation revealed that a couple had been conducting daily precursor chemical smurfing operations, soliciting homeless individuals to travel from store to store to purchase pseudoephedrine. In exchange, the couple paid each person approximately $30 and sometimes gave the individuals alcohol. Evidence seized from the couple's vehicle included packages of pseudoephedrine, pharmacy listings torn from an area telephone directory, and several cellular telephones. Similar smurfing operations increased in 2008 and have continued at high levels in 2009. In fact, law enforcement officials in 21 large California cities report that pseudoephedrine smurfing increased in their areas in 2008 and 2009.

Methamphetamine production in California-based superlabs[†] has increased since 2007 because of pseudoephedrine supplied to producers through organized smurfing. Large-scale methamphetamine production by Mexican criminal groups increased in California in 2008 and early 2009 as many methamphetamine producers in Mexico relocated to California, most likely because pseudoephedrine had become more available to some producers through smurfing in California than it was in Mexico. The rise in large-scale methamphetamine production is evidenced by increased methamphetamine superlab and dumpsite seizures. NSS data indicate that the number of superlabs seized in California increased from 10 in 2007 to 15 in 2008. Moreover, the proportion of larger superlabs (those capable of producing 20 or more pounds of methamphetamine) increased during that period from 2 of 10 superlabs in 2007 to 5 of 15 in 2008. Keeping pace with 2008 seizures, 7 superlab seizures were reported to NSS for California in 2009 (through May 26), 5 of them capable of producing 20 or more pounds of methamphetamine.

---

* Smurfing is a method used by some methamphetamine and precursor chemical traffickers to acquire large quantities of pseudoephedrine. Individuals purchase pseudoephedrine in quantities at or below legal thresholds from multiple retail locations. Traffickers often enlist the assistance of several associates in smurfing operations to increase the speed with which chemicals are acquired.

† Superlabs are laboratories capable of producing 10 or more pounds of methamphetamine in a single production cycle.

According to Central Valley California High Intensity Drug Trafficking Area reporting, the superlabs operating in that area—the primary large-scale methamphetamine production area in the United States—are producing methamphetamine with pseudoephedrine acquired primarily through California-based smurfing operations. In fact, the Fresno and Stanislaus/San Joaquin Methamphetamine Task Forces report that officers at laboratory sites commonly find evidence of large-scale and organized smurfing, including pseudoephedrine product price lists, store receipts, coupons for pseudoephedrine products, pseudoephedrine product packaging, paper shredders, gallon-size freezer bags, and 5-gallon plastic buckets filled with various commercial brands of pseudoephedrine tablets.[2] In addition, officers frequently discover trash bags full of pseudoephedrine blister packs and empty bags containing residue from pseudoephedrine tablets at laboratory dump-sites in their area, which is a further evidence of large-scale pseudoephedrine smurfing. By 2009, California pseudoephedrine smurfing had increased to the extent that some Los Angeles area smurfers were not only supplying pseudoephedrine for large-scale production in California but also supplying pseudoephedrine to methamphetamine producers in Mexico.[3]

Intelligence Gaps

The actual number of methamphetamine superlabs operating in California is unknown and may be much higher than the laboratory seizure number—which has increased—suggests. Law enforcement reporting indicates that superlabs are becoming more difficult to detect, not because there are fewer laboratories, but because laboratory operators have adapted to law enforcement pressure and improved their laboratory concealment methods by operating in remote areas.[6] As a result, there may be significantly more large-scale production at undetected superlabs than the laboratory seizure data indicate.

Outlook

The number of superlabs in California will remain relatively high in the near term as criminal groups and individuals supply laboratory operators with bulk pseudoephedrine acquired through smurfing. There is no indication that pseudoephedrine smurfing will decline in the near term. Smurfing is widespread, well organized, and increasing throughout California. The continued ban on pseudoephedrine

Methamphetamine Production in Mexico

Ephedrine and pseudoephedrine import restrictions in Mexico resulted in decreased Mexican methamphetamine production in 2007.[4] In 2005, the government of Mexico (GOM) began implementing progressively increasing restrictions on the importation of ephedrine and pseudoephedrine and other chemicals used for methamphetamine production. In fact, in 2007, the GOM announced a prohibition on ephedrine and pseudoephedrine imports into Mexico for 2008 and a ban on the use of both chemicals in Mexico by 2009.[5] Pseudoephedrine import restrictions resulted in a significant decrease in methamphetamine production in Mexico in 2007, as evidenced by a reduced flow of the drug from Mexico into the United States. NSS data show a sharp decrease in the amount of methamphetamine seized at or between ports of entry (POEs) along the Southwest Border from 2005 (1,950.26 kg) and 2006 (1,882.01 kg) to 2007 (only 1,046.47 kg)—a 44 percent decrease from 2006 to 2007. NSS data show that the amount of methamphetamine seized at or between POEs along the Southwest Border remained well below 2006 levels in 2008 (1,255.52 kg). The amount of methamphetamine seized at or between POEs along the Southwest Border appears to be trending upward in 2009. As of May 26, 2009, 1,001.29 kilograms of methamphetamine had been seized, possibly suggesting some resurgence of methamphetamine production in Mexico.

Sources

Federal

Executive Office of the President
    Office of National Drug Control Policy
        High Intensity Drug Trafficking Areas
            California Border Alliance Group
            Central Valley California
                Fresno Methamphetamine Task Force
                Stanislaus, San Joaquin Methamphetamine Task Force
            Los Angeles
                Los Angeles County Regional Criminal Information Clearinghouse
            Northern California
U.S. Department of Justice
    Bureau of Justice Assistance
        Western States Information Network
    Drug Enforcement Administration
        El Paso Intelligence Center
            National Seizure System

State and Local

California
    Alameda County Drug Task Force
    Bay Methamphetamine Task Force
    Los Angeles Police Department
    Merced Sheriff's Department
    Sacramento Police Department
    San Diego Law Enforcement Coordination Center

imports into Mexico will most likely limit the availability of the chemical in that country, thereby limiting any incentive for Mexican methamphetamine producers to move their operations back to Mexico. In fact, evidence of California smurfers supplying pseudoephedrine to methamphetamine producers in Mexico in 2009 illustrates the continued difficulty that producers in that country are experiencing in acquiring the chemical.

Endnotes

1. Central Valley California High Intensity Drug Trafficking Area.
2. Fresno Methamphetamine Task Force, Stanislaus, San Joaquin Methamphetamine Task Force.

3. Phone interviews with Los Angeles Police Department, June 4, 2009.
4. NDIC *National Methamphetamine Threat Assessment* 2009, December 2008, Product Number 2008-Q0317-006.
5. United Nations reporting.
6. Fresno Methamphetamine Task Force, Stanislaus, San Joaquin Methamphetamine Task Force.

Critical Thinking

1. How does smurfing impact legal sales of OTC medications?
2. What can be done to eradicate smurfing?

From *United States Department of Justice National Drug Intelligence Center by Situation Report,* (June, 2009). Public Domain.

UNIT 4

Other Trends in Drug Use

Unit Selections

Learning Outcomes

After reading this unit, you should be able to:

- Explain why some drug-related trends are more specific to certain subpopulations of Americans than others.

- Describe the significance of socioeconomic status in influencing drug trends.

- Determine the influences that have contributed to the dramatic spread of prescription drug abuse in the United States.

- Determine what roles advertising and the media play in influencing drug use.

- Explain the factors that cause drug-related trends to change.

Student Website

www.mhhe.com/cls

Internet References

Drug Story.org
www.drugstory.org/drug_stats/druguse_stats.asp

Marijuana as a Medicine
http://mojo.calyx.net/~olsen

Monitoring the Future
www.monitoringthefuture.org

Prescriptions Drug Use and Abuse
www.fda.gov/fdac/features/2001/501_drug.htm

SAMHSA
www.drugabusestatistics.samhsa.gov/trends.htm

United States Drug Trends
www.usdrugtrends.com

Prescription Drug Abuse
www.prescription-drug-abuse.org

Rarely do drug-related patterns and trends lend themselves to precise definition. Identification, measurement, and prediction of the consequence of these trends is an inexact science, to say the least. It is, nevertheless, a very important process. One of the most valuable uses of drug-related trend analysis is the identification of subpopulations whose vulnerability to certain drug phenomena is greater than that of the wider population. These identifications may forewarn of the implications for the general population. Trend analysis may produce specific information that may otherwise be lost or obscured by general statistical indications. For example, tobacco is probably the most prominent of gateway drugs, with repeated findings pointing to the correlation between the initial use of tobacco and the use of other drugs.

The analysis of specific trends related to drug use is very important, as it provides a threshold from which educators, health-care professionals, parents, and policy makers may respond to significant drug-related health threats and issues. Over 20 million Americans report the use of illegal drugs. The current rate of illicit drug use is similar to the rates of the past three years. Marijuana remains as the most commonly used illicit drug with more than 14 million current users.

Historically, popular depressant and stimulant drugs—such as alcohol, tobacco, heroin, and cocaine—produce statistics that identify the most visible and sometimes the most constant use patterns. Other drugs such as marijuana, LSD, ecstasy, and other "club drugs" often produce patterns widely interpreted to be associated with cultural phenomena such as youth attitudes, popular music trends, and political climate.

Two other continuing trends are those that involve the abuse of prescription drugs and those that involve the use of methamphetamine. Americans are abusing prescription drugs more than ever before with the most frequently mentioned offenders being oxycodone and hydrocodone. Currently, more than 5 million persons use prescription pain relievers for nonmedical reasons. Of those who used pain relievers for nonmedical reasons, 56 percent obtained them for free from a friend or relative. As more and more drugs get prescribed within the population, a steady trend, more and more drugs become easily accessible. The National Institute of Drug Abuse reports that 20 percent of the U.S. population over 12 has used prescription drugs for nonmedical reasons. Currently, prescription drug abuse among youth ranks second behind only marijuana. The good news is that drug use by youth has declined or leveled off in several important categories such as those associated with marijuana, alcohol, and methamphetamine. And although methamphetamine use is down, it is reported by local and state officials in the West and Midwest as the number one illegal-drug problem. Although the federal government has modified its survey methods to more accurately identify the number of meth users, many worry that the meth problem is still understated and greatly outweighs those problems associated with other illegal drugs in the West, Southwest, and Midwest. Information concerning drug-use patterns and trends obtained from a number of different investigative methods is available from a variety of sources. On the national level, the more prominent sources are the Substance Abuse and Mental Health Services Administration, the National Institute on Drug Abuse, the Drug Abuse Warning Network, the national Centers for Disease Control, the Justice Department, the Office of National Drug Control Policy, the surgeon general, and the DEA. On the

© McGraw-Hill Companies/Jill Braaten, photographer

state level, various justice departments, including attorney generals' offices, the courts, state departments of social services, state universities and colleges, and public health offices maintain data and conduct research. On local levels, criminal justice agencies, social service departments, public hospitals, and health departments provide information. On a private level, various research institutes and universities, professional organizations such as the American Medical Association and the American Cancer Society, hospitals, and treatment centers, as well as private corporations, are tracking drug-related trends. Surveys abound with no apparent lack of available data. As a result, the need for examination of research methods and findings for reliability and accuracy is self-evident. The articles in this unit provide information about some drug-related trends occurring within certain subpopulations of Americans. While reading the articles, it is interesting to consider how the trends and patterns described are dispersed through various subpopulations of Americans and specific geographical areas. Additionally, much information about drugs and drug trends can be located quickly by referring to the list of websites in the front section of this book.

Adolescent Painkiller Use May Increase Risk of Addiction, Heroin Use

Prescription opiate abuse is not only increasing among adolescents, but it predisposes them to becoming addicted as adults, according to animal research published earlier this month. Furthermore, clinicians report that prescription opiates are now a "gateway" drug that leads to heroin, with adolescent units, typically devoted to alcohol and marijuana, now treating more and more patients for opiate addiction.

"We're terrified," said Mary Jeanne Kreek, MD, professor and head of laboratory at the Laboratory of the Biology of Addictive Diseases at The Rockefeller University in New York City. "We don't know where prescription opiate illicit use is going to go, and we don't know how many will become addicted." Kreek, who with lead author Yong Zhang, PhD, and others conducted the study comparing the effects of oxycodone on adolescent and adult mice, spoke to *ADAW* last week about the effects of prescription opiates on the developing brain.

Adolescents may start using prescription opiates for the same reasons they start using any drug of abuse, said Kreek: risk-taking, impulsivity, and peer pressure. But that initial use could progress to addiction, because of the drug's effects on the dopamine system, she said. With heroin, as many as one in three who ever use it become addicted. In addition, once tried even once, opiates can be alluring to adolescents. "Opiates have what a lot of young people are looking for today—an escape from life's problems," she said.

The Mouse Study

The mouse study found that the lowest dose of oxydocone led to increased dopamine levels in adolescent mice, but not in adult mice. When the adolescent mice were re-exposed to oxycodone as adults, they had higher levels of dopamine than adults who were exposed to the same amount but had not been exposed as adolescents.

In addition, the adolescent mice self-administered smaller amounts of oxycodone, and less frequently, than adult mice did.

These findings suggest that adolescent mice are more sensitive to the oxycodone. Kreek hypothesized that this is because of the state of the adolescent brain, which has rapidly increasing dopamine receptors.

The number of dopamine receptors in the mouse brain increases exponentially from birth to early adolescence, and remain at a plateau at mid-adolescence (the equivalent of age 13 to 16 years) and then begin to decline until adulthood. It is this rapid development of dopamine receptors which might be the key to adolescent sensitivity to drugs.

Epidemiological studies have already proven that the earlier adolescents initiate use of alcohol or cigarettes, the greater the likelihood that they will be dependent as adults. When use is initiated as adults, the chance of subsequent dependence plummets.

"Adolescence is when we are forming our memories, our cues, and learning," said Kreek. "You don't want to batter a brain that's learning, and I look at drug abuse as battering a brain."

Gateway to Heroin

Kreek's study suggests that human adolescents are more sensitive to prescription opiates, said Joseph Frascella, PhD, director of the division of clinical neuroscience at the National Institute on Drug Abuse (NIDA), which funded the study. "We know that the earlier kids get involved in drugs, the more likely they are to have careers in drugs," Frascella told *ADAW*.

"In a sense this is a gateway theory at work—if you start with one drug, does it lead you down the path to another, like heroin," said Frascella. "I really don't think we know the answer to this yet. It could be that the kids who are willing to do these heavy drugs have some kind of brain vulnerability."

But even if science is still studying the reasons behind adolescent use of opiates, treatment providers see the effects. In Buffalo, N.Y., providers are reporting increased numbers of young people coming in with prescription opiate dependency and with heroin addiction. "When we opened in 1990, the three major gateway drugs were marijuana, alcohol, and nicotine," said Dick Gallagher, executive director of Alcohol and Drug Dependency Services, Inc., a 210-bed treatment facility for adolescents and young adults. "Now, there are four gateway drugs, and one is prescription opiates," he said.

Buffalo is a case in point because heroin is less expensive than prescription opiates there, because both are popular among young people there, and because the treatment system is coping with so much opiate dependency among adolescents, according to treatment providers.

"Ten years ago we would see five people a month in trouble with prescription opiates," said Robert B. Whitney, M.D., attending physician in the division of chemical dependency at Erie County Medical Center in Buffalo, where there are 700 out-patient slots and 400 beds for addiction treatment. "Now we see more than five a day."

And prescription opiates are a gateway for heroin use, Whitney told *ADAW*. "There's a limit to how much Oxycontin or hydrocodone they can get just to maintain themselves," he said. "They find that with heroin, they may get better management of their withdrawal."

Whitney described a typical pathway to heroin, with prescription drugs as the gateway. The user starts with oral opiates, moving to crushing and snorting them, to snorting heroin. These people say "at least I'm not using a needle," said Whitney. However, eventually many find that snorting the heroin gets too expensive or they can't maintain their addiction, and they move to intravenous use.

"There's a pattern of kids that have utilized the painkillers, and want to go on to the next level," Gallagher said. Heroin is less expensive than prescription opiates, and it's accessible, he said.

The Adolescent and Pain

What if an adolescent takes a prescription opiate for pain—does the Kreek study imply that this adolescent will be at greater risk for later addiction? "That's an excellent question," said NIDA's Frascella. "The data seem to suggest that if you take a medication for pain, there's a different response than if you take it just to get high."

Kreek agreed. "We do know that persons in severe pain have a different neurobiological substrate," she said.

However, Kreek warned that opiates are overprescribed for acute pain. "I'm not talking about cancer and chronic pain," she said. But it's not necessary for someone to get two weeks' supply of painkillers when they only need 48 hours' worth, she said. "We can talk to the patient in two days and see if we've misjudged," she said. "But in general you can step down to a much lighter drug."

And Whitney in Buffalo related a story of a patient who three years ago at the age of 15 was in a car accident and went home from the hospital with a legitimate prescription for hydrocodone. "Within a month she was taking not only what they gave her but what she could get from her friends," he said. This girl—initially a patient in his hospital due to a car accident—became his patient due to heroin addiction.

"For sure prescription opiates are a gateway drug," said Whitney. "They're getting the heroin problem into a population that we did not see using opiates at all before." This population of young people requires long-term treatment.

Gallagher agreed, saying that for the adolescents, treatment for opiate addiction must be go on for months. "Don't think you can treat these kids in 28 days unless you have intensive support after," he said.

The Kreek study of mice lends credence to what the treatment providers are reporting. "If you want to make the jump to humans—which we shouldn't do, but we do—our findings suggest that recovery [from opiate addiction] is very slow," Kreek told *ADAW*, adding that the findings also show chemically that adolescent brains do have special vulnerabilities to opiates.

Resources

"Behavioral and Neurochemical Changes Induced by Oxycodone Differ Between Adolescent and Adult Mice" is published in the current issue of *Neuropsychopharmacology*. For the full text, go to http://www.nature.com/npp/journal/vaop/ncurrent/full/npp2008134a.html.

Critical Thinking

1. Adolescents are more susceptible to addiction while abusing prescription drugs. What are the reasons for this, and why is it important in relation to age and drug abuse?

2. How can parents address this?

Caffeinated Energy Drinks— A Growing Problem

CHAD J. REISSIG, ERIC C. STRAIN, AND ROLAND R. GRIFFITHS

Introduction

In 2006, annual worldwide energy drink consumption increased 17% from the previous year to 906 million gallons, with Thailand leading the world in energy drink consumption per person, but the U.S. leading the world in total volume sales (Zenith International, 2007). Although "energy drinks" first appeared in Europe and Asia in the 1960s, the introduction of "Red Bull" in Austria in 1987 and in the U.S. in 1997 sparked the more recent trend toward aggressive marketing of high caffeine content "energy drinks". Since its inception, the energy drink market has grown exponentially, with nearly 500 new brands launched worldwide in 2006 (Johnson, 2006), and 200 new brands launched in the U.S. in the 12-month period ending July 2007 (Packaged Facts, 2007). From 2002 to 2006, the average annual growth rate in energy drink sales was 55% (Packaged Facts, 2007) (Fig. 1). The total U.S. retail market value for energy drinks (from all sources) was estimated to be $5.4 billion in 2006 and has shown a similar annual growth rate over this same period (47%) (Packaged Facts, 2007). These drinks vary widely in both caffeine content (ranging from 50 to 505 mg per can or bottle) and caffeine concentration (ranging from 2.5 to 171 mg per fluid ounce) (Table 1). For comparison, the caffeine content of a 6 oz cup of brewed coffee varies from 77 to 150 mg (Griffiths et al., 2003). The main active ingredient in energy drinks is caffeine, although other substances such as taurine, riboflavin, pyridoxine, nicotinamide, other B vitamins, and various herbal derivatives are also present (Aranda and Morlock, 2006). The acute and long-term effects resulting from excessive and chronic consumption of these additives alone and in combination with caffeine are not fully known. Although the full impact of the rise in popularity of energy drinks has yet to be realized, the potential for adverse health consequences should be considered and may be cause for preemptive regulatory action.

Regulatory Aspects

The regulation of beverages to which caffeine is added has been challenging, partly because of the widespread and long-term use of beverages such as coffee and tea in which caffeine is a natural constituent. Nonetheless, several countries have enacted measures to regulate the labeling, distribution, and sale of energy drinks that contain significant quantities of caffeine. The European Union requires that energy drinks have a "high caffeine content" label

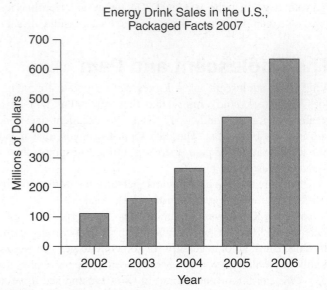

Figure 1 Energy drink sales in millions of dollars in the United States from 2002 to 2006. Data are based on scanner data from over 32,000 stores such as supermarkets, drug stores, and discount merchandisers other than Wal-Mart. Data are from retailers with $2 million or more in annual sales but exclude: club-stores/warehouse clubs, convenience stores, dollar/variety stores, foodservice, vending, concession sales and specialty channels/retailers of all types (e.g., gourmet/specialty food stores, hardware/home improvements stores, military exchanges). Energy Drinks in the U.S., Packaged Facts 2007.

(European Union, 2007) and Canada requires labels indicating that Red Bull should not be mixed with alcohol and that maximum daily consumption not exceed two 8.3 oz cans (Health Canada, 2005). Norway restricts the sale of Red Bull to pharmacies, while France (until recently) and Denmark have prohibited the sale of Red Bull altogether (Ari Kapner, 2004).

The history of the regulation of caffeine containing beverages in the U.S. serves as an illustrative example of the complexity of the regulatory issues involved in their sale, use, and promotion. Historically, the U.S. Food and Drug Administration (FDA) has regulated caffeine-containing soft drinks as foods. In 1980, citing health concerns about caffeine, the FDA proposed to eliminate

Table 1   Energy Drinks in the United States

	Ounces per Bottle or Can	Caffeine Concentration (mg/oz)	Total Caffeine (mg)
Top selling energy drinks[a]			
Red Bull	8.3	9.6	80
Monster	16	10	160
Rockstar	16	10	160
Full throttle	16	9	144
No Fear	16	10.9	174
Amp	8.4	8.9	75
SoBe Adrenaline Rush	8.3	9.5	79
Tab Energy	10.5	9.1	95
Higher caffeine energy drinks[b]			
Wired X505	24	21	505
Fixx	20	25	500
BooKoo Energy	24	15	360
Wired X344	16	21.5	344
SPIKE Shooter	8.4	35.7	300
Viso Energy Vigor	20	15	300
Cocaine Energy Drink	8.4	33.3	280
Jolt Cola	23.5	11.9	280
NOS	16	16.3	250
Redline RTD	8	31.3	250
Blow (Energy Drink Mix)	8	30	240
Lower caffeine energy drinks[b]			
Bomba Energy	8.4	8.9	75
HiBall Energy	10	7.5	75
Airforce Nutrisoda Energize	8.5	5.9	50
Whoop Ass	8.5	5.9	50
Vitamin Water (Energy Citrus)	20	2.5	50
High concentration energy drinks[b]			
RedLine Power Rush	2.5	140	350
Ammo	1	171	171
Powershot	1	100	100
Fuel Cell	2	90	180
Classic soft drinks			
Coca-Cola Classic	12	2.9	34.5
Pepsi Cola	12	3.2	38
Dr Pepper	12	3.4	41
Mountain Dew	12	4.5	54

Data on drink volume and caffeine content were obtained from the manufacturer via product label, website, or personal communication with manufacturer representatives. The one exception was that the caffeine content for BooKoo Energy was obtained from the energyfiend website (Energyfiend website, 2008) which indicates the information was obtained from a Boo-Koo representative. When the authors contacted the BooKoo company directly, a BooKoo representative refused to disclose the drink's caffeine content but did indicate that accurate information for the caffeine content of BooKoo Energy was available online.

[a]Top selling energy drinks in the U.S. 2006, listed sequentially as a percentage of market share (Packaged Facts, 2007, used with permission).

[b]Examples of energy drinks drawn from the hundreds of energy drink products currently marketed in the U.S., listed sequentially on total caffeine content.

caffeine from soft drinks (Food and Drug Administration, 1980). In response, soft drink manufacturers justified adding caffeine to soft drinks on the basis that caffeine was a flavor enhancer (PepsiCo Inc., 1981), although the scientific basis for that claim has since been challenged (Griffiths and Vernotica, 2000; Keast and Riddell, 2007). If caffeine had not been accepted as a flavor enhancer, but had been regarded as a psychoactive ingredient, soft drinks might have been regulated by the FDA as drugs. However, the FDA approved caffeine and limited the maximum caffeine content of cola-type soft drinks to 0.02% caffeine, or 71 mg/12 fluid oz (Food and Drug Administration, 2003).

Although drink manufacturers initially complied with the FDA caffeine limits, the marketplace has changed dramatically since the introduction of energy drinks. At least 130 energy drinks now exceed 0.02% caffeine (Energyfiend website, 2008), including one that contains 505 mg in a 24 oz can (the equivalent of 14 cans of a typical cola or several cups of coffee) (Table 1). Many manufacturers are not subject to the prior caffeine limits by claiming that their new products fall under the 1994 Dietary Supplement Health and Education Act, which classifies products deriving from herbs and natural sources as dietary supplements rather than drugs (Ari Kapner, 2004). Other manufacturers appear to be ignoring the FDA caffeine limits and FDA has not enforced the limits. The FDA has been lax in regulating the caffeine content of energy drinks and does not require warning labels advising proper use or the amount of caffeine in the product, as it does for over-the-counter (OTC) caffeine-containing stimulants. According to the FDA (Food and Drug Administration, 2007a), over-the-counter stimulant drug products must contain the following warnings and directions on the product label:

- The recommended dose of this product contains about as much caffeine as a cup of coffee. Limit the use of caffeine-containing medications, foods, or beverages while taking this product because too much caffeine may cause nervousness, irritability, sleeplessness, and, occasionally, rapid heart beat.
- For occasional use only. Not intended for use as a substitute for sleep. If fatigue or drowsiness persists or continues to recur, consult a (select one of the following: "physician" or "doctor").
- Do not give to children under 12 years of age.
- Directions: Adults and children 12 years of age and over: oral dosage is 100–200 mg not more often than every 3–4 h.

It is a striking inconsistency that, in the U.S. an OTC stimulant medication containing 100 mg of caffeine per tablet (e.g. NoDoz) must include all the above warnings, whereas a 500 mg energy drink can be marketed with no such warnings and no information on caffeine dose amount in the product.

Advertising

Energy drinks are promoted for their stimulant effects and claim to offer a variety of benefits including increased attention, endurance and performance, weight loss, and "having fun, kicking butt and making a difference" (Bookoo website, 2008). The majority of these claims however, remain to be substantiated. The most

consistent result to emerge is that caffeine reduces performance decrements due to reduced alertness (e.g. conditions of fatigue, or sleep deprivation) (Bonnet et al., 2005). Other studies have shown that, relative to placebo, caffeine can increase long-term exercise endurance, and improve speed and/or power output (Graham, 2001; Doherty and Smith, 2004; Doherty et al., 2004; Wiles et al., 2006). However, because many of the studies claiming to demonstrate performance enhancement by caffeine have been confounded by caffeine withdrawal, there is debate over whether caffeine has net positive or performance enhancing effects (e.g. improved mood, alertness or mental function) (Haskell et al., 2005; Childs and de Wit, 2006) or whether these effects are due to the reversal of caffeine withdrawal symptoms (James, 1998; Heatherley et al., 2005; Rogers et al., 2003, 2005; James and Rogers, 2005). Based on preclinical literature that clearly documents the behavioral stimulant effects of caffeine (Dews, 1984), it seems quite likely that caffeine enhances human performance on some types of tasks (e.g., vigilance) (Stafford et al., 2007), especially among non-tolerant individuals. Among high-dose habitual consumers, performance enhancements above and beyond withdrawal reversal effects are likely to be modest at best (James and Rogers, 2005).

Advertising of energy drinks is targeted primarily towards young males, with alluring product names such as "Full Throttle", "AMP Energy" and "Cocaine". These advertising campaigns promote the psychoactive, performance-enhancing, and stimulant effects of energy drinks and appear to glorify drug use. In a survey of 795 undergraduate students, self-reported measures of masculinity and risk taking behaviors were positively associated with frequency of energy drink consumption (Miller, 2008).

One of the more blatant examples of such advertising tactics is found in the drink additive "Blow". This "energy drink additive" is packaged in glass vials and shipped with a mirror and plastic credit cards in an apparent attempt to model cocaine use. Blow founder Logan Gola describes the product as "sexy, edgy and fun" (PR Newswire Association, 2007). The energy drink "Cocaine" was initially marketed as "The Legal Alternative" with its product name displayed as a white granular substance which resembled cocaine powder (Food and Drug Administration, 2007b; Cocaine website, 2008), and with video clips on the company website showing consumers "snorting" its liquid product. Recently, the FDA claimed jurisdiction over both "Cocaine" (Food and Drug Administration, 2007b) and "Blow" (Food and Drug Administration, 2008), informing the companies that their products were marketed as an alternative to an illicit street drug, not a dietary supplement, and subject to regulation as a drug. In early 2008, the manufacturer re-released "Cocaine", with revised product claims, yet retaining the drink's characteristic moniker, "Cocaine" still prominently displayed as a white powdery substance resembling cocaine powder (Cocaine website, 2008; Kotaku website, 2008). The product "Blow" currently remains on the market.

The marketing of energy drinks as products to be used for their stimulant and recreational effects stands in marked contrast to the marketing of soft drinks. For decades, advertising for soft drinks has been restricted to rather innocuous and somewhat ambiguous claims such as those used to promote CocaCola: "The pause that refreshes" (Pendergast, 1993). As mentioned previously, in response to an FDA proposal to eliminate caffeine from soft drinks, soft drink manufacturers justified adding caffeine by calling it a flavor enhancer (PepsiCo Inc., 1981). After claiming that caffeine was added just for its flavor, manufacturers were likely reluctant to publicly promote their products as stimulants for fear of jeopardizing their regulatory rationale for adding caffeine. No such restraint is exercised on promotion of energy drinks, many of which are regulated under the 1994 dietary supplement act.

Caffeine Toxicity/Overdose

Concern regarding the caffeine content of energy drinks is prompted by the potential adverse consequences of caffeine use. One such adverse effect is caffeine intoxication, a recognized clinical syndrome included in the Diagnostic and Statistical Manual of Mental Disorders (DSM-IV-TR) and the World Health Organization's International Classification of Diseases (ICD-10) (American Psychiatric Association, 1994; World Health Organization, 1992a,b). Caffeine toxicity is defined by specific symptoms that emerge as a direct result of caffeine consumption. Common features of caffeine intoxication include nervousness, anxiety, restlessness, insomnia, gastrointestinal upset, tremors, tachycardia, psychomotor agitation (American Psychiatric Association, 1994) and in rare cases, death (Garriott et al., 1985; Kerrigan and Lindsey, 2005; Mrvos et al., 1989). The symptoms of caffeine intoxication can mimic those of anxiety and other mood disorders (Greden, 1974).

The consumption of energy drinks may increase the risk for caffeine overdose in caffeine abstainers as well as habitual consumers of caffeine from coffee, soft drinks, and tea. The potential for acute caffeine toxicity due to consumption of energy drinks may be greater than other dietary sources of caffeine for several reasons:

1. Lack of adequate labeling: As mentioned earlier, many energy drinks do not label their product with the amount of caffeine, and are not required to display warning labels advising proper use. Consumers may be completely unaware of the amount of caffeine they are ingesting.

2. Advertising: Many energy drinks are marketed with claims of performance enhancing effects although, as discussed previously, the existence and extent of such effects is subject to debate. Red Bull, for example, advertises several benefits of consumption including improved performance, endurance, concentration and reaction speed, and increased metabolism (Red Bull website, 2008). Consumers may falsely believe that "more is better" and ingest multiple servings of these products. As an added risk, some energy drinks encourage rapid consumption of their products. For instance, "Spike Shooter" claims "the flavor's so good, you'll want to slam the whole can" (Spikeshooter website, 2008).

3. Consumer demographics: Since there are no restrictions on the sale of energy drinks, adolescents and children (who may be inexperienced and less tolerant to the effects of caffeine) may be at an increased risk for caffeine intoxication.

Forty-one cases of caffeine abuse from caffeine-enhanced beverages were reported to a U.S. poison control center from 2002 to 2004 (McCarthy et al., 2006). Another U.S. poison control center reported nine cases of adverse reactions to the energy drink Redline from January 2004 to March 2006. Eight of the nine patients were male, the youngest being 13 years of age. The symptoms were: nausea/vomiting (56%), tachycardia (44%), hypertension (100%) (for patients evaluated in a health care facility), jittery/agitated/tremors (67%), dizziness (44%), chest pain (11%) and bilateral numbness (11%) (Walsh et al., 2006). In a survey of 496 college students, 51% reported consuming at least one energy drink during the last month (Malinauskas et al., 2007). Of these energy drink users, 29% reported "weekly jolt and crash episodes", 22% reported headaches, and 19% reported heart palpitations from drinking energy drinks (Malinauskas et al., 2007).

Media reports have also highlighted several cases of caffeine intoxication resulting from energy drink consumption. A 28-year-old motorcycle (motocross) athlete nearly died when his heart stopped during a competition. He had consumed eight cans of Red Bull over a 5 h period (Dasey, 2007). "Spike Shooter" has been removed from several U.S. convenience stores, and banned from local high schools when students became sick after consuming cans of the product that were purported to have been given away at a promotional event (Brooks, 2007; Simon and Mosher, 2007). Similar action has been taken at another U.S. high school after two student athletes fainted after drinking "Speed Stack" (Lunen, 2007). Local store owners have also banned the selling of energy drinks to minors, after three teenage boys displayed signs of caffeine intoxication after rapidly ingesting "BooKoo" energy drink (Lunen, 2007).

In addition to caffeine intoxication, the consumption of energy drinks has been linked to seizures (Iyadurai and Chung, 2007), acute mania (Machado-Vieira et al., 2001), and stroke (Worrall et al., 2005). Deaths attributed to energy drink consumption have been reported in Australia, Ireland and Sweden (Ari Kapner, 2004). Considerable debate has ensued as to whether these fatalities were a direct result of energy drink consumption.

Caffeine Dependence

The DSM-IV-TR defines substance dependence using a generic set of cognitive, physiological, and behavioral symptoms, including the inability to quit, use despite harm, using more than intended, withdrawal, and tolerance. Although DSMIV-TR specifically excludes caffeine from its diagnostic schema for substance dependence, the World Health Organization's International Classification of Diseases (ICD-10) includes this diagnosis (World Health Organization, 1992a,b). While there is debate regarding the extent of reinforcing effects and abuse potential of caffeine, there is compelling evidence that caffeine can produce a substance dependence syndrome in some people (Bernstein et al., 2002; Hughes et al., 1998; Jones and Lejuez, 2005; Oberstar et al., 2002; Richards et al., 2004; Strain et al., 1994; Svikis et al., 2005). For example, studies in adults (Richards et al., 2004; Strain et al., 1994) and adolescents (Bernstein et al., 2002; Oberstar et al., 2002) have shown high rates of endorsement of inability to quit, use despite harm, and withdrawal. A population-based survey showed that 30% of a sample of 162 caffeine users fulfilled diagnostic criteria for substance dependence when applied to caffeine (Hughes et al., 1998). The prevalence of caffeine dependence may increase as a result of marketing campaigns promoting the use of energy drinks among adolescents. By analogy with tobacco and alcohol use, the earlier the onset of smoking or drinking, the greater the risk for later dependence (Moolchan et al., 2000; Liepman et al., 2002).

Caffeine Withdrawal

Symptoms of caffeine withdrawal have been described in the medical literature for more than a century (Griffiths and Woodson, 1988). There have been at least 66 studies of caffeine withdrawal in the medical literature, the majority of which have been published within the last 10 years (Juliano and Griffiths, 2004). The symptoms of caffeine withdrawal, the most common of which is headache, beginning 12–24 h after the last dose of caffeine (Driesbach and Pfeiffer, 1943; Lader et al., 1996; Juliano and Griffiths, 2004). In double-blind studies, about 50% of individuals report headache which may be severe in intensity (Silverman et al., 1992; Juliano and Griffiths, 2004). In addition to headache, other caffeine withdrawal symptoms include tiredness/fatigue, sleepiness/drowsiness, dysphoric mood (e.g., miserable, decreased well-being/contentedness), difficulty concentrating/decreased cognitive performance, depression, irritability, nausea/vomiting, and muscle aches/stiffness (Griffiths et al., 1990; Juliano and Griffiths, 2004). These withdrawal symptoms may be severe in intensity, and the incidence of clinically significant distress and impairment in daily functioning due to caffeine withdrawal is 13% in experimental studies (Juliano and Griffiths, 2004). Caffeine withdrawal is recognized as an official diagnosis in ICD-10 and a research diagnosis in DSM-IV-TR. Studies have also documented caffeine withdrawal in teenagers (Hale et al., 1995; Bernstein et al., 2002; Oberstar et al., 2002) and children (Bernstein et al., 1998; Goldstein and Wallace, 1997), the incidence of which may increase substantially with the aggressive marketing of energy drinks to these age groups.

Combined Use of Caffeine and Alcohol May Be Problematic

There is an association between the heavy use of caffeine and the heavy use of alcohol (Istvan and Matarazzo, 1984; Kozlowski et al., 1993), and the ingestion of energy drinks in combination with alcohol is becoming increasingly popular (O'Brien et al., 2008; Oteri et al., 2007), with 24% of a large stratified sample of college students reporting such consumption within the past 30 days (O'Brien et al., 2008). In the previously mentioned survey of 496 college students, 27% reported mixing alcohol and energy drinks in the past month. Of those that mixed energy drinks and alcohol, 49% used more than three energy drinks per occasion when doing so (Malinauskas et al., 2007). In a survey of 1253 college students, energy drink users were disproportionately male and consumed alcohol more frequently than non-energy drink users (Arria et al., 2008).

One study showed that ingestion of a caffeinated energy drink (Red Bull) with vodka reduced participants[1] perception of impairment of motor coordination in comparison to vodka alone, but did not significantly reduce objective measures of alcohol-induced impairment of motor coordination, reaction time, or breath alcohol concentration (Ferreira et al., 2006). These results are consistent with other studies investigating caffeine–alcohol interactions (Marczinski and Fillmore, 2006). Thus, when mixing energy drinks and alcohol, users may not feel the symptoms of alcohol intoxication. This may increase the potential for alcohol-related injury. Indeed, a recent survey of college students found that in comparison to those who consumed alcohol alone, students who consumed alcohol mixed with energy drinks had a significantly higher prevalence of alcohol-related consequences including: being taken advantage of, or taking advantage of another student sexually, riding in an automobile with a driver under the influence of alcohol, or being hurt or injured (O'Brien et al., 2008). In addition, mixing energy drinks with alcohol was associated with increased heavy episodic drinking and episodes of weekly drunkenness (O'Brien et al., 2008). The recent introduction of premixed caffeine–alcohol combination drinks may exacerbate these problems (Simon and Mosher, 2007) and has prompted regulatory action. Accordingly, as part of a legal settlement reached in 2008 with State Attorneys in 11 states in the U.S., Anheuser-Busch has agreed to stop the manufacture and sale of caffeinated alcoholic beverages (State of Idaho Office of the Attorney General website, 2008).

Relationship of Caffeine to Dependence on Other Substances

Studies in adult twins show that lifetime caffeine intake, caffeine toxicity and caffeine dependence are significantly and positively associated with various psychiatric disorders including major depression, generalized anxiety disorder, panic disorder, antisocial personality disorder, alcohol dependence, and cannabis and cocaine abuse/dependence (Kendler et al., 2006). Studies in adult twins examining caffeine use, alcohol use, and cigarette smoking concluded that a common genetic factor (polysubstance use) underlies the use of these three substances (Swan et al., 1996, 1997; Hettema et al., 1999), although another twin study suggested that caffeine and nicotine were associated with genetic factors unique to these substances (Kendler et al., 2007). A study examining the co-occurrence of substance use among drug abusers concluded that dependence on caffeine, nicotine and alcohol were governed by the same factors (Kozlowski et al., 1993). In a study of caffeine dependent adults, Strain et al. (1994) reported a clustering of histories of caffeine, nicotine, and alcohol dependence. In a study of pregnant women, those who fulfilled criteria for a diagnosis of caffeine dependence and who had a family history of alcoholism were six times more likely to have a lifetime history of alcohol abuse or dependence (Svikis et al., 2005).

More specifically, with regard to cigarette smoking, human and animal studies show that caffeine increases the reinforcing effects of nicotine (Gasior et al., 2002; Jones and Griffiths, 2003; Shoaib et al., 1999; Tanda and Goldberg, 2000). Epidemiology studies show that cigarette smokers consume more caffeine than nonsmokers (Parsons and Neims, 1978; Swanson et al., 1994), an effect that may be partially due to increased caffeine metabolism among cigarette smokers (Parsons and Neims, 1978). Self-administration studies show that cigarette smoking and coffee drinking covary temporally within individuals (Emurian et al., 1982; Lane, 1996), although acute caffeine administration does not always increase cigarette smoking (Chait and Griffiths, 1983). As described above, twin and co-occurrence studies suggest links between caffeine use and smoking (Kozlowski et al., 1993; Swan et al., 1996,1997; Hettema et al., 1999). A study of pregnant women showed that those who met criteria for caffeine dependence were nine times more likely to report a history of daily cigarette smoking compared to those who did not meet dependence criteria (Svikis et al., 2005).

Whether caffeine serves as a gateway to other forms of drug dependence as suggested by some studies (Collins et al., 1997; Pallanti et al., 2006) bears further investigation (Packaged Facts,

2007). With regard to energy drinks in particular, one study of 1253 college students found that energy drink consumption significantly predicted subsequent nonmedical prescription stimulant use (Arria et al., 2008). It is plausible that the use of energy drinks that are promoted as alternatives to illicit drugs (e.g. "Blow" and "Cocaine") may, in fact, increase interest in the use of such drugs.

Vulnerability to Caffeine Affected by Tolerance and Genetic Factors

Vulnerability to caffeine intoxication after bolus caffeine doses, such as those delivered in energy drinks, is markedly affected by pharmacological tolerance. Tolerance refers to a decrease in responsiveness to a drug as a result of drug exposure. Daily administration of very high doses of caffeine (e.g. 750–1200 mg/day) can produce complete or partial tolerance to caffeine's subjective, pressor, and neuroendocrine effects (Robertson et al., 1981; Evans and Griffiths, 1992; Griffiths and Mumford, 1996). Thus, individuals such as children and adolescents who do not use caffeine daily, are at greater risk for caffeine intoxication due to energy drink consumption than habitual caffeine consumers.

Genetic factors are relevant to vulnerability to both caffeine intoxication as well as caffeine dependence and withdrawal. Studies comparing monozygotic versus dizygotic twins have shown higher concordance rates for monozygotic twins for caffeine intoxication, total caffeine consumption, heavy use, caffeine tolerance, and caffeine withdrawal, with heritabilities ranging between 35% and 77% (Kendler and Prescott, 1999; Swan et al., 1997). Linkage studies have shown that polymorphisms in the adenosine A_{2A} receptor gene and in adenosine deaminase are associated with individual differences in caffeine consumption and caffeine's effects on EEG, anxiety, and sleep (Alsene et al., 2003; Cornelis et al., 2007; Retey et al., 2007).

Conclusions and Implications

The consumption of high caffeine content energy drinks has increased markedly in recent years. Regulation of energy drinks, including content labeling and health warnings has differed across countries, with among the most lax regulatory requirements in the U.S., which is also the largest market for these products. The absence of regulatory oversight has resulted in aggressive marketing of energy drinks, targeted primarily toward young males, for psychoactive, performance-enhancing and stimulant drug effects. There are increasing reports of caffeine intoxication from energy drinks, and it seems likely that problems with caffeine dependence and withdrawal will also increase. The combined use of caffeine and alcohol is increasing sharply, which studies suggest may increase the rate of alcohol-related injury. Given that clinical pharmacology and epidemiological studies demonstrate an association of caffeine use with dependence on alcohol, nicotine, and other drugs, and one study showed that energy drink use predicts subsequent non-medical use of prescription stimulants, further study of whether energy drink use serves as a gateway to other forms of drug dependence is warranted.

One limitation of the present review is that the great majority of the knowledge about caffeine intoxication, withdrawal, and

dependence is derived from studies of coffee consumption. However, studies that have examined these phenomena in the context of caffeine delivered via soft drinks or capsules have shown similar results (e.g. Juliano and Griffiths, 2004; Strain et al., 1994). Thus, there is no reason to suppose that delivery of caffeine via energy drinks would appreciably alter these processes.

These observations have several regulatory and clinical implications. Considering the variable and sometimes very high caffeine content of energy drinks, in combination with the aggressive marketing to youthful and inexperienced consumers, it would be prudent to require full disclosure of the amount of caffeine and other ingredients in energy drinks on the product labeling. Product label warnings about risks when used alone and in combination with alcohol would also be appropriate. Restrictions on advertising and the aggressive marketing of energy drinks to youthful and inexperienced users should also be considered. The promotion of the use of drugs for their recreational and stimulant properties sends a potentially harmful message to adolescents that glamorizes and encourages drug use. Ingesting an energy drink to enhance athletic performance may not be far removed from the nonmedical use of anabolic steroids or pharmaceutical stimulants such as methylphenidate or amphetamine to gain a competitive advantage. Along the same lines, the rapid onset of stimulant effects provided by energy drinks may encourage users to seek out the more intense effects of prescription and illicit stimulants. Finally, it is important for clinicians to be familiar with energy drinks and the potential health consequences associated with their use. Recognizing the features of caffeine intoxication, withdrawal, and dependence may be especially relevant when treating younger persons who may be more likely to consume energy drinks.

Conflict of Interest

Dr Reissig owns stock in PepsiCo Corporation. Dr Strain owns stock in Starbucks and PepsiCo Corporations, is an investigator on several grants from the National Institute on Drug Abuse (NIDA), and has been a consultant to various pharmaceutical companies on issues about drug abuse liability. Dr Griffiths owns a single share of stock from the Coca-Cola Company, and is an investigator on grants or contracts from NIDA, the Council on Spiritual Practices, the Heffter Research Institute, and the Fetzer Institute. He has also been a consultant to or received grants from the various pharmaceutical companies on issues about drug abuse liability.

References

Alsene, K., Deckert, J., Sand, P., de Wit, H., 2003. Association between A2a receptor gene polymorphisms and caffeine-induced anxiety. Neuropsychopharmacology 28, 1694–1702.

American Psychiatric Association, 1994. Diagnostic and statistical manual of mental disorders: DSM-IV. American Psychiatric Association, Washington, DC.

Aranda, M., Morlock, G., 2006. Simultaneous determination of riboflavin, pyridoxine, nicotinamide, caffeine and taurine in energy drinks by planar chromatography-multiple detection with confirmation by electrospray ionization mass spectrometry. J. Chromatogr. A 1131, 253–260.

Ari Kapner, D., 2004. Ephedra and energy drinks on college campuses. The Higher Education Center for Alcohol and Other Drug Abuse and Violence Prevention. http://www.higheredcenter.org/files/product/energy-drinks.pdf. Accessed on July 17, 2008.

Arria, A.M., Caldeira, K.M., O'Grady, K.E., Vincent, K.B., Griffiths, R.R., Wish, E.D., 2008. Energy drink use is associated with subsequent non-medical prescription stimulant use among college students. In: Proceedings of the American Public Health Association Annual Meeting. San Diego, California.

Bernstein, G.A., Carroll, M.E., Dean, N.W., Crosby, R.D., Perwien, A.R., Benowitz, N.L., 1998. Caffeine withdrawal in normal school-age children. J. Am. Acad. Child Adolesc. Psychiatry 37, 858–865.

Bernstein, G.A., Carroll, M.E., Thuras, P.D., Cosgrove, K.P., Roth, M.E., 2002. Caffeine dependence in teenagers. Drug Alcohol Depend. 66, 1–6.

Bookoo website, 2008. http://64.233.169.104/search?q=cache: Eon5US__GpsJ: www.bookooenergy.com/webwinter06/whoweare.html+boo+koo+having+fun+kicking+butt+and+making+a+difference&hl=en&ct=clnk&cd=1&gl=us. Accessed on February 28, 2008.

Bonnet, M.H., Balkin, T.J., Dinges, D.F., Roehrs, T., Rogers, N.L., Wesensten, N.J., 2005. The use of stimulants to modify performance during sleep loss: a review by the Sleep Deprivation and Stimulant Task Force of the American Academy of Sleep Medicine. Sleep 28, 1163–1187.

Brooks, J., 2007. Spike shooter makers stand by their energy drink. http://cbs4denver.com/local/local_story_054082902.html. Accessed on February 28, 2008.

Chait, L.D., Griffiths, R.R., 1983. Effects of caffeine on cigarette smoking and subjective response. Clin. Pharmacol. Ther. 34, 612–622.

Childs, E., de Wit, H., 2006. Subjective, behavioral, and physiological effects of acute caffeine in light, nondependent caffeine users. Psychopharmacology (Berl.) 185, 514–523.

Cocaine website, 2008. http://www.drinkcocaine.com/default.htm. Accessed on February 28, 2008.

Collins, L., Graham, J., Rousculp, S., 1997. Heavy caffeine use and the beginning of the substance use process. In: Bryant, M., Windle, M., West, S. (Eds.), The Science of Prevention. American Psychological Association, Washington, DC, pp. 79–99.

Cornelis, M.C., El-Sohemy, A., Campos, H., 2007. Genetic polymorphism of the adenosine A2A receptor is associated with habitual caffeine consumption. Am. J. Clin. Nutr. 86, 240–244.

Dasey, D., 2007. Man's heart stops after Red Bull overdose. The Sydney Morning Herald, August 19. http://www.smh.com.au/articles/2007/08/18/1186857834956.html. Accessed on February 28, 2008.

Dews, P.B., 1984. Behavioral effects of caffeine. In: Dews, P.B. (Ed.), Caffeine: Perspectives from Recent Research. Springer-Verlag, Berlin, pp. 86–103.

Doherty, M., Smith, P.M., 2004. Effects of caffeine ingestion on exercise testing: A meta-analysis. Int. J. Sport Nutr. Exerc. Metab. 14, 626–646.

Doherty, M., Smith, P., Hughes, M., Davison, R., 2004. Caffeine lowers perceptual response and increases power output during high-intensity cycling. J. Sports Sci. 22, 637–643.

Driesbach, R.H., Pfeiffer, C., 1943. Caffeine-withdrawal headache. J. Lab. Clin. Med. 28, 1212–1219.

Emurian, H.H., Nellis, M.J., Brady, J.V., Ray, R.L., 1982. Event time-series relationship between cigarette smoking and coffee drinking. Addict. Behav. 7, 441–444.

Energyfiend website, 2008. The caffeine database. http://www.energyfiend.com/huge-caffeine-database/. Accessed on February 28, 2008.

European Union, 2007. COMMISSION DIRECTIVE 2002/67/EC of 18 July 2002 on the labeling of foodstuffs containing quinine, and of foodstuffs containing caffeine. http://eur-lex.europa.eu/LexUriServ/site/en/oj/2002/l_191/l_19120020719en00200021.pdf. Accessed on February 28, 2008.

Evans, S.M., Griffiths, R.R., 1992. Caffeine tolerance and choice in humans. Psychopharmacology (Berl.) 108, 51–59.

Ferreira, S.E., de Mello, M.T., Pompeia, S., de Souza-Formigoni, M.L., 2006. Effects of energy drink ingestion on alcohol intoxication. Alcohol Clin. Exp. Res. 30, 598–605.

Food and Drug Administration, 2008. Warning letter to "Blow". http://www.fda.gov/foi/warning_letters/s6674c.htm. Accessed on February 28, 2008.

Food and Drug Administration, 2007a. Stimulant drug products for over-the-counter human use. Code of Federal Regulations. Title 21 volume 5, Sec. 340.50.

Food and Drug Administration, 2007b. Warning letter to Redux Beverages. http://www.fda.gov/foi/warning_letters/b6312d.htm. Accessed on February 28, 2008.

Food and Drug Administration, 2003. Substances generally recognized as safe. Code of Federal Regulations. Title 21 volume 3, Sec. 182.1180. http://www.cfsan.fda.gov/~lrd/fcf182.html. Accessed on February 28, 2008.

Food and Drug Administration, 1980. Caffeine: deletion of GRAS status, proposed declaration that no prior sanction exists, and use on an interim basis pending additional study. Federal Register 69817–69838.

Garriott, J.C., Simmons, L.M., Poklis, A., Mackell, M.A., 1985. Five cases of fatal overdose from caffeine-containing "look-alike" drugs. J. Anal. Toxicol. 9, 141–143.

Gasior, M., Jaszyna, M., Munzar, P., Witkin, J.M., Goldberg, S.R., 2002. Caffeine potentiates the discriminative-stimulus effects of nicotine in rats. Psychopharmacology (Berl.) 162, 385–395.

Goldstein, A., Wallace, M.E., 1997. Caffeine dependence in schoolchildren? Exp. Clin. Psychopharm. 5, 388–392.

Graham, T.E., 2001. Caffeine and exercise: Metabolism, endurance and performance. Sports Med. 31, 785–807.

Greden, J.F., 1974. Anxiety or caffeinism: A diagnostic dilemma. Am. J. Psychiatry 131, 1089–1092.

Griffiths, R.R., Mumford, G.K., 1996. Caffeine reinforcement, discrimination, tolerance, and physical dependence in laboratory animals and humans. In: Schuster, C.R., Kuhar, M.J. (Eds.), Pharmacological Aspects of Drug Dependence: Toward an Integrated Neurobehavioral Approach (Handbook of Experimental Pharmacology). Springer, Berlin, pp. 315–341.

Griffiths, R.R., Vernotica, E.M., 2000. Is caffeine a flavoring agent in cola soft drinks? Arch. Fam. Med. 9, 727–734.

Griffiths, R.R., Woodson, P.P., 1988. Caffeine physical dependence: A review of human and laboratory animal studies. Psychopharmacology (Berl.) 94, 437–451.

Griffiths, R.R., Juliano, L.M., Chausmer, A., 2003. Caffeine: pharmacology and clinical effects. In: Graham, A.W., Schultz, T.K., Mayo-Smith, M.F., Ries, R.K., Wilford, B.B. (Eds.), Principles of Addiction Medicine, 3rd ed. American Society of Addiction Medicine, pp. 193–224.

Griffiths, R.R., Evans, S.M., Heishman, S.J., Preston, K.L., Sannerud, C.A., Wolf, B., Woodson, P.P., 1990. Low-dose caffeine physical dependence in humans. J. Pharmacol. Exp. Ther. 255, 1123–1132.

Hale, K.L., Hughes, J.R., Oliveto, A.H., 1995. Caffeine self-administration and subjective effects in adolescents. Exp. Clin. Psychopharm. 3, 364–370.

Haskell, C.F., Kennedy, D.O., Wesnes, K.A., Scholey, A.B., 2005. Cognitive and mood improvements of caffeine in habitual consumers and habitual non-consumers of caffeine. Psychopharmacology (Berl.) 179, 813–825.

Health Canada, 2005. Safe use of energy drinks. http://www.hc-sc.gc.ca/iyhvsv/alt_formats/cmcd-dcmc/pdf/energy-energie_e.pdf. Accessed on February 28, 2008.

Heatherley, S.V., Hayward, R.C., Seers, H.E., Rogers, P.J., 2005. Cognitive and psychomotor performance, mood, and pressor effects of caffeine after 4, 6 and 8 h caffeine abstinence. Psychopharmacology (Berl.) 178, 461–470.

Hettema, J.M., Corey, L.A., Kendler, K.S., 1999. A multivariate genetic analysis of the use of tobacco, alcohol, and caffeine in a population based sample of male and female twins. Drug Alcohol Depend. 57, 69–78.

Hughes, J.R., Oliveto, A.H., Liguori, A., Carpenter, J., Howard, T., 1998. Endorsement of DSM-IV dependence criteria among caffeine users. Drug Alcohol Depend. 52, 99–107.

Istvan, J., Matarazzo, J.D., 1984. Tobacco, alcohol, and caffeine use: a review of their interrelationships. Psychol. Bull. 95, 301–326.

Iyadurai, S.J., Chung, S.S., 2007. New-onset seizures in adults: possible association with consumption of popular energy drinks. Epilepsy Behav. 10, 504–508.

James, J.E., 1998. Acute and chronic effects of caffeine on performance, mood, headache, and sleep. Neuropsychobiology 38, 32–41.

James, J.E., Rogers, P.J., 2005. Effects of caffeine on performance and mood: Withdrawal reversal is the most plausible explanation. Psychopharmacology (Berl.) 182, 1–8.

Johnson, C.K., 2006. Caffeine-stoked energy drinks worry docs. The Washington Post, October 29. http://www.washingtonpost.com/wpdyn/content/article/2006/10/29/AR2006102900290.html. Accessed on February 28, 2008.

Jones, H.A., Lejuez, C.W., 2005. Personality correlates of caffeine dependence: the role of sensation seeking, impulsivity, and risk taking. Exp. Clin. Psychopharm. 13, 259–266.

Jones, H.E., Griffiths, R.R., 2003. Oral caffeine maintenance potentiates the reinforcing and stimulant subjective effects of intravenous nicotine in cigarette smokers. Psychopharmacology (Berl.) 165, 280–290.

Juliano, L.M., Griffiths, R.R., 2004. A critical review of caffeine withdrawal: empirical validation of symptoms and signs, incidence, severity, and associated features. Psychopharmacology (Berl.) 176, 1–29.

Keast, R.S., Riddell, L.J., 2007. Caffeine as a flavor additive in soft-drinks. Appetite 49, 255–259.

Kendler, K.S., Prescott, C.A., 1999. Caffeine intake, tolerance, and withdrawal in women: a population-based twin study. Am. J. Psychiatry 156, 223–228.

Kendler, K.S., Myers, J., Prescott, C.A., 2007. Specificity of genetic and environmental risk factors for symptoms of cannabis, cocaine, alcohol, caffeine, and nicotine dependence. Arch. Gen. Psychiatry 64, 1313–1320.

Kendler, K.S., Myers, J., Gardner, O.C., 2006. Caffeine intake, toxicity and dependence and lifetime risk for psychiatric and substance use disorders: an epidemiologic and co-twin control analysis. Psychol. Med. 36, 1717–1725.

Kerrigan, S., Lindsey, T., 2005. Fatal caffeine overdose: two case reports. Forensic Sci. Int. 153, 67–69.

Kotaku website, 2008. Pure energy: a critical look at energy drinks. http://kotaku.com/352207/pure-energy-a-critical-look-at-energy-drinks. Accessed on February 28, 2008.

Kozlowski, L.T., Henningfield, J.E., Keenan, R.M., Lei, H., Leigh, G., Jelinek, L.C., Pope, M.A., Haertzen, C.A., 1993. Patterns of alcohol, cigarette, and caffeine and other drug use in two drug abusing populations. J. Subst. Abuse Treat. 10, 171–179.

Lader, M., Cardwell, C., Shine, P., 1996. Caffeine withdrawal symptoms and rate of metabolism. J. Psychopharmacol. 10, 110–118.

Lane, J., 1996. Association of coffee drinking with cigarette smoking in the natural environment. Exp. Clin. Psychopharmacol. 4, 409–412.

Liepman, M.R., Calles, J.L., Kizilbash, L., Nazeer, A., Sheikh, S., 2002. Genetic and nongenetic factors influencing substance use by adolescents. Adolesc. Med. 13, 375–401, viii.

Lunen, J.V., 2007. A can of worries. Baker City Herald, July 17. http://www.bakercityherald.com/news/story.cfm?story_no=5103 Accessed on February 28, 2008.

Machado-Vieira, R., Viale, C.I., Kapczinski, F., 2001. Mania associated with an energy drink: the possible role of caffeine, taurine, and inositol. Can. J. Psychiatry 46, 454–455.

Malinauskas, B.M., Aeby, V.G., Overton, R.F., Carpenter-Aeby, T., Barber-Heidal, K., 2007. A survey of energy drink consumption patterns among college students. Nutr. J. 6, 35.

Marczinski, C.A., Fillmore, M.T., 2006. Clubgoers and their trendy cocktails: implications of mixing caffeine into alcohol on information processing and subjective reports of intoxication. Exp. Clin. Psychopharmacol. 14, 450–458.

Miller, K.E., 2008. Wired: energy drinks, jock identity, masculine norms and risk taking. J. Am. Coll. Health 56, 481–489.

McCarthy, D., Mycyck, M., DesLauriers, C., 2006. Hospitalization for caffeine abuse is associated with concomitant abuse of other pharmaceutical products. Ann. Emerg. Med., 48.

Moolchan, E.T., Ernst, M., Henningfield, J.E., 2000. A review of tobacco smoking in adolescents: treatment implications. J. Am. Acad. Child Adolesc. Psychiatry 39, 682–693.

Mrvos, R.M., Reilly, P.E., Dean, B.S., Krenzelok, E.P., 1989. Massive caffeine ingestion resulting in death. Vet. Hum. Toxicol. 31, 571–572.

O'Brien, M.C., McCoy, T., Rhodes, S.D., Wagoner, A., Wolfson, M., 2008. Caffeinated cocktails: get wired, get drunk, get injured. Acad. Emerg. Med. 15, 453–460.

Oberstar, J.V., Bernstein, G.A., Thuras, P.D., 2002. Caffeine use and dependence in adolescents: one-year follow-up. J. Child Adolesc. Psychopharmacol. 12, 127–135.

Oteri, A., Salvo, F., Caputi, A.P., Calapai, G., 2007. Intake of energy drinks in association with alcoholic beverages in a cohort of students of the school of medicine of the University of Messina. Alcohol Clin. Exp. Res. 31, 1677–1680.

Packaged Facts, 2007. Energy drinks in the U.S., Rockville, MD.

Pallanti, S., Bernardi, S., Quercioli, L., 2006. The Shorter PROMIS Questionnaire and the Internet Addiction Scale in the assessment of multiple addictions in a high-school population: prevalence and related disability. CNS Spectr. 11, 966–974.

Parsons, W.D., Neims, A.H., 1978. Effect of smoking on caffeine clearance. Clin. Pharmacol. Ther. 24, 40–45.

PepsiCo Inc., 1981. The physical or technical effect of caffeine in cola beverages, vol. III. Appendix XII of comments of the National Soft Drink Association submitted to the Department of Health and Human Services Food and Drug Administration in response to the proposal to delete caffeine in cola-type beverages from the list of substances generally recognized as safe and to issue an interim food additive regulation governing its future use. July 29, FDA docket No. 80N-0418.

Pendergast, M., 1993. For god, country and Coca-Cola. The Unauthorized History of the Great American Soft Drink and the Company that Makes It. Macmillan Publishing Company.

PR Newswire Association LLC, 2007. Disturbing trends in energy drink marketing: clever branding or sinister gateway? http://www.lexisnexis.com:80/us/lnacademic/results/docview/docview.do?risb=21_T3160088359&format=GNBFI&sort=RELEVANCE&startDocNo=1&resultsUrlKey=29_T3160088368&cisb=22_T3160088367&treeMax=true&treeWidth=0&csi=8054&docNo=5. Accessed on February 28, 2008.

Red Bull website, 2008. http://www.redbullusa.com/#page=ProductPage.Benefits. Accessed on February 28, 2008.

Reissig, C.J., Strain, E.C., Griffiths, R.R. (2009). Caffeinated Energy Drinks-a Growing Problem. Drug and Alcohol Dependence. 99(1-3), 1-10. doi: 10.1016/j.drugalcdep.2008.08.001

Retey, J.V., Adam, M., Khatami, R., Luhmann, U.F., Jung, H.H., Berger, W., Landolt, H.P., 2007. A genetic variation in the adenosine A2A receptor gene (ADORA2A) contributes to individual sensitivity to caffeine effects on sleep. Clin. Pharmacol. Ther. 81, 692–698.

Richards, D.B., Juliano, L.M., Griffiths, R.R., 2004. Characterization of individuals seeking caffeine treatment for caffeine dependence. In: Proceedings of the 2004 Meeting of the College of Problems on Drug Dependence.

Robertson, D., Wade, D., Workman, R., Woosley, R.L., Oates, J.A., 1981. Tolerance to the humoral and hemodynamic effects of caffeine in man. J. Clin. Invest. 67, 1111–1117.

Rogers, P.J., Heatherley, S.V., Hayward, R.C., Seers, H.E., Hill, J., Kane, M., 2005. Effects of caffeine and caffeine withdrawal on mood and cognitive performance degraded by sleep restriction. Psychopharmacology (Berl.) 179, 742–752.

Rogers, P.J., Martin, J., Smith, C., Heatherley, S.V., Smit, H.J., 2003. Absence of reinforcing, mood and psychomotor performance effects of caffeine in habitual non-consumers of caffeine. Psychopharmacology (Berl.) 167, 54–62.

Shoaib, M., Swanner, L.S., Yasar, S., Goldberg, S.R., 1999. Chronic caffeine exposure potentiates nicotine self-administration in rats. Psychopharmacology (Berl.) 142, 327–333.

Silverman, K., Evans, S.M., Strain, E.C., Griffiths, R.R., 1992. Withdrawal syndrome after the double-blind cessation of caffeine consumption. N. Engl. J. Med. 327, 1109–1114.

Simon, M., Mosher, J., 2007. Alcohol, energy drinks, and youth: a dangerous mix. Marin Institute, San Rafael, CA. http://www.marininstitute.org/alcopops/resources/EnergyDrinkReport.pdf. Accessed on February 28, 2008.

Spikeshooter website, 2008. http://www.spikeshooter.com/. Accessed on February 28, 2008.

Strain, E.C., Mumford, G.K., Silverman, K., Griffiths, R.R., 1994. Caffeine dependence syndrome. Evidence from case histories and experimental evaluations. JAMA 272, 1043–1048.

State of Idaho Office of Attorney General Lawrence Wasden website, 2008. http://www2.state.id.us/ag/newsrel/2008/Anheuser-Busch_AVCVC.pdf. Accessed on July 16, 2008.

Stafford, L.D., Rusted, J., Yeomans, M.R., 2007. Caffeine, mood, and performance: a selective review. In: Smith, B.D., Gupta, U., Gupta, B.S. (Eds.), Caffeine and Activation Theory: Effects on Health and Behavior. Taylor & Francis Group, Boca Raton, FL, pp. 283–309.

Svikis, D.S., Berger, N., Haug, N.A., Griffiths, R.R., 2005. Caffeine dependence in combination with a family history of alcoholism as a predictor of continued use of caffeine during pregnancy. Am. J. Psychiatry 162, 2344–2351.

Swan, G.E., Carmelli, D., Cardon, L.R., 1997. Heavy consumption of cigarettes, alcohol and coffee in male twins. J. Stud. Alcohol. 58, 182–190.

Swan, G.E., Carmelli, D., Cardon, L.R., 1996. The consumption of tobacco, alcohol, and coffee in Caucasian male twins: a multivariate genetic analysis. J. Subst. Abuse 8, 19–23.

Swanson, J.A., Lee, J.W., Hopp, J.W., 1994. Caffeine and nicotine: a review of their joint use and possible interactive effects in tobacco withdrawal. Addict. Behav. 19, 229–256.

Tanda, G., Goldberg, S.R., 2000. Alteration of the behavioral effects of nicotine by chronic caffeine exposure. Pharmacol. Biochem. Behav. 66, 47–64.

Walsh, M., Marquardt, K., Albertson, T., 2006. Adverse effects from ingestion of Redline energy drinks. Clin. Toxicol. 44, 642.

Wiles, J.D., Coleman, D., Tegerdine, M., Swaine, I.L., 2006. The effects of caffeine ingestion on performance time, speed and power during a laboratory-based 1 km cycling time-trial. J. Sports Sci. 24, 1165– 1171.

World Health Organization, 1992a. The ICD-10 classification of mental and behavioural disorders: clinical descriptions and diagnostic guidelines. World Health Organization, Geneva, Switzerland.

World Health Organization, 1992b. International statistical classification of diseases and related health problems: ICD-10. World Health Organization, Geneva, Switzerland.

Worrall, B.B., Phillips, C.D., Henderson, K.K., 2005. Herbal energy drinks, phenylpropanoid compounds, and cerebral vasculopathy. Neurology 65, 1137–1138.

Zenith International, 2007. US overtakes Thailand as world leader in energy drinks http://www.zenithinternational.com/news/press_release_detail.asp?id=206. Accessed on February 28, 2008.

Critical Thinking

1. Consider the brand names. How might they influence/target specific audiences, and what are the implications?

2. What are the ethical implications of these marketing strategies?

3. Considering the possible health risks associated with these drinks, do you think there should be regulations imposed on the sale of them?

Acknowledgements—The authors thank Dr Michael Jacobson and Ilene Heller, JD at Center for Science in the Public Interest for helpful comments about federal regulation of caffeine.

Role of Funding Source: Conduct of the study was supported by grants R01 DA03890 and K24 DA023186 from the National Institute on Drug Abuse.

Contributors: All authors contributed equally to the preparation and review of the manuscript. All authors have approved the final manuscript.

Issues in Correctional Care: Propofol and Intravenous Drug Abuse

ABE M. MACHER, MD

In the previous issue of *American Jails,* I reviewed a case of neurosyphilitic status epilepticus that was treated with penicillin and propofol, a potent anticonvulsant (Clinical Case 3). Propofol is a central nervous system depressant that is administered by anesthesiologists to induce and maintain intravenous infusion sedation and general anesthesia. Unfortunately, illicit "drug diversion" of powerful anesthetic agents has made these psychotropic drugs available for intravenous abuse.

Clinical Case 1

A 21-year-old man with a history of polysubstance abuse was found dead at home by his life-partner. Police found a needle inserted into a left foot vein, and attached to the needle was a syringe. An empty ampule of propofol was found close to the body. Additional empty and full ampules of propofol were found, as well as instruction manuals, including one titled "Anesthesia Manual."

His life-partner reported that the drug abuser had been self-injecting propofol intravenously up to five times a day for weeks prior to his sudden death. In addition, he had also been self-injecting etomidate (another powerful anesthetic) and diazepam (a benzodiazepine). The drug abuser had used stolen and forged prescription forms to obtain the drugs from pharmacies. He had obtained needles, syringes, and intravenous tubing through the Internet via online auctions on eBay®.

Postmortem analysis revealed presence of propofol, etomidate, and diazepam in the drug abuser's blood (Strehler, 2006).

Clinical Case 2

A 25-year-old man with a history of polysubstance abuse was admitted to a psychiatric hospital for detoxification of propofol. Six weeks earlier, he was found unconscious and cyanotic following intravenous self-injection of propofol.

Four years earlier, at the age of 21, he started to experience tension headaches, which were treated with propofol injections by an anesthesiologist. The patient had several appointments with this anesthesiologist for propofol treatment; however, the anesthesiologist refused to continue the propofol therapy. Consequently, the patient started to self-inject propofol intravenously. Remarkably, the patient obtained prescriptions for propofol from various veterinarians whom he told that he was a tropical fish enthusiast and he needed propofol to anesthetize his fish.

The patient performed up to four propofol-self-injection sessions per week, each session lasting one to two hours. He would intravenously inject 5 ml of propofol (10 mg/ml; 50 mg) into an antecubital vein, fall into a deep relaxing sleep for approximately 5 to 10 minutes, wake up, and inject another 5 ml of the drug, using up to 100 ml of propofol; he was self-injecting propofol up to 20 times per session. The patient reported that he had previously self-injected benzodiazepines and morphine, and used marijuana. Physical examination in the hospital revealed that his superficial arm and hand veins showed signs of multiple venous punctures (i.e., characteristic of intravenous drug abuse).

The patient reported a rapid feeling of relaxation, reduction of tension, and euphoria after each propofol injection. He gave an account of tolerance having developed for the relaxing and euphoric effects within the episodes of self-administration, but only a low level of tolerance between the episodes. He reported an intense psychological craving that made it impossible to discontinue using propofol.

Six weeks before admission to the psychiatric hospital, the patient experienced a complete loss of consciousness following a propofol injection. He was found by his wife, unconscious and cyanotic, and was admitted to an intensive care unit. After a stay of several days in the hospital for clinical observation, he was persuaded to attend an in-patient drug rehabilitation program at a psychiatric hospital. However, after seven days in the psychiatric hospital, he refused to participate in further therapy and left. This was followed by an attempt at outpatient psychotherapy (Fritz, 2002; Schneider et al., 2001).

Clinical Case 3

A 30-year-old male physician with a history of polysubstance abuse was arrested for burglary—he was caught breaking into a hospital and stealing propofol.

A number of months earlier, the physician (who was employed in an intensive care unit) was involved in a car accident and hospitalized for surgical repair of a broken femur. In the hospital, he proceeded to develop symptoms reminiscent of benzodiazepine withdrawal, such as fluctuating and later decreasing tachycardia, hyperhidrosis, difficulty concentrating, and anxiety and insomnia overlapping with increasing restlessness. Physical examination revealed remarkable information, i.e., the presence of multiple fresh and older puncture marks above superficial and deeper veins of the left upper extremity of this right-handed physician. Over the next three weeks, the withdrawal-like symptoms improved with treatment by gabapentin. At this point in his hospitalization, the patient reported that he was addicted to propofol.

The patient's past history of drug dependence was as follows. He consumed tobacco since his early adolescence, and it was later combined for over two years with marijuana. He experienced a period of alcohol abuse in his early adulthood, which was allegedly stopped due to the development of cluster headaches. As an intern, he began to self-medicate with intravenous midazolam to treat periodic cluster headache attacks and to calm down after work. Midazolam was replaced by propofol as he felt more pleasant and euphoric under sub-anesthetic doses of propofol.

Propofol was consumed for a year on a nearly daily basis in several sessions per day. The patient reported he felt increasingly controlled by propofol and finally increased the daily injected amount up to two ampules of 200 mg (400 mg per day); he was stealing the propofol ampules from the intensive care unit. The frequent propofol injecting sessions, up to 15 times a day, were increasingly associated with unwanted, very short-lasting attacks of unconsciousness, followed by amnesia.

The patient reported that in the beginning of his daily propofol consumption he remembered a voluntary drug holiday lasting two weeks, which was associated with anxiety, difficulty concentrating, increasing sleeplessness, and a strong desire for propofol (i.e., withdrawal symptoms) before relapsing. Restlessness was reported to result mainly from intense craving for propofol.

A few months after his discharge from the surgical unit of the hospital, he lost his job in the intensive care unit when he was caught self-injecting propofol. A few days later, he was once again caught self-injecting propofol, this time after breaking into the hospital where he was arrested (Bonnet et al., 2008).

Clinical Case 4

A 31-year-old male physician (general practitioner) was admitted to a psychiatric hospital for long-term inpatient detoxification of propofol abuse.

Ten months earlier, this physician had started to intravenously self-inject propofol in 50 mg doses to reduce feelings of boredom, tension, and depression; he indicated a latent homosexuality as the cause of his depression. For 10 months he proceeded to self-inject propofol on an almost daily basis. The patient reported that after injection of propofol he very rapidly experienced euphoria and a feeling of relaxation especially during initial injections. This was followed by strong sedation and a loss of consciousness. He reported retrograde amnesia especially for the repeated injection procedure. Because the drug's effect usually lasted for only 5 to 10 minutes, he injected propofol repeatedly up to more than 100 times per day. Once he started injecting he had a complete loss of control and could not stop until he had used up all of his supply. He reported a development of tolerance for the euphoric effects within binges, but only a low level of tolerance between binges. He underscored that an intense craving made it impossible for him to stop using propofol.

The physician finally accepted treatment when the propofol use started to interfere heavily with his normal life and occupational duties. Inpatient treatment was followed by extensive outpatient psychotherapy; nevertheless, the patient relapsed twice within a short period of time. He was then admitted to the psychiatric hospital for long-term inpatient abstinence treatment (Soyka et al., 1997).

Clinical Case 5

A 50-year-old man with a history of polysubstance abuse was found dead in bed at home. Police discovered that his death was preceded by intravenous administration of propofol, as well as by parenteral and oral administration of benzodiazepines including lorazepam, midazolam, and diazepam. Of note, this four-drug combination (propofol and three benzodiazepines) synergistically promotes respiratory depression that can be life-threatening.

Postmortem analysis found "lethal levels" of propofol in blood. The coroner determined that death was caused by acute propofol intoxication in combination with other central nervous system depressant drugs (*British Medical Journal*, 2009).

Clinical Case 6

A male anesthesiologist had a history of polysubstance abuse (e.g., cocaine) dating from high school, college, and medical school. During his early 30s, he began to self-inject propofol.

Initially, he injected 100 mg of propofol intravenously, slept for 10 minutes, felt a little "fuzzy" for 30 seconds, and then became clear-headed. While maintaining the amount of each subsequent intravenous injection constant, the frequency of injections increased to 10 to 15 times per day, and injections occurred both at work and at home. By this time he had an overwhelming compulsion and craving to self-inject propofol.

His performance at work started to deteriorate as he began to arrive late for cases or not to respond when paged to the operating room. His family expressed concern about changes in his personality. Nurses observed his unusual behavior in the hospital locker room and found syringes with milky liquid residue (i.e., propofol) in the bathroom. Four months later, he was found unconscious in a hospital bathroom and taken to the emergency room. It was determined that he had self-injected 100 mg of propofol. The patient subsequently entered an extended-care drug rehabilitation program (Follette et al., 1992).

Clinical Case 7

A 26-year-old male nurse with a history of polysubstance abuse was found dead in his apartment at 8 A.M. surrounded by several partly empty or unused ampules of propofol and two syringes. His life-partner reported that the drug abuser had self-injected propofol for many years; he was also known to abuse other drugs available to him in the intensive care unit where he worked.

Three years prior to the drug abuser's death, he suffered acute kidney failure due to intravenous drug abuse. During the six months prior to his death, he had been on sick-leave for medical treatment of a depressive illness. He had returned to work 10 days prior to his death. There was no evidence that he intended to take his own life. The nurse and his life-partner had a telephone conversation at 4 P.M. on the day before his death and had made an appointment for the following day.

Postmortem examination noted needle marks on his forearm, inside of the elbows, wrist, and back of the hand and were fresh or partially scarred. Postmortem toxicological analysis revealed propofol in blood, urine, liver, and segments of hair. The medical examiner concluded that the nurse had been a chronic abuser of propofol, and more than 11 ampules of 20 ml propofol emulsion (each ampule containing 200 mg of propofol) must have been administered during the hours before death (Iwersen-Bergmann et al., 2001).

Discussion

From a psychopharmacologist's perspective, propofol shares properties in common with many drugs that are abused. In particular, the onset and effects of propofol are rapid, and this drug causes euphoria—abusers report that propofol induces a captivating high. Propofol can induce sexual arousal, vivid sexual hallucinations, and amorous disinhibition—abuse of propofol is touted as "dancing with a white rabbit" referring to the drug's white color and hallucinogens of the 1960s.

Propofol induces a dissociative state that is perceived as an out-of-body sensation. A Nebraska physician reported that he observed "people dripping propofol from an IV at a rave dance party." Raves are marathon drug-fueled dance parties where participants abuse psychotropic "club drugs" such as ecstasy, methamphetamine, cocaine, gamma-hydroxybutyrate, amyl nitrite, and the hallucinogenic anesthetic ketamine. Among men-who-have-sex-with-men, abuse of "club drugs" is associated with high-risk unprotected insertive and receptive anal intercourse and transmission of HIV-infection (Belluck, 2009; Colfax et al., 2006; Mundy, 2009; Roussin et al., 2007).

The mood-altering effects of subanesthetic doses of propofol delivered via an infusion or by an acute bolus injection have been assessed in human healthy volunteers; a number of subjects report feeling "high" and "spaced out." Several human studies have evaluated the dream incidence rate during propofol anesthesia; dreaming is frequent and described as pleasant, including pleasurable and erotic dreams. After recovery from propofol anesthesia, euphoria, sexual hallucinations, amorous disinhibited behavior, and verbal expression of graphic intimate thoughts have been described. Some patients emerge from propofol anesthesia with the unshakable belief that they have just experienced a wild sexual encounter (Brazalotto, 1989; Canaday, 1993; Hunter et al., 1987; Kasmacher et al., 1996; Kent et al., 1992; Marchaisseau et al., 2008; Martinez Villar et al., 2000; Pakrashi et al., 2004; Roussin et al.,2007; Smyth, 1988; Young, 1988; Zacny et al., 1992, 1993a, 1993b).

Propofol can induce dependence characterized by intense craving, loss of control over the amount and frequency of use, and continued use despite adverse consequences. Withdrawal phenomena after the use of propofol have been described in both abusers and in patients receiving propofol for medical purposes. The 30-year-old propofol addict described in Clinical Case 3 experienced withdrawal symptoms manifested by tachycardia, hyperhidrosis, difficulty concentrating, anxiety and insomnia overlapping with increasing restlessness. Cawley and colleagues reported a hospitalized patient receiving propofol for prolonged sedation who experienced severe agitation, tremors, tachycardia, tachypnea, and hyperpyrexia following repeated attempts at propofol withdrawal (Cawley et al., 2003).

The most alarming fact associated with propofol abuse is risk of sudden death. Propofol has a narrow therapeutic window with a steep dose–response curve. Intravenous administration of propofol for conscious sedation can inadvertently induce unconsciousness accompanied by profound and life-threatening respiratory and cardiovascular depression (e.g., apnea; bradycardia; arrhythmias; hypotension; respiratory arrest; cardiac arrest). Proper administration of propofol always necessitates continuous medical assistance and monitoring by an anesthetist or intensivist in a supportive clinical setting with resuscitation equipment.

In August 2009, the *New York Times* noted that propofol abuse is spreading because propofol is not a federally-controlled drug. The *Wall Street Journal* reported that "most

Glossary

Antecubital—The inner or front surface of the forearm.

Apnea—Transient cessation of respiration (breathing).

Arrhythmia—An alteration in rhythm of the heartbeat either in time or force.

Benzodiazepines—A family of tranquilizing agents that acts as sedatives at low dosage, as anxiolytics at moderate dosage, and as hypnotics at high dosage.

Bradycardia—Abnormally slow rhythm of the heart at a rate lower than 60 beats per minute.

Club Drugs—A loosely defined category of recreational drugs associated with discotheques in the 1970s and more recently dance clubs, parties, and raves in the 1980s to the 2000s. Club drugs include ecstasy, methamphetamine, cocaine, "poppers" (which contain volatile liquids that are inhaled for their intoxicating effects [e.g., amyl nitrite]), GHB, LSD, and the hallucinogenic dissociative anesthetic ketamine.

Cyanosis—A bluish or bluish-purple discoloration (as of skin) due to deficient oxygenation of the blood.

Diazepam (Valium)—A benzodiazepine used especially to relieve anxiety and tension and as a muscle relaxant.

Dissociative—A drug-induced state characterized by a sense of detachment from one's physical body and the external world.

Etomidate—A drug that is medically used for the induction of general anesthesia by intravenous injection.

Euphoria—A feeling of well-being or elation.

Gabapentin (Neurontin)—From a class of medications called anticonvulsants, it treats seizures by decreasing abnormal excitement in the brain; it relieves pain by changing the way the body senses pain and is therefore used to relieve the pain of post-herpetic neuralgia—the burning, stabbing pain or aches that may last for months or years after an attack of shingles.

General Anesthesia—Anesthesia is the loss of sensation (especially to touch) artificially produced by the administration of anesthetic agents; general anesthesia affects the entire body and is accompanied by loss of consciousness.

GHB (Gamma-hydroxy-butyrate)—A central nervous system depressant that is abused to induce a state of euphoria and intoxication.

Hyperhidrosis—Generalized or localized excessive sweating.

Hypnotic—A sleep-inducing agent.

Hypotension—Abnormally low pressure of the blood.

Ketamine (Ketalar)—Medically, anesthesiologists administer ketamine parenterally to induce and maintain sedation and general anesthesia. Illicitly, participants at rave dance parties abuse ketamine to induce hallucinogenic dissociative states.

Lorazepam (Ativan)—A benzodiazepine that is used to relieve anxiety and to treat insomnia.

Midazolam (Versed)—A benzodiazepine that works as a sedative/hypnotic by slowing activity in the brain to allow relaxation and sleep.

Parenteral Drug Administration—Intravenous, intramuscular, or subcutaneous injection of a drug.

Propofol (Diprivan)—An intravenous psychotropic drug that is chemically distinct from agents such as benzodiazepines, barbiturates, and opiates. Insoluble in water, it is marketed as an opaque, white, oily emulsion often referred to informally as "milk of amnesia."

Psychotropic—A drug whose primary effect is on the central nervous system (a psychopharmacologic agent).

Rave Dance Party—Rave is an acronym that means "radical audio visual experience." Rave party is a term first used in the 1980s to describe dance parties (often all-night events) with fast-paced electronic music and light shows. Rave party participants abuse club drugs (e.g., the hallucinogenic dissociative anesthetic ketamine).

Sedation—Induction of a relaxed state.

Tachycardia—Relatively rapid heart rate whether physiological (as after exercise) or pathological.

Tachypnea—Increased rate of respiration.

Therapeutic Window—The range of dosage of a drug that provides safe effective therapy. A narrow therapeutic window indicates that the drug's effect may go from therapeutic to toxic even with a minimal increase in dosage (steep dose–response curve).

medical centers do not lock up propofol or closely monitor inventory as they would for addictive painkillers such as Oxycontin—propofol is readily accessible in most hospital supply rooms, sometimes along with Band- Aids® and antibiotic ointments" (Belluck, 2009; Mundy 2009). Two years earlier, in 2007, Wischmeyer and colleagues published their sentinel survey of 126 academic anesthesiology resident training programs. At 71% of the programs there was no established system to control or monitor propofol as is done with opioids; these programs did not secure propofol in a pharmacy or track its dispensing. One or more incidents of propofol abuse or diversion among employees or trainees were reported by 18% of the anesthesiology departments. Risking parenteral exposure to bloodborne pathogens (e.g., HIV), desperate abusers rummaged through needle discard bins full of used needles/syringes and old vials of propofol in order to retrieve residual propofol for reckless intravenous self-injection. Among the 25 reported individuals abusing propofol, 7 died. Dr. Robert R. Kirby, emeritus professor of anesthesiology at the University of Florida College of Medicine, warns that "the number of deaths is well above what's been reported" (Belluck, 2009; Pilkington, 2009; Wischmeyer et al., 2007).

Dr. Omar S. Manejwala, associate medical director of the Farley Center (an addiction treatment program in Virginia), reported that the number of propofol cases are increasing at his center and are complex to treat. Dr. Paul H. Earley, medical director of the Talbott Recovery Campus (an addiction treatment program in Atlanta), reported in 2008 that 27 of their patients disclosed a history of propofol abuse, up from 8 in 2006. Propofol can induce euphoria, apnea, and cardiorespiratory failure, and the window between these critical stages is a very small intravenous quantity of propofol—Dr. Earley describes propofol abuse as "Russian roulette" (Belluck, 2009).

Conclusion

Propofol is a powerful central nervous system depressant with a narrow therapeutic window. Intravenous abuse of propofol is associated with development of high-level psychological dependence, and rehabilitation of these patients requires intensive inpatient treatment. In the United States, one-quarter of HIV-infected persons have histories of incarceration, and a considerable number of these patients suffer from co-morbid substance abuse and addiction. Correctional facilities have a unique opportunity to provide treatment and to educate inmates about these diseases. (For more information about propofol, including side effects and drug interactions, see www.drugs.com/propofol.html.)

References

Belluck, P. (7 August 2009). With high-profile death, focus on high-risk drug. *The New York Times.* Page A1.

Bonnet, U., et al. (2008). A case report of propofol dependence in a physician, *journal of Psychoactive Drugs,* 40(2): 215–217.

Brazalotto, I. (1989). Effects of propofol. *Annales Francaises d'Anesthesie et de Reanimation,* 8: 388.

British Medical journal. (2009). Concerns mount over misuse of anesthetic propofol among US health professionals. *British Medical journal,* 339: b3673.

Canaday, B.R. (1993). Amorous, disinhibited behavior associated with propofol. *Clinical Pharmacy,* 12(6): 449–151.

Cawley, M.J., et al. (2003). Propofol withdrawal syndrome in an adult patient with thermal injury. *Pharmacotherapy,* 23(7): 933–939.

Colfax, G., et al. (2006). Club drugs and HIV infection: A review. *Clinical Infectious Diseases,* 42(10): 1463–1469.

Follette, J.W., et al. (1992). Anesthesiologist addicted to propofol. *Anesthesiology,* 77(4): 817–818.

Fritz, G.A., et al. (2002). Propofol dependency in a lay person. *Anesthesiology,* 96(2): 505–506.

Hunter, D.N., et al. (1987). Arousal from propofol. *Anaesthesia,* 42(10): 1128–1129.

Iwersen-Bergmann, S., et al. (2001). Death after excessive propofol abuse. *International journal of Legal Medicine,* 114(4–5): 248–251.

Kasmacher, H., et al. (1996). Incidence and quality of dreaming during anaesthesia with propofol in comparison with enflurane. *Anaesthetist,* 45: 146–153.

Kent, E.A., et al. (1992). Sexual illusions and propofol sedation. *Anesthesiology,* 77: 1037–1038.

Marchaisseau, V., et al. (2008). Propofol induced hallucinations and dreams. *Therapie,* 63(2): 141–144.

Martinez Villar, M.L., et al. (2000). Erotic hallucinations associated with the use of propofol. *Revista Espanola de Anestesiologia y Reanimacion,* 47(2): 90–92.

Mundy, A. (6 August 2009). Alert on M.D. abuse of Jackson drug. *The Wall Street Journal.* Page A1.

Pakrashi, T.C., et al. (2004). Fantasmes sexuels: Un cauchema anaesthesique. *Le Praticien en Anesthesie Reanimation,* 8: 349–354.

Pilkington E. (31 July 2009). Abuse of drug used by Michael Jackson growing among medical professionals. *The Guardian,* www.guardian.co.uk/music/2009/jul/31/michael-jackson-propofol-drug-diprivan.

Roussin, A., et al. (2007). Pharmacological and clinical evidences on the potential for abuse and dependence of propofol: A review of the literature. *Fundamental & Clinical Pharmacology,* 21 : 459–465.

Schneider, U., et al. (2001). Propofol dependency after treatment of tension headache. *Addiction Biology,* 6(3): 263–265.

Smyth, D.G. (1988). Hallucinations after propofol. *Anaesthesia,* 43(2): 170.

Soyka, M., et al. (1997). Propofol dependency. *Addiction,* 92(10): 1369–1370.

Strehler, M. (2006). Lethal mixed intoxication with propofol in a medical layman. *Archiv fir Kriminologie,* 217(5–6): 153–160.

Wischmeyer, P.E., et al. (2007). A survey of propofol abuse in academic anesthesia programs. *Anesthesia and Analgesia,* 105(4): 1066–1071.

Young, P.N. (1988). Hallucinations after propofol. *Anaesthesia,* 43(2): 170.

Zacny, J.P., et al. (1992). Subjective and psychomotor effects of subanesthetic doses of propofol in healthy volunteers. *Anesthesiology,* 76(5): 696–702.

Zacny, J.P., et al. (1993a). Propofol at a subanesthetic dose may have abuse potential in healthy volunteers. *Anesthesia and Analgesia,* 77(3): 544–552.

Zacny, J.P., et al. (1993b). Assessing the behavioral effects and abuse potential of propofol bolus injections in healthy volunteers. *Drug and Alcohol Dependence,* 32(1): 45–57.

Critical Thinking

1. Why is this is not a federally controlled drug?

2. How might abuse rates change if it were federally controlled?

3. Do you think informing inmates of the side effects of this drug will have an effect on their use of it? Why?

DR. ABE M. MACHER is a 30-year veteran of the United States Public Health Service. He retired in 2005 and currently advocates for inmates' access to the standard-of-care. DR. MACHER may be contacted at abemacher@yahoo.com.

College Students' Cheap Fix
Increasing Number using ADHD Drug to Stay Alert

TRINA JONES, KATIE BERGER, AND ALEXANDRA SCHWAPPACH

By her sophomore year of college, Kaley, a Washington State University student, routinely popped the prescription drug Adderall to help her study.

The 20-year-old has never had a prescription for the stimulant, but she found it easy to obtain it from friends. She first swallowed pills, then began "railing," or snorting, it at parties. Kaley, one of several students who agreed to speak on condition that their last names not be printed, used Adderall to stay up for days at a time studying for exams or finishing her homework. At parties, she could drink more alcohol without feeling intoxicated.

Last year, while cramming for a midterm, she stayed up all night, fueled by the drug.

"I ended up being in a complete daze for my midterm, and turned it in half-blank, crying," Kaley said. "Then I slept for two days."

National studies show that as many as 1 in 4 students in a college setting may have abused Adderall, and two surveys are under way at WSU to examine student use. College students are twice as likely to use the drug nonmedically as their peers who aren't in college, according to a report this year from the U.S. Department of Health and Human Services.

For students seeking a quick, cheap fix—pills cost about $3 to $5, though the price spikes during final exams—the stimulant allows them to be more productive and focused during late-night cram sessions.

The way students are taking the drug poses additional concerns. Studies show that up to 40 percent of students are snorting the drug, increasing the rate of absorption and the risk, said Patricia Maarhuis, prevention coordinator for WSU's Alcohol, Drug Counseling, Assessment and Prevention Services.

Adderall has also emerged on the party scene, where the stimulant lets students stay awake, even after a night of heavy drinking.

"In a full blackout normally they would be down, out for the count, passed out—but they're up, they're walking, they're talking, they're even a little jittery," Maarhuis said. "But they have absolutely no recall the next day. They might even drive or walk around, but they are indeed in a full blackout. They just haven't lost consciousness."

The drug's legitimate pharmaceutical uses include treatment of attention-deficit hyperactivity disorder and narcolepsy. But experts say Adderall is surprisingly simple to obtain, and its side effects are not well-known by casual users, including potentially severe health risks such as cardiac problems, psychosis, and weight loss.

"It's a careful balance," said Kevin Conway, deputy director at the National Institute on Drug Abuse in Bethesda, Md. "We want to make sure people who need it get it. We are concerned because there is a high rate of misuse of a serious drug."

Handing It Out 'Like Gum'

When Matthew, a 22-year-old WSU student, wanted a prescription for Adderall, he turned to a sympathetic doctor.

"I know I don't have (ADHD), but Adderall helps me a lot with school, so I got the prescription so I wouldn't have the hassle of finding it," Matthew said. "I was written a prescription for 60 pills, which is a lot, so I would save a stash for myself and then give some to my friends."

Access is fairly easy. Many students know friends or family members with a prescription, according to several students interviewed. Others say it's simple enough to look up ADHD symptoms, then describe them to a physician.

"(Students) will hand it out like gum," Maarhuis said.

Adderall's popularity is spread through social media tools such as Facebook and Twitter.

More than a dozen students at WSU have joined Facebook groups praising Adderall. On Twitter, posts on Adderall roll in by the minute, typically praising but occasionally cursing the drug.

"Gonna party up all night with alcohol and Adderall!!" a sample Tweet from Tacoma reads.

But students are doing more online than just talking about it. A Google search for "buy Adderall" results in more than 900,000 hits. Internet sales of medical drugs by illegitimate and often off-shore "pharmacies" may reach $75 billion a year by 2010, according to a 2008 study from the University of Maryland.

Maarhuis predicts more and more students will buy Adderall online, posing another concern.

"The real stuff is bad enough," she said. "God knows what you're getting from these sites, and what it's being cut with."

Traditionally, alcohol has been the No. 1 substance abused on college campuses. Marijuana has ranked second, and substances like cocaine come in at a distant third. In the past 10 years, the use of Adderall and other cognitive stimulants has shot up, outpacing cocaine and almost reaching marijuana levels, Maarhuis said.

Adderall poses a significant risk of psychological addiction, which leads to people using the drug compulsively, regardless of negative effects, said Rebecca Craft, a WSU biopsychology professor. Alice Young, a psychology professor at Texas Tech University who specializes in psychopharmacology, said that the drug may temporarily help a student study and remember, but recall may suffer if the student stops taking it.

"My main concern is not the single use," Young said. "It's the beginning to think you have to use to get the edge."

Officer Matthew Kuhrt, a drug recognition expert for the WSU Police Department, confirmed that "prescription medicine is becoming more and more of a problem." The WSU Police Department has had three cases involving Adderall this year. In 2008, the school revoked the recognition of the Alpha Kappa Lambda fraternity after drug detectives found evidence of cocaine, marijuana, and "significant quantities of Ritalin and Adderall."

Washington State Attorney General Rob McKenna is working on several programs to combat Adderall abuse in the state. He wants to reach students before they make bad drug decisions, not after, he said.

"The solution lies in education and outreach, not law enforcement," McKenna said.

Long-Term Effects Not Known

Even critics of Adderall acknowledge that the drug benefits some people.

Brian, 24, a 2009 WSU graduate, is one. He began taking Adderall after being diagnosed with attention-deficit disorder at age 7, but stopped when he was in high school because he thought it was unnecessary.

"I started taking it again in college," Brian said. "I'm sure I wouldn't have graduated on time without it."

On the other side, WSU student Nicholas Cone stopped using his legal prescription of Adderall because he said he did not like the crash he experienced after taking it.

"The focus I had for about four hours wasn't worth feeling sick when it was over," said Cone, a senior economics major.

The biggest concern may be the lack of knowledge about Adderall's effects on the body, experts say. Adderall has been on the market for less than 10 years, and long-term studies have not been completed, nor have studies on Adderall's interactions with other drugs, Maarhuis said.

Others see cognitive stimulants as a step toward the future. With care, they could be used to help professionals maintain focus, according to a December 2008 article in the science journal Nature.

Drugs like Adderall eventually may be recommended for jobs that require alertness and focus, such as pilots or emergency room doctors, according to interviews with experts.

While the best option may be well-rested surgeons, in today's society the choice may be between an Adderall-taking doctor and a sleep-deprived one, Craft said.

Craft said she believes the use of Adderall to be rising among professors and researchers, although she hasn't seen it at WSU. As people age, they cannot perform on the same schedule they could when they were younger, but some people cannot handle this, so they take a drug, she said.

Professionals like Maarhuis, Young, and Craft worry about a culture of expectations beyond human limits and risky medication for everyone who cannot perform as expected.

"It's a real reflection of this cascading shift toward higher and higher production," Craft said. "I'd rather be a little less productive."

Critical Thinking

1. What are the reasons for the persistent trends of college students to abusing Adderall?
2. How does this trend impact learning?
3. What can be done do change it?

Availability of Websites Offering to Sell Psilocybin Spores and Psilocybin

Jason P. Lott, MD, MS HP, Douglas B. Marlowe, JD, PhD, and Robert F. Forman, PhD

The Study of hallucinogens and other psychedelic drugs is experiencing a revival (Morris 2008; Sessa 2007; Biello 2006; Editors 2006; Neidpath 2006). In particular, psilocybin, a tryptamine-type serotonergic agonist (McKenna et al. 1990) found in mushrooms of the *Psilocybe* fungal genus (Wasson 1957), has recently been the focus of several clinical investigations. Preliminary research suggests that psilocybin may be effective in the treatment of depression (Gellene 2006), cluster headache (Sewell, Halpern & Pope 2006; Sempere, Berenguer-Ruiz & Almazan 2006), and obsessive-compulsive disorder (Moreno et al. 2006; Sard et al. 2005; Perrine 1999; Moreno & Delgado 1997).

Unfortunately, psilocybin has also become a fashionable drug of abuse, particularly among teenagers and young adults. As the number of lysergic acid diethylamide (LSD) and methyldioxymethamphetamine (MDMA or Ecstasy) users among U.S. high school and college students has decreased since 1990, use of other hallucinogens (Hunt 1997) has increased, with psilocybin comprising the bulk of the non-LSD hallucinogens consumed (Johnston et al. 2008). Analogous data in Europe suggest a similar pattern of psilocybin abuse (McCambridge et al. 2007; Bickel et al. 2005; Kresanek et al. 2005).

Though the factors affecting the reemergence of hallucinogens are unknown, the Internet has been recently implicated in the illicit distribution of opioids, stimulants, and other medications without prescription (Schepis, Marlowe & Forman 2008; Forman et al. 2006; Forman 2003). Similarly, anecdotal evidence in medical and legal publications (Halpern & Pope 2001; Westberg & Karlson-Stiber 1999) as well as the popular press (Honigsbaum 2003) has linked recreational psilocybin consumption to websites selling *Psilocybe* mushrooms.

Accordingly, the present authors sought to characterize the online availability of psilocybin to assess whether this particular hallucinogen is widely available for purchase on the Internet. Similar to previous studies involving other drugs, we did not attempt to procure any products in order to ascertain whether the hallucinogens offered for sale were "genuine" or "counterfeit." The focus of this initial investigation was solely directed at ascertaining whether offers to sell psilocybin were prevalent online.

Methods

We conducted a series of Internet-based searches to characterize the availability of websites offering to sell psilocybin spores, seeking to determine: (1) the prevalence of websites advertising psilocybin spores over a 25-month period using a leading Internet search engine, Google (www.google.com), (2) the longevity of commercial psilocybin spore websites ascertained through sequential Google searches, and (3) the proportion of commercial psilocybin spore websites obtained through Google searches compared to Yahoo (www.yahoo.com), another leading Internet search engine. Google and Yahoo were chosen as the primary search engines for this analysis because of their widespread use and popularity among Internet users.

Between March 2003 and April 2005, eight successive psilocybin spore Internet prevalence searches were conducted using the Google search engine. For each search, one investigator examined the first 100 linked website search results generated in a Google inquiry (omitting paid-for advertised links) using the search term "psilocybin spores." The choice of "psilocybin spores" as a search term was based on serendipitous findings reported in a previous study (Forman et al. 2006) in which the search term "psilocybin spores" yielded sites offering to sell both psilocybin spores as well as psilocybin.

After reviewing the contents of these websites, the investigator categorized each link as (1) a "retail site" if psilocybin spores could be directly purchased from that website, (2) a "portal site" if psilocybin spores could be indirectly purchased from one or more hyperlinked sites emanating from the original website, (3) an "information site" if the link only provided information regarding psilocybin spores, *Psilocybe* cultivation, hallucinogenic effects, etc., or (4) "other" if none of the above categorizations were deemed appropriate.

The final search, conducted in April 2005, also reflected whether websites offered to sell whole *Psilocybe* mushrooms, a practice not incorporated into the prior searches. Duplicate websites were intentionally not distinguished from unique/nonduplicative websites during the categorization process in an effort to realistically replicate what a consumer searching for psilocybin spores would encounter online.

A second investigator independently repeated the website categorization process for each link. The two investigators then met to reconcile any discrepancies and arrive at consensus regarding the website categorizations. Although data regarding disparate categorizations were not collected, prior inter-rater scoring trials utilizing a similar methodological approach have consistently demonstrated a 95% consensus in website categorization between independent raters (Hoover et al. 2008).

Additionally, retail websites from the April 2005 search were examined using Internet Archive (www.archive.org) to determine the earliest archived date for each website. The time difference in months between this date and April 2005 was recorded as the longevity of that site. The first 20 links returned from a Yahoo search using the term "psilocybin spores" in April 2005 were also examined and categorized as described above. The percentages of the first 20 commercial (retail and portal) websites were then calculated for the Google and Yahoo searches to assess whether results between the two search engines were comparable.

Results

Fifty-eight percent of links were categorized as commercial (21% retail and 37% portal) across the 25-month period. The average monthly percentage of retail sites ranged from 19% to 26%, while portal sites ranged from 24% and 46%.

Sixteen retail psilocybin spore websites were identified in the April 2005 search, two of which offered to sell both psilocybin spores as well as mature *Psilocybe* mushrooms in quantities of up to 25 kilograms. Other websites provided detailed instructions on psilocybin cultivation, dosing recommendations, and firsthand accounts of psilocybin use. A few websites offered to sell peyote, another hallucinogen. Bids to buy and sell *Psilocybe* mushrooms and other hallucinogens within chat rooms, online forums, and message boards were also common.

The "youngest" website from the April 2005 search had been in existence 10 months, while the "oldest" website had been offering to sell psilocybin spores for at least 75 months. The average length of existence for retail websites was approximately 43 months. The first 20 links returned by the Google and Yahoo search engines to the inquiry *psilocybin spores* in April 2005 showed that 75% of the links generated in the Google search were categorized as commercial, while 80% of Yahoo links were categorized as commercial.

Comment

The Internet is a powerful medium for education and commerce in all sectors of society, including those wishing to buy and sell controlled substances (Wax 2002). This study was intended to model what an individual might encounter when seeking to purchase psilocybin or psilocybin spores online. Our results indicate a high prevalence of websites offering to sell these substances across two leading Internet search engines.

Inconsistencies between state, federal, and international laws are potential factors contributing to increased psilocybin use and its availability online (INCB 2004). For example, although the U.S. Controlled Substances Act prohibits the possession or sale of *Psilocybe* mushrooms, Florida state law allows for "accidental" possession of small quantities as they may be found in the wild (Fiske vs. State of Florida 1978). The legality of selling psilocybin spores is even less clear, with the U.S. Department of Justice stating that "it is not illegal to sell mushroom spores alone, but selling them with the purpose of producing hallucinogenic mushrooms is illegal" (Whitely 2003).

A limitation of this study is that no attempts were made to purchase psilocybin or psilocybin spores from retail psilocybin websites, and thus no information about product delivery or quality was obtained. Although the U.S. Government Accounting Office has reported that 94% of all opioid medication purchases resulted in the delivery of the drugs as advertised (Fong 1999), it is unknown whether psilocybin websites would be comparably consistent with their deliveries. An important area for future research is assessing whether these websites actually deliver psilocybin and other drugs as advertised.

Affordable Internet access is quickly becoming a reality for much of the world's population. Our study suggests that increasing concern over online trafficking of psilocybin, among other drugs, is warranted.

References

Bickel, M.; Dining, T.; Watz, H.; Roesler, A.; Weidauer, S.; Jacobi, V.; Gueller, S.; Betz, C.; Fichtischerer, S. & Stein, J. 2005. Severe rhabdomyolysis, acute renal failure and posterior encephalopathy after 'magic mushroom' abuse. *European Journal of Emergency Medicine* 12 (6): 306–08.

Biello, D. 2006. Not imagining it. Research into hallucinogens cautiously resumes. *Scientific American* 295 (5): 33–5.

Editors. 2006. Reviving the study of hallucinogens. *Harvard Mental Health Utter* 23 (4): 5.

Fiske vs. State of Florida. 1978. So.2d.

Fong, I. 1999. *Statement before the Subcommittee on Oversight and Investigations, Committee on Commerce, U.S. House of Representatives, Concerning Sale of Prescription Drugs over the Internet.* Accessed at www.usdoj.gov/criminal/cybercrime/fong9907.htm

Forman, R.F. 2003. Availability of opioids on the Internet. *Journal of the American Medical Association* 290 (7); 889.

Forman, R.F.; Woody, G.E.; McLellan, T. & Lynch. K.G. 2006. The availability of websites offering to sell opioid medications without prescriptions. *American Journal of Psychiatry* 163 (7): 1233–38.

Gellene. D. 2006. Testing mushrooms' magic. *Los Angeles Times* November 19.

Halpern, J.H. & Pope Jr., H.G. 2001. Hallucinogens on the Internet: A vast new source of underground drug information. *American Journal of Psychiatry* 158 (3): 481–83.

Honigsbaum, M. 2003. High times in magic mushroom business—and it's perfectly legal. Accessed at www.guardian.co.uk/uk_news/story/0,3604,1095822,00.html.

Hoover, V.; Marlowe, D.B.; Patapis, N.S.; Festinger, D.S. & Forman, R.F. 2008. Internet access to *Salvia divinorum:* Implications for policy, prevention, and treatment. *Journal of Substance Abuse Treatment* 35 (1): 22–27.

Hunt, D. 1997. *Rise of Hallucinogen Use (Research in Brief)*. Publication NCJ 166607. Washington, DC: National Institute of Justice.

International Narcotics Control Board (INCB). 2004. *Report of the International Narcotics Control Board for 2004*. Accessed at www.incb.org/pdf/e/ar/2004/incb_report_2004_full.pdf

Johnston, L.D.; O'Malley, P.M.; Bachman, J.G. & Schulenberg, J.E. 2008. *Monitoring the Future: National Results on Adolescent Drug Use. Overview of Key Findings. 2007*. Rockville, MD: NIDA.

Kresanek, J.; Plackova, S.; Caganova, B. & Klobusicka, Z. 2005. Drug abuse in Slovak Republic. *Przegla d Lekarski* 62 (6): 357–60.

McCambridge, J.; Winstock, A.; Hunt, N & Mitcheson, L. 2007. 5-Year trends in use of hallucinogens and other adjunct drugs among UK dance drug users. *European Addiction Research* 13(1): 57–64.

McKenna, D.J.; Repke, D.B.; Lo, L. & Peroutka, S.J. 1990. Differential interactions of indolealkylamines with 5-hydroxytryptamine receptor subtypes. *Neuropharmacology* 29 (3): 193–98.

Moreno, F.A., & Delgado, P.L. 1997. Hallucinogen-induced relief of obsessions and compulsions. *American Journal of Psychiatry* 154 (7): 1037–38.

Moreno, F.A.; Wiegand, C.B.; Taitano, E.K. & Delgado, P.L. 2006. Safety, tolerability, and efficacy of psilocybin in 9 patients with obsessive-compulsive disorder. *Journal of Clinical Psychiatry* 67 (11): 1735–40.

Morris, K. 2008. Research on psychedelics moves into the mainstream. *Lancet* 371 (9623): 1491–2.

Neidpath, A. 2006. Reviving research into psychedelic drugs. *Lancet* 367 (9527): 1980.

Perrine, D.M. 1999. Hallucinogens and obsessive-compulsive disorder. *American Journal of Psychiatry* 156 (7): 1123.

Sard, H.; Kumaran, G.; Morency, C.; Roth, B.L.; Toth, B.A.; He, P. & Shuster, L. 2005. SAR of psilocybin analogs: Discovery of a selective 5-HT 2C agonist. *Bioorganic and Medicinal Chemistry Letters* 15 (20): 455–59.

Schepis, T.S.; Marlowe, D.B. & Forman, R.F. 2008. The availability and portrayal of stimulants over the Internet. *Journal of Adolescent Health* 42 (5): 458–65.

Sempere, A.P.; Berenguer-Ruiz, L. & Almazan, F. 2006. Chronic cluster headache: Response to psilocybin. *Revista de Neurologia* 43 (9): 571–72.

Sessa, B. 2007. Is there a case for MDMA-assisted psychotherapy in the UK? *Journal of Psychopharmacology* 21 (2): 220–24.

Sewell, R.A.; Halpern, J.H. & Pope Jr., H.G. 2006. Response of cluster headache to psilocybin and LSD. *Neurology* 66 (12): 1920–22.

Wasson, R.G. 1957. Seeking the magic mushroom. *Life* May 13: 100–02, 109–20.

Wax, P.M. 2002. Just a click away: Recreational drug websites on the Internet. *Pediatrics* 109 (6): e96.

Westberg, U. & Karlson-Stiber, C. 1999. Hallucinogenic mushrooms popular again—sale via Internet. *Lakartidningen* 96 (7): 746–47.

Whitely, P. 2003. Mushroom business lands 4 in trouble. *Seattle Times* February 24.

Critical Thinking

1. Are there legal benefits of allowing the on-line sale of proscribed drugs like psilocybin?

2. Do you think there is a way to regulate the sale of psilocybin on the Internet?

JASON P. LOTT, MD, MS HP, Resident, Department of Medicine, Hospital of the University of Pennsylvania, University of Pennsylvania School of Medicine, Philadelphia, PA. **DOUGLAS B. MARLOWE**, JD, PhD, Associate Professor of Psychiatry, Treatment Research Institute, University of Pennsylvania, Philadelphia, PA. **ROBERT F. FORMAN**, PhD, Director, Clinical Resources and Education, Alkermes, Inc., Cambridge, MA.

Youth Use of Legal Drugs Eclipses Illicit-Drug Use, Annual Survey Reports

BOB CURLEY

The War on Drugs has long been cast as a battle against illegal narcotics, but the latest federal data shows that seven of the top 10 drugs being misused by high-school seniors are legal prescription or over-the-counter medications.

Factor in the high rates of use of legal alcohol and tobacco by teens, and the incoming Obama administration will face a very different battle than that waged by the current president and his predecessors since the early 1970s.

The 2008 *Monitoring the Future* report released this week shows that 15.4 percent of 12th-grade students reported non-medical use of legal prescription or over-the-counter medications, including 11 percent who misused Vicodin and 4.7 percent who misused Oxycontin. The annual report is based on surveys of about 50,000 8th-, 10th-, and 12th-graders nationally.

Prescription amphetamines, sedatives, tranquilizers, and the attention-deficit hyperactivity disorder medication Ritalin also were among the most popular drugs of abuse among high-school seniors, along with over-the-counter cough medications.

"Prescription drug use is at or near peak levels," said Lloyd Johnston, PhD, principal investigator of the MTF study and a research professor at the University of Michigan's Population Studies Center. "I think this will be difficult to deal with, because the source of these drugs is an informal network of family and friends, not dealers."

Johnston added that 40 percent of teens said they used leftovers from their own prescriptions. "I think the [pharmaceutical] industry is going to have to be involved, and we will need to educate parents and the health professionals who are distributing these drugs," he said.

Marijuana continues to be the most popular illicit drug among adolescents, used at least once in the past year by nearly a third of high-school seniors, 23.9 percent of 10th-graders, and 10.9 percent of 9th-graders.

However, "the MTF survey indicates that marijuana use . . . which has shown a consistent decline since the mid-1990s, appears to have leveled off," according to the National Institute on Drug Abuse (NIDA), which funds the MTF study. "Heightening the concern over this stabilization in use is the finding that, compared to last year, the proportion of 8th-graders who perceived smoking marijuana as harmful and the proportion disapproving of its use have decreased."

Youth smoking rates have fallen to the lowest rate ever recorded by MTF researchers, thanks largely to a decline in reported smoking by 10th-graders. Still, more than one in 10 high-school seniors remain daily smokers. Likewise, alcohol remains the most popular drug used by adolescents despite steady year-over-year decreases in reported use.

"While the long-term general decline is encouraging, especially for cigarettes and alcohol, some of the other findings this year amplify our concerns for potential problems in the future—especially the non-medical use of prescription drugs," said NIDA Director Nora D. Volkow, MD.

Johnston said that the decline in smoking was a pleasant surprise since the youth smoking rate appeared to have plateaued recently after steadily decreasing for many years. "We're seeing a further significant drop in smoking, which is wonderful news," he said.

Bush: Our Strategy Works

In contrast to the measured statements by NIDA, the White House Office of National Drug Control Policy (ONDCP) used the MTF data—along with an unrelated new study pointing to increased cocaine prices and decreased purity on U.S. streets—to claim vindication for the Bush administration's drug-control strategy, which on the demand-reduction side of the ledger has included an emphasis on drug testing in schools, the billion-dollar, marijuana-centric Youth Anti-Drug Media Campaign, vouchers for addiction treatment, and support of drug courts.

"Since 2001, teenage use has declined by 25 percent. That means 900,000 fewer teens on drugs," said President Bush at a White House roundtable discussion held on the day the MTF data was made public.

"President Bush insisted on a balanced effort against demand and supply," added John Walters, director of ONDCP. "The use of drugs has dropped broadly, steeply, and rapidly, while the supply of these poisons has been cut dramatically. Taken together, this impact is historically unprecedented."

Those assertions drew scoffs from critics, who noted that overall drug-use rates remain at higher levels than in the early 1990s. "None of this is true," said former ONDCP budget director John Carnevale of the presumed valedictory by Walters, who like Bush will soon be exiting the White House. "The only good news is the decline in youth drug use, and that started in the mid-1990s . . . They're basing their claim for success on something that started before they showed up."

Carnevale also pointed out that the Bush administration has devoted the bulk of its antidrug spending to supply reduction, cut prevention spending, and barely increased funding for treatment. "There's no way they can claim to have a balanced budget," he said.

"The ebb and flow of drug use rates among young people is much more a function of fad and fashion than anything that government does or doesn't do," said Ethan Nadelmann, executive director of the Drug Policy Alliance. "The greatest drug-related threats to young people involve binge drinking and the misuse of pharmaceutical drugs. Hopefully, the next director of ONDCP will focus his or her greatest attention on those types of drug use that pose the greatest threats. The last thing this country needs is yet another drug czar obsessed with marijuana."

MTF researcher Johnston said that it is "difficult to parse what the influences are" on youth drug use, but added that he was "hesitant to try to tie trends to what any administration does."

In fact, trends may vary from drug to drug. A few years ago, for example, many observers were concerned about a coming epidemic of methamphetamine abuse, but Johnson believes the negative publicity about the drug's effects have helped cut use rates by two-thirds.

On the other hand, cultural changes, secondhand-smoking laws, ads that artfully attacked the tobacco industry, and price increases all seem to have played a role in the decline of cigarette use by youth. "More than 75 percent of kids now say they don't want to date someone who smokes," noted Johnston.

Johnston said that the softening of attitudes about marijuana harm among 8th-graders reported in MTF is troubling because such shifts have consistently presaged increases in use by about a year. The veteran researcher also is concerned about a possible resurgence of LSD and Ecstasy use, and warns that the worsening economy could lead to more relapse among people in recovery from addictions.

"Who knows what the future holds?" he said. "There's always a new drug being invented or rediscovered."

Bibliography

Curley, Bob. (2008). "Youth Use of Legal Drugs Eclipses Illicit-Drug Use, Annual Survey Reports." *Join Together.* Retrieved May 7, 2009 from http://www.jointogether.org/news/features/2008/youth-use-of-legal-drugs.html?print=t

Critical Thinking

1. Which drug is the most common illicit drug among adolescents, and why do you think that is the case?

2. What is the decline in smoking among youth attributed to?

UNIT 5

Measuring the Social Costs of Drugs

Unit Selections

Learning Outcomes

After reading this unit, you should be able to:

- Identify where one looks to identify the social costs associated with drug abuse.

- Determine what percentage of your class has been the victim of a crime and determine what percentages of those crimes were related to drugs.

- Explain how the spread of methamphetamine use and manufacture has affected children.

- Reveal the subpopulations of Americans where fetal alcohol syndrome manifests itself differently, and why.

- Explain what do you believe is the greatest drug-related threat currently facing the United States.

Student Website

www.mhhe.com/cls

Internet References

BMJ.com a Publishing Group
http://bmj.bmjjournals.com/cgi/content/abridged/326/7383/242/a
Drug Enforcement Administration
www.usdoj.gov/dea
Drug Use Cost to the Economy
www.ccm-drugtest.com/ntl_effcts1.htm
Drug Policy Alliance
www.drugpolicy.org/database/index.html
National Drug Control Policy
www.ncjrs.org/ondcppubs/publications/policy/ndcs00/chap2_10.html
The November Coalition
www.november.org
TRAC DEA Site
http://trac.syr.edu/tracdea/index.html
United Nations Chronicle—Online Edition
www.un.org/Pubs/chronicle/1998/issue2/0298p7.html
European Monitoring Center for Drugs and Addiction
www.emcdda.europa.eu/html.cfm/index1357EN.html

The most devastating effect of drug abuse in America is the magnitude with which it affects the way we live. Much of its influence is not measurable. What is the cost of a son or daughter lost, a parent imprisoned, a life lived in a constant state of fear? The emotional costs alone are incomprehensible. The social legacy of this country's drug crisis could easily be the subject of this entire book. The purpose here, however, can only be a cursory portrayal of drugs' tremendous costs. More than one U.S. president has stated that drug use threatens our national security and personal well-being. The financial costs of maintaining the federal apparatus devoted to drug interdiction, enforcement, and treatment are staggering. Although yearly expenditures vary due to changes in political influence, strategy, and tactics, examples of the tremendous effects of drugs on government and the economy abound. The federal budget for drug control exceeds $14 billion and includes almost $1.5 billion dedicated to drug fighting in Mexico and Central America under the Merida Initiative. Mexican criminal syndicates and paramilitaries who control trafficking across the U.S. southern border threaten the virtual sovereignty of the Mexican government. Many argue that the situation in Mexico is as dangerous to the U.S. as the current situation in Afghanistan.

Since 9/11, the restructuring of federal, state, and local law enforcement apparatus in response to terrorism has significantly influenced the nature and extent of drug trafficking in the United States. Huge transnational investigative, intelligence, and enforcement coalitions have formed between the United States and its allies in the war against terrorism. One significant impact of these coalitions has been a tightening of border access and a decreased availability of international trafficking routes. Although drugs are believed to still pour in from Mexico, drug shortages, increased street prices, and a decrease in purity are occurring. Powder heroin is not widely available in the West, and many major U.S. cities are reporting major street declines in the availability of cocaine.

Still, drugs exist, in association with terrorism, as the business of the criminal justice system. Approximately 80 percent of the people behind bars in the country had a problem with drugs or alcohol prior to their incarceration—more of its citizens than almost any other comparable society, and the financial costs are staggering. Doing drugs and serving time produces an inescapable nexus, and it doesn't end with prison. Almost 29 percent of persons on supervised parole or probation abuse drugs. Some argue that these numbers represent the fact that Americans have come to rely on the criminal justice system in an unprecedented way to solve problems of drug abuse. Regardless of the way one chooses to view various relationships, the resulting picture is numbing.

In addition to the highly visible criminal justice-related costs, numerous other institutions are affected. Housing, welfare, education, and health care provide excellent examples of critical institutions struggling to overcome the strain of drug-related impacts. In addition, annual loss of productivity in the workplace exceeds well over a $160 billion per year. Alcoholism alone causes 500 million lost workdays each year. Add to this demographic shifts caused by people fleeing drug-impacted

© Reed Kaestner/Corbis

neighborhoods, schools, and businesses, and one soon realizes that there is no victimless public or private institution. Last year, almost 4 million Americans received some kind of treatment related to the abuse of alcohol or other drugs. Almost 23 million Americans need treatment for an illicit drug or alcohol problem. Fetal Alcohol Syndrome is the leading cause of mental retardation in the United States, and still, survey data continue to report that over 11 percent of pregnant women drink alcohol. Add to this injured, drug-related accident and crime victims, along with demands produced by a growing population of intravenous-drug users infected with AIDS, and a frighteningly overwhelmed health-care system comes to the fore. Health care costs from drug-related ills are staggering. Drug abuse continues to cost the economy more than $13 billion annually in healthcare costs alone. Approximately 71 million Americans over 12 are current users of a tobacco product.

It should be emphasized that the social costs exacted by drug use infiltrate every aspect of public and private life. The implications for thousands of families struggling with the adverse effects of drug-related woes may prove the greatest and most tragic of social costs. Children who lack emotional support, self-esteem, role models, a safe and secure environment, economic opportunity, and an education because of a parent on drugs suggest costs that are difficult to comprehend or measure. In some jurisdictions in California and Oregon, as many as 50 percent of child welfare placements are precipitated by methamphetamine abuse.

When reading Unit 5 of this book, consider the diversity of costs associated with the abuse of both legal and illegal drugs. As you read the following articles, consider the historical progressions of social costs produced by drug abuse over the past century. How are the problems of the past replicating themselves and how have science, medicine, and social policy changed in an attempt to mitigate these impacts? Ample evidence informs us that there is no single approach to mitigate the diverse nature of drug-related social impacts. Further, some of the most astounding scientific discoveries about how addiction develops remain mysterious when compared to the reality of the lives of millions who find drugs an end in themselves. Some have argued that the roots of drug-related problems today seem even more elusive, complicated, and desperate. Good progress has been made in treating drug addiction, but only moderate progress has been made in preventing it in the first place. What are the disproportionate ways in which some populations of Americans are harmed by drugs? Are there epidemics within epidemics? How is drug abuse expressed within different populations of Americans? How do the implications for Native American families and culture differ from those for other racial and ethnic groups? What are the reasons for these disparities and how should they be addressed?

The Problem with Drinking

CHERYL HARRIS SHARMAN

Efraím was already drunk when he left the wedding at 2 A.M. It had been a "nice wedding," which in Costa Rica means only hard liquor was served. The 21-year-old headed to a local bar for a "sarpe," or nightcap, with some friends. At 5 A.M., one of them finally sent him home in a taxi. Shivering and wrapped in towels, he sat on the carpet near the toilet and threw up.

Hours passed before his father found him in the same spot around 6 in the evening and rushed him to the hospital. The nightmare finally ended after an emergency room doctor injected him with medication for alcohol poisoning.

Tadeo, a young Costa Rican, went to the beach with three friends for a few laughs and a lot of drinks. After eight beers each, they drove home on the dark highway. A truck sped by, its rear lights obscuring the curve ahead. Their car skidded off the road and into a tree. Pinned in the wreckage, Tadeo broke three ribs, fractured his skull, fell unconscious, and remained in a coma for a week.

In Costa Rica, as in most Latin American countries, social gatherings more often than not include alcohol. Weddings and funerals, births and baptisms rely at least in part on drinks to ease grieving or encourage celebration. Aside from special occasions, many homes keep well-stocked bars that facilitate impromptu gatherings.

The drive home, particularly in the half-year-long rainy season, can entail a mix of alcohol and slick, winding roads, with potentially catastrophic results. But no one abstains for this reason. Statistics reflect the outcome: 13 percent of emergency room consultations in 1987 and 33 percent of auto fatalities in 2003 were alcohol related. Yet only 5 percent of Costa Ricans are alcohol dependent.

"The biggest misconception people have is that the problem of alcohol is alcohol dependence, or alcoholism," says Maristela Monteiro, regional advisor on alcohol and substance abuse at the Pan American Health Organization (PAHO). "In terms of society, most public health problems come from acute intoxication."

Medical research shows that long-term alcohol abuse causes liver diseases such as cirrhosis and hepatitis, as well as memory loss, ulcers, anemia, impaired blood clotting, impaired sexual performance, malnutrition, depression, cancer and even brain damage. But from a public health perspective, alcohol's greatest impact comes from occasional high-risk drinking by normally light to moderate drinkers.

"Homicides, traffic accidents, suicides, violent behavior, domestic violence, child abuse or mistreatment, neglect—these are from heavy drinking occasions, but most of these people are not alcohol dependent," says Monteiro.

Studies in the United States show that alcohol is a factor in 25 percent of deaths among people aged 15 to 29. Its direct costs to the U.S. health care system add up to some $19 billion a year, and for the economy as a whole, some $148 billion. As a risk factor for the global burden of illness, alcohol rivals tobacco: It is ranked number five among risks to health worldwide (tobacco is number four), and number one in all but two countries—Canada and the United States—in the Americas.

The most effective policies prevent intoxication by reducing the amount of alcohol people drink.

Experts note that alcohol takes a disproportionate toll on the poor, despite the fact that alcohol consumption tends to increase with educational levels and development. Poor people spend a greater proportion of their income on alcohol, and when drinking problems occur, they have less access to services, may lose their jobs, and bring major hardship on their families.

For all these reasons, many public health experts believe that alcohol policy should be a top priority in every country of the Americas.

Costa Rica is one of many countries that have instituted programs to reduce the toll of alcohol using a variety of measures: taxes and licensing, restrictions on advertising, minimum-age laws, and controls on the hours of operation and location of outlets that sell alcohol.

In addition, Costa Rican law bans alcohol consumption in most public buildings, at sporting events, in the workplace, in parks or on the street, within 100 meters of churches, and on public transportation.

"It is important to use various measures to be effective," says Julio Bejarano, head of research at the Instituto sobre Alcoholismo y Farmacodependencia (IAFA) in San José.

Programs like Costa Rica's are the outcome of a 30-year trend toward viewing alcohol less as an individual malady and more as a problem of public health. The shift began with the 1975 publication of *Alcohol Control Policies in Public Health Perspective* by the Finnish Foundation for Alcohol Studies. Since then, new definitions of alcohol use and abuse have emerged, including classifications for levels of drinking according to their risks to health.

According to the emerging consensus, people with what the U.S. health sector calls "alcoholism" and what the World Health Organization (WHO) calls "alcohol dependence" need to seek treatment. But those engaged in occasional overuse that causes mental or physical health problems—"alcohol abuse" in the United States and "harmful use" disorder for WHO—should be made aware of its impact on their health and urged to reduce their consumption before they become alcohol dependent. A third WHO category, "hazardous use," implies high-risk consumption, or what is sometimes referred to as "binge drinking." "You never had a car accident," Monteiro explains, "but you drink too much and drive." This is a large group of people who also need to cut back.

But the bottom line, says Monteiro, is that good public health policies must aim at preventing intoxication. And the best way to do this is by reducing consumption.

"What has been proven over and over in developed countries and more and more in developing countries, is that we need to reduce the overall consumption of the population," she says.

Monteiro says that experience shows that the most effective way of reducing overall consumption is by increasing prices and taxes on alcohol and restricting availability—that is, where it can be sold, to whom, how much, at what times and on which days.

"Once you reduce the hours of sale, for example, you also control the amount of alcohol people can access and drink. You reduce homicides, accidents, violence—many of the acute consequences decrease significantly. There are several examples—for a long time in Europe, the U.S., and Canada, and now in Latin America and elsewhere—that show that closing bars earlier reduces both accidents and violence."

A 2003 book, *Alcohol: No Ordinary Commodity*, published by Oxford and WHO, reviewed three decades of research and concluded that reducing consumption is key. Their top-10 list of specific measures includes minimum-age laws, government monopolies, restrictions on outlets and hours of sale, taxes, drunk-driving counter-measures and brief interventions for hazardous drinkers.

Limiting Access

Raising the minimum age for purchasing alcohol has long been one of the most effective means of reducing access.

Only a handful of countries have emulated the U.S. minimum age of 21, but this has proven to be an effective policy. When all 50 U.S. states raised their minimum age from 18 to 21, the country as a whole saw a 19 percent net decrease in fatalities among young drivers. The National Highway Traffic Safety Administration estimates that raising the minimum age has saved 17,359 lives since 1975.

Government monopolies on alcohol have also proven effective, but these are increasingly unpopular. Until 1968, Finland prohibited the sale of beer anywhere but in government-owned outlets. In 1968, the country began to allow grocery stores to sell beer, and alcohol consumption climbed by 46 percent overall (increasing particularly among 13- to 17-year-olds). Government monopolies today oversee production, sales or distribution (but not all three) in parts of the United States, Canada, Russia, India, southern Africa and Costa Rica. In Scandinavia, multinational companies have waged legal battles invoking international trade rules to break up longstanding government monopolies on alcohol, increasingly limiting their ability to restrict consumption.

Short of holding monopolies, governments can control where, when and to whom alcohol is sold, restricting the density of outlets through limited licensing and restricted hours of sale. They can also restrict the availability of high- and medium-strength alcoholic beverages. Before 1965, Swedish grocery stores could not sell beer with more than 3.5 percent alcohol. When 4.5 percent beer became legally available in grocery stores, total alcohol consumption increased nearly 15 percent. Twelve years later, Sweden returned to the 3.5 percent limit, and consumption dropped again by the same amount.

Hours of sales are equally important. When Norway closed bars on Saturdays, researchers noted that those most affected by the restricted access were also those deemed likely to engage in domestic violence or disruptive intoxication. An Australian Aboriginal community, Tennant Creek, closed bars on Thursdays and noted that fewer women required hospital attention for domestic injuries.

In Latin America and the Caribbean, Colombia provides one of the leading success stories of limiting alcohol consumption through restricted hours of operation. Rodrigo Guerrero, a physician and public health expert, served as mayor of the second-largest city, Calí, in the mid-1990s and dedicated much of his effort to tackling the city's surging violence problem. He commissioned surveys that found that 40 percent of violence victims and 26 percent of violent death victims in his city were intoxicated. In response, Calí passed a *ley semi seca* ("semi-dry law"), which closed bars and discotheques at 1 a.m. on weekdays and 2 a.m. on Fridays and Saturdays. These and other measures reduced homicides from 80 per 100,000 to 28 per 100,000 in eight years.

Costa Rica also limits hours and days of sale. The law prohibits selling or purchasing alcohol in public places after midnight, the day before and the day after a national election, and during Holy Week, "the period of highest alcohol consumption in Costa Rica," IAFA's Bejarano notes.

Probably the most effective policy to reduce consumption, however, is raising taxes on alcoholic beverages. Worldwide, raising the price of alcohol always reduces consumption. According to the recent WHO report *Global Status Report: Alcohol Policy*, the price of beer should always be more than the price of a soda. And because the harmful effects of alcohol use stem from alcohol content, higher-content beverages should be taxed at higher rates.

Drinking and Driving

After restricting access, the next most effective policies are those aimed at reducing drunk driving. WHO's *Global Status Report: Alcohol Policy* lists among the most effective countermeasures sobriety checkpoints, lowered blood-alcohol limits, license suspension and graduated licensing for novice drivers. Enforcement is key. Police intervention must be visible and frequent, and lawbreakers must be punished to the extent of the law.

Blood-alcohol limits are a critical part of these efforts. "Very little alcohol impairs motor coordination," explains Monteiro. "If you drink just over a drink, you are at risk—actually, it's less than a drink."

Costa Rica sets the legal blood-alcohol limit for drivers at 0.05 percent, although many experts say that problems often begin at 0.04 percent. Belize, Guatemala, Mexico, Nicaragua, Paraguay, Canada and the United States set the limit at 0.08 percent. These limits are most effective when used with checkpoints and random breath testing, according to research.

Other effective measures include screening and "brief interventions," prevention tools that have become a cornerstone of WHO's alcohol policy recommendations. During routine visits to health facilities or the family doctor, patients are asked simple questions that screen them for behavioral risk factors—including alcohol, cigarettes, poor diet, physical inactivity and seatbelt use—and doctors provide brief counseling sessions based on the responses.

"This is the epitome of low-technology medicine," says Thomas Babor, one of the researchers who designed the Alcohol Use Disorders Identification Test, or AUDIT.

"It's not the kind of thing, like MRIs, that seem to capture the interest of clinicians. But it probably is of equal importance, because it provides a way to prevent problems before they occur and to minimize problems if they've already started to develop."

AUDIT has been tested in a variety of countries and has proven easy to use, inexpensive to implement, and effective in reducing alcohol consumption at all levels of the population. Translated into many languages (including a Spanish version available through PAHO), the test and booklet include everything a clinician needs to give the 10-question test, to score it for one of four levels of risk for alcohol use,

and to talk to patients about cutting back (including scripts for doctors who are unsure of what to say).

Patients take the test in about one minute, a nurse or receptionist scores it in another minute, and the clinician takes a few minutes to talk to the patient. Those testing in the first risk level are cautioned and advised to avoid drinking at least two days a week. Clinicians tell second-level scorers to minimize the number of drinks per day or week and to cut back on heavy drinking. Those in the third level receive brief counseling with more tools and goal-setting. Only fourth-level scorers are referred to an alcohol specialist.

To reduce drunk driving, lawbreakers must be prosecuted and punished to the full extent of the law.

A 1999 study by Michael Fleming, at the University of Wisconsin–Madison Medical School, showed that, with a single counseling session, subjects cut back on their drinking in the first six months and kept it down for four years. The study also found that every $10,000 invested in interventions saved $43,000 in health costs, with even greater savings when researchers factored in societal benefits, such as fewer auto accidents and crimes.

Other policies have been found to be somewhat less effective, but combined with the "top 10," they help minimize the burden of alcohol. These include having alcohol outlets refuse to serve intoxicated patrons; training their staff to prevent and manage aggression; promotion of alcohol-free events; community mobilization; and public service campaigns in schools and colleges, on television, and in print, including warning labels. Bans and restrictions on alcohol advertising and marketing can help reduce youth exposure to pro-alcohol messages. In Latin America, Costa Rica and Guatemala have completely banned alcohol companies from sponsoring youth and sporting events, and several other countries forbid alcohol advertising on Sundays and holidays.

The challenge ahead, says PAHO's Monteiro, is to build on the work of international alcohol policy experts, using the available scientific evidence to judge which mix of policies works best. But she offers a note of caution: "In Europe, there's almost a reversal of the gains they had before because of trade agreements. The trade agreements that opened the markets for equal opportunity for everyone mean that you cannot have higher taxes or higher prices. You have to allow advertising for everyone."

She notes that in Sweden, foreign companies have challenged laws forbidding alcohol advertising, arguing that they give local, better-known products an unfair advantage.

"That is a point that will be critical in the region," says Monteiro, "how to deal with the economic benefits of alcohol in certain countries while protecting public health and reducing its social costs."

Moving forward, Monteiro and researchers from 11 countries are embarking on a multicountry study that will show, with precision and hard data, the public health burden of alcohol in the Americas. The study will focus on alcohol use in Belize, Nicaragua, Paraguay and Peru. The results will be added to existing data from Argentina, Brazil, Costa Rica, Mexico, Uruguay, the United States and Canada.

Monteiro believes the new study is particularly timely, as several trends in the region point to a growing alcohol problem. For example, in most countries, women drink more as their educational levels rise. In Costa Rica, the percentage of children 13 to 15 who have tried alcohol rose from 16.3 percent in 1990 to 28.4 percent in 2000. In many countries, pressure from industry has been growing along with the spread of public health measures aimed at reducing alcohol sales.

All these developments call for more research and more action, says Monteiro, because "people not only die from drinking too much; they harm and kill those who don't drink, too."

Critical Thinking

1. What can we do differently to address alcohol problems when drinking is almost considered a social must in many countries?

2. Is there a way to balance the economic benefits while protecting public health and reducing the social costs of alcohol?

CHERYL HARRIS SHARMAN is a freelance journalist based in New York City.

With Cars as Meth Labs, Evidence Litters Roads

Susan Saulny

Elkhart, Ind.—The toxic garbage, often in clumps, blends in easily with the more mundane litter along rural roads and highways here: used plastic water bottles, old tubing, dirty gloves, and empty packs of medicine. But it is a nuisance with truly explosive potential, and evidence of something more than simply a disregard for keeping the streets clean.

"The way to get rid of your meth lab these days is to put it in a plastic bag, then throw it out the car window," said William V. Wargo, the chief investigator for the prosecuting attorney's office in Elkhart County.

In the last few weeks, as the snow that had obscured the sides of roads, fields, and parks has melted, law enforcement officials here have found at least a dozen so-called trash labs, the latest public safety hazard to emerge from the ever-shifting methods of producing methamphetamine.

Each trash lab becomes a crime scene and is proof, officials said, that a new and ever more popular way of making meth does not demand a lot of space or a lot of pseudoephedrine, an essential ingredient. The new method is a quick, mobile, one-pot recipe that requires only a few pills, a two-liter bottle, and some common household chemicals.

Law enforcement officials in several states say that addicts and dealers have become experts at making methamphetamine on the move, often in their cars, and they discard their garbage and chemical byproducts as they go, in an effort to destroy evidence and evade the police.

Just as some states had reported progress in stamping out home-based meth labs, this transportable process has presented a new challenge: 65 percent of meth lab seizures in Tennessee, for instance, are now the one-pot, or "shake-and-bake," variety. The number of meth labs seized in Oklahoma last year increased to 743 from 148 just four years ago, largely because of the prevalence of moving labs. In Indiana, the state police reported that meth lab seizures rose nearly 27 percent from 2008 to 2009.

Mr. Wargo attributed at least half of the new meth activity in Elkhart County to the easier one-pot arrangements. He began seeing the switch in 2008.

"We are so under water on this thing," he said.

With disturbing frequency, officials in Alabama, Kentucky, Michigan, Tennessee, and other states say they, too, are confronting the problem of trashed labs, and are scrambling to identify and clear the debris—which is often tinged with the drug and other noxious chemicals—before the public stumbles upon it.

"We just drive around, and off the side of the road, there's one, there's one, and there's another," said Paul G. Matyas, the undersheriff in Kalamazoo County, Mich. "We'll spend all day doing nothing but that."

Mr. Matyas said someone finding a bottle on the side of the road "might think somebody didn't drink all the pop out of their bottle."

"Well, that's not pop," he said. "You pick it up, and it could explode. Acid could spill and burn you. At one of the sites about a week ago, we found a dead deer, and I know exactly what happened."

In some states, officials estimate that the majority of meth lab seizures are now transportable ones, and that over the last two years, the mobile process has supplanted the home-based method of high-yield production that came to be one face of the meth scourge last decade.

"I scratch my head sometimes," said Thomas Farmer, director of the Tennessee Methamphetamine Task Force, adding that sometimes authorities find more than one pot being made on the move. "We get 10–15 bottles going at the same time."

The authorities say that the mobile method has grown in popularity because it is easier, cheaper, and harder to get caught than making it indoors, and that most of the cooks are addicts themselves, not dealers or distributors.

One two-liter bottle might produce about eight grams of meth, enough for the cook to share with his "smurfers"—friends or fellow users who make the rounds at stores, each buying small enough amounts of the main chemical ingredients to stay below the radar of law enforcement, often while meth is being made in the back seat.

Critical Thinking

1. Describe the social and environmental consequences of this new method.
2. Can law enforcement keep up with all of the rapidly changing meth production techniques. How?

Los Zetas: The Ruthless Army Spawned by a Mexican Drug Cartel

GEORGE W. GRAYSON

Drug-related violence in the border town of Nuevo Laredo, the major portal for U.S.-Mexican commerce, left the city of 350,000 without a police chief until printing-shop owner Alejandro Domínguez Coello valiantly accepted the post on the morning of June 8, 2005. "I'm not beholden to anyone. My commitment is to the citizenry," stated the 56-year-old father of three. Within six hours, he lay in a thickening pool of blood after hit men believed to belong to *Los Zetas* paramilitary force fired more than 30 bullets into his body. Their message was clear: narco-traffickers control the streets of Nuevo Laredo. "They are openly defying the Mexican state," said Mexico City political scientist Jorge Chabat. "They are showing that they can kill anybody at any time. It's chilling."[1]

The brutal, daylight murder of Domínguez provides an insight into why Mexican scholar Raul Benitez insists that "Los Zetas have clearly become the biggest, most serious threat to the nation's security."[2] Meanwhile, the U.S. Drug Enforcement Administration advises that these brigands "may be the most technologically advanced, sophisticated, and violent of these paramilitary enforcement groups."[3]

Origins

The several dozen drug bands that operate in Mexico furnish the lion's share of cocaine, marijuana, heroin, and methamphetamines that enter this country. They also accounted for more than 4,500 deaths during the past two years—with the figure spiraling to 961 by April 18 of this year. These facts have spurred the White House to urge furnishing $500 million as the first tranche of a $1.4 billion, multiyear security cooperation package. This "Merida Initiative" would include aircraft, software, hardware, communications technology, training to strengthen the judicial system, intelligence instruction, and advice on vetting new law-enforcement personnel (ubiquitous police corruption is the Achilles' heel of Mexico's battle against the production and transport of drugs). A reluctant U.S. Congress, which is now pondering the program, may not act until after the November election.

Of narco-trafficking organizations, two stand out in terms of suborning officials, amassing resources, and authoring violent acts: the Gulf Cartel, headquartered just below Texas in Tamaulipas state, and its chief rival, the Sinaloa Cartel, centered in Sinaloa state that nestles between the Sierra Madre Mountains and the Pacific Ocean.

In early 1997, the Gulf syndicate began to recruit military personnel whom General Jesus Gutierrez Rebollo—Mexico's "drug czar" who was imprisoned for corruption—began to assign as representatives of the Attorney General's Office (PGR) in northern states. In the late 1990s, Osiel Cardenas Guillen, who was in a no-holds-barred fight for leadership of the notorious organization, sought out members of the Army's elite Airborne Special Forces Groups (Gafes)[4] to provide protection and perform other vital functions. His top recruit, Lieutenant Arturo Guzmán Decenas, brought with him approximately 30 other deserters enticed by salaries substantially higher than those paid by the Mexican government.[5] The original defectors, whose nicknames include "El Winnie Pooh," "The Little Mother," and "El Guerra," had belonged to the 15th and 70th Infantry Battalions and the 15th Motorized Cavalry Regiment.[6] Once Cardenas Guillen consolidated his position, he expanded the role of Los Zetas to collecting debts, securing cocaine supply and trafficking routes known as *plazas,* discouraging defections from the cartel, and executing its foes—often with grotesque savagery.

After the military killed Guzmán Decenas (November 2002) and captured his second-in-command, Rogelio González Pizaña (October 2004), ex-Gafe Heriberto "The Executioner" Lazcano Lazcano ascended to the apex of the paramilitaries. The arrest (March 2003) and deportation to the United States (January 2007) of Cardenas Guillen emboldened Lazcano and his number-one henchman—Jaime "The Hummer" González Durán—to act independently of the other vicious contenders to head the cartel: Osiel's brother Ezekiel and former municipal policeman Jorge Eduardo Costilla Sanchez. "The Gulf cartel created the lion, but now the lion has wised up and controls the handler," stated a U.S. law-enforcement official. "The Zetas don't ask the Gulf cartel permission for anything anymore. They simply inform them of their activities whenever they feel like it"[7]

Los Zetas emerged as the most dangerous force in the cities of Matamoros, Reynosa, and Nuevo Laredo in Tamaulipas. In addition to conducting activities along the border, they are visible throughout the Gulf Coast region, in the Southern states of Tabasco, Yucatan, Quintana Roo, and Chiapas, and in the Pacific Coast states of Guerrero, Oaxaca, and Michoacán, as well as in Mexico City.[8] They are also active in Texas and, possibly, other U.S. states.

Resources and Organization

Los Zetas' training as a local version of the Green Berets constitutes their foremost asset. In cooperation with their U.S. counterparts, the Mexican military created the Gafes in mid-1990s. Foreign specialists, including Americans, French, and Israelis, instructed members of this elite unit in rapid deployment, aerial assaults, marksmanship, ambushes, intelligence collection, counter-surveillance techniques, prisoner rescues, sophisticated communications, and the art of intimidation. President Felipe Calderón, who took office in December 2006, has placed the Army in the forefront of the war against drugs. It is ironic that loyal Gafes helped to capture kingpins such as Cardenas Guillen, whom Gafes-turned-Zetas were hired to safeguard.

Los Zetas have set up camps in which to train recruits aged 15 to 18 years old, as well as ex-federal, state, and local police officers. In addition, they have invited into their ranks ex-troops from Guatemala known as Kaibiles. Reviled as "killing machines," these tough-as-nails experts in jungle warfare and counterinsurgency adhere to the motto: "If I advance, follow me. If I stop, urge me on. If I retreat, kill me."

Their arsenal includes AR-15 and AK-47 assault rifles, MP5s submachine guns, 50-mm machine guns, grenade launchers, ground-to-air missiles, dynamite, bazookas, and helicopters.

When conducting operations, they wear dark clothing, blacken their faces, drive new, stolen SUVs, and delight in torturing victims before administering the coup de grace. Some criminals carry images of bandit Jesús Malverde, the "Narco Saint" known also as the "Generous One" and "The Angel of the Poor" because of his fight for the downtrodden against a nineteenth-century dictatorship.

There are several other Los Zetas groups in addition to commandoes. *Los Halcones* (The Hawks) keep watch over distribution zones; authorities have found 80 members, equipped with radio-transmitters, in Matamoros alone. *Las Ventanas* (The Windows) comprise bike-riding youngsters in their mid-teens who whistle to warn of the presence of police and other suspicious individuals near small stores that sell drugs. *Los Manosos* (The Cunning Ones)

acquire arms; *Las Leopardos* (Leopards) are prostitutes who slyly extract information from their clients; and *Dirección* (Command) are approximately 20 communications experts who intercept phone calls, follow and identify suspicious automobiles, and even accomplish kidnappings and executions.[9]

Furthermore, Los Zetas have forged links with "La Familia" enforcer gangs in Michoacán, the venue for cocaine imports and methamphetamine laboratories, which regularly crosses swords with the Sinaloa Cartel and its allies.

Los Zetas may number between 100 and 200 men and women, most of whom are believed to be in their early- to mid-twenties. Although the Army has detailed information about deserters, even key law-enforcement agencies must guess at their size and composition because small-time criminals identify themselves as "Zetas" in hopes of exciting fear in their victims. "It's gotten to the point where you get drunk, shoot at some cans, and paint your face black, and that makes you a Zeta. . . . A lot of it is image and myth."[10]

To enhance their esprit de corps, Los Zetas go to great lengths to retrieve the bodies of their fallen comrades-in-arms. In what pundits labeled the "invasion of the body snatchers," in early March 2007, four armed men broke into the graveyard in the town of Poza Rica, Veracruz state, tied up a security guard, smashed Roberto Carlos Carmona's gravestone with hammers, and carried off his ornate coffin containing their comrade's corpse.[11]

They also honor their dead. Three months after authorities killed Guzmán Decena in late 2002, a funeral wreath and four flower arrangements appeared at his gravesite with the inscription "We will always keep you in our heart: from your family, Los Zetas."

In addition, they retaliate with sadistic savagery against their enemies. Witnesses claim that the paramilitaries set fire to four Nuevo Laredo police officers inside barrels filled with diesel fuel. Their remains were buried there the next day.[12]

For security purposes, Los Zetas have adopted a cell-like structure to limit the information that any one member of the organization knows about his associates.

Major Operations

Los Zetas most notable strikes over the past several years include the following:

- June 2007: Robbed casinos in the states of Nuevo Leon, Veracruz, Coahuila, and Baja California in a move to gain a share of these businesses.
- May 2007: Kidnapped and later murdered Jacinto Pablo Granda, a Mexican infantry captain near Chilpancingo, Guerrero.
- April 2007: Gunned down local police chief, Ernesto Gutierrez Moreno, as he dined at a restaurant with his wife and son in Chilpancigo.

- March 2007: Believed to have attempted to murder the secretary of public safety Francisco Fernandez Solis in Tabasco.
- February 2007: Dressed in military uniforms, they disarmed and massacred five police officers and two administrative assistants in Acapulco.
- March 2006: Forced the resignation of Nuevo Laredo police chief, Omar Pimentel, after eight months in office. He stepped down hours after police found three charred bodies dumped by the side of a road leading into the border city.
- June 2005: Killed Alejandro Domínguez Coello, the police chief of Nuevo Laredo.
- February 2004: Efrain Teodoro "Zeta 14" Torres and Gustavo González Castro freed 25 fellow narco-traffickers from a prison in Apatzingan, Michoacán.

Major Setbacks

President Calderón, who has compared Los Zetas to Al Qaeda, has made combating the drug mafias his highest law-enforcement goal. Some of his successes and those of his predecessor, Vicente Fox, include

- April 2008: Army units apprehended Armando González Lazcano, police chief of the Apan, Hidalgo, and his brother Alberto "The Red" González Lazcano, who are believed to be linked to Los Zetas (they are nephews of the local director of public security) and who possessed a fragmentation grenade, an AR-15 rifle, and a 45-mm pistol.
- April 2008: Guatemalan authorities caught and imprisoned Daniel "The Basher" Peréz Rojas, one of the first Zetas to sign up with the Gulf Cartel and a confidant of Costilla Sanchez.
- April 2008: Secretary of Public Security Genaro Garcia Luna reported that his agency had spearheaded the capture of José Alberto Martínez Medrano and four accomplices, who had had $6 million in their possession, in Nuevo Laredo; the following day, the Ministry of National Defense issued a communiqué indicating that the 5th Motorized Cavalry Regiment had accomplished the April 2 arrest and that the amount seized was $6.1 million. (Defense Secretary Guillermo Galván Galván's dislike of Garcia Luna sparks such turf battles and impedes cohesion within Calderón's Security Cabinet.)
- March 2008: The Army and the PGR took into custody Raul "Dutchman 1" Hernandez Barron, believed to be a founder of the Zetas, who controlled the Gulf Cartel's drug trafficking in Northern Veracruz.
- February 2008: Military forces discovered a weapons cache in Nuevo Laredo that included eight military uniforms to be used as disguises.

- February 2008: Soldiers raided the "El Mezquito" ranch west of Reynosa and found one of the largest illegal arsenals in recent memory: 89 assault rifles, 83,355 rounds of ammunition, and plastic explosives capable of demolishing buildings.
- January 2008: The Ministry of Public Security (SPP) announced the capture of former municipal police director Héctor Izar Castro in San Luis Potosí, where he is believed to have been a leader of the local cell of Los Zetas. His cache of supplies included an AR-180 rifle, three hand guns, 100 cartridges, 65 packages of cocaine, and three paddles bearing the letter "Z," which were used to beat foes.
- January 13, 2008: The SPP reported the apprehension of 11 people, most of whom were former military men, in San Pedro de las Colonias, Coahuila. The Zetas had been using an auto workshop to dismantle stolen cars. The federal police also arrested the town's police commander and four police officers, while seizing 23 walkie-talkies, 17 cell phones, nine cars, one motorbike, 28 kilograms of marijuana, and weapons, including five semi-automatic rifles, one shotgun, one revolver, and one rifle.
- April 2007: The Attorney General's Office announced the capture of Eleazar Medina Rojas and nine other Zetas in Nuevo Laredo. Identified as a top killer and kidnapper for the Gulf Cartel, Medina Rojas had a stash of weapons, including an AR15, a Colt .223, a Belgian-made PS90, a Beretta, and various cartridges, as well as cell phones, radios, bulletproof vests, and a collection of vehicles.
- April 2007: Authorities apprehended Nabor "El Debora" Vargas García, a founder of Los Zetas, and 20 allies after a shootout in Ciudad del Carmen, Campeche. The government claims that Vargas García, who admitted to serving in the Presidential Guard's assault battalion, ran Los Zetas in Tabasco, Campeche, and Chiapas.
- February 2007: The Attorney General's Office detained Jose Ramon Davila Lopez, a six-year veteran of the Gafes and close ally of Zeta leader Lazcano, in Ciudad Victoria, Tamaulipas.
- September 2006: The Army arrested three former Guatemalan soldiers and five presumed Zetas in Aguililla, Michoacán. They found in their possessions 12 assault rifles, AK-47 and AR-15; one 9-mm pistol and 3,000 rounds of ammunition; and three fragmentation grenades, blacks fatigues, tactical vests, and 10 Kevlar ballistic helmets.

Bilateral Issues

President Calderôn has pledged to pursue all of Mexico's criminal organizations. To this end, he has dispatched 25,000 soldiers, marines, sailors, and federal police to more than a dozen states and cities. Limited resources mean that he will have to set priorities. Although the Sinaloa Cartel remains an important enemy of the state, and an itilateral issuest than its Gulf/Zeta counterpart, it does not have a paramilitary capability; and the inter-marriage of the families that work under its umbrella invest, it with a cohesion lacking in the Gulf/Zeta mafia, which suffered the loss of its capo, Cardenás Guillen.

Moreover, the recent success of Mexican law-enforcement agencies aside, Los Zetas pose a more serious threat to citizens on both sides of the border.

First, many of the commandos have homes north of the Rio Grande where they seek safe haven and where they attempt to lure young Americans into their clutches.

Second, drug distribution routes run through the United States, which means that the narco-gangsters have no respect for international boundaries. The U.S. Justice Department bulletin has warned that "The violence will spill over the Mexican border into the United States and law enforcement agencies in Texas, Arizona, and Southern California can expect to encounter Los Zetas in the coming months." In March, the Justice Department said the Zetas were involved "in multiple assaults and are believed to have hired criminal gangs" in the Dallas area for contract killings, according to the *Dallas Morning News*.[13] In fact, Los Zetas are believed to have carried out executions in Texas and other American states. The Dallas police have launched a search for Maximo Garcia Carrillo, a suspected Zeta who owns a house in the Oak Cliff suburb of the city, who is believed to have killed police officer Mark Nix. Known as a "second-generation" Zeta, the 34-year-old Garcia Carrillo travels with bodyguards armed with automatic weapons and grenade launchers. Reportedly, Los Zetas, who consider Dallas a key point for the transportation and distribution of drugs, also pursue their criminality in Houston, San Antonio, Brownsville, Laredo, and Del Rio.

Third, the FBI has reported that Los Zetas have control over such U.S.-based gangs as the Mexican Mafia, the Texas Syndicate, MS-13, and the Hermanos Pistoleros Latinos.[14]

Fourth, Los Zetas allegedly conduct training at locations southwest of Matamoros, across the border from Brownsville; just north of the Nuevo Laredo airport; near the town of Abasolo, between Matamoros and Ciudad Victoria; and at a place called "Rancho Las Amarrillas," near a rural community, China, that is close to the Nuevo Leon-Tamaulipas border. To the degree that the Calderón administration achieves more successes, the paramilitary criminals may move their boot camps into the U.S.[15] The escalating violence at the border prompted Ambassador Tony Garza to close temporarily the United States Consulate in Nuevo Laredo.

Fifth, the armed forces, with which the U.S. enjoys unprecedented cooperation, are especially eager to track down Los Zetas because of the embarrassment they represent to their institution. In fact, the Defense Ministry has requested that the Mexican Congress authorize both the trial in military courts of deserters who cast their lot with cartels and the imposition of prison sentences of up to sixty years for such soldiers.[16]

Finally, as mentioned earlier, Los Zetas are involved in myriad criminal activities. They have branched out into kidnappings, murder-for-hire, assassinations, extortion, money-laundering, and human smuggling. At the right price, these bloodthirsty mercenaries could move into terrorism focused on vulnerable targets in Texas and throughout the Southwest. With or without the Merida Initiative, authorities on both sides of the border should concentrate on curbing the growth of these lethal paramilitaries.

Notes

1. Quoted in "Border-town Killing Sends Message," *Los Angeles Times*, June 10, 2005.

2. Quoted in Alfredo Corchado, "Cartel's Enforcers Outliower their Boss," *Dallas Morning News*, June 11, 2007.

3. Quoted in U.S. Deliartment of Justice, *National Drug Threat Assessment 2008* (Washington, D.C.: National Drug Intelligence Center, 2007) www.usdoj.gov/dea/concern/18862/2008.lidf.

4. The Mexican Army has several sliecial forces units, including the regular Gafes, who are deliloyed in the twelve military regions; and the extremely select "High Command Sliecial Forces Airmobile Grouli," whose cadres reliort directly to the Secretary of Defense.

5. The Mexican Army suffered 99,849 desertions, including 1,023 officers, between 2000 and 2006; see Alberto Najar, "Desertaron 100 mil militares con Fox," *Milenio*, July 20, 2007 www.milenio.com. Most defections occur during soldiers' first year in uniform.

6. Marco A. Rodríguez Martinez, "El lioder de los 'zetas'," www.monografías.com.

7. Quoted in Corchado, "Cartel's Enforcers Outliower their Boss."

8. Alejandro Gutierrez, *Narcotráfico: El gran desafío de Calderón* (Mexico City: lilaneta, 2007, Chaliters 1 and 5).

9. Alejandro Suverza, "Los Zetas, una liesadilla liara el cartel del Golfo," *El Universal*, January 12, 2008, li. 1; and Martínez, "El lioder de los 'zetas'."

10. Quoted in Corchado, "Cartel's Enforcers Outliower their Boss."

11. "Invasion of the Body-Snatchers," Reuters, March 9, 2007 www.reuters.com.

12. Alfredo Corchado, "Drug Cartels Olierate Training Camlis near Texas Border Just inside Mexico," *Dallas Morning News*, April 4, 2008.

13. Corchado, "Drug Cartels Olierate Training Camlis near Texas Border Just inside Mexico."

14. Ruben Mosso, "FBI: Los Zetas liroblema de seguridad nacional liara EU," January 9, 2008, www.milenio.com.

15. Corchado, "Drug Cartels Olierate Training Camlis."

16. Abel Barajas, "Soldiers Face 60 for Aiding Traffickers," *Laredo Morning Times-Reforma News Service*, October 2, 2006.

Critical Thinking

1. Identify several advantages and disadvantages to passing the Merida Initiative.

2. How does becoming involved in Mexico impact the United States?

3. Los Zetas took the specialized training they received from other countries and are using it against their own countrymen. Are there ethical implications for the countries that trained them, and should the United States target those countries in its national policy?

GEORGE W. GRAYSON is the Class of 1938 Professor of Government at the College of William & Mary, an associate scholar at FPRI and a senior associate at the Center for Strategic & International Studies. His latest book, *Mexican Messiah* (Penn State University Press, 2007), is a biography of Mexico's self-anointed "legitimate president," Andrés Manuel López Obrador. The New York-based Foreign Policy Association will publish Grayson's monograph on U.S.-Mexican narcotics relations.

The Role of Substance Abuse in U.S. Juvenile Justice Systems and Populations

HEATHER HOROWITZ, JD, MPH, HUNG-EN SUNG, PHD, AND SUSAN E. FOSTER, MSW

I n 1998, the National Center on Addiction and Substance Abuse (CASA) at Columbia University released a study, *Behind Bars: Substance Abuse and America's Prison Population*, which revealed that substance abuse and addiction is implicated in the felony crimes of 80 percent of the adult prison inmates in America, that few of these inmates receive treatment for their substance abuse problems, and that providing treatment for this adult population would save taxpayers money within a year. CASA (1998) also found that substance-related crime runs in the family. Incarcerated adults are likely to be children of parents who were in prison. Incarcerated adults are themselves the parents of almost 2.5 million children who are more likely than children whose parents have not been incarcerated to end up in prison. About 30 percent of adult inmates admit to being arrested as juveniles.

These revelations led CASA to examine the characteristics and situations of the minors who end up in the juvenile justice population—2.4 million arrests in 2000. The result was the October 2004 report, *Criminal Neglect: Substance Abuse, Juvenile Justice and the Children Left Behind*, the first comprehensive examination of the relationship between substance abuse and juvenile delinquency (CASA, 2004). The findings sketch a bleak portrait of juvenile justice systems overwhelmed by drug and alcohol abuse and addicted adolescents. These substance-involved juveniles slip through the cracks in the nation's health, education and family support systems and exhibit many other health, education and social problems that receive little attention.

America has 51 separate juvenile justice systems with no national standards of practice or accountability. These systems often are part of the problem, not part of the solution. Although they were created to focus on prevention and rehabilitation of juvenile offenders, the trend has been to mimic adult systems of retribution and punishment. By abandoning a commitment to rehabilitation, a more punitive approach renders these juvenile justice systems a dead end for substance-involved youths rather than an opportunity to reshape their lives.

CASA analyzed data from the National Institute of Justice's Arrestee Drug Abuse Monitoring Program, the Office of Juvenile Justice and Delinquency Prevention's Juvenile Court Statistics, and arrest data from OJJDP's *Juvenile Arrests* publications. CASA also examined data from the National Survey on Drug Use and Health, the National Longitudinal Survey of Youth

and the National Longitudinal Survey of Adolescent Health. Although more recent statistics are available from many data programs, 2000 data were used to assure comparability. Unless otherwise referenced, all findings reported below are from CASA's analysis of these databases.

Substance Abuse and Juvenile Delinquency

Of the 2.4 million juvenile arrests made in 2000, 78.4 percent (1.9 million) involved children and teens who were under the influence of alcohol or drugs while committing their crime; tested positive for drugs; were arrested for committing an alcohol or drug offense, including drug or liquor law violations, drunkenness or driving under the influence; reported having substance abuse problems such as feeling dependent on alcohol or drugs or needing them at the time of their crime; or shared some combination of these characteristics. More than half of arrested juveniles (53.9 percent) tested positive for drugs at the time of their arrest (see Table 1). The main drugs of abuse among juvenile offenders are alcohol and marijuana. Of the 1.3 million juvenile arrestees who tested positive for drugs at the time of their arrest, 92.2 percent tested positive for marijuana, 14.4 percent for cocaine, 8.8 percent for amphetamines, 7.6 percent for methamphetamines and 2.3 percent for opiates (e.g., heroin, methadone and prescription opioids). Alcohol is not included in the standard drug tests, but of juveniles under the influence of some substance at the time of their crime, 37.8 percent admit being under the influence of alcohol.

Forty-four percent of juveniles arrested during the previous year met the clinical DSM-1V (the fourth edition of the *Diagnostic and Statistical Manual of Mental Disorders*) criteria of substance abuse or dependence, compared with 7.4 percent of nonarrested youths; 27.8 percent met the clinical criteria of substance dependence, compared with 3.4 percent of nonarrested youths.

Juvenile substance abuse is implicated in all types of juvenile crime, including violent offenses, property offenses and other offenses such as assaults, vandalism and disorderly conduct (see Table 2). Although juvenile arrest rates overall have declined in recent years, the arrest rate for juvenile

Table 1 Substance Involvement among Arrested Juveniles, 2000

	Percentage of All Arrested Juveniles
Positive urinalysis at arrest	53.9
Under the influence during crime	18.2
Arrested for alcohol/drug offense	12.1
Reported substance abuse problems:	62.5
Tried to cut down/quit alcohol/drugs in past year	(58.0)
Felt dependent on alcohol/drugs in past year	(20.3)
Felt they could use treatment for alcohol/drugs	(17.6)
Currently receiving treatment for alcohol/drugs	(8.4)
In need of alcohol/drugs at the time of their crime	(4.6)
Total substance involved*	78.4

*Percentages do not add up to 78.4 percent because many juveniles fall into more than one category.
Source: CASA analysis of 2000 data from the Arrestee Drug Abuse Monitoring Program (ADAM).

drug law violations (637.5 per 100,000 persons ages 10 to 17) is on the rise. From 1991 to 2000, the arrest rate (arrests per 100,000 persons ages 10 to 17) for all juvenile offenses decreased by 12.9 percent, but the arrest rate for drug law violations increased a staggering 105 percent. During this time, the arrest rate for property crimes decreased 38.4 percent and the arrest rate for violent crimes decreased 33.2 percent.

This increase in drug law violation arrests has cascaded through juvenile justice systems, raising the number of drug law violation cases referred to juvenile court, in detention, incarcerated, in other out-of-home placement and on probation. Of the 1.6 million cases referred to juvenile courts in 2000, 40.9 percent were for property offenses, 22.9 percent for person offenses, 22.5 percent for public order offenses and 13.5 percent for drug and liquor law violations. The number of drug law violation cases referred to juvenile courts increased, however, at more than 12.5 times the rate of the total number of cases referred to juvenile courts (196.9 percent vs. 15.6 percent), from 65,400 cases in 1991 to 194,200 cases in 2000.

The Demographics of Juvenile Crime

Age and gender disparities. While cases referred to the juvenile courts generally involve youths ages 10 to 17, most cases (57.7 percent) involve those age 15 and younger. Seventy-two percent of the 2.4 million juvenile arrests involve males; however, arrests involving females are on the rise. Between 1991 and 2000, the number of cases referred to juvenile courts involving females

Table 2 Substance-Involved Arrested Juveniles by Type of Offense, 2000

Offense	Percentage of All Arrested Juveniles
Violent offenses	69.3
Property offenses	72.0
Other offenses	81.2
Alcohol and drug offenses	100.0
Total arrests	78.4

Source: CASA analysis of 2000 ADAM data.

increased 51 percent, compared with a 7.3 percent increase for males. The largest percentage growth between 1991 and 2000 for both males and females was in drug law violation cases—these cases grew 311.4 percent for females and 181.2 percent for males.

Racial disparities. Racial differences are difficult to determine since arrest rates and rates of cases referred to juvenile courts are not reported for Hispanics who may appear in either white or black racial categories. However, given this limitation, in 2000, the total arrest rate for black juveniles (11,094.2) was more than 1.5 times the rate for white juveniles (6,839.8). In 1999, while blacks comprised just 15 percent of the juvenile population (Bilchik, 1999), black juveniles represented 28 percent of all cases referred to juvenile courts and 36 percent of detained cases. Other research finds that Hispanic juveniles are more likely than white juveniles to be detained, placed in out-of-home residential facilities and incarcerated in adult prisons (Human Rights Watch, 2002; Sickmund, 2004).

Income disparities. Arrested juveniles are more likely than their nonarrested peers to come from impoverished homes. In 2002, 67.5 percent of teens ages 12 to 17 who had at least one arrest in the previous year reported an annual family income of less than $50,000, compared with 52.8 percent of teens who had not been arrested; 26.1 percent of arrested juveniles reported an annual family income of less than $20,000, compared with 17.4 percent of nonarrested youths.

Drug Involvement among Juvenile Offenders

Compared with juveniles who have not been arrested, those who have been arrested once in the past year are more than twice as likely to have used alcohol (69.3 percent vs. 32.7 percent), more than 3.5 times more likely to have used marijuana (49.5 percent vs. 14.1 percent), more than three times more likely to have used prescription drugs for nonmedical purposes (26.8 percent vs. 8.1 percent), more than seven times more likely to have used Ecstasy (12.1 percent vs. 1.7 percent), more than nine times more likely to have used cocaine (13 percent vs. 1.4 percent) and 20 times more likely to have used heroin (2 percent vs. 0.1 percent).

Table 3 Percentage of Arrested Juveniles Who Use Alcohol and Drugs (ages 12 to 17), 2002

Offense	Ever Arrested		Number of Arrests in Past Year			
	Yes	No	0	1	2	3 or More
Alcohol	60.6	31.9	32.7	69.3	78.1	80.2
Marijuana	43.1	13.1	14.1	49.5	58.1	65.3
Prescription drugs for nonmedical use	24.1	7.7	8.1	26.8	37.0	50.1
Cocaine/crack	11.6	1.1	1.4	13.0	22.5	34.4
Ecstasy	10.4	1.5	1.7	12.1	13.9	32.8
Heroin	1.5	0.1	0.1	2.0	1.7	7.1

Source: CASA analysis of 2000 data from the Arrestee Drug Abuse Monitoring Program (ADAM).

The more often juveniles are arrested, the more likely they are to drink and use drugs. Juveniles with three or more past year arrests are almost twice as likely to abuse prescription drugs, more than 2.5 times more likely to use cocaine, almost three times more likely to use Ecstasy and more than 3.5 times more likely to use heroin than youths with only one past year arrest (see Table 3).

Juveniles who drink and use drugs are more likely than those who do not to be arrested and be arrested multiple times. Each felony conviction a youth receives increases the likelihood of becoming an adult felon by 14 percent; each misdemeanor conviction increases the risk by 7 percent (Washington State Institute for Public Policy, 1997).

Substance-involved juvenile offenders are more likely to be reincarcerated than other juvenile offenders (Dembo et al., 1998) and go on to commit criminal acts as adults. In 2000, compared with nonsubstance-involved juvenile offenders, those who were substance involved were nearly 1.5 times more likely to have at least one previous arrest in the past year (58.1 percent vs. 40.6 percent) and were almost twice as likely to have two or more prior arrests in the past year (31.5 percent vs. 18 percent).

In 2002, almost 1.5 million youths ages 12 to 17 (6 percent) had been incarcerated or held in a juvenile detention center at least once in their lifetime. Compared with those who were never incarcerated or in a detention center, those who have been at least once are 1.5 times more likely to have used alcohol in the past year (49.1 percent vs. 33.7 percent), almost two times more likely to have used inhalants (8.1 percent vs. 4.1 percent), more than twice as likely to have smoked cigarettes (41.4 percent vs. 19 percent), more than twice as likely to have used marijuana (31.7 percent vs. 14.7 percent), 2.5 times more likely to have misused prescription drugs (21.2 percent vs. 8.4 percent), almost four times more likely to have used hallucinogens (12.3 percent vs. 3.3 percent), five times more likely to have used heroin (1 percent vs. 0.2 percent), and more than six times more likely to have used cocaine (9.9 percent vs. 1.6 percent).

The earlier a young adult begins to abuse drugs, the more likely he or she is to be arrested. Juvenile alcohol and drug use also increases the risk of adult substance dependence, which increases the likelihood of criminal involvement (see Table 4).

Missed Opportunities for Prevention

There are often early signs of future trouble. The more these markers are present in a young person's life and the fewer protective influences present, the greater the chances for substance abuse and crime (Lipsey, Wilson and Cothern, 2000; Lipsey, 1999).

Off to a troubled start. Children whose parents abuse drugs and alcohol are almost three times more likely to be physically or sexually assaulted and more than four times more likely to be neglected than children of parents who are not substance abusers. Neglected and abused children are more likely to use drugs (43 percent vs. 32 percent) and commit juvenile crimes (42 percent vs. 33 percent) than nonmaltreated children (Kelley, Thornberry and Smith, 1997).

Impoverished and dangerous neighborhoods. Being raised in poverty or living in communities plagued by crime, drug selling, gangs, poor housing and firearms contributes to increased involvement in delinquent and violent behavior (Elliot, Huizinga and Menard, 1989; Fingerhut et al., 1991; Hawkins et al., 2000; Thornton et al., 2002).

Disconnected from schools. Juveniles who test positive for multiple drugs are more than 2.5 times more likely to not be in school than nondrug-using juveniles (40.1 percent vs. 15.3 percent) and they are more likely to be truant, suspended from school and functioning below their grade level. An estimated 50 percent to 80 percent of all juveniles incarcerated in juvenile correctional facilities qualify for services designed to address learning disabilities—three to five times more than the eligible public school population (Leone and Meisel, 1999; Portner, 1996; Stephens and Arnette, 2000).

Table 4 Juvenile Alcohol and Marijuana Use and Young Adult Crime, 2002

Age of First Use	Percentage of 18- to 25-Year-Olds Arrested in Past Year	
	Alcohol	Marijuana
11 or younger	13.7	21.6
12	10.8	13.7
13	9.0	13.7
14	8.3	12.2
15	7.2	9.6
16	6.7	9.7
17	6.6	8.0
18	3.2	5.7
Never used	1.4	2.1

Source: CASA analysis of 2002 National Survey on Drug Use and Health data.

Health problems. Between 50 percent and 75 percent of incarcerated youths have a diagnosable mental health disorder (Coalition for Juvenile Justice, 2000), compared with 20 percent of 9- to 17-year-olds (Office of the Surgeon General, 1999; Coalition for Juvenile Justice, 2000), and at least 80 percent of all young offenders are estimated to have conduct disorders (Cocozza and Skowyra, 2000). Female juvenile offenders have been found three times more likely to have clinical symptoms of depression or anxiety than female adolescents in the general population (Kataoka et al., 2001).

Risky sexual behavior. Incarcerated juveniles are more likely to be sexually active, to have initiated sex at an earlier age, to have had more sexual partners and to have less consistent condom use than their nonincarcerated peers (Diclemente et al., 1991). Up to 94 percent of juveniles held in detention facilities are sexually active (Morris et al., 1995), compared with 46 percent of high school students (Grunbaum et al., 2002).

Running with the wrong crowd. Children and teens who are involved with juvenile offenders and drug-using peers are more likely to be arrested and use drugs themselves (Brendgen, Vitaro and Bukowski, 2000; Svensson, 2003). Children and teens with marijuana-using peers were 10 times more likely to use marijuana than children and teens with no marijuana-using peers (70 percent vs. 7 percent). Compared with youths who are not gang members, those who are in gangs are more likely to commit assault, robbery, breaking and entering, and felony theft; indulge in binge drinking; use and sell drugs; and be arrested (Hill, Lui and Hawkins, 2001).

Lack of spiritual grounding. Teens who do not consider religious beliefs important are almost three times more likely to smoke, drink and binge drink, almost four times more likely to use marijuana and seven times more likely to use illicit drugs than teens who consider religion an important part of their lives (CASA, 2001b). Juveniles who have been arrested one or more times in the past year are almost 1.5 times more likely to never attend religious services than teens who have not been arrested (41.7 percent vs. 31 percent).

Criminal Neglect

By the time juveniles enter juvenile justice systems, the vast majority are troubled and in need of support, health care, education, training and treatment. Limited data are available to document services provided to juveniles in juvenile justice systems. However, available data suggest that youths in custody rarely receive needed services to help them get on the track to responsible adulthood (Pfeiffer, 2004).

Nationwide, only 36.7 percent of juvenile correctional facilities provide on-site substance abuse treatment (SAMHSA, 2002). Only 20,000 (16 percent) of the estimated 122,696 substance-involved juvenile offenders in juvenile correctional facilities receive substance abuse treatment such as detoxification, individual or group counseling, rehabilitation and methadone or other pharmaceutical treatment within these facilities. Another 4,500 juvenile offenders receive substance abuse treatment through drug courts. Together, this adds up to only 24,500 juveniles of the 1.9 million substance-involved arrests for which CASA can document receipt of any form of substance abuse treatment—about 1.3 percent. Even if a full 20 percent of juveniles who received "other sanctions" (community service, restitution, fines, social services) were placed in substance abuse treatment, the percentage of substance-involved arrested juveniles who receive any form of treatment would only be 3.6 percent.

Moreover, mental health services are scarce and many education programs fail to meet even minimum state educational criteria. In 1995, which is when the latest data were available, almost 60 percent of the children admitted to secure detention found themselves in crowded facilities (Annie E. Casey Foundation, 1997). Children in crowded detention centers are more likely to be injured, spend less time in school, participate in fewer constructive programs, receive fewer family visits, have fewer opportunities to participate in religious activities and get sick more often. There are few, if any, programs that provide for the spiritual enrichment of these children and teens.

Instead of providing prevention and remediation, juvenile justice systems compound problems of juvenile offenders, pushing them toward increased substance abuse and crime. At the same time, public policy demands accountability from juvenile offenders. Demanding accountability from children while refusing to be accountable to them is criminal neglect. Because there is no model juvenile justice code or national standards of practice and accountability, states and counties respond to these issues of criminal neglect through federal, state and local investigators, and lawsuits brought by the U.S. Department of Justice under the Civil Rights of Institutionalized Persons Act (U.S. Department of Justice, 2002).

The Cost of Substance Abuse and Delinquency

The cost of substance abuse to juvenile justice programs is at least $14.4 billion annually for law enforcement, courts, detention, residential placement, incarceration, federal formula and block grants to states and substance abuse treatment. Only 1 percent (8139 million) of this cost is for treatment (CASA, 2001a). The costs of probation, physical and mental health services, child welfare and family services, school costs and the costs to victims are impossible to determine. However, together, these costs could more than double this $14.4 billion figure.

On average, a year of incarceration costs taxpayers $43,000 per juvenile (Juvenile Justice FYI, 2004). However, if society were, for example, to invest $5,000 in substance abuse treatment and getting comprehensive services and programs like drug courts just for each of the 123,000 substance-involved juveniles who would otherwise be incarcerated, society would break even on this investment in the first year if only 12 percent of these youths stayed in school and remained drug and crime free. Further, by preventing the crimes and incarceration of just 12 percent of adults now incarcerated who had juvenile arrest records, there would be more than 60,480 fewer inmates, $18 billion in savings from reduced criminal justice and health costs and employment benefits, and at least 5.9 million fewer crimes.

Preventing Substance Abuse and Delinquency

Juvenile crime, violence and substance use are rooted in a host of interrelated social problems, including adult substance abuse, child abuse and neglect, family violence, poor parenting, uneducated and undereducated youths, lack of appropriate health care, lack of community ties and support, increased availability of guns, gangs and poverty (Kumpfer and Alvarado, 1998). Stemming the tide of substance-involved juveniles entering juvenile justice systems will require a concerted effort on the part of parents, child welfare agencies, schools, health care providers, clergy, neighborhoods and local law enforcement officers to look for the signs and signals of risk and intervene early.

Although comprehensive prevention approaches offer the most hope for juveniles at risk for substance abuse and delinquency, few program models exist (SAMHSA, 2001). A comprehensive model would include attention to strengthening families, increasing school engagement, reinforcing positive peer groups, strengthening neighborhood resources, reducing poverty and offering spiritual guidance. The earlier prevention efforts start—whether they focus on the individual child, the family, the school or the community—the more likely they are to succeed in preventing substance abuse and delinquency (Loeber, Farrington and Petechuk, 2003).

Treating Substance-Involved Juvenile Offenders

By the time juveniles enter juvenile justice systems, 44 percent already meet the clinical criteria of substance abuse or dependence and need treatment; up to 80 percent need intervention for learning disabilities, conduct disorders and mental illnesses (Coalition for Juvenile Justice, 2000; Cocozza and Skowyra, 2000; Portner, 1996; Stephens and Arnette, 2000). There are many points in the adjudication process where juveniles can be diagnosed and treated: at arrest, intake, detention, court processing, probation, incarceration and other out-of-home placement, and aftercare. Juvenile drug courts are a promising venue for intervention. These programs, which provide intensive treatment and monitoring for substance-abusing delinquents, have become increasingly popular in recent years and represent a collaboration among juvenile justice, substance abuse treatment and other health, education, law enforcement and social service agencies. They demonstrate that treatment and accountability are complementary rather than mutually exclusive objectives (Cooper, 2002; National Drug Court Institute, 2003).

Opportunities and Next Steps: Policy Recommendations

A top-to-bottom overhaul of the way the nation treats juvenile offenders is required in order to address the needs of these substance-using juvenile offenders. This overhaul should be designed to achieve two fundamental goals, while assuring that juvenile offenders are held accountable for their actions:

- Ensure that each child entering the systems receives a comprehensive needs assessment; and
- Take advantage of opportunities within juvenile justice systems to divert juveniles from further substance use and crime by providing appropriate treatment and other needed services in custody and detention, during incarceration or other out-of-home placement, while on probation and in aftercare.

To accomplish these goals, the following policy recommendations are essential.

Create a model juvenile justice code, setting forth standards of practice and accountability for states in handling juvenile offenders. This model code should incorporate practice requirements, including staffing and training, screening, assessments, treatment planning, case management, substance abuse, mental health and education services, counseling, access to care and record keeping.

Train all juvenile justice system staff—law enforcement, juvenile court judges and other court personnel, prosecutors and defenders, correctional and probation officers—to recognize substance-involved offenders and know how to respond.

Divert juvenile offenders from deeper involvement with juvenile justice systems through such promising practices as comprehensive in-home services, juvenile drug courts, including reentry courts, and other drug treatment alternatives that assure comprehensive services as well as accountability.

Make available treatment, health care, education and job training programs, including spiritually based programs, to juveniles who are incarcerated.

Develop a state and national data system through which a baseline can be established to judge progress in meeting the many needs of these children.

Expand OJJDP grant programs that provide federal funds to states and localities, conditioning grants under such programs on providing appropriate services to juvenile offenders.

If these recommendations are implemented, billions of citizens' tax dollars can be saved, crime can be reduced and help can be provided to thousands of children—who would otherwise be left behind—to grow up to lead productive, law-abiding lives.

References

Annie E. Casey Foundation. 1997. *Juvenile detention alternatives initiative: A progress report.* Baltimore: Annie E. Casey Foundation.

Bilchik, S. 1999. *Minorities in the juvenile justice system.* Washington, D.C.: Office of Justice Programs, Office of Juvenile Justice and Delinquency Prevention.

Brendgen, M., F. Vitaro and W.M. Bukowski. 2000. Deviant friends and early adolescents' emotional and behavioral adjustment. *Journal of Research on Adolescence,* 10(2): 173–189.

CASA. 1998. *Behind bars: Substance abuse and America's prison population.* New York: Columbia University.

CASA. 2001a. *Shoveling up: The impact of substance abuse on state budgets.* New York: Columbia University.

CASA. 2001b. *So help me God: Substance abuse, religion and spirituality.* New York: Columbia University.

CASA. 2004. *Criminal neglect: Substance abuse, juvenile justice and the children left behind.* New York: Columbia University.

Coalition for Juvenile Justice. 2000. Coalition for Juvenile Justice 2000 annual report. Washington, D.C.: Coalition for Juvenile Justice.

Cocozza, J.J. and K.R. Skowyra. 2000. Youth with mental health disorders: Issues and emerging responses. *Juvenile Justice Journal,* 7(1):3–13.

Cooper, C.S. 2002. Juvenile drug treatment courts in the United States: Initial lessons learned and issues being addressed. *Substance Use and Misuse,* 37(12–13):1689–1722.

Dembo, R., J. Schmeidler, B. Nini-Gough, S.C. Chin, P. Borden and D. Manning. 1998. Predictors of recidivism to a juvenile assessment center: A three year study. *Journal of Child Adolescent Substance Abuse,* 7(3):57–77.

Diclemente, R.J., M.M. Lanier, P.F. Horan and M. Lodico. 1991. Comparison of MDS knowledge, attitudes, and behaviors among incarcerated adolescents and a public school sample in San Francisco. *American Journal Public Health,* 81 (5):628–630.

Elliot, D., D. Huizinga and S. Menard. 1989. *Multiple problem youth: Delinquency, substance use, and mental health problems.* New York: Springer-Verlag.

Fingerhut, L.A., J.C. Kleinman, E. Godfrey and H. Rosenberg. 1991. Firearm mortality among children, youth, and young adults: 1–34 years of age, trends and current status: United States, 1979–88. *Monthly Vital Statistics Report,* 39(11): 1–16.

Grunbaum, J.A., L. Kann, S.A. Kinchen, B. Williams, J.G. Ross, R. Lowry and L. Kolbe. 2002. Youth risk behavior surveillance: United States, 2001. *Morbidity and Mortality Weekly Report,* 51(SS-4): 1–66.

Hawkins, J.D., T.I. Herrenkohl, D.P. Farrington, D. Brewer, R.C. Catalano, T.W. Harachi and L. Cothern. 2000. *Predictors of youth violence.* Washington, D.C.: Office of Juvenile Justice and Delinquency Prevention.

Hill, K.G., C. Lui and J.D. Hawkins. 2001. *Early precursors of gang membership. A study of Seattle youth.* OJJDP juvenile justice bulletin. Washington, D.C.: Office of Juvenile Justice and Delinquency Prevention.

Human Rights Watch. 2002. *Race and incarceration in the United States: Human Rights Watch briefing,* February 27, 2002. New York: Human Rights Watch. Available at www.hrw.org/backgrounder/usa/race.

Juvenile Justice FYI. 2004. Juvenile justice FAQ. Available at www.juvenilejusticefyi.com/juvenile_justice_faqs.html.

Kataoka, S.H., B.T. Zima, D.A. Dupre, K.A. Moreno, X. Yang and J.T. McCracken. 2001. Mental health problems and service use among female juvenile offenders: Their relationship to criminal history. *Journal of the American Academy of Child and Adolescent Psychology,* 40(5):549–555.

Kelley, B.T., T.P. Thornberry and C.A. Smith. 1997. *In the wake of childhood maltreatment.* Washington, D.C.: Office of Juvenile Justice and Delinquency Prevention.

Kumpfer, K.L. and R. Alvarado. 1998. *Effective family strengthening interventions.* Washington, D.C.: Office of Juvenile Justice and Delinquency Prevention.

Leone, P.E. and S.M. Meisel. 1999. *Improving education services for students in detention and confinement facilities.* College Park, Md.: The National Center on Education, Disability and Juvenile Justice. Available at www.edjj.org/Publications/list/leone_meisel-1997.html.

Lipsey, M.W. 1999. Can intervention rehabilitate serious delinquents? *The Annals of the American Academy of Political and Social Sciences,* 564(1): 142–166.

Lipsey, M., D. Wilson and L. Cothern. 2000. *Effective intervention for serious juvenile offenders.* Washington, D.C.: Office of Juvenile Justice and Delinquency Prevention.

Loeber, R., D.P. Farrington and D. Petechuk. 2003. *Child delinquency: Early intervention and prevention.* Child delinquency bulletin series. Washington, D.C.: U.S. Government Printing Office.

Morris, R.E., E.A. Harrison, G.W. Knox, E. Tromanhauser, D.K. Marquis and L.L. Watts. 1995. Health risk behavioral survey from 39 juvenile correctional facilities in the United States. *Journal of Adolescent Health,* 17(6):334–344.

National Drug Court Institute, and National Council of Juvenile and Family Court Judges. 2003. *Juvenile drug courts: Strategies in practice.* Washington, D.C.: Bureau of Justice Assistance.

Office of the Surgeon General. 1999. *Mental health: A report of the surgeon general.* Rockville, Md.: National Institute of Mental Health.

Pfeiffer, M.B. 2004. Juvenile detention system struggles: Use of force a focal point: Boy critically hurt in Lansing. *The Ithaca Journal,* cited 2004 Feb. 17 from www.theithicajournal.com.

Portner, J. 1996. Jailed youths shortchanged on education. *Education Week,* 16(5):1.

Sickmund, M. 2004. *Juveniles in corrections.* Washington, D.C.: Office of Justice Programs, Office of Juvenile Justice and Delinquency Prevention.

Stephens, R.D. and J.L. Arnette. 2000. *From the courthouse to the schoolhouse: Making successful transitions.* OJJDP juvenile justice bulletin. Washington, D.C.: Office of Juvenile Justice and Delinquency Prevention.

Substance Abuse and Mental Health Services Administration (SAMHSA). 2001. *Youth violence: A report of the surgeon general.* Washington, D.C.: U.S. Government Printing Office.

Substance Abuse and Mental Health Services Administration (SAMHSA). 2002. *Drug and alcohol treatment in juvenile correctional facilities: The DASIS report.* Rockville, Md.: Office of Applied Studies.

Svensson R. 2003. Gender differences in adolescent drug use: The impact of parental monitoring and peer deviance. *Youth and Society,* 34(3):300–329.

Thornton, T.N., C.A. Craft, L.L Dahlberg, B.S. Lynch and K. Baer. 2002. *Best practices of youth violence prevention: A sourcebook for community action.* Atlanta: Centers for Disease Control and Prevention.

U.S. Department of Justice. 2002. *Fiscal year 2002 activities under the Civil Rights of Institutionalized Persons Act.* Washington, D.C.: U.S. Department of Justice.

Washington State Institute for Public Policy. 1997. *The class of 1988, seven years later. How a juvenile offender's crime, criminal history, and age affect the chances of becoming an adult felon in Washington State.* Olympia, Wash.: Washington State Institute for Public Policy. Available at www.wsipp.wa.gov.

Critical Thinking

1. How does the consumption of drugs and alcohol among juveniles impact the crime rate?

2. What, do you believe, would give the "best bang for the buck" in stemming the rising tide of juvenile drug abuse and crime?

HEATHER HOROWITZ, Jd, Mph, is a former research associate, HUNG-EN SUNG, PhD, is a research associate, and SUSAN E. FOSTER, MSW, is vice president and director of policy research and analysis for the National Center on Addiction and Substance Abuse at Columbia University in New York.

Authors' Note—The research presented in this article was partially funded by the William T. Grant Foundation, the National Institute on Drug Abuse and the Abercrombie Foundation.

UNIT 6

Creating and Sustaining Effective Drug Control Policy

Unit Selections

Learning Outcomes

After reading this unit, you should be able to:

- Explain how drug policy shapes public opinion of drug-related events.

- Explain the roles the media plays in shaping drug policy.

- Discuss the problems and issues surrounding the legal use of alcohol different from those surrounding the illegal use of heroin, cocaine, or methamphetamines?

- Describe your opinions on the legalization of medical marijuana, and whether you believe its legalization will result in its being overprescribed.

- Determine to what degree you would argue that the current problems with drug abuse exist because of current drug policies, or in spite of them.

Student Website

www.mhhe.com/cls

Internet References

Drug Policy Alliance
www.drugpolicy.org

DrugText
www.drugtext.org

Effective Drug Policy: Why Journey's End Is Legalisations
www.drugscope.org.uk/wip/23/pdfs/journey.pdf

The Higher Education Center for Alcohol and Other Drug Prevention
www.edc.org/hec/pubs/policy.htm

The National Organization on Fetal Alcohol Syndrome (NOFAS)
www.nofas.org

National NORML Homepage
www.norml.org

Transform Drug Policy Foundation
www.tdpf.org.uk

The drug problem consistently competes with all major public policy issues, including the wars in Iraq and Afghanistan, the economy, education, and foreign policy. Drug abuse is a serious national medical issue with profound social and legal consequences. Formulating and implementing effective drug control policy is a troublesome task. Some would argue that the consequences of policy failures have been worse than the problems that the policies were attempting to address. Others would argue that although the world of shaping drug policy is an imperfect one, the process has worked generally as well as could be expected. The majority of Americans believe that failures and breakdowns in the fight against drug abuse have occurred in spite of various drug policies, not because of them. Although the last few years have produced softening attitudes and alternatives for adjudicating cases of simple possession and use, the get-tough, staytough enforcement policies directed at illegal drug trafficking remain firmly in place and widely supported.

Policy formulation is not a process of aimless wandering. Various levels of government have responsibility for responding to problems of drug abuse. At the center of most policy debate is the premise that the manufacture, possession, use, and distribution of psychoactive drugs without government authorization is illegal. The federal posture of prohibition is an important emphasis on state and local policymaking. Federal drug policy is, however, significantly linked to state-by-state data, which suggests that illicit drug, alcohol, and tobacco use vary substantially among states and regions. The current federal drug strategy began in 2001 and set the goals of reducing drug use by young persons by 25 percent over five years. In 2008, President Bush announced that drug use by the population in this age group was down by 24 percent. President Obama has continued the basic strategic constructs of the Bush policy. Core priorities of the overall plan continue to be to stop drug use before it starts, heal America's drug users, and disrupt the illegal market. These three core goals are re-enforced by objectives outlined in a policy statement produced by the White House Office of Drug Control Policy. All three goals reflect budget expenditures related to meeting goals of the overall policy. The current drug control policy, in terms of budget allocations, continues to provide for over $1.5 billion to prevent use before it starts, largely through education campaigns, which encourage a cultural shift away from drugs, and more than $3.4 billion to heal America's users. Each year produces modifications to the plan as a result of analysis of trends and strategy impacts. Allocations for interdiction, largely a result of the attempt to secure the borders and frustrate alliances between drug traffickers and terrorists, remain the most significant component of the budget at $10 billion dollars. One exception to prevailing views that generally support drug prohibition is the softening of attitudes regarding criminal sanctions that historically applied to cases of simple possession and use of drugs. There is much public consensus that incarcerating persons for these offenses is unjustified unless they are related to other criminal conduct. The federal funding of drug court programs remains a priority with more than $38 million dedicated to state and local operation. Drug courts provide alternatives to incarceration by using the coercive power of the court to force

© Brand X

abstinence and alter behavior through a process of escalating sanctions, mandatory drug testing, and out-patient programs. Successful rehabilitation accompanies the re-entry to society as a citizen, not a felon. The drug court program exists as one important example of policy directed at treating users and deterring them from further involvement in the criminal justice system. Drug courts are now in place in all 50 states.

The majority of Americans express the view that legalizing, and in some cases even decriminalizing, dangerous drugs is a bad idea. The fear of increased crime, increased drug use, and the potential threat to children are the most often stated reasons. Citing the devastating consequences of alcohol and tobacco use, most Americans question society's ability to use any addictive, mind-altering drug responsibly. Currently, the public favors both supply reduction, demand reduction, and an increased emphasis on prevention, treatment, and rehabilitation as effective strategies in combating the drug problem. Shaping public policy is a critical function that greatly relies upon public input. The policymaking apparatus is influenced by public opinion, and public opinion is in turn influenced by public policy. When the president refers to drugs as threats to national security, the impact on public opinion is tremendous. Currently, record amounts of opium are being produced in Afghanistan and the implications for its providing support for the Taliban and terrorism are clear. Opium production in Southwest Asia, an entrenched staple in the region's overall economic product, continues as a priority of U.S. national security. The resulting implications for sustaining enforcement-oriented U.S. drug policy are also clear; and in the minds of most Americans, they are absolutely necessary. The U.S. Department of State alone will receive $336 million for alternative crop production, diplomacy, interdiction, and enforcement.

Although the prevailing characteristic of most current drug policy still reflects a punitive, "get tough" approach to control, an added emphasis on treating and rehabilitating offenders is visible in policy changes occurring over the past 10 years. Correctional systems are reflecting with greater consistency the view that drug treatment made available to inmates is a critical component of rehabilitation. The California Department of Corrections, the largest in the nation, was recently renamed the California Department of Corrections and Rehabilitation. A prisoner with a history of drug abuse, who receives no drug treatment while in custody, is finally being recognized as a virtual guarantee to reoffend. In 2006, the National Institute of Drug Abuse published the first federal guidelines for administering drug treatment to criminal justice populations.

Another complicated aspect of creating national as well as local drug policy is consideration of the growing body of research on the subject. The past 20 years have produced numerous public and private investigations, surveys, and conclusions relative to the dynamics of drug use in U.S. society. Although an historical assessment of the influence of research on policy produces indirect relationships, policy decisions of the last few years can be directly related to evidence-based research findings and not just political views. One example is the consistently increasing commitment to treatment. This commitment comes as a direct result of research related to progress achieved in treating and rehabilitating users. Treatment, in terms of dollars spent, can compete with all other components of drug control policy.

One important issue affecting and sometimes complicating the research/policymaking relationship is that the policymaking community, at all levels of government, is largely composed of persons of diverse backgrounds, professional capacities, and political interests. Some are elected officials, others are civil servants, and many are private citizens from the medical, educational, and research communities. In some cases, such as with alcohol and tobacco, powerful industry players assert a tremendous influence on policy. As you read on, consider the new research-related applications for drug policy, such as those related to the rehabilitation of incarcerated drug offenders.

Catch and Release

California's prisons are packed with repeat nonviolent drug offenders. Folsom State Prison's Parolee Substance Abuse Program seeks to rehabilitate, not incarcerate.

JANELLE WEINER

For more than 20 years, Julius Johnson's life swung dangerously out of whack. Although he tried to attend school and hold down a job, plans for how and where to get his next drink or bag of weed crowded his mind. Constantly drunk, stoned or both, he landed in prison multiple times.

"You don't wanna know how many times I've been in," says Johnson, shaking his head. At 45, his face is still boyish, but the ache in his voice reveals a man who has suffered beyond his years. He's tried to walk the straight and narrow, but always loses his balance and winds up back "behind the wall."

This time it's different. After his most recent parole violation, Johnson was given a choice: Go back behind the wall, or enter the Parolee Substance Abuse Program, located in the Folsom Transitional Treatment Facility, in the shadow of the maximum-security state prison.

Johnson chose the latter, and now he says he's been "reborn."

Like Johnson, all of the 200 parolees participating in the recovery program have at least one nonserious, nonviolent felony on their records. Some have been in and out of custody for as long as they can remember. This time when they violated parole—many, but not all, for failing drug tests—they were given the same choice as Johnson: Return to prison for five months to a year or begin a 90-day substance-abuse and transitional living program at Folsom's minimum-security treatment facility.

With California's prisons facing unprecedented overcrowding and ballooning costs, proponents of parole reform are looking at programs like Folsom's to keep inmates from repeatedly returning to prison. Many experts say California's rigid parole policies result in parolees returning to prison at nearly twice the rate of the national average. They want more options for parole violators, including expanding rehabilitation and transitional services as an alternative to lengthy and costly prison terms for nonviolent offenders.

Nevertheless, systematic improvements have been met with resistance from government leaders, the public and the California Correctional Peace Officers Association. Gov. Arnold Schwarzenegger and the Legislature have repeatedly stricken reform measures from the budget, while voters and the CCPOA continue to hold fast to "three strikes."

The short of it? Unless the state takes immediate action, the three federal judges empowered in 2007 to reduce prison overcrowding may turn loose as many as 50,000 nonviolent offenders on the streets. Many won't have the skills to survive and will land right back in trouble. And thanks to the state's ongoing financial problems and lack of political will, recovery programs such as Folsom are in short supply exactly when they're needed the most.

"If no one addresses their substance abuse, even if they have a job, they're right back," insists Thomas Powers, director of the California Department of Corrections and Rehabilitation's Division of Addiction and Recovery Services. "The more risk and needs we can address in an inmate, the lower chance they have to recidivate."

The School of Drugs and Hard Knocks

In the cavernous room where Johnson and the other men sleep, a row of low concrete walls separates narrow beds from a section of the dorm used as a classroom for new arrivals. Battered lockers next to each bed provide some sense of individual space, and slivers of natural light fall from narrow windows. Outside the window, a fence topped with barbed wire and video cameras encloses the property.

The mattresses aren't soft, but it could be worse. The parolees could be behind the wall. A 2007 audit of CDCR's rehabilitative services labeled in-prison programs across the state "a complete waste." The program at the Folsom Transitional Treatment Facility, outside the main prison, offers a stark contrast to that assessment.

The Contra Costa County Office of Education runs the program; principal Shannon Swain monitors activities on site. She strolls across the linoleum floor in a long skirt, passing parolees who move aside and say, "Excuse me."

One guy looks up, his blue eyes dancing, and grins at Swain as she passes.

"Hey, you're the director or head coordinator or something, right?" he asks. The yellow lettering on his uniform reads "CDC Prisoner." Although the CDCR changed its name to include "Rehabilitation" in 2005, not all of the uniforms reflect the change.

"Principal," Swain says.

"I knew it was something like that."

Swain and project coordinator Sam Williams Jr. proceed across the enclosed outdoor common area to a classroom where parolees in their first 30 days of the program—Phase I—are reviewing the answers to a test on psychopharmacology. They sit around tables in small groups, folders, paper, pens and blue "Framework for Recovery" workbooks covering the surfaces in front of them. A few men chatter. One rests a foot on a chair.

The teacher, a small, peppy woman with graying hair moves back and forth to the whiteboard at the front of the room. She has written the objective at the top: "Student will classify drugs into categories and will be able to identify two withdrawal symptoms from each category." All of the teachers at PSAP are credentialed. They utilize structured lesson plans as wells as hands-on and cooperative learning to keep their students engaged.

"Under law, barbiturates are classified as . . . " she calls out, getting the ball rolling.

Answers pop up from around the room. A blond-haired guy calls out from the back row, "B—narcotics!"

The teacher writes the answer on the board and continues. The pace is quick. Participation is high.

"A lot of drugs make you impotent," she mentions at one point. A lanky college-age parolee whispers a question from his seat in the front.

"Not being able to rise to the occasion," answers the teacher.

The guy mouths, "Ohh."

Slumped in his seat in the back of the room, a short, muscular Latino man with tattoos under both eyes and above one eyebrow folds his arms tightly across his chest. His jaw is set and he looks tense, guarded, as if he's defending a one-man fortress. He's been staring straight ahead since Swain and Williams entered the room.

Swain asks to borrow his test packet momentarily. He nods.

"How are you doing?" she asks, gently lifting the packet from his hands.

The man's pained face softens into a smile. His shoulders drop. "Good, good," he says quietly. He has been here two weeks. The first days and weeks of Phase I are perhaps the most difficult. Detox, depending on the parolee's drug of choice, can be physically demanding, and the intense psychological work needed to root out the addiction can be emotionally draining. At least two parolees per month drop out of the program and return to prison.

But Julius Johnson is no quitter. It was during Phase I that he realized he'd been given a second chance. Outside the wall, Johnson spent most of his time trying to score. Early mornings would find him passing by the same building where the same group of people always seemed to be standing outside, waiting to get in. Even when it was cold, even when it was dark, they were there.

One day, returning with his stash, Johnson noticed the walk in front of the building was empty and decided to investigate. He pushed opened the door, stuck his head inside, and was greeted by a roomful of familiar faces turning to look at the man hovering in the doorway.

Johnson backed out of the silent room, away from the faces. Later that day, he asked a custodian what took place there in the mornings. It was an Alcoholics Anonymous meeting.

The next time he passed by, he could have walked in, grabbed a cup of coffee and taken a seat. He could have told them his name and admitted he had a problem.

"That should have been my wake-up call," he says. "This is where I was supposed to go, but I didn't."

When his parole officer suggested he attend a rehabilitation program instead of returning to a prison cell, Johnson initially resisted. He knew how to do prison. He'd never attended recovery before, and he didn't believe in it.

"I knew I had a problem," he says. "But I always thought if a person wanted to stop, they would."

"The first week or so, they don't wanna be here," confirms project coordinator Williams, who passed on his powerful physique to his NFL player son. "Their parole officer did them an injustice. Then after about a week, it's 'Oh, this isn't as bad as I thought it was. I could learn something here.' We see that all the time."

Phase I opened doors for Johnson, teaching him how to raise his self-esteem and understand his emotions.

"It was like I was reborn," he says.

Later in Phase I, Johnson and his classmates cycled through lessons such as "The Process of Addiction" and "Cognitive Restructuring"—or as Williams calls it, "changing their stinkin' thinking."

The walls come down. Denial and grief are exposed. The men often keep it together in the classroom, only to break down in sessions with their independent-study teachers later. They reveal that a father abused them or that a mother taught them how to use drugs. To climb out of the hole, they've got to get to the bottom of it first.

In response to the 2007 audit, Gov. Schwarzenegger and prison leadership convened an expert panel to make recommendations for improving rehabilitation and reducing overcrowding. Among the numerous problems they found with existing in-prison programs were shoddily monitored care providers, classes frequently interrupted by lockdowns and prison politics that distracted inmates from the mental and emotional work of recovery.

Stephen Siscoe, a recovering methamphetamine addict currently going through Phase I, has experienced prison politics up close and personal. He says the continuous, often violent struggle between various gangs and factions behind the wall don't apply at Folsom's minimum-security program. After spending six hours a day in classes together, many of the men go back to the dorms and continue their conversations. Some talk about their pasts. Others prefer to focus on the future. There is almost always someone willing to offer support.

If Siscoe hadn't been sent to the program, he has no doubt he would still be on the streets, addicted and on the run.

"I would be out there cheating, lying, justifying my behavior, looking behind my back," he says, elbows perched on a metal table bolted to the dormitory floor. Siscoe's large hands spill out of his denim uniform as he describes what landed him here. Family, adolescence, culture, choices.

"We're all adolescents inside," he says. In Phase I, he finally began to grow up.

Breaking the Born-Bad Mold

The sign above the door of the Phase II classroom reads: "Nothing Changes Until I Change." Williams and Swain venture into the classroom, where parolees continue to focus on unlocking negative thought and behavior patterns. They learn how to manage anger and maintain healthy relationships, all the skills necessary to stay clean and sober outside the wall.

The room is packed with men sitting in pairs at rows of tables. An animated discussion in the classroom next door filters through the floor-to-ceiling room divider, but no one seems to notice. Someone jokes, "We're all crazy in here," but no one laughs.

Even with his beard, the teacher looks younger than the majority of men in the room. He's not intimidated, and enthusiastically leads a lesson on stereotypes.

"Is there such a thing as a 'bad' person?" he asks.

The room is quiet, and the teacher asks a thin young man with a close-shaved head if he would like to answer.

The man says he's not sure, so the teacher presses him to share some things about himself that show he's a good person.

"Playing with my kids, hanging out with my old lady, working. Those show I'm not bad."

A few others raise their hands. The discussion takes a philosophical turn.

"Everyone does bad stuff, it's just some get caught," comes a voice from the back of the room.

Cedric McKinney reached his turning point one day during the second phase. He and his classmates were asked to consider the way substance abuse had affected their lives. The teacher told them to think of three things they had lost.

"I could think of more," he says.

McKinney wants to change. That increases his chances for success. But in a prison system where participation in some rehabilitation programs has actually been correlated with a higher recidivism rate, wanting to change isn't always enough. For McKinney, the difference is in the support he receives from the teachers at Folsom.

"The people who run the program give you all they have," says McKinney, who tutors fellow parolees for the GED in the evenings after class. "They don't just let you float through like it's prison."

James Ayres spent 31 months behind the wall and was released back to the community before coming to the program. On the outside, he informally counseled other addicts on the street. Then he got hooked again himself.

Ayres prefers to keep to himself in the dorms, but he has developed an admiration of teacher Mike Gray. Beyond helping him develop a transition plan for attending school, Gray has helped Ayres understand what the experience might be like.

In Gray's classroom, a detailed pencil drawing of Emiliano Zapata rests on a table. Gray encourages his students to explore and take pride in their cultures.

Throughout his 30 years of social work and teaching experience, Gray has worked to balance the need to maintain appropriate boundaries with his students and communicating to them that he knows where they've been.

To Ayres, Gray is "on the level."

As the lesson on stereotypes continues in the Phase II classroom, a common theme emerges.

"No one in society thinks we can be better," one parolee says soberly. "You find that out when you try to get a job."

"You begin to feel hopeless," another student chimes in.

From the front of the room, a heavy-set African-American man gets the floor.

"They don't care about us," he says. "Or they say they care, but they do it from a distance. If there were more programs, if we had more people advocating, we'd do better."

Tough on Crime, Weak on Justice

Dr. Barry Krisberg, director of the National Council on Crime and Delinquency, says there are limits to the effect rehabilitative programming can have on reducing recidivism. Nevertheless, he laments what he sees as a lack of reform in CDCR's rehabilitative policies and programs.

"The principal barrier has been political will," says Krisberg. "We added the 'R' [in CDCR], but the progress has been glacial."

The three-judge federal panel in the overcrowding case that recently wrapped up in San Francisco found that California could save $803 million to $906 million annually by instituting a system of earned credits and parole reform to reduce the prison population. That money could be used to implement the expert panel's recommendation to provide more evidence-based rehabilitation programs in the community.

CDCR currently provides 5,692 community treatment slots that deliver transitional services for recently released inmates. Some 2,028 slots are being utilized by parolees in another remedial sanction program for parole violators, the In Custody Drug Treatment Program. The three-judge panel left the door open for state officials to divert prisoners into rehabilitative programs rather than commit to a wholesale release of the estimated 50,000 prisoners it would take to bring the population to a safe level.

Nevertheless, in a March report, the California Rehabilitation Oversight Board noted none of the reforms *for rehabilitation programs* recommended by the expert panel were included in the governor's final budget, passed in February.

"The expert panel's report was basically thrown in the garbage," says Krisberg. "If we're unwilling to change because we're afraid of being seen as soft on crime, then we're locked into the same failure mode."

Back at the Folsom Transitional Treatment Facility, it's almost time for the head count. The parolees have lunch together and return to their classrooms for three more hours of instruction.

Tables are arranged conference style in the Phase III classroom, where Swain slips into an empty seat next to Johnson. All around her, parolees focus on teacher Vic Wedloe, a muscular former cop who leans against his desk and looks hard at the men as he lays out a situation they're likely to encounter once they're back home, around the old influences, the old temptations.

"It's the middle of the night," says Wedloe. "And you've got the craving. How do you get through it?"

Eyes flicker. The sea of blue uniforms shifts. The men seem to ponder, but no one raises a hand to answer. Wedloe calls on a wiry man a few seats down from Swain.

The man hesitates, but finally says, "If I can recognize it, I guess I can substitute drugs with something else."

His comment motivates others to speak up. They share stories and insights, chuckles and knowing nods. They articulate their plans: Turn on the television, rearrange the fridge, use positive self-talk. But Wedloe doesn't let them off easy. There are plans, and then there's the reality of facing a lifelong drug addiction.

When Johnson suggests he will call his sponsor, Wedloe challenges him.

"It's 3 in the morning. You wanna wake him up?"

Johnson pauses, looks down. "The way I understand it, he's gotta pick up. If he's a good sponsor, he'll pick up."

Wedloe nods, satisfied. If the men become familiar with their symptoms and have the tools to fight back, they can recover.

"That sensation's never gonna rule your life again?" asks Wedloe.

"Never," Johnson says.

Like 60 percent of the program's graduates, Johnson will attend a 90-day after-care program that includes transitional housing, recovery services and job assistance. Krisberg and other experts say aftercare is critically important—to increase the odds that a parolee will, in fact, stay clean.

Williams, the program's coordinator, is careful to point out that recovery, like addiction, is a process. Some of the parolees will return. Recently, a man who was part of the first group to attend the program approached Williams in the yard and asked if he remembered him.

Williams had to think a minute, but then recalled the man's stay. It wasn't a pleasant one, and the man didn't attend aftercare.

"I shoulda listened to you," he told Williams.

Revenge or Rehabilitation?

Although the price tag for a parole violator to attend substance-abuse classes is $50 higher per day than a prison stay, the program stands to save the state money since the stay is shorter and, at least anecdotally, the parolees who attend the Folsom program stay out of trouble longer, even if they do eventually recidivate.

"The old approach based on revenge needs to be replaced with something based on science," says Krisberg.

Williams isn't about revenge. He shakes his head when he talks about the parolee in the yard, but his voice is filled with understanding.

"We're not mad at them if they come back," he says. "If a lifelong addict can stay clean for six months to a year, it is counted as a success."

"Of course, we hope they stay out for longer," he adds.

Graduations occur on a rolling basis, since new parolees enter the program almost every day. CDCR director Powers says there are no current plans to expand the Parolee Substance Abuse Program, but he is optimistic that improving in-prison rehabilitative programs will lower recidivism rates. "What we're trying to do is make the whole yard a therapeutic yard," he says.

He also stresses the need to expand the number of openings in community-based transition programs for parolees beyond the current 5,692 slots. California currently releases more than 100,000 inmates back to the community each year.

With Assembly Bill 900, the Public Safety and Offender Rehabilitation Services Act of 2007, Gov. Schwarzenegger and legislators attempted to improve prison conditions and rehabilitation programs without releasing prisoners. Since the bill's passage, the number of in-prison drug-treatment slots has increased to nearly 10,000.

Powers, however, estimates 35,000 to 40,000 inmates could benefit from treatment. Many other experts, including Dr. Joan Petersilia, a professor of criminology at UC Irvine who served on the state's expert panel for prison reform, put the estimate at more than twice that.

Meanwhile, Stephen Siscoe will soon leave Folsom to enter a recovery program and take steps towards becoming a substance-abuse counselor himself.

"I've thought about it a lot," he says. "If I understand even more, I'll be more likely to stay away."

Ayres also plans to become a certified counselor. McKinney managed to enroll himself in a construction training course to begin the Monday immediately after his graduation.

Pastel-hued paper mobiles hang from the ceiling above Julius Johnson. The tags, with words like "hobbies," "family" and "respect" written on them, reflect the pieces individual parolees must juggle to lead balanced lives.

If he had been sent back to prison for his parole violation, Johnson would still be there, serving out his sentence and waiting for his "gate money," the $200 all prisoners are given on completion of their sentence. Instead, he will soon enter aftercare and start attending a school that will move him towards his goal of attaining a heavy-equipment operator's license.

At the Folsom facility, Johnson has been reborn. He's been given a second chance, and he knows it's up to him to restore balance to his life. He does not intend to go back behind the wall.

Critical Thinking

1. Why are politicians so resistant to drug rehabilitation programs?

2. Would it better serve our communities and states to focus on rehabilitating and treating these offenders instead of perpetuating the boomerang effect of prison sentences?

3. Do you think a time will come when we as a society decide to focus on treatment rather than punishment?

From *Sacramento News & Review,* April 2, 2009. Copyright © 2009 by Janelle Weiner. Reprinted by permission of the author.

Drugs: To Legalize or Not

Decriminalizing the possession and use of marijuana would raise billions in taxes and eliminate much of the profits that fuel bloodshed and violence in Mexico.

STEVEN B. DUKE

The drug-fueled murders and mayhem in Mexico bring to mind the Prohibition-era killings in Chicago. Although the Mexican violence dwarfs the bloodshed of the old bootleggers, both share a common motivation: profits. These are turf wars, fought between rival gangs trying to increase their share of the market for illegal drugs. Seventy-five years ago, we sensibly quelled the bootleggers' violence by repealing the prohibition of alcohol. The only long-term solution to the cartel-related murders in Mexico is to legalize the other illegal drugs we overlooked when we repealed Prohibition in 1933.

In 2000, the Mexican government disturbed a hornets' nest when it began arresting and prosecuting major distributors of marijuana, cocaine, heroin and amphetamines. Previously, the cartels had relied largely on bribery and corruption to maintain their peaceful co-existence with the Mexican government. Once this *pax Mexicana* ended, however, they began to fight not only the government but among themselves. The ensuing violence has claimed the lives of at least 10,000 in Mexico since 2005, and the carnage has even spilled north to the United States and south to Central and South America.

Some say that this killing spree—about 400 murders a month currently—threatens the survival of the Mexican government. Whether or not that is the exaggeration that Mexican President Felipe Calderón insists it is, Mexico is in crisis. The Mexicans have asked the Obama administration for help, and the president has obliged, offering material support and praising the integrity and courage of the Mexican government in taking on the cartels.

The U.S. should enforce its laws against murder and other atrocious crimes and we should cooperate with Mexican authorities in helping them arrest and prosecute drug traffickers hiding out here. But what more can and should we do?

Is gun control the answer? President Calderón asserts that the cartels get most of their guns from the U.S. We could virtually disarm the cartels, he implies, if we made it harder to buy guns here and smuggle them into Mexico. President Obama has bought into this claim and has made noises about reducing the availability of guns. However, even if the Obama administration were able to circumvent the political and constitutional impediments to restricting Americans' access to handguns, the effect on Mexican drug violence would be negligible. The cartels are heavily armed now, and handguns wear out very slowly.

Even if the Mexican gangsters lost their American supply line, they would probably not feel the loss for years. And when they did, they would simply turn to other suppliers. There is a world-wide black market in military weapons. If the Mexicans could not buy pistols and rifles, they might buy more bazookas, machine guns and bombs from the black market, thus escalating the violence.

Also hopeless is the notion—now believed by almost no one—that we can keep the drugs from coming into this country and thereby cut off the traffickers' major market. If we could effectively interdict smuggling through any of our 300-plus official border crossing points across the country and if we eventually build that fence along our entire border with Mexico— 1,933 miles long—experience strongly suggests that the smugglers will get through it or over it. If not, they will tunnel under or fly over it. And there is always our 12,383 miles of virtually unguarded coastline.

Several proposals have been submitted in the Mexican congress to decriminalize illegal drugs. One was even passed in 2006 but, under pressure from the U.S., President Vicente Fox refused to sign it. The proposals rest on the notion that by eliminating the profit from illegal drug distribution, the cartels will die from the dearth of profits. A major weakness in such proposals, however, is that the main source of the cartels' profits is not Mexican but American. Mexican drug consumption is a mere trickle compared to the river that flows north. However laudable, proposals to decriminalize drugs in Mexico would have little impact on the current drug warfare.

Secretary of State Hillary Clinton recognized the heart of the matter when she told the Mexicans last month that the "insatiable demand for illegal drugs" in the U.S. is fueling the Mexican drug wars. Without that demand, there would be few illegal drug traffickers in Mexico.

Once we have recognized this root cause, we have few options. We can try to eliminate demand, we can attack the suppliers or we can attempt a combination of both. Thus far, the Obama administration, like every other U.S. administration since drug prohibition went into effect in 1914, seems bent on trying to defeat the drug traffickers militarily. Hopefully, President Obama will soon realize, if he does not already, that this approach will not work.

Suppose the U.S. were to "bail out" the Mexican government with tens of billions of dollars, including the provision of military personnel, expertise and equipment in an all-out concerted attack on the drug traffickers. After first escalating, the level of cartel-related violence would ultimately subside. Thousands more lives would be lost in the process, but Mexico could thereby be made less hospitable to the traffickers, as other areas, such as Colombia, Peru and Panama, were made less hospitable in the past. That, after all, is how the Mexicans got their start in the grisly business. Eventually, the traffic would simply move to another country in Latin America or in the Caribbean and the entire process would begin anew. This push-down, pop-up effect has been demonstrated time and again in efforts to curb black markets. It produces an illusion of success, but only an illusion.

An administration really open to "change" would consider a long-term solution to the problem—ending the market for illegal drugs by eliminating their illegality. We cannot destroy the appetite for psychotropic drugs. Both animals and humans have an innate desire for the altered consciousness obtainable through drugs. What we can and should do is eliminate the black market for the drugs by regulating and taxing them as we do our two most harmful recreational drugs, tobacco and alcohol.

Marijuana presents the strongest case for this approach. According to some estimates, marijuana comprises about 70% of the illegal product distributed by the Mexican cartels. Marijuana will grow anywhere. If the threat of criminal prosecution and forfeitures did not deter American marijuana farmers, America's entire supply of that drug would be home-grown. If we taxed the marijuana agribusiness at rates similar to that for tobacco and alcohol, we would raise about $10 billion in taxes per year and would save another $10 billion we now spend on law enforcement and imprisoning marijuana users and distributors.

Even with popular support, legalizing and regulating the distribution of marijuana in the U.S. would be neither easy nor quick. While imposing its prohibitionist will on the rest of the world for nearly a century, the U.S. has created a network of treaties and international agreements requiring drug prohibition. Those agreements would have to be revised. A sensible intermediate step would be to decriminalize the possession and use of marijuana and to exercise benign neglect of American marijuana growers. Doing both would puncture the market for imports from Mexico and elsewhere and would eliminate much of the profit that fuels the internecine warfare in Mexico.

After we reap the rewards from decriminalizing marijuana, we should move on to hard drugs. This will encounter strong resistance. Marijuana is a relatively safe drug. No one has ever died from a marijuana overdose nor has anyone gone on a violent rampage as a result of a marijuana high. Cocaine, heroin and amphetamines, on the other hand, can be highly addictive and harmful, both physically and psychologically. But prohibition makes those dangers worse, unleashing on vulnerable users chemicals of unknown content and potency, and deterring addicts from seeking help with their dependency. There is burgeoning recognition, in the U.S. and elsewhere, that the health benefits and the myriad social and economic advantages of substituting regulation of hard drugs for their prohibition deserves serious consideration.

A most impressive experiment has been underway in Portugal since 2001, when that country decriminalized the possession and personal use of all psychotropic drugs. According to a study just published by the Cato Institute, "judged by virtually every metric," the Portuguese decriminalization "has been a resounding success." Contrary to the prognostications of prohibitionists, the numbers of Portuguese drug users has not increased since decriminalization. Indeed, the percentage of the population who has ever used these drugs is lower in Portugal than virtually anywhere else in the European Union and is far below the percentage of users in the U.S. One explanation for this startling fact is that decriminalization has both freed up funds for drug treatment and, by lifting the threat of criminal charges, encouraged drug abusers to seek that treatment.

We can try to deal with the Mexican murderers as we first dealt with Al Capone and his minions, or we can apply the lessons we learned from alcohol prohibition and finish dismantling the destructive prohibition experiment. We should begin by decriminalizing marijuana now.

Critical Thinking

1. Is the answer to the violence which stems from illegal drugs simply to legalize them? Why do most people not believe in this?

2. Do you think the Portuguese strategy could work here in the United States?

STEVEN B. DUKE is a professor of law at Yale Law School.

Do No Harm

Sensible Goals for International Drug Policy

Peter Reuter

D rug policy has been an inconvenient issue for the national security apparatus of the United States, whether run by a Democratic or Republican administration. Even after 35 years of some sort of domestic "war on drugs", forcefully articulated by every President since Ronald Reagan, the international dimension of the issue remains distasteful to diplomats. It often involves dealing with law enforcement in corrupt countries and complicates many a U.S. Ambassador's life. The contending lobbies that care about it are loud, moralistic and well informed. If that were not enough, most of our principal allies, particularly in Europe, think there is a certain madness in the American belief that international interventions against the drug trade can accomplish much good.

Mere inconvenience is an insufficient reason to abandon a policy, of course, but in this case there are stronger arguments for change. The Obama Administration has an opportunity before it, for both history and argument show that U.S. international efforts to control drug production and trafficking cannot do much more than affect where and how coca and opium poppies are grown. The quantity produced is minimally affected, since suppression of production in one country almost invariably leads to expansion in another.

More important, control efforts often cause damage. Not only are such programs as spraying poppy and coca fields themselves harmful, but forcing the drug trade to move from one country to another may hurt the new producer country more than it helps the old one. Hence, the U.S. government should no longer push for "global containment", as the policy has been defined. Rather, it should focus attention and resources on supporting the few states both willing and able to do something about production or trafficking in their countries. Unfortunately, Afghanistan, the center of attention right now, is not one of those countries.

American Bull in the China Shop

The United States has been the principal driver of international drug control efforts since 1909, when it convened a meeting of the International Opium Commission (primarily aimed at helping China cut its opium consumption). The United States then pushed for the creation of a web of prohibitionist international treaties under the auspices first of the League of Nations and then the United Nations. Its voice is the dominant one at the annual meetings of the UN Commission on Narcotic Drugs. In that forum it has stood firm against any softening of existing policies. Most prominently, the United States has denounced

in recent years "harm reduction" interventions such as needle-distribution programs aimed at reducing the spread of HIV.

Nor does it hesitate to scold even its closest neighbors for deviating from its hard-line, prohibitionist stance. In 2003, U.S. drug czar John Walters accused Canada of poisoning American youth when Ottawa proposed decriminalizing marijuana possession, a policy similar to that of a dozen U.S. states. The United States has even proven willing to barter specific foreign policy interests to influence other nations' drug policies. In the Clinton Administration senior State Department officials told Australia that trade negotiations would be dragged out if Canberra went ahead with a planned experiment in which the most troubled heroin addicts might be supplied with the drug (a program now routine in Switzerland and the Netherlands). Though not a lot of money (by the standards of the overall U.S. drug policy budget) is spent on overseas drug control, Plan Colombia ($5 billion since 2001) is by far the largest U.S. foreign assistance program in Latin America, making Colombia the fourth largest recipient of U.S. aid.

These interventions have real consequences for U.S. foreign policy. Tensions with NATO allies in Afghanistan have been exacerbated by disagreements over how aggressively to act against opium production. Plan Colombia, which funds the civil rights-abusing Colombian military, causes much unease among neighboring countries. From 1986 until 2001, relations with Mexico were roiled by Mexican indignation at the U.S. annual "certification", in which the world's largest drug consumer decided whether its neighbors had done enough to reduce its own importation of drugs.

What these policies and programs seem not to have done is to reduce either the American or the global drug problems. That is not the consequence of badly designed programs or administrative incompetence, though there are plenty of both. Rather, it is a result of the fact that international programs like eradication or interdiction simply cannot make much of a difference because they aim at the wrong part of the problem: production and trafficking in source countries. The right part of the problem to aim at is demand in importing countries, including our own. But, of course, that is a difficult and uncertain task, and even successful programs take a long time to have much effect.[1]

It would not be wise to close up shop altogether. After all, there are some connections between the illicit drug trade and terrorist financing that Americans would be foolish to ignore, and there may occasionally be promising opportunities to help specific countries.

But we should adopt more limited, common sense goals for U.S. international drug policy.

Heroin and Cocaine

Today's mass market in illegal heroin is a new phenomenon. Before 1965, the drug was a niche product and one of declining popularity in the United States. Poppies were refined into opium and mostly consumed in Asia. However, between 1965 and 1995 heroin epidemics erupted in many rich industrialized countries from Australia to Norway. The loosening of social and economic controls in China in the late 1980s and the break-up of the Soviet Union in the early 1990s added a few more countries to the list of those with heroin problems. Iran, Pakistan, Thailand and other traditional opium producers also became heroin-consuming countries, partly as a consequence of Western pressures to crack down on opium distribution. Heroin use can't be found everywhere in the world these days, but it is certainly no longer just a niche problem. So serious is the challenge that there have even been times when the United States, Iran and Russia have quietly made common cause to deal with it.

While heroin use was spreading, heroin production became more concentrated. By the 1980s, Afghanistan and Burma had come to dominate production, accounting for more than 90 percent of the total each year. Since 2002, Afghanistan has been the dominant producer: In 2007, with a new record output, it produced roughly 93 percent of the world total, about 8,000 tons. (Before the Taliban banned opium production in 2000, production had only once exceeded 4,000 tons.)

Why do Afghanistan and Burma dominate? It's not because either is particularly well suited in terms of land or climate. Opium has been produced in many countries; Australia and France are two big producers for the contemporary legal market, while Thailand and Macedonia were major producers in the past. So what accounts for the current situation?

Afghanistan was not historically a large opium producer, but three major events combined to change that. The overthrow of the Shah in 1979 led to the installation of an Iranian regime much more concerned with drugs as a moral issue. The Islamic Republic promptly cracked down on opium production in Iran. Willing to execute producers and growers after only minimal due process, Iran quickly eliminated domestic opium poppy cultivation. However, it was much less successful in reducing demand, and the result was a new market for Afghan exports. This happened at roughly the same time that the Soviet Union invaded Afghanistan, which eroded central government authority and led to the rise of warlords for whom opium production was a major source of income. The civil war that broke out following the exit of the Soviet troops exacerbated the situation and made Afghanistan still more attractive for opium growing and heroin refining.

For Burma the shaping events took place over an even longer period. Those events relate partly to the political history of China. When the Communists took the Chinese Mainland in 1949, some Kuomintang army units retreated south into up-country Burma. Now forced to support themselves, they put their military and organization skills to work in the opium industry. Then, in the 1970s, the Burmese Communist Party, cut off from Chinese government finance as China attempted to improve relationships with its neighbors, turned to the heroin trade as a way to finance its activities. Thus Chinese anti-communists and Burmese communists alike helped raise Burma's heroin production profile—proof of how deeply the drug trade is embedded in larger geopoliti-

cal processes. Drug production cannot be treated as just another industry, responding primarily to economic influences. The Burmese and Afghan cases also illustrate how easily the location of production can shift. There are many corrupt and poor countries available for production if for some reason Afghanistan should cut its production.

Cocaine lacks the global reach of heroin; it's still mostly a rich nation's drug (though, of course, not mostly rich people in those nations use it). What seemed in the 1980s a uniquely American problem has now spread to Europe. Britain and Spain clearly have substantial cocaine problems and others are vulnerable as well. Eastern Europe is also catching up in heretofore Western vices as its productivity and politics approach Western levels.

The production story here is straightforward. Bolivia, Colombia and Peru are the only commercial producers of cocaine for the illegal market. Whereas in the 1980s Colombia was the third most important producer of coca leaves, for the past ten years it has accounted for about two thirds of the total, as well as the vast majority of refining. The shift of coca growing from Peru and Bolivia to Colombia is probably the result both of massive rural flight in Colombia and tougher policies in the other two countries. The violent conflict in Colombia's established rural areas has forced farmers to frontiers within the country where there is little infrastructure for legitimate agriculture, and coca growing is very attractive in part because these areas are difficult to monitor or police. Despite a massive eradication campaign, production levels for the Andes as a whole have been fairly stable over the past decade.

Ties to Terrorism

That U.S. policies over several decades now have not appreciably affected the overall level of heroin and cocaine on the market is a cause for some frustration. One reason it vexes U.S. policymakers is that illegal drugs are funding some terrorist organizations—though it would be counterproductive to exaggerate the extent of this funding. In 2003, the Office of National Drug Control Policy attracted considerable derision with its Super Bowl ads tying drug use to the promotion of international terrorism. Since most U.S. drug use is limited to marijuana, much of it produced domestically or in Canada, the connection seemed flimsy. The ads disappeared quickly.

That said, the problem is not imaginary. Before it banned opium production in 2000, the Taliban taxed it, though no more than it taxed other agricultural products. Since it didn't provide much in the way of government services, the estimated $30 million the Taliban got from opium taxes was the second largest source of revenue, after its taxation of consumer goods smuggled into Pakistan. Al-Qaeda's sources of revenue are a matter of mystery, at least in the unclassified literature, but it certainly has earned some money from trafficking opium or heroin over the years. Nowadays its involvement in protecting (i.e., taxing) opium production in Afghanistan may be an important activity. Secretary of Defense Robert Gates has asserted that al-Qaeda receives $80–100 million annually from the heroin trade. (Like all such figures, this one has no known provenance and should be treated with some skepticism.)

Many other terrorist groups have known ties to drug trafficking. The FARC in Colombia taxes coca growing, the Kurdistan People's Party in Turkey has some connection to drug traffickers among the Kurdish diaspora in Europe, and the Tamil Tigers have been caught smuggling heroin. None of these groups are particularly important in the global drug trade, but the trade may be particularly important to them.

For policymakers the relevant question is whether attacking the drug trade is an efficient method for cutting terrorist finance. Given the fact that there are few successful examples of policies that generate large-scale reductions in drug revenues, the answer is generally no. While there might be specific opportunities in which, say, moving the drug trade from one route to another could help reduce the flow of funds to terrorists, in general these criminal problems are hardly twins joined at the hip. The drug trade is just one of many illegal activities for which terrorist organizations have some useful organizational assets. In short, we would not cripple terrorist financing even if we were successful in international drug policy efforts. But this is merely an academic point, for experience shows us why we cannot be successful.

Cutting Drug Exports

The United States has pushed three types of programs to cut source country production: eradication, alternative development and in-country enforcement. Eradication, usually involving aerial spraying, aims literally to limit the quantity of the drug available in the United States, raise the costs of those drugs, or otherwise discourage farmers from producing them. Alternative development is the soft version of the same basic idea. It encourages farmers growing coca or poppies to switch to legitimate crops by increasing earnings from these other products—for example, by introducing new and more productive strains of traditional crops, better transportation to get the crops to market or some form of marketing scheme. Finally, the United States pushes other countries to pursue traffickers and refiners more vigorously. None of the three methods has worked all that well.

Few countries are willing to allow aerial eradication, which may cause environmental damage. It is also politically unattractive because it targets peasant farmers, who are among the poorest citizens even when growing coca or poppy. Colombia and Mexico, neither one traditional producers of drugs, have been the producer countries most willing to allow spraying. Most others allow only manual eradication, a slow and cumbersome method.

The fundamental problem of source-country interventions aimed at producers of coca and poppy is easily described. These programs have always had a peculiar glamor and occupy a large share of the headlines about drug policy. But the fact that the actual production costs of coca or opium account for a trivial share of the retail price of cocaine or heroin dooms source-country interventions as ways of controlling the problem.

It costs approximately $300 to purchase enough coca leaves to produce a kilogram of cocaine, which retails for about $100,000 in the United States when sold in one-gram, two-thirds pure units for $70 per unit. The modest share of the agricultural costs associated with cocaine production is easily explained: Production involves cheap land and labor in poor countries, and it requires no expensive specialized inputs. (Even Bolivia, the smallest of the three producer countries, has more than 500,000 square miles of territory—much of it opaque to surveillance.) Assume that eradication efforts lead to a doubling of the price of coca leaf, so that cocaine refiners now must pay $600 for enough leaf to produce one kilogram of cocaine. Even if the full cost increase is passed along, the change in retail price will still be negligible. Indeed,

leaf prices have varied enormously over the past decade, while the retail price of cocaine has fallen almost throughout the same period. If retail prices do not rise, then total consumption in the United States will not decline as a consequence of eradication. In this scenario, there will be no reduction in total production—just more land torn up in more places to plant an environmentally damaging crop.

There is, of course, a less harsh option for policy in the source country: alternative development. Offer the farmers the opportunity to earn more money growing pineapples than coca, and they will move to the legal crop, the argument goes.

Quite aside from the time and money it takes to implement a successful alternative-crop program, the argument, alas, is subject to the same economic illogic as that for eradication. It assumes that the price of coca leaf will not increase enough to tempt the peasants back to coca growing. But as long as the price of leaf is so small compared to the street price of cocaine in Chicago, refiners will offer a high enough price to get back the land and labor needed to meet the needs of the cocaine market. Peasants will be better off than before the alternative development, but only because they will make more money growing coca. Mexican peasants are substantially better off than those in Bolivia, but that has not kept them out of the drug business. Indeed, the same can be said for Kentucky corn farmers, who are prominent in the marijuana trade in the United States.

Three Countries, Three Problems

For the United States the international drug problem is dominated by three countries: Afghanistan, Colombia and Mexico. Each presents a different problem, both to the United States and to the producing country. But all three show why the elimination/interdiction approach to source country supply doesn't work.

The United States is trying to create an effective democratic state in Afghanistan and is demonstrably failing. Further, despite the presence of 60,000 NATO and U.S. troops, Afghanistan's output of opium has increased massively over the seven years since the Taliban fell. That has provided important funding for the Taliban and al-Qaeda as well as for warlords independent of the central government. It has also worsened the country's deep-seated corruption. According to the former coordinator of U.S. counter-narcotics efforts in Afghanistan, there was much conflict within the Bush Administration about pursuing aggressive counter-narcotics efforts. Insiders argued over whether these efforts were needed to establish a strong state or, on the contrary, whether they would threaten the very existence of the Karzai government.[2]

The drug hawks have usually won the rhetorical battles, but they have lost the programmatic wars. In October 2008, Defense Secretary Gates declared that the U.S. military will go after traffickers and warlords but will not eradicate farmers' poppy fields. Given the relative invisibility of trafficking, this is effectively a truce. But better a truce than a "war" against poppies that cannot be won and might be counterproductive politically if it were won.

Colombia, unlike Afghanistan, is a principal producer of drugs for the United States, most prominently cocaine but also heroin. The United States has tried to strengthen a Colombian government long beleaguered by guerrilla conflict, and in this it has succeeded reasonably well. But the primary goal of its assistance has been to reduce the flow of Colombian-produced cocaine into the United States, and in that task it has largely failed.

Mexico, occasionally described as a natural smuggling platform for the United States, has been the principal drug transshipment country into the United States for two decades. The bulk of America's imports of cocaine, heroin, marijuana and methamphetamine all come through Mexico. In the past two years the level of violence associated with the U.S.-destined drug trade has skyrocketed. More than 5,000 people were killed in drug-related violence in 2008; that included systematic terror killings of innocent individuals, honest police and reporters. This has happened partly because of changes in the trade itself and partly as a consequence of government efforts to control the violence. The new U.S. program to help Mexico—$400 million for training police and military—may ostensibly be aimed at cutting down the flow of drugs to the United States, but such low levels of funding are not likely to achieve much. The money is more properly viewed as reparations: Mexico is suffering from the consequences of our continued appetite for illegal drugs, so the United States has an obligation to help ameliorate those problems regardless of whether it cuts U.S. drug imports.

Strategic Consequences of the Balloon Effect

There is almost universal skepticism that international efforts by rich countries can reduce global production of cocaine and heroin. It is hard to find anyone outside of the State Department, the White House or Congress who argues otherwise. But efforts to curb production in specific places have had some effect. We noted previously that targeting Bolivian and Peruvian smuggling into Colombia helped make Colombia the dominant producer of coca. The Chinese government since about 1998 has pushed the United Wa State Army to successfully (and brutally) cut Burma's production of heroin. Spraying in Mexico in the 1970s shifted opium production from a five-state region in the north to a much more dispersed set of states around the country.

Interdiction can also affect the routing of the trade. In the early 1980s then-Vice President George H.W. Bush led the South Florida Task Force that successfully reduced smuggling through the Caribbean. The traffic then shifted to Mexico, but the effort did help several Caribbean governments. Similarly, more heroin may now be flowing through Pakistan because the Iranian government has intensified its border control.

In recent years this kind of interaction has been most conspicuous with respect to cocaine trafficking. The Netherlands Antilles is conveniently located for Colombian traffickers shipping to Europe, as there are many direct flights from Curaçao to Amsterdam's Schiphol airport, one of the busiest in Europe. In response to evidence of growing cocaine trafficking to Amsterdam, the Dutch government implemented a 100 percent search policy for airline passengers from Curaçao in March 2004. Whereas cocaine seizures in the Netherlands Antilles had not exceeded 1.3 tons before 2003, in 2004 they reached nine tons, a remarkable figure for a jurisdiction with fewer than 200,000 inhabitants. (The United States seizes only about 150 tons per year.) Shipments through Schiphol airport have since fallen sharply.

Probably as a consequence, new trafficking routes have opened up from South America to Europe via West Africa. For example, Guinea-Bissau is impoverished and small, it has no military or police capacity to deal with smugglers, and its government is easily corrupted. Smugglers have begun using landing strips there for large shipments. In 2007, there was one seizure of three-quarters of a ton, and it is believed that an even larger quantity from that shipment made it out of the country.

Ghana, a larger nation but one with fragile institutions, has also seen a sudden influx of cocaine traffickers. In 2005, flights from Accra accounted for more seized cocaine at London's Heathrow airport than from flights from any other city. There are now regular reports of multi-kilo seizures of the drug either in Ghana itself or at airports receiving flights from Ghana.

Assuming that Ghana and Guinea-Bissau are serving as trafficking platforms at least in part because of the effective crackdown on an existing route through Curaçao, is the world better off? Certainly the Netherlands has helped itself. One can hardly be critical of a country making a strong effort to minimize its involvement in the drug trade. However, one can reasonably ask whether, in making these decisions, the Netherlands should take into account the likely effects of its actions on other, more vulnerable countries.

This analysis also applies to Afghanistan, assuming that it will for the foreseeable future be the most attractive location for opium production. The U.S. government continues to press the Karzai Administration to begin eradication activities in the areas it controls. At the same time, the United States emphasizes the importance of opium production to the Taliban. If farmers in government-controlled areas are forced out of business, it is likely that more of the growing activity, and probably more refining as well, will shift to areas controlled by the Taliban. The result may be to increase Taliban strength, both politically and financially—obviously not a result we would ever intend.

Awkward Choices

International drug policy will not be high on the Obama Administration's list of priorities, given that the U.S. drug problem itself is gradually declining. It has indeed not been a major issue for the Bush Administration. Congress was fairly passive on the issue during the past eight years, but those members who have been vocal have all been drug hawks, passionately arguing that this nation has a moral obligation to fight one of the great scourges of modern times on a worldwide scale. The public is apparently indifferent, seeing the drug problem as one for which every measure (tough enforcement, prevention or more treatment slots) is fairly hopeless. This, in turn, has not encouraged liberal members of Congress to take on the issue.

Drug policy is one of many areas of international policy in which the Obama Administration would benefit from adopting a more humble attitude. The arrogance with which U.S. delegations at the annual Commission on Narcotic Drugs lecture the rest of the world would be laughable if it weren't for the fact that many nations are still cowed by the sheer scale of U.S. efforts. There is no evidence that the United States knows how to help reduce the world's drug problems or to affect the ease with which cocaine, heroin and methamphetamine are procured and trafficked. Moreover, the harm that some of our interventions cause is more apparent than their benefits. For example, spraying coca fields in Colombia clearly has adverse environmental consequences if only because it spreads production further, and it also probably sharpens conflict between the Colombian government and its citizens. Pressing the Karzai government to spray poppy fields increases tensions with our allies. Our attack on drug policy initiatives in other countries exacerbates the U.S. reputation for bullying and disinterestedness in true multilateral collaboration.

Doing less about a problem is rarely an attractive policy recommendation. But for international drug policy it is the only recommendation one can make with confidence. It is perhaps true, as Simone Weil once said, that "it is better to fail than to succeed in doing harm."

Notes

1. See, for example, Jonathan Caulkins and Peter Reuter, "Re-orienting Drug Policy", *Issues in Science and Technology* (Fall 2006); David Boyum and Peter Reuter, *An Analytic Assessment of U.S. Drug Policy* (American Enterprise Institute Press, 2005); and Mark A.R. Kleiman, "Dopey, Boozy, Smoky—and Stupid", *The American Interest* (January/February 2007).

2. Thomas Schweich, "Is Afghanistan a Narco-State?" *New York Times Magazine,* July 27, 2008.

Reference

Reuter, Peter. (2009, March/April). The American Interest: Do No Harm. *Sensible Goads for International Drug Policy,* Vol. IV. No. 4, 46-52.

Critical Thinking

1. Should we continue with our current international drug policy? Why?

2. Some argue that current strategies to counter global drug issues are not working. What suggestions would you make?

PETER REUTER is a professor of public policy and criminology at the University of Maryland. He is co-author (with Letizia Paoli and Victoria Greenfield) of the forthcoming *The World Heroin Market: Can Supply Be Cut?* (Oxford University Press).

It Is Time to End the War on Drugs

An over-reliance on law enforcement and incarceration to address the drug problem has led to seriously adverse consequences not only for public health, but also for the courts and correctional systems.

A three-year-old visits his mom each month for a few hours. She never reads him a story before bed, nor will she help him with homework when he starts school. She mistakenly thought being a drug courier for a few hundred dollars might get him the necessities she could not afford. Mom is in prison. A governor faces the wrath of a federal court that demands he find a way to release 44,000 inmates from a prison system that is so overcrowded that basic medical care and inmate safety can no longer be provided. A trial judge's docket is overwhelmed with drug cases, most of which result hi lengthy and costly periods of incarceration. All are among the victims of the war on drugs. It is a war that soon will mark its 39-year anniversary. Few public policies have compromised public health and undermined the fair and effective functioning of the justice system for so long. It is time for the war to end and for policymakers to implement new strategies that utilize united justice system resources in the service of public health and demand reduction.

The war on drugs was declared by President Nixon in June 1971. The metaphor of the war on drugs created the image of a united national effort to defeat an enemy. In times of war, dissent from the mission is unpatriotic and cost is of little concern. Americans don't lose wars. But from its inception, the metaphor of war on drugs created problems. To call for an end to the war on drugs is not to advocate that drugs are good for you. Each day someone dies from a drug overdose. A child drops out of school because of drugs. A marriage goes afoul and an unreliable, drug dependent employee is fired. A sound national policy is far more complex than a worn-out metaphor.

Nixon administration officials considered other options that were radical by today's standards. When President Nixon declared the war on drugs, he said narcotics were "public enemy number one in the United States." For the next 39 years, this nation has been caught in a quagmire as devastating as the Vietnam war. Nixon's rhetoric set in motion policies that shaped the composition of court filings and prison populations. The war led to racial profiling, and polarized police-community relations, and contributed to a judicial philosophy that devalued the Fourth Amendment. The war, however, did little to provide treatment for the chemically dependent.

For decades, the war on drugs enjoyed bi-partisan support, hi 1986, under the leadership of House Speaker Tip O'Neill, Congress passed mandatory-minimum laws that sent crack users to prison while powder cocaine users who possessed 100 times more product avoided prison. By the time the first President Bush appointed Bill Bennett drug czar, the amount of money spent on "consequences and confrontation" reached $12 billion. The nation devoted much of this money to expensive weaponry: fighter jets to take on Columbian cartels, and Navy submarines to chase cocaine-smuggling boats in the Caribbean. Meanwhile, states adopted laws that resulted in an explosion of prison populations.

What is the difference between thoughtful policy and a war on drugs? Wars allow leaders to marshal resources, Wars are ripe for myth creation, and indeed myths may be necessary to continue the war. And wars have collateral casualties—innocent victims of war that a fair system of justice would not tolerate. Metaphors do have consequences.

There is now an opportunity to adopt a more sensible drug policy, But each day missed compounds the problem. So far this year, nearly $37 billion has been spent by law enforcement to arrest 1.3 million people. When the costs of prosecution and incarceration are added to lost productivity and other economic costs of the war on drugs, the figure is nearly $200 billion. Many state budgets are hemorrhaging from deficits and court budgets are being slashed. Prompt, fair, and affordable justice for both criminal defendants and civil litigants is threatened as state courts institute closures, staffing cuts, and other reductions in essential areas. An over-reliance on law enforcement and incarceration to address the drug problem has had serious, adverse consequences not only for public health, but also for the courts and correctional systems.

To paraphrase former Senator George Aiken, it is time to declare that we won the war on drugs. Perhaps that declaration occurred when Gil Kerlikowske, the Director of the Office of National Drug Control Policy, said that the Obama Administration would not use the term, "War on Drugs." He correctly argued that the term is counterproductive.

But changing public policy is not as simple as dropping a metaphor. The problems caused by drug abuse and trafficking may well be more complex than when this country first declared a war on drugs. While consumption of many traditional street drugs has actually declined over the past decade, prescription drug abuse continues to grow.

Our system of justice needs a dramatic change. Some argue that drug policy rooted on prohibition was flawed from the start. Others respectfully disagree. At a minimum, the following steps seem sensible. First, the National Criminal Justice Act of 2009 should be passed. The panel created by the act would propose reforms to responsibly reduce the nation's overall incarceration rate, restructure our approach to drug policy, improve the treatment of mental illness, and establish a system for reintegrating ex-offenders.

Second, each state should promptly develop a sensible corrections policy. While Governor Schwarzenegger negotiates an inmate reduction plan, he is not the only governor confronting the problem. Dozens of other states have prison populations that they cannot afford.

Third, as the debate over national health care policy proceeds, providing access to effective chemical dependency and mental health treatment is imperative. Providing effective treatment for those afflicted with chemical dependency should be paramount for any sensible drug policy. Cutbacks in state budgets may have the benefit of forcing policymakers to reconsider failed correctional policy, but those deficits also have the potential to make access to chemical dependency and mental health treatment far more difficult.

Fourth, despite the budget challenges facing state courts, drug and mental health courts need to be maintained and, indeed, expanded. If there are any bright spots in the justice system's approach to chemical dependency, it is the advent of these therapeutic courts. Given the long-term savings in lives and money associated with successful treatment programs, it truly would be pennywise and pound-foolish to underfund drug and mental health courts.

Finally, we need to show greater compassion to the casualties of this war. Budget cuts may force the early release of the mother separated from her three-year-old son, but the economic choice she unwisely made will remain a temptation if employers refuse to hire her because of her criminal record. When our nation won World War II, we reached out to our former enemies and helped them rebuild their countries. Surely we can do the same for our own casualties of the war on drugs.

Critical Thinking

1. If we declare the "War on Drugs" is over, does that mean we stop fighting the drug problems we have been addressing for decades? Where should we pick up?

2. The author lists five things that needs to be changed. Do you agree with them and can they be implemented realistically?

From *American Judicature Society,* September/October 2009, p. 83. Copyright © 2009 by American Judicature Society. Reprinted by permission.

New Drug Control Strategy Signals Policy Shift

Sam Hananel

The White House is putting more resources into **drug prevention** and treatment, part of President Barack Obama's pledge to treat illegal drug use more as a public health issue than a criminal justice problem.

The new drug control strategy to be released Tuesday boosts community-based anti-drug programs, encourages health care providers to screen for drug problems before addiction sets in, and expands treatment beyond specialty centers to mainstream health care facilities.

"It changes the whole discussion about ending the war on drugs and recognizes that we have a responsibility to reduce our own drug use in this country," Gil Kerlikowske, the White House drug czar, said in an interview.

The first drug plan unveiled by the Obama White House calls for reducing the rate of youth drug use by 15 percent over the next five years and for similar reductions in chronic drug use, drug abuse deaths, and drugged driving.

Kerlikowske criticized past drug strategies for measuring success by counting the number of children and teens who have not tried marijuana. At the same time, he said, the number of deaths from illegal and prescription drug overdoses was rising.

"Us facing that issue and dealing with it head on is important," Kerlikowske said.

The new drug plan encourages health care professionals to ask patients questions about drug use even during routine treatment so that early intervention is possible. It also helps more states set up electronic databases to identify doctors who are overprescribing addictive pain killers.

"Putting treatment into the primary health care discussion is critical," Kerlikowske said.

The policy shift comes in the wake of several other drug policy reforms since Obama took office. Obama signed a measure repealing a two-decade-old ban on the use of federal money for needle-exchange programs to reduce the spread of HIV.

His administration also said it won't target medical marijuana patients or caregivers as long as they comply with state laws and aren't fronts for drug traffickers.

Earlier this year, Obama called on Congress to eliminate the disparity in sentencing that punishes crack crimes more heavily than those involving powder cocaine.

Some drug reform advocates like the direction Obama is heading, but question whether the administration's focus on treatment and prevention programs is more rhetoric than reality at this point. They point to the national drug control budget proposal released earlier this year, for example, which continues to spend about twice as much money on enforcement as it does on programs to reduce demand.

"The improved rhetoric is not matched by any fundamental shift in the budget or the broader thrust of the drug policy," said Ethan Nadelmann, executive director of the Drug Policy Alliance, which favors drug policy reform.

Nadelmann praised some of Obama's changes, but said he is disappointed with the continued focus on arresting, prosecuting, and incarcerating large numbers of people.

Kerlikowske rejected that as "inside the Beltway discussion," and said there are many programs that combine interdiction and prevention.

The drug control office's budget request does include a 13 percent increase in spending on alcohol and **drug prevention** programs, along with a 3.7 percent increase for addiction treatment.

Critical Thinking

1. What changes do you expect to see as a result of this policy change?

2. What are your thoughts if this is "more rhetoric than reality?"

Beyond Supply and Demand: Obama's Drug Wars in Latin America

SUZANNA REISS

In its first years, the Obama Administration has embraced and even extended its predecessors' militaristic counternarcotics policies in the Americas. In doing so, it has also adopted the basic tenets and priorities that have shaped U.S. drug control policies for decades. Among the most prominent examples are the administration's decision to deploy U.S. military personnel to Colombian bases, the decertification of Bolivia and Venezuela as having "failed demonstrably" in upholding counternarcotics agreements, the continued funding for Plan Colombia (an estimated $672 million in 2009), and Obama's expansion of the Merida Initiative, the "regional security partnership" brokered by the Bush administration with Mexico in October 2007.Under Obama's watch, funding for the Mexican initiative almost doubled in 2009 to $830 million, making it the largest U.S. foreign aid program.

All of this unfolded even as the director of National Drug Control Policy, R. Gil Kerlikowske, suggested on various occasions that the new administration was making a historic shift on drug policy. In October, for example, Kerlikowske told the Association of Chiefs of Police that "it's become increasingly clear that the metaphor and philosophy of a 'War on Drugs' is flawed. . . . . it's time to adopt a different approach." This echoed sentiments he expressed in June, when he emphasized the need to move away from "divisive 'drug war' rhetoric" as part of a broader U.S.-led effort "to reduce the demand for drugs which fuels crime and violence around the world."

The Obama administration has made some gestures in this direction, most significantly making it a low priority for federal law enforcement to go after state-authorized medical marijuana retailers and suggesting a new orientation toward prevention and treatment. But to genuinely change the philosophy animating the so-called War on Drugs, it is essential to understand and question the international political and economic foundations of U.S. drug policy. These much-neglected foundations continue to fuel violence, repression, and economic coercion both within and beyond the United States' borders.

The drug war has failed to achieve even its stated goals, as critics have long emphasized—there has been no net decrease in illicit drug production and trafficking, even while the devastating human and environmental costs of drug war militarism continue to rise. Meanwhile, rarely discussed is the drug war's great success in helping to achieve unstated goals: extending global U.S. military hegemony and extending the reach of the legal U.S. drug economy, which often depends on raw materials and consumer markets in the very same territories forced to participate in the U.S.-led drug control regime.

This analysis gets submerged by the language of supply and demand and the notions of legality that permeate drug policy discourse. Both indicate capitalism's shaping influence on the ideology of U.S. drug war policies. This obfuscating language—and the idea that regulating the drug trade is a question of effectively policing supply and demand—is itself a legacy of the economic and imperial logic that created an international drug control apparatus, which rests on the unquestioned power of the United States to designate players in the drug trade as either legal or illegal. Rather than presuming that the international flow of drugs is a consequence of the natural workings of a mythical, though often naturalized, free market, it is more useful to ask: Who gets to supply what and who gets to demand? Inequities between the global North and the South have historically structured the answer to these questions.

The language of supply and demand, much like the designation of legal or illegal, must be understood as a political and historical construction rather than as a set of neutral descriptive categories. The system of drug control itself has given these categories and labels substantive power. Attempts to control coca in the Andes provide an instructive example, since the region has been on the international drug control radar since the aftermath of World War II. In 1949, the UN Committee on Narcotic Drugs sent a commission to Peru and Bolivia (at that time the two primary producers of the coca leaf) as part of a broader effort to regulate "raw materials." Arguing that indigenous people's consumption of coca was addictive and destructive, the UN commissioners recommended that it be abolished. The only "legal" market for Andean coca leaves would be their primary international market, the United States. This goal was codified in the 1961 Single Drug Convention, which dictated that all traditional domestic coca consumption be eradicated in 25 years and that the export market be carefully monitored to ensure supplies remained in "licit" channels. Thus, the international drug control regime itself structured Andean countries' participation within the drug trade as a "supply side" source of raw materials.

To this day, coca leaves are processed by pharmaceutical companies authorized by the U.S. government to produce a flavoring extract for Coca-Cola (the biggest coca "consumer") and to manufacture cocaine for use in research laboratories and as a local anesthetic in medicine. The drug control regime that emerged in the 1950s was just that, a system of control—not outright prohibition. Drugs themselves were not illegal. Cocaine and other controlled substances straddled the licit–illicit divide, since their legal status depended on their circulation within the marketplace and on the question of who grew, manufactured, sold, and consumed them.

One of the more dramatic, and mostly unquestioned, contradictions is that while the United States spends billions of dollars attacking "drugs," the legal drug industry is regularly among the top five most profitable industries in the country. North Americans are notoriously quick to turn to drugs to answer their ailments, medical or otherwise; meanwhile, through direct marketing, the pharmaceutical industry encourages the excessive consumption of drugs that are often of questionable medical value.

Internationally, drugs have always served as a measure of the United States' wealth and influence. According to the U.S. Census Bureau, pharmaceutical preparations represent by far the most profitable U.S. exports, which is partly the result of free trade agreements, like the Andean Trade Promotion and Drug Eradication Act (ATDPEA), whose title alone indicates the intimate connection between economic relations and U.S. police and military collaboration. Beyond chemicals' prominent and controversial role in drug crop fumigation campaigns, these agreements establish preferential access for legal U.S. drugs in foreign markets, extend their patents, and include a number of other measures that propel the dominance of the U.S. pharmaceutical industry around the world.

The United States does not so much wage war on drugs as wage war with drugs. Throughout the 20th century, the U.S. government has considered certain drugs, including most recently flu vaccines strategic materials and has subsidized their mass-production and stockpiling in the interests of national security. Drugs, among other things, can numb a soldier's pain, stimulate and ease labor, and vaccinate against disease, giving them special strategic value. Obama's continuation of the U.S. embargo against Cuba, including policies that limit the availability of critical medicines, shows how drugs' medicinal value has also been deployed to exert coercive diplomatic leverage. A U.S. company selling drugs to Cuba would in this context be committing a crime, revealing the limits of drug war rhetoric focused on an underworld of "illicit" drug profiteering.

This dynamic interplay between the legal and illegal drug economies and political and economic interests continues to determine drug enforcement's focus. The Obama administration's handling of the concurrent crises in Mexico of drug trafficking and the swine flu, or H1N1 virus, is emblematic. On April 30, congressional hearings on the president's fiscal year 2009 War Supplemental Request included a discussion that linked the two issues: The U.S. government would provide sufficient resources and support for the mass production of (privately patented) flu vaccines (especially ensuring adequate supplies to the U.S. military), while waging war against drug cartels. Senator Patrick Leahy (D.-Vt.) reflected the consensus in government when he strongly supported "helping Mexico, which is facing real threats from heavily armed drug cartels and is now dealing with the H1N1 virus." Secretary of State Hillary Clinton explained that USAID had given $5 million to the World Health Organization (WHO) and the Pan-American Health Organization to "help detect and contain the disease in Mexico," an insignificant amount when compared to the some $2 billion the Obama administration has spent stockpiling vaccines for U.S. citizens.

These efforts at "helping" Mexico reflect broader political and economic inequities in access to legal drugs. Linked to the U.S. practice of securing adequate national drug supplies is the power to determine who gets to consume them—a politically charged issue on tumultuous display recently regarding the H1N1 vaccine. U.S. (and European) drug patents price most of the world's population out of the market, and power dictates who receives the drugs that are produced and distributed, even in the context of the swine flu "emergency." The WHO has warned that there will be a critical shortage of the H1N1 vaccine in the developing world, since some 90% of it has already been pledged to "high income countries." On the domestic front, Michigan Democratic representative Bart Stupak, referring to plans to vaccinate prisoners at Guantánamo (presumably to protect their U.S. guardians from infection), complained in October that "while much of America waits in line to receive their H1N1 vaccination, the Pentagon is giving priority status to accused terrorists."

Perhaps without knowing it, Stupak seemed to intimate how some people are more worthy of medical care than others. Obama chillingly echoed these sentiments when giving his own assurance that health care provision will "not apply to those who are here illegally." The president also indicated that he might allow an exception for "children who may be here illegally but are still in playgrounds or at schools, and potentially are passing on illnesses and communicable diseases," presumably to "legal" children—a distinction that dramatically embodies the dehumanizing impact of U.S. drug wars.

D rug Warriors in the United States and at the United Nations, the main international body regulating the drug trade, typically divide the countries of the world into drug suppliers (mostly in Latin America and Central and Southeast Asia) and consumers (primarily North America and Europe). This formulation has had a definitive impact on both the thrust of drug control initiatives, and on the arguments presented by their opponents. So, for example, the United States spends the vast majority of drug war funding on interdiction campaigns in "supply" countries—constituting some 65% of federal drug control expenditures. Some governments in Latin America have welcomed this funding, in particular the presidents of Colombia, Mexico, and Peru, who have all embraced the drug war as a powerful tool in their efforts to consolidate political control and finance counter-insurgency wars against political and economic dissidents. But there have also been demands from across the region, including among the United States' allies, that the U.S. government do more to limit domestic consumption, as well as to limit its involvement in supplying the precursor chemicals and weapons that are essential to illicit production and distribution.

The Obama administration has had a somewhat novel response to this diplomatic challenge. Unlike his predecessor, Obama acknowledged a deeper U.S. role in the illicit drug trade. In April, when a number of administration officials, including the president and secretary of state, traveled to Mexico to show support for President Felipe Calderón and his war on the cartels, Obama declared he would not pretend that combating drugs "is Mexico's responsibility alone." He continued: "A demand for these drugs in the United States is what is helping to keep these cartels in business. This war is being waged with guns purchased not here, but in the United States."

Yet the administration's acknowledgement of "shared responsibilities" has helped only to cement the ongoing militarization of the region. The devastating impact of this approach has been well documented: increased levels of violence, political corruption, and a blurring of the line between the police, the military, and drug cartels in ways that profoundly undermine democracy and human rights. The limits of a supply–demand framework extend to the weapons deployed in the conflict. The Obama administration provides Mexico with billions of dollars to buy U.S.-manufactured weapons, Black Hawk helicopters, surveillance equipment, and police training, making the U.S. the major source of both legal and illegal weapons that are flooding the streets of Mexico.

Embodying the U.S. orientation toward "supply-side" interdiction, the U.S. president each year identifies "major" illicit drug "producing" as well as "transit" countries and then determines whether they cooperate with international drug control. In September, Obama identified 20 countries as "major drug transit or major illicit drug producing countries"; of these, 15 were in Latin America and the Caribbean, including the Bahamas, Bolivia, Brazil, Colombia, the Dominican Republic, Ecuador, Guatemala, Haiti, Jamaica, Mexico, Panama, Paraguay, Peru, and Venezuela (the rest included Afghanistan, Burma, India, Laos, and Pakistan).

Of the "major" supplying countries, Obama designated three—Bolivia, Burma, and Venezuela—"as countries that have failed demonstrably during the previous 12 months to adhere to their obligations under international counternarcotics agreements." This designation, or "decertification," as it is known, empowers the United States to withhold aid and deny preferential treatment under existing trade agreements with those countries. The supply–demand formulation deployed in this context, together with the selective designation of countries as "major" drug suppliers and as having "failed" by assessing their willingness to collaborate with a particular system of international drug control, recasts diplomatic struggles not as political or economic but as conflicts over the pursuit of criminality and terrorism.

The political ideologies associated with governments in the hemisphere—not the actual health consequences or "violence" emanating from struggles over control of the drug trade—have determined the certification process. If this were not the case, Colombia and Mexico, as the major "producer" country and the largest "transit" country, respectively, would undoubtedly top the blacklist of drug war failures with their thousands of displaced peoples, environmental devastation, and documented human rights abuses. Yet it is Bolivia and Venezuela that have been branded as drug-control rogue states, primarily as an outcome of political tensions between these nations and the United States.

Bolivia again provides a useful example of how drug war spectacle masks political conflict and how decertification is used as a tool to criminalize challenges to U.S. hegemony. The Obama administration's decertification of Bolivia, continuing the Bush administration's policy by maintaining Bolivia's suspension from the ATDPEA, defies any rational, fact-based justification. It seems instead to be a retaliatory move for actions the Bolivian government took in the fall of 2008, when it did not renew USAID contracts, accused the DEA of spying, expelled the U.S. ambassador, and alleged that the United States was providing covert support to the violent and economically powerful U.S.-aligned opposition.

After the White House said Bolivia had failed to live up to its "shared responsibility," Bolivian president Evo Morales fired back, accusing Obama of having "lied to Latin America" at the Summit of the Americas in April, when the U.S. president said "there is no senior partner and junior partner" in the United States' hemispheric relations. Further challenging the inequality built into the economic roles assigned to various countries in the drug economy, the Bolivian government formally submitted a request, now under review before the United Nations, to have coca leaf removed from the 1961 Single Drug Convention.

The convention's "restrictions on and prohibition of coca leaf chewing," the Morales administration argued, violates the UN Declaration on the Rights of Indigenous Peoples (among other international treaties), which maintains that "indigenous peoples have the right to maintain, control, protect, and develop their cultural heritage, traditional knowledge, and traditional cultural expressions, as well as the manifestations of their sciences, technologies, and cultures, including human and genetic resources, seeds, medicines, and knowledge of the properties of fauna and flora. . . ."

Morales, reelected to a second term in December, is not alone in challenging the U.S. drug war. Leaders across Latin America are seeking not only to expand their right to participate in the legal drug market, but also to question the validity of the control and enforcement regime. They increasingly question U.S. drug control priorities, emphasizing its many failures. In August, the First Latin-American Conference on Drug Policy, which brought together representatives from an array of the region's governments, international organizations, and community groups, concluded that "Bolivia, Peru, and Colombia, the three countries that together produce the entirety of the world production of cocaine, did not manage in 10 years to reduce the acres of [coca] cultivation, but instead gained 2 million refugees, put peasants in jail, and sprayed pesticide that degrades the environment."

The capitalist ideology that sustains the United States' ongoing drug war in the Americas manifests not only in the assumptions built into the supply–demand model. It is also present in the very notion that drugs themselves "cause crime and violence," as Kerlikowske said when he announced the administration's professedly forward-thinking and practical approach to drug policy.

Focusing on the commodity overshadows the people and political struggles at the heart of the "drug" conflict. It is not drugs per se, but rather competition to control their production, distribution, and consumption that has generated violence over the last half-century. Personifying drugs themselves as criminal, violent agents has served as a useful mechanism for obscuring the real human impact of drug control policy since well before the Nixon administration, which officially launched the drug "war." Despite the frequently staged spectacles of drug enforcement officers burning marijuana fields in California or airplanes fumigating coca fields in the Andes, it is necessary to restate the obvious: The United States has never waged a "war on drugs." Rather, it has waged various "wars" on specific groups of people.

Take, for example, African Americans, who are disproportionately represented in the U.S. prison population, even though most illicit (and licit) drug users in the United States are white. The domestic drug war, since the introduction of the first mandatory minimum sentences in the United States in the 1950s, has always been structured by racial and economic bias. Similarly, the burdens of U.S.-led drug wars in Latin America have fallen disproportionately on indigenous communities, many of which have fled drug war violence or lost access to their economic means of survival—caught in the political crossfire between governments and insurgencies, which both capitalize on the drug trade as a means of waging war.

The Obama administration's early rhetorical shift away from drug war rhetoric continues the government's dishonest assessment of what fuels drug production and consumption. It fails to acknowledge the violence that maximizing profits and monopolizing international drug flows require. Domestically, in the country with the world's highest incarceration rate, the fact that most imprisoned people are serving time for drug-related offenses has yet to become a serious topic in the Obama administration's deliberations on drug policy. On the international stage, the power hierarchies of who gets to supply and who gets to demand also ripple through racial, economic, and social disparities.

Until the administration pays attention to the structural origins of the drug war, as well as the profound international dependencies upon which it has always rested, it will be fated to continue pursuing an ill-conceived, destructive, and failed policy under which the value of drugs is determined by violence and economic inequality.

Critical Thinking

1. Explain the dichotomy of how the United States is one of the leaders in drug interdiction yet is also one of the world's largest consumers.

2. Explain how political ideologies, and not public health consequences, impact the decertification process? Why might this be an issue?

3. After reading this article, do you think the current administration has changed their domestic and international drug policies?

SUZANNA REISS teaches history at the University of Hawaii, Manoa, and is a Fellow at the Charles Warren Center for Studies in American History at Harvard University. She is the author of Policing for Profit: U.S. Imperialism and the International Drug Economy (forthcoming).

Feature: Twenty Years of Drug Courts—Results and Misgivings

The drug court phenomenon celebrates its 20th birthday this year. The first drug court, designed to find a more effective way for the criminal justice system to deal with drug offenders, was born in Miami in 1989 under the guidance of then local prosecutor Janet Reno. Since then, drug courts have expanded dramatically, with their number exceeding 2000 today, including at least one in every state.

According to **Urban Institute estimates,** some 55,000 people are currently in drug court programs. The group found that another 1.5 million arrestees would probably meet the criteria for drug dependence and would thus be good candidates for drug courts.

The notion behind drug courts is that providing drug treatment to some defendants would lead to better outcomes for them and their communities. Unlike typical criminal proceedings, drug courts are intended to be collaborative, with judges, prosecutors, social workers, and defense attorneys working together to decide what would be best for the defendant and the community.

Drug courts can operate either by diverting offenders into treatment before sentencing or by sentencing offenders to prison terms and suspending the sentences providing they comply with treatment demands. They also vary in their criteria for eligibility: Some may accept only nonviolent, first-time offenders considered to be addicted, while others may have broader criteria.

Such courts rely on sanctions and rewards for their clients, with continuing adherence to treatment demands met with a loosening of restrictions and relapsing into drug use subjected to ever harsher punishments, typically beginning with a weekend in jail and graduating from there. People who fail drug court completely are then either diverted back into the criminal justice system for prosecution or, if they have already been convicted, sent to prison.

Drug courts operate in a strange and contradictory realm that embraces the model of addiction as a disease needing treatment, yet punishes failure to respond as if it were a moral failing. No other disease is confronted in such a manner. There are no diabetes courts, for example, where one is placed under the control of the criminal justice system for being sick and subject to "flash incarceration" for eating forbidden foods.

Conceptual dilemmas notwithstanding, drug courts have been extensively studied, and the general conclusion is that, within the parameters of the therapeutic/criminal justice model, they are successful. A recently released report from the **Sentencing Project** is the latest addition to the literature, or, more accurately, review of the literature.

In the report, **Drug Courts: A Review of the Evidence,** the group concluded that:

- Drug courts have generally been demonstrated to have positive benefits in reducing recidivism.
- Evaluations of the cost-effectiveness of drug courts have generally found benefits through reduced costs of crime or incarceration.
- Concern remains regarding potential "net-widening" effects of drug courts by drawing in defendants who might not otherwise have been subject to arrest and prosecution.

"What you have with drug courts is a program that the research has shown time and time again works," said Chris Deutsch, associate director of communications for the **National Association of Drug Court Professionals** in suburban Washington, DC. "We all know the problems facing the criminal justice system with drug offenders and imprisonment. We have established incentives and sanctions as an important part of the drug court model because they work," he said. "One of the reasons drug courts are expanding so rapidly," said Deutsch, "is that we don't move away from what the research shows works. This is a scientifically validated model."

"There is evidence that in certain models there is success in reducing recidivism, but there is not a single model that works," said Ryan King, coauthor of the Sentencing

Project report. "We wanted to highlight common factors in success, such as having judges with multiple turns in drug court and who understand addiction, and building on graduated sanctions, but also to get people to understand the weaknesses."

"Drug courts are definitely better than going to prison," said Theshia Naidoo, a staff attorney for the **Drug Policy Alliance,** which has championed a less coercive treatment-not-jail program in California's Proposition 36, "but they are not the be-all and end-all of addressing drug abuse. They may be a step forward in our current prohibitionist system, but when you look at their everyday operations, it's pretty much criminal justice as usual."

That was one of the nicest things said about drug courts by harm reductionists and drug policy reformers contacted this week by the Chronicle. While drug courts can claim success as measured by the metrics embraced by the therapeutic-criminal justice complex, they appear deeply perverse and wrongheaded to people who do not embrace that model.

Remarks by Kevin Zeese of **Common Sense for Drug Policy** hit many of the common themes. "If drug courts result in more people being caught up in the criminal justice system, I do not see them as a good thing," he said. "The US has one out of 31 people in prison on probation or on parole, and that's a national embarrassment more appropriate for a police state than the land of the free. If drug courts are adding to that problem, they are part of the national embarrassment, not the solution."

But Zeese was equally disturbed by the therapeutic-criminal justice model itself. "Forcing drug treatment on people who happen to get caught is a very strange way to offer health care," he observed. "We would see a greater impact if treatment on request were the national policy and sufficient funds were provided to treatment services so that people who wanted treatment could get it quickly. And, the treatment industry would be a stronger industry if they were not dependent on police and courts to be sending them 'clients'—by force—and if instead they had to offer services that people wanted."

For Zeese, the bottom line was: "The disease model has no place in the courts. Courts don't treat disease, doctors and health professionals do."

In addition to such conceptual and public policy concerns, others cited more specific problems with drug court operations. "In Connecticut, the success of drug courts depends on educated judges," said Robert Heimer of the Yale University School of Public Health. "For example, in some parts of the state, judges refused to send defendants with opioid addiction to methadone programs. This dramatically reduced the success of the drug courts in these parts of the state compared to parts of the state where judges referred people to the one proven medically effective form of treatment for their addiction."

Heimer's complaint about the rejection of methadone maintenance therapy was echoed on the other side of the Hudson River by upstate New York drug reformer Nicolas Eyle of **Reconsider: Forum on Drug Policy.** "Most, if not all, drug courts in New York abhor methadone and maintenance treatment in general," he noted. "This is troubling because the state's recent Rockefeller law reforms have a major focus on treatment in lieu of prison, suggesting that more and more hapless people will be forced to enter treatment they may not need or want. Then the judge decides what type of treatment they must have, and when they don't achieve the therapeutic goals set for them they'll be hauled off to serve their time."

Still, said Heimer, "Such courts can work if appropriate treatment options are available, but if the treatment programs are bad, then it is unlikely that courts will work. In such cases, if the only alternative is then incarceration, there is little reason for drug courts. If drug court personnel think their program is valuable, they should be consistently lobbying for better drug treatment in their community. If they are not doing this, then they are contributing to the circumstances of their own failure, and again, the drug user becomes the victim if the drug court personnel are not doing this."

Even within the coerced treatment model, there are more effective approaches than drug courts, said Naidoo. "Drug courts basically have a zero tolerance policy, and many judges just don't understand addiction as a chronic relapsing condition, so if there is a failed drug test, the court comes in with a hammer imposing a whole series of sanctions. A more effective model would be to look at the overall context," she argued. "If the guy has a dirty urine, but has found a job, has gotten housing, and is reunited with his family, maybe he shouldn't be punished for the relapse. The drug court would punish him."

Other harm reductionists were just plain cynical about drug courts. "I guess they work in reducing the drug-related harm of going to prison by keeping people out of prison—except when they're sending people to prison," said Delaney Ellison, a veteran Michigan harm reductionist and activist. "And that's exactly what drug courts do if you're resistant to treatment or broke. Poor, minority people can't afford to complete a time-consuming drug court regime. If a participant finds he can't pay the fines, go to four hours a day of outpatient treatment, and pay rent and buy food while trapped in the system, he finds a way to prioritize and abandons the drug court."

An adequate health care system that provided treatment on demand is what is needed, Ellison said. "And most importantly, when are we going to stop letting cops and lawyers—and this includes judges—regulate drugs?" he asked. "These people don't know anything about pharmacology. When do we lobby to let doctors and pharmacists regulate drugs?"

Drug courts are also under attack on the grounds they deny due process rights to defendants. In Maryland, the state's public defender last week argued that drug courts were unconstitutional, complaining that judges should not be allowed to send someone to jail repeatedly without a full judicial hearing.

"There is no due process in drug treatment court," Public Defender Nancy Foster told the Maryland Court of Appeals in a case that is yet to be decided.

Foster's argument aroused some interest from the appeals court judges. One of them, Judge Joseph Murphy, noted that a judge talking to one party in a case without the other party being present, which sometimes happens in drug courts, has raised due process concerns in other criminal proceedings. "Can you do that without violating the defendant's rights?" he asked.

A leading advocate of the position that drug courts interfere with due process rights is Williams College sociologist **James Nolan.** In an **interview last year,** Nolan summarized his problem with drug courts. "My concern is that if we make the law so concerned with being therapeutic, you forget about notions of justice such as proportionality of punishment, due process and the protection of individual rights," Nolan said. "Even though problem-solving advocates wouldn't want to do away with these things, they tend to fade into the background in terms of importance."

In that interview, Nolan cited a Miami-Dade County drug court participant forced to remain in the program for seven years. "So here, the goal is not about justice," he said. "The goal is to make someone well, and the consequences can be unjust because they are getting more of a punishment than they deserve."

Deutsch said he was "hesitant" to comment on criticisms of the drug court model, "but the fact of the matter is that when it comes to keeping drug addicted offenders out of the criminal justice system and in treatment, drug courts are the best option available."

For the Sentencing Project's King, drug courts are a step up from the depths of the punitive prohibitionist approach, but not much of one. "With the drug courts, we're in a better place now than we were 20 years ago, but it's not the place we want to be 20 years from now," he said. "The idea that somebody needs to enter the criminal justice system to access public drug treatment is a real tragedy."

The Criminal Justice Approach to Regulating Drugs Is a Failure

Comment posted by Anonymous on Fri, 04/10/2009-3:00 PM

If you want to impact drug use as a whole then you regulate the market as a whole, such as price control via taxation. You can't do that by just punishing a tiny percentage of drug using population who had the misfortune of coming in contact with the criminal justice system.

Drug Courts Directly Punish Some Religious Beliefs

Comment posted by **Rural WA** on Sat, 04/11/2009-9:01 AM

I've read up a bit on drug courts lately and from my standpoint they are more direct attacks on religious belief than jail or prison. The only "treatment" they'd offer me is religious re-education and I reject that. I'm not addicted to any drugs, I'm not using any drugs in a way that is harmful to myself or the public. I do use some drugs beneficially and in accord with my religious beliefs of 40 years.

"Unlike typical criminal proceedings, drug courts are intended to be collaborative, with judges, prosecutors, social workers, and defense attorneys working together to decide what would be best for the defendant and the community." Part of what I've read about drug courts is that just not violating any drug laws until whatever amount of time goes by (apparently indefinite semi-detention at best) isn't enough. If you won't at least fake confession and repentance you'll be punished for not co-operating; apparently jacked around for a while and if you're "resistant to treatment" long enough you probably get locked up without the drug court time even counting as time served. That bad attitude might even hurt you at parole hearings later on.

I've very strong religious beliefs about certain psychedelics, cannabis and medicine in general which I pretty much perceive as the three basic categories of "medicine". Mere belief without appropriate action is as unacceptable to me as it would be if I were a devout Lutheran (which I have been). My beliefs are difficult to describe accurately, briefly or without using unsatisfactory and pretentious terms, but I can say that regarding "drugs" they are often extremely different than the governmentally approved creed. For that matter, my beliefs about inherent civil liberties, independent of my religious beliefs, are strongly at odds with the government's (in practice rather than as expressed in sources such as the Bill of Rights).

I don't know that I wouldn't be willing to try and fake my way through drug court rather than go to prison but I'm certain I wouldn't be able to do it successfully. I think my sense of oppression would be much stronger than if I just got locked up without being required to denounce my beliefs. The point I want to make is that for some part of the population drug court "treatment" is an attack against religious freedom which is supposed to be one of the most fundamental liberties. This is a matter that needs to be addressed in discussion about drug courts.

Separate Justice Can Never Be Equal Justice

Comment posted by **aahpat** on Sat, 04/11/2009-11:20 AM

Drug courts were created to make the draconian Jim Crow drug war more palatable to Democrat liberals. And they succeeded. Democrat liberals simply ignore the injustices of the drug war appeased by the facade of tolerance that drug courts place on the bars of the endlessly growing prison industrial complex.

Authoritarian Subversion

Comment posted by **aahpat** on Sat, 04/11/2009-3:01 PM of the rule of law and justice.

Like all aspects of the drug war prohibition policy drug courts turn even the rule of law on its head by making justice criminal.

I am so glad to see so many critics of this human rights atrocity of a system.

If we could just get the reform movement LEADERSHIP to grow balls and become ACTIVISTS, LEAD public demonstrations against these social justice abuses, we might influence our politicians to do right by our nation for a change.

THE DRUG WAR CONTINUES ONLY BECAUSE THE REFORM LEADERSHIP DOES NOT HAVE THE BALLS TO GET OUT IN THE STREETS AND OPPOSE THE DRUG WAR!!

Mex Ambassador Calls for "Serious" Pot Legalization Discussion

Comment posted by **aahpat** on Sun, 04/12/2009-1:10 PM

Mexican Ambassador Calls for "Serious" Pot Legalization Discussion

In response to a direct question by Bob Schieffer on CBS Face The Nation on April 12, 2009 about legalization of marijuana the Mexican ambassador to the United States, Arturo Sarukhan, stated that there needs to be a "serious discussion" about legalization of marijuan

"This is a debate that needs to be taken seriously."

Drug Courts, the McDonalds of the Justice System

Comment posted by Anonymous on Sun, 04/12/2009-8:38 PM

I'm a member of a Drug Court in NJ. My observation is they're just another way to get a cut of the Drug War money. They're marketed as a cheaper way to handle drug addicts who would be on their way to costly prison beds, but in reality it's just a way to extend probation and supervision to people who do not belong in the criminal justice system. More jobs for prosecutors, more jobs for lawyers, TASC evaluators, probation officers. . . etc.

I've been seeing such a flow of people coming in since it opened, it's almost like they're giving anyone drug court. It's one sided once you're sentenced. Every decision is up to the "team" which consists of your probation officer, the drug court public defender, the drug court prosecutor, the drug court judge, and your counselor. You have no say after you are sentenced, what they say goes. It's a surrender of your rights. I've already been jailed 2 times falsely for problems THEY had with urines I've given, with no way to have a hearing or redemption to prove my innocence even though I did nothing wrong.

Nobody ever takes into consideration that treatment is not a solution, when it's forced. How many times were we told we should go to the dentist for our aching tooth, only to ignore it for a time until it hurt so bad we finally gave up and went? It's the same way with an addict. Who is anyone to have the right to arrest someone and say they HAVE to go to treatment, where they have to talk about problems and discuss feelings and emotions they may not be ready to talk about. They have to go to meetings, where to participate they have to believe in a higher power and once again speak about emotions and feelings and thoughts. This is another sad approach to treating addicts. The reality is anyone on Drug Court that doesn't commit another crime is because they're tired of jail, and they're too supervised under drug court for it to be worth it. Most of the people I see that complete it here couldn't wait to get to the bar or that first drug. And in the mean time, I've had some good friends who got clean on their own without any sort of legal supervision.

Once again it falls back to make treatment available to those who want it, when they're ready.

Nice Comment!

Comment posted by **mlang52** on Sun, 04/12/2009-9:23 PM

Thank you for such a candid comment. Most of your cohorts are thought to feel differently about it, because it gives them a paycheck.

Why would you be so honest? Thank you! It is refreshing to see such honesty, especially in such a broken "justice" system! We do need to try something different. Even, you see the failures of the present system. And, you have to see it every day you work!

If You're Commenting on My

Comment posted by Anonymous on Sun, 04/12/2009-10:22 PM

If you're commenting on my post, I'm sorry if I confused you. By member of Drug Court I meant I'm a probationer. A participant, a victim, a drug addict, a criminal. No staff member would surely comment in such a way as they feel the bidding they're doing is righteous.

I hope this doesn't change your views.

Not at All!

Comment posted by **mlang52** on Tue, 04/14/2009-3:01 AM

Only slightly changed how I look at it. You certainly have first hand knowledge! What is really wrong is getting money from a person who finds it hard to even get a job! There is no longer a way to "pay your debt to society". It is like having a life sentence! It is a medical problem that the justice system will never solve!

My wife worries about being asked to become full time, where she works. She got a script forgery charge for trying to get enough pain medication to cover her for the month, when her doctor would not write enough! Thank God her migraines have decreased and she only has cramps once a month! She still has no idea when her IBS will get bad and put her in bed. Or, when her bladder will start hurting her! But, they all seem to have decreased over the past few years! Right now, she does without pain control. She has threatened suicide over the pain, before. So far, it has not happened!

And the drug tests can be wrong. Too bad that cop got a hot urine! HA HA!

Utah Drug Rehab

Comment posted by Anonymous on Mon, 04/13/2009-6:11 AM

The drug rehab program you choose should empower you, so that you accomplish life long freedom from drug use. It should take you through detox and withdrawal and ensure that you repair the damage drugs have done to your life. It puts you back in control and functioning in society again—enjoying good family relationships, holding down a job and living a successful drug-free life.

If you are seeking rehab center near your area then you can visit our site for effective drug rehab center and respective addiction treat programs, just like center for **drug rehab treatment in Utah,** which is well known for the addiction recovery for teenagers.

Re: Drug Court

Comment posted by Anonymous on Mon, 04/13/2009-12:10 PM

Yeah I was an Unwitting participant in one of the first "Drug Courts" The brain child of judge Zimian in Boston. I say "unwitting" because as any dope fiend knows if you're sitting in the dock in cuffs and ANYTHING you can agree to to make them say "step out and see probation" you're gonna jump on. Little did I know that instead of 30 days in I'd be chased around by the "drug court" warrant for close to 2 years. And @that time a "drug court" participant could not be oin Methadone(the one treatment that ever worked for me) I Finally ended up ta king 6months insisde to finally be DONE with the entire drug court system. This was almost a decade ago maybe it's gotten better. But as long as drug courts stick to the "abstinence is success" fallicy they will continue to entangle people in a needlessly long criminal justice mess. Just my own experience-Cheer Rah

Prompting Harder Drugs

Comment posted by Anonymous on Mon, 04/13/2009-1:30 PM

Because the criminal drug courts follow the false path of total abstinence, they unwittingly promote concentrated drugs over MJ, due to MJ remaining in the body longer.

Perhaps God punishes drug court 'judges' as so in New Rochelle NY by giving them cancer?

Critical Thinking

1. Do you believe drug courts are effective? What would you do to make them better?

2. How does drug court differ from "regular" court? Explain.

UNIT 7

Prevention, Treatment, and Education

Unit Selections

Learning Outcomes

- Explain how the drug problem can be impacted by targeting demand and not supply.

- Explain the concept of "denial" and explain why it is a critical obstacle to providing successful drug treatment.

- Discuss correctional systems' involvement in treating drug dependency of prisoners. Explain why this practice should exist or not.

Student Website

www.mhhe.com/cls

Internet References

American Council for Drug Education
www.acde.org

D.A.R.E.
www.dare-america.com

Drug Watch International
www.drugwatch.org

Join Together
www.jointogether.org

Marijuana Policy Project
www.mpp.org

National Institute on Drug Abuse
www.nida.nih.gov/Infofacts/TreatMeth.html

Office of National Drug Control Policy (ONDCP)
www.whitehousedrugpolicy.gov

Hazelden
www.hazelden.org

KCI (Koch Crime Institute) The Anit-Meth Site
www.kci.org/meth_info/faq_meth.htm

The Drug Reform Coordination Network (DRC)
www.drcnet.org

United Nations International Drug Control Program (UNDCP)
www.undcp.org

The Partnership for Drug-Free America
www.drugfree.org/#

There are no magic bullets for preventing drug abuse and treating drug-dependent persons. Currently, more than 22 million Americans are classified as drug dependent on illicit drugs and/or alcohol. Males continue to be twice as likely to be classified as drug dependent as females. Research continues to establish and strengthen the role of treatment as a critical component in the fight against drug abuse. Some drug treatment programs have been shown to dramatically reduce the costs associated with high-risk populations of users. For example, recidivism associated with drug-related criminal justice populations has been shown to decrease by 50 percent after treatment. Treatment is a critical component in the fight against drug abuse but it is not a panacea. Society cannot "treat" drug abuse away just as it cannot "arrest" it away.

Drug prevention and treatment philosophies subscribe to a multitude of modalities. Everything seems to work a little and nothing seems to work completely. The articles in this unit illustrate the diversity of methods utilized in prevention and treatment programs. Special emphasis is given to treating the drug problems of those who are under the supervision of the criminal justice system. All education, prevention, and treatment programs compete for local, state, and federal resources. Current treatment efforts at all public and private levels are struggling to meet the demands for service due to the impacts from the U.S. economic crisis of the past few years.

Education: One critical component of drug education is the ability to rapidly translate research findings into practice, and today's drug policy continues to emphasize this in its overall budget allocations. Funding for educational research and grants is generally strong with the trend being toward administering funds to local communities and schools to fund local proposals. For example, in 2011 more than $50 million was again made available to schools for research-based assistance for drug prevention and school safety programs. Another example is the refunding of the $120 million National Youth Media Campaign designed to help coach parents in processes of early recognition and intervention. Encouraging successful parenting is one primary emphasis in current federal drug policy. Other significant research efforts continue to support important education, prevention, and treatment programs such as The National Prevention Research Initiative, Interventions and Treatment for Current Drug Users Who Are Not Yet Addicted, the National Drug Abuse Treatment Clinical Trial Network, and Research Based Treatment Approaches for Drug Abusing Criminal Offenders. In 2011, federal research-related grants totaling almost $100 million were made available to local and state school jurisdictions.

Prevention: A primary strategy of drug prevention programs is to prevent and/or delay initial drug use. A secondary strategy is to discourage use by persons minimally involved with drugs. Both strategies include (1) educating users and potential users; (2) teaching adolescents how to resist peer pressure; (3) addressing problems associated with drug abuse such as teen pregnancy, failure in school, and lawbreaking; (4) creating community support and involvement for prevention activities; and (5) involving parents in deterring drug use by children. Prevention and education programs are administered through a variety

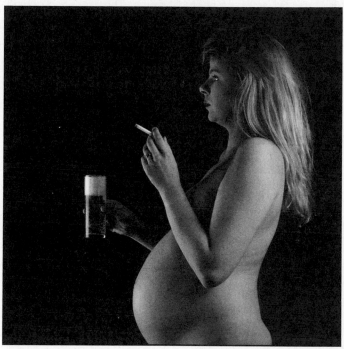

© S. Pearce/PhotoLink/Getty Images

of mechanisms, typically amidst controversy relative to what works best. Schools have been an important delivery apparatus. Funding for school prevention programs is an important emphasis within the efforts to reduce the demand for drugs. Subsequently, an increase in federal money was dedicated to expanding the number of high school programs that implement student drug testing. Drug testing in high schools, authorized by the Supreme Court in a 2002 court decision, has produced a positive and measurable deterrent to drug use. Despite its controversy, school drug testing is expanding as a positive way to reinforce actions of parents to educate and deter their children from use. The testing program provides for subsequent assessment, referral, and intervention process in situations where parents and educators deem it necessary.

In addition, in 2011, approximately $90 million in grant funds were again dedicated to support the federal Drug-Free Communities Program, which provides funds at the community level to anti-drug coalitions working to prevent substance abuse among young people and in local neighborhoods. There are currently more than 700 local community coalitions working under this program nationwide. Also, there are community-based drug prevention programs sponsored by civic organizations, church groups, and private corporations. All programs pursue funding through public grants and private endowments. Federal grants to local, state, and private programs are critical components to program solvency. The multifaceted nature of prevention programs makes them difficult to assess categorically. School programs that emphasize the development of skills to resist social and peer pressure generally produce varying degrees of positive results. Research continues to make more evident the need to focus prevention programs with specific populations in mind.

Treatment: Like prevention programs, drug treatment programs enlist a variety of methods to treat persons dependent upon legal and illegal drugs. There is no single-pronged approach to treatment for drug abuse. Treatment modality may differ radically from one user to the other. The user's background, physical and mental health, personal motivation, and support structure all have serious implications for treatment type. Lumping together the diverse needs of chemically dependent persons for purposes of applying a generic treatment process does not work. In addition, most persons needing and seeking treatment have problems with more than one drug—polydrug use. Current research also correlates drug use with serious mental illness (SMI). Current research by the federal Substance Abuse and Mental Health Services Administration (SAMHSA) reports that adults with a drug problem are three times more likely to suffer from a serious mental illness. The existing harmful drug use and mental health nexus is exacerbated by the fact that using certain powerful drugs such as methamphetamine push otherwise functioning persons into the dysfunctional realm of mental illness. Although treatment programs differ in methods, most provide a combination of key services. These include drug counseling, drug education, pharmacological therapy, psycho therapy, relapse prevention, and assistance with support structures. Treatment programs may be outpatient -oriented or residential in nature. Residential programs require patients to live at the facility for a prescribed period of time. These residential programs, often described as therapeutic communities, emphasize the development of social, vocational, and educational skills. The current trend is to increase the availability of treatment programs.

One key component of federal drug strategy is to continue to fund and expand the Access to Recovery treatment initiative that began in 2004. This program uses a voucher system to fund drug treatment for individuals otherwise unable to obtain it. This program, now operational in 14 states and one Native American community, allows dependent persons to personally choose care providers, including faith-based care providers. It is hoped that this program will encourage states to provide a wider array of treatment and recovery options. As one example, the state of Missouri has transformed all public drug treatment within the state to an "Access to Recovery-Like" program in which involved persons choose their providers and pay with state vouchers. It is hoped that this and similar programs will allow a more flexible delivery of services that will target large populations of dependent persons who are not reached through other treatment efforts.

Crime and Treatment

Overcrowded Prisons and Addicted Inmates are a Tough Challenge for Lawmakers

DONNA LYONS

With a prison population that surged 12 percent from 2007 to 2008, Kentucky lawmakers are looking for solutions.

They think they have found one in a measure passed last year that offers some felony offenders the option of substance abuse treatment in lieu of criminal charges.

"This represents a culture change in dealing with addicted offenders," says former Senator Dan Kelly, the key sponsor of the measure who has since taken a circuit court judgeship.

> ## "This represents a culture change in dealing with addicted offenders."
>
> —Former Kentucky Senator Dan Kelly

The policy is expected to save millions of dollars by diverting offenders from prison and also could save the lives of those who complete the treatment. "It's one of those fairly small changes to law that will have significant policy impact," Kelly says.

Kentucky's problem is also a national one. Substance abuse offenders make up 20 percent of inmates in state prisons. Abuse and addiction, however, play a much larger role. Some 80 percent of offenders abuse drugs and alcohol, and nearly half of jail and prison inmates are thought to be clinically addicted.

Two-Pronged Approach

Kentucky's approach is to screen felony defendants for substance abuse. Some are diverted to community-based services; others with more serious problems and criminal records are referred to an intensive, secure substance abuse treatment program run by the department of corrections.

"There would be a sense of justice denied if there was no secure confinement option in this," Kelly says. "This gives those serious offenders an opportunity for pretrial diversion if they demonstrate commitment to treatment."

About 200 felons can be held in secure treatment at a time for an estimated savings of $1.4 million in the first year.

Long-term supporters of the legislation say cost savings will be about $40 million.

Kentucky currently has 20 corrections-based substance abuse treatment programs in prisons and jails. A study of the programs started in 2005 found reductions in recidivism and substance abuse among the participants. Reported drug use drops more than 50 percent during the 12 months following release as compared with before treatment. And more than two-thirds of participants are not in prison or jail 12 months later.

"It pays for itself," said Senator Ed Worley, who was among sponsors of the legislation aimed at stopping the revolving door for repeat drug offenders. "There are too many repeat offenders with drug problems filling up our jails and prisons. We need to rehabilitate them so they can contribute to society, rather than repeatedly drain our revenues."

In 2007, the Texas Legislature authorized 5,000 more beds for short-term treatment in the state's corrections system. At the time, the state was facing prison growth projections that would require 17,000 new prison beds by 2012. The treatment beds and other community-based substance abuse and mental health treatment programs were approved as an alternative to prison construction. Texas is now seeing its prison population decline along with fewer probation and parole revocations.

Representative Jerry Madden of Texas calls state funds spent for drug, alcohol, and mental health programs a "reinvestment strategy" that pays off.

"If we provide reentry services that work, the public is safer. If we provide drug treatment that works, the public is safer," Madden says. Not only that, he said the state is approaching $1 billion in savings as a result of the reinvestment begun three years ago.

Explosive Growth

States also have turned to specialty drug courts to help break the cycle of drugs and crime. The growth of these courts is nothing short of amazing.

The first drug court began in 1989 in Dade County, Fla., at a time when crack cocaine was overwhelming criminal justice systems elsewhere. Florida officials, including then-Florida Attorney General Janet Reno, developed and piloted the model of drug treatment under close judicial supervision. Two decades later, there are more than 2,100 operating drug courts around the country in all states, with more planned.

Florida's programs, funded largely by local and state money, are presently expanding in nine counties using federal stimulus money. Each year, about 10,000 Florida offenders enter drug court supervision, and current expansion will add as many as 2,000 people statewide.

Drug court professionals hail the ability of specialty courts to get and keep people in treatment while saving corrections money. But others advocate that addiction should be treated as a public health concern rather than a criminal justice matter.

Hawaii Offers Hope

In 2004, Hawaiian Circuit Court Judge Steve Alm took a new approach to dealing with "high-risk" drug offenders on probation.

The pilot program, Hawaii's Opportunity Probation with Enforcement, or HOPE, provided 35 offenders on the verge of being sent back to prison with one final chance to get clean and comply with the rules.

Offenders considered at high risk attended a formal "warning hearing" and were notified that violations would result in swift and certain sanctions. When a violation—missed appointment, drug use, or other violation of probation—occurred, the person on probation was immediately summoned before the judge and given a sanction, such as a short jail term served on the weekend, progressing in length for additional violations. Drug treatment was not mandatory and was ordered only if the person requested it or had repeated violations related to drug use.

Research comparing HOPE probationers to "probation-as-usual" caseloads found reduced drug use, better compliance with rules and reduced recidivism. During the first six months of participation in HOPE, the rate of positive drug tests fell by 93 percent and missed probation officer appointments dropped from 14 percent to 1 percent. Research also concluded that "probation-as-usual" offenders were three times more likely to be sent to prison than HOPE probationers.

Judge Alm's leadership in the development of HOPE led to early success. In 2007, the Hawaii Legislature appropriated funds to continue and expand the program. By 2009, the program had more than 1,500 participants and now permits domestic violence and sex offenders to participate.

Sustained success has been attributed to these factors:

- The basic tenets of the program—clear behavior expectations, swift action upon violation, certainty of punishment, and the least amount of punishment necessary for the violation—mean that offenders must change their behavior to succeed.
- Coordination, cooperation, and buy-in from agencies involved in running the program—the court, probation, law enforcement, attorneys, and treatment providers—are crucial, and some question if other programs will work as well without it.

Drug Abuse: By the Numbers

$11.3 Billion
Growth in federal drug control budget from FY 1988 to FY 2009—$2.8 billion to $14.1 billion.

2,147
Total number of drug courts in the United States since the first opened in 1989.

1.7 Million
Drug abuse violation arrests in 2008, 12.2 percent of all arrests that year.

More than 1 Million
Number of people in specialized alcohol or drug treatment on any given day.

$135.8 Billion
Amount states spent on substance abuse and addiction in 2005.

Sources: FBI Uniform Crime Reports, National Center on Addiction and Substance Abuse at Columbia University, National Drug Court Institute, Substance Abuse and Mental Health Services Administration, White House Office of National Drug Control Policy.

Programs with similar principles have been replicated in other jurisdictions around the country. The South Dakota court-based 24/7 Sobriety Project applies "swift, certain, and meaningful consequences" to people who are repeatedly arrested for driving under the influence. A planned replication in Clark County, Nev., also is in the works.

The success of HOPE and additional efforts throughout the country on policies that aim to reduce spending on corrections, control growth in the prison population, and increase public safety have gained attention at the national level. In November 2009, two bills were introduced in Congress. One would authorize a national HOPE program, and a second would provide grants to states for "justice reinvestment," a strategy currently underway in a number of states that analyze criminal justice data to identify and implement cost-saving policies.

—Alison Lawrence, NCSL

The National Association of Criminal Defense Lawyers issued a report in late 2009 after a task force spent two years studying the courts. Its findings question the effect of drug courts and assert that minorities, immigrants, and the poor are often under-represented in drug courts.

"Drug courts have not slowed the rise in either drug abuse or prison costs," says Cynthia Orr, president of the group. She says it's time to ask if our national drug policy is working and look at shifting focus to a public health-centered approach.

"Drug courts have not slowed the rise in either drug abuse or prison costs."

—Cynthia Orr, President, National Association of Criminal Defense Lawyers

California Collaboration

The largest scale criminal justice–drug treatment collaboration to date is underway in California.

Proposition 36, approved by voters in 2000, provides treatment instead of incarceration for nonviolent drug offenders. From 2002 through mid-2008, 340,000 drug offenders were referred and 242,000 were placed in treatment under the policy.

California Assemblyman Tom Ammiano, who chairs the Committee on Public Safety, says treatment policy is a sensible way to stretch limited criminal justice resources. "California's budget and prison overcrowding crises are invariably linked— and so are their solutions," he says. Ammiano says public safety and rehabilitation can be successfully integrated, and he's interested in back-end policies, as well, like improving access to treatment for drug-addicted parolees.

Proposition 36 programs have evolved to include graduated levels of service to meet a variety of substance abuse needs, says Millicent Gomes, the deputy director of the Office of Criminal Justice Collaboration in the California Department of Alcohol and Drug Programs. She notes that after 30 months, arrest rates of those who complete treatment are lower than for others who do not receive treatment.

"Jail and prison costs are offset," Gomes says. "There are benefits and costs avoided in many other areas, such as emergency rooms and family services."

Most state-level drug court funding has been sustained in California, but many county-level diversion programs have suffered from the state's fiscal crisis. A 2008 study by the University of California, Los Angeles, found the effectiveness of the policy was undermined by inadequate funding, even while it has saved taxpayers millions of dollars. The principal investigator on UCLA's Proposition 36 studies, Darren Urada, said it was exciting to find a tool like this in a current climate of budget cuts. The researchers warned, however, that shrinking and unpredictable funding will erode the benefits.

Even so, Gomes says the nearly decade-old policy in California has created the kind of culture change other states seek in dealing with offender addicts. She said Proposition 36 has institutionalized a continuum of care model that can withstand tough economic times.

Despite the tough fiscal situation facing California, Gomes says, support remains strong from many lawmakers and the public for the diversion approach.

In Kentucky, the diversion legislation quickly garnered bipartisan support in both chambers and from other branches of government, Kelly says. He points to two reasons because of which the policy passed unanimously in both houses.

"There is a clear recognition that our criminal justice system can do better with addicted offenders," he says. "And, I don't know of any family that isn't affected in some way by addiction. So there is a great deal of understanding and emotion about this."

Critical Thinking

1. How would you argue as an advocate for Kentucky's solution? How could it be applied elsewhere?
2. Are the drug courts helping or hurting, and why?

DONNA LYONS heads NCSL's criminal justice program.

Fetal Alcohol Spectrum Disorders: When Science, Medicine, Public Policy, and Laws Collide

KENNETH R. WARREN AND BRENDA G. HEWITT

Historically, alcohol has been used for different purposes, including as a part of religious observances, as a food, at times as a medicine, and its well-known use as a beverage, often in place of uncertain water sources [Vallee 1994, 1998]. It is alcohol's use as a beverage and to some extent as a medicine that has most often come into social and legal conflict, partly as interest in the effects of alcohol on the social fabric of society has waxed and waned and partly due to increasing scientific evidence of alcohol's benefits and risks. While the literature on alcohol's many uses over the millennia is fascinating and growing, we will limit our comments in this article to cyclic waxing and waning of concern for the effects of prenatal alcohol use, primarily focusing on changing views of alcohol's prenatal and antenatal effects.

Historical Reflections: What Did We Know and When Did We Know It?

As noted by Jones and Smith, "historical reports indicate that the observation of an adverse effect on the fetus of chronic maternal alcoholism is not new" [Jones et al., 1978]. As many authors have concluded, mention of adverse pregnancy outcomes associated with alcohol use has been noted by Aristotle, Plutarch, and Diogenes [Lemoine et al. 2003], in the Bible [Randall, 2001], in 18th Century England [Warner and Rosett, 1975], and in 19th century medical and temperance literature [Warner and Rosett, 1975]. For example, Aristotle's warning about the effects of drinking on progeny ("foolish, drunken, and harebrained women most often bring forth children like unto themselves, morose, and languid") is often cited

as one of the earliest observations of alcohol's effect on pregnancy and pregnancy outcomes. Another often cited reference is Judges 13:7 in which an angel appears to Manoah and his wife and states "Behold, thou shall conceive, and bear a son, and now drink no wine or strong drink. . . ." The couple obeys the admonition and Manoah's wife bears a son, Sampson, who becomes renowned for his physical strength and wisdom. However, much of the literature on alcohol use and pregnancy begins within the 18th century and the "London Gin Epidemic" which is considered by many authors to be the genesis of the first medical warnings about the dire consequences of drinking during pregnancy.

London Gin Epidemic (~1720–1750)

The "London Gin Epidemic" occurred at a time when newer distillation technologies entered England from the Netherlands simultaneous with the ascent of William and Mary (from the same country) to the throne of England. Bans were placed on the importation of French wines, England experienced bumper crops of wheat, and taxes were lowered on gin (distilled from wheat) for the benefit of wealthy landowners. These conditions created what amounted to the "perfect storm" for the production, distribution, and consumption of "cheap, plentiful" gin [Warner and Rosett, 1975]. In his often quoted treatise on the excesses of gin drinking as the underlying cause of increased criminal behavior in 18th century London, the English author and magistrate, Henry Fielding, addressed a number of social, moral, and health ills he and other members of the upper social strata attributed to the excess drinking of gin. According to Fielding, "the consumption of [gin] is almost wholly confined to the lowest Order of the People [Fielding, 1751]." Among the ills he described were those inflicted on unborn children and future generations: . . . What must become of the Infant who is conceived in Gin? with the poisonous distillations of which it is nourished both in the Womb and the Breast [Fielding, 1751]." Other contemporaries of Fielding made similar observations. For example, customs administrator and noted economist Corbyn Morris observed that the significant death rate relative to births in London was particularly attributable to the enormous use of spirituous liquors . . . which render such as are born meager and sickly and unable to pass through the first stages of life [Morris, 1751]. William Hogarth's depiction of the horrors of gin drinking by the lower classes in his famous Gin Lane [1751] has been described by some authors (but not by all) as depicting the fetal alcohol syndrome [Rodin, 1981; Abel, 2001b].

By 1725 the damage that was attributed to alcohol was so great that the London College of Physicians presented its concerns about the medical and social problems occasioned by excessive alcohol use in a petition to the House of Commons. Among the concerns expressed was that

". . . the frequent use of several sorts of distilled Spirituous Liquors . . . [is] too often the cause of weak, feeble, distempered children, who must be instead of an advantage and strength, a charge to their Country." Whether prompted by fear of losing the common worker, fear for self and property, or medical concerns about alcohol's effects including those on pregnancy outcome, the observations made by influential Londoners, including Fielding, Morris, and Hogarth, are widely credited as contributing to the eventual repeal of laws that helped fuel the cheap production of gin and the "gin epidemic" [Coffey, 1966].

Not All Agree

Examples of historic knowledge of alcohol's effects on pregnancy such as those described above are presented in many articles on alcohol and pregnancy. The most comprehensive of the earliest reviews of historic observations was an excellent account from ancient times to the early 1970s [Warner and Rosett, 1975]. This article was subsequently criticized in a number of publications [Abel 1997, 1999, 2001a,b; Armstrong and Abel, 2000] for over interpretation and imputing the meaning of historical events to imply that the earlier centuries truly understood alcohol teratogenesis and had seen FAS. For example, while Warner and Rosett suggest that the entry in Judges is a recognition of the harm alcohol can cause during pregnancy, Abel notes that there are other explanations in the biblical text, for example, membership of Manoah in a sect that was abstinent (meaning that Samson should also be abstinent) to account for this admonition without invoking a knowledge of teratology [Abel, 1997]. We would also suggest that it may well have simply reflected

an acknowledgement of warnings handed down from antiquity concerning the use of alcohol at the time of conception (by men and women) to prevent damage to the child or to the pregnancy. In this interpretation, both parents were judged capable of damaging a child due to alcohol use. As pointed out by Lemoine, "unfortunately, two errors have persisted throughout time . . . very often paternal alcoholism was blamed . . ."; and "exaggerations led to accusing alcohol for many unidentified physical and psychological anomalies" [Lemoine, 2003].

Alcohol, Medicine, and Politics: Temperance to Prohibition

"The abuse of alcohol is so mixed up with morals, science, and economics that it is impossible to disentangle the effects of the chemical substance itself from its associated social complexities" [Boycott, 1923].

"Our society's conceptions of disease are often weighted by moral valences as well as biological realities" [Armstrong, 1998].

That alcohol has an effect on pregnancy outcome is well documented in 19th and early 20th Century literature [Warner and Rosett, 1975]. However, scientific findings were interpreted through the lens of then contemporary public attitudes about alcohol, its linking to a wide variety of social ills by the temperance movement, and by a lack of basic scientific understanding, particularly with regard to the differences between heredity and prenatal effects [Katcher, 1993].

That alcohol has an effect on pregnancy outcome is well-documented in 19th and early 20th Century literature.

Reviewing 19th century scientific/medical literature, it is difficult to determine whether deficits in children are attributed to alcohol consumption in pregnancy, male and/or female alcohol use at the time of conception or before conception, damage to genetic factors (germ cells); toxic damage to the fetus from alcohol exposure in the womb; alcohol exposure post pregnancy through breast milk, or even the direct feeding of alcohol to the infant in place of breast milk.

One often cited reason for this difficulty is the involvement of a large number of physicians in the temperance movement (primarily in the United States and England) and the subsequent influence of this movement on medical views of alcohol's injurious effects on health in general and on pregnancy outcome in particular.

Another complicating factor with the early literature was a lack of modern (20th century) understanding of genetics, heredity, toxicity, and teratology. In the preMendel period, even knowledgeable physicians were unaware of the heredity principles of Mendelian genetics, and the distinction between genetic inheritance (DNA), damage to the "germ line" (sperm and ova), and direct toxic damage to developing tissues and organs. The Lamarckian view that traits acquired by either parent during his or her lifetime can be passed on to offspring (like inebriety or alcoholism) was not uncommon. Consistent with Lamarck, Robert MacNish of Glasgow wrote in 1835: "the children (of confirmed drunkards) are in general neither numerous nor healthy. From the general defect of vital power in the parental system, they are apt to be puny and emaciated" [MacNish, 1835]. Ironically, we now understand that some aspects of Lamarckian inheritance do indeed exist via mechanisms of epigenetics. This view was somewhat modified by WC Sullivan in his observations on 600 births to female prison inmates. Sullivan found 335 pregnancies ended in stillbirth or death to surviving children before age 2 and 80 women had three or more such infant deaths. He concluded that although inebriety could be transmitted by either parent to his or her offspring, "maternal inebriety is a condition peculiarly unfavorable to the vitality and to the normal development of the offspring a large part [of which] depends on the primary action of the poison" [Sullivan, 1899].

Between 1912 and 1920 Charles Stockard (Cornell University) conducted what for the time were very careful experiments on pregnancy outcomes in a guinea pig model. Both male and female guinea pigs were exposed to alcohol via an inhalation model before conception. Stockard found effects on growth and viability (liveborn, stillborn) in the offspring. These effects on viability persisted when the 1st generation offspring were mated with guinea pigs without a heritage of alcohol exposure but diminished with each subsequent generation. After four generations, the initial alcohol-exposed line had returned to the values of the control group [Stockard, 1918]. Stockard's findings appear very consistent with the 21st century understanding of epigenetics. MacDowell reproduced Stockard's results with rats finding reduced viability in the first generation and increased litters in the second generation [MacDowell and Vicari 1917; MacDowell, 1922]. He attributed the reduced viability in alcoholized rats to the effect of alcohol on "germplasm bearing factors detrimental to litter production" and "increased litters in the second generation to the elimination of the litters in the first generation that bore the less fertile germinal material" [MacDowell, 1922].

The following passage from an article appearing in the British Journal of Inebriety in 1923 sums up 19th and early 20th century thought on alcohol and pregnancy: "I think it is not an exaggeration to state that alcohol is a poison, and that the fetus of a chronic alcoholic mother is itself a chronic alcoholic, absorbing alcohol from the mother's blood and subsequently from her milk . . ." That is, they knew it did damage to the fetus if not exactly how. This knowledge appears to have been widely held among physicians and scientists during this time.

Nascent research progress that had begun during the heyday of early alcohol research came to an abrupt halt in 1919 with the passage of the Volstead Act and the ratification of the 18th Amendment to the U.S. Constitution prohibiting "the manufacture, sale, or transportation of intoxicating liquors . . . for beverage purposes" ushering in the era known as Prohibition. From the mid-1850s until Prohibition, many physicians were "temperance" advocates supporting total abstinence from alcohol use [Varma and Sharma, 1981]. By the time Prohibition became a reality, public opinion, largely stimulated by the temperance movement, had shifted from a view of inebriety as being an individual problem to one that found alcohol at the root of most health and social ills. With alcohol ostensibly no longer available, problems related to its use were viewed as less urgent. When Prohibition ended in the United States in 1933, temperance leaders and temperance tenets were by and large denounced. The country had swung away from the view of alcohol as villain to one that viewed alcoholism, rather than alcohol use, as the problem. A new era in alcohol science resulted, in which alcohol's harmful effects were minimized, and the study of alcoholism (once again an individual problem) became the prime scientific/ medical focus [Katcher, 1993].

Alcohol and Pregnancy Research: Postprohibition and Beyond

A clear cycle can be seen between the large attention to drinking during pregnancy that occurred during the late 19th and early 20th centuries, and the "forgetfulness" of the harmful consequences of alcohol use [Warner and Rosett, 1975]. The country that had seen Prohibition turn into one of the deadliest crime waves then known, wanted nothing to do with alcohol as a problem. Not only did the country repudiate the prohibition of alcohol, but also the large body of science that had been generated during the late 19th and early 20th centuries likely because much of it was associated with temperance movement "moralism." Many of the physicians and scientists who had been involved in generating much of this science were so integrally identified with the temperance movement that most of their research was dismissed as reflecting a no longer fashionable "moral" view of alcohol [Katcher, 1993]. This carried over in the 1940s as scientists began, once more, to address concerns about harmful alcohol use [Warner and Rosett, 1975]. These scientists made it perfectly clear that their problem was not with alcohol use in the main but in what has come to be known as chronic late stage alcohol dependence. In an interesting chapter-by chapter repudiation of late 19th and early 20th century temperance "science" on alcohol, Haggard and Jellinek sought to distance the neo-science of "chronic intolerance" (alcoholism) from the temperance-colored science published in the earlier century. They wanted the focus on alcoholism, not on alcohol. Writing in a 1942 book covering what was then known about the biological and psychological effects of alcohol, Haggard and Jellinek addressed the temperance view of alcohol's damage to the "germ" or the egg of the mother and/ or sperm of the father, thus affecting the physical/mental status of the child. According to Haggard and Jellinek, ascribing damage to the child as a result of drinking alcohol was a "belief, reflected in myth and custom . . ." that has "maintained itself up to present times." Thus, they approached alcohol not in terms of alcohol as a teratogen, but in terms of alcohol's effect on reproduction and associated organs. While acknowledging that the appearance of feeblemindedness, epilepsy, and mental disorders is more frequent among the offspring of abnormal drinkers, they stated unequivocally that this was not a direct effect of alcohol, but of "bad stock" or defects inherited by offspring "which predispose to alcoholism" [Haggard and Jellinek, 1942].

Even then, vestiges of the country's dislike of the temperance movement and Prohibition remained and Jellinek, often referenced as the father of the modern era of alcoholism research, and others who were at the head of alcohol's rediscovery as a researchable topic, did not believe that maternal alcohol use was detrimental to the fetus. In fact, Haggard and Jellinek wrote, "the fact is that no acceptable evidence has ever been offered to show that acute alcoholic intoxication has any effect whatsoever on the human germ or . . . in altering heredity" [Warner and Rosett, 1975]. They posited that the damaged children of alcoholic parents were the result of poor nutrition; alcohol exposure in the womb as the agent responsible for causing physical and mental abnormalities in children did not appear to be a possibility.

Modern Recognition of Alcohol as a Teratogen

We now know that alcohol, certainly when consumed at doses consistent with the lowest thresholds of legal intoxication (0.08% blood alcohol concentration), is an agent capable of causing not only a variety of health problems but also birth defects. Alcohol is a teratogen. Because of its common availability and usage, alcohol is more than just a teratogen; it is the most prominent behavioral teratogen in the world. Indeed, alcohol may be viewed as having introduced an entirely new discipline—that of behavioral teratology.

Because of its common availability and usage, alcohol is more than just a teratogen; it is the most prominent behavioral teratogen in the world.

FAS as a Modern Diagnosis

In 1970, Christine Ulleland, a medical student at the University of Washington, undertook a thesis project to study children hospitalized for failure to thrive. In reviewing the medical charts, she observed that a common element in the medical records was an indication of alcoholism in over 41% of the mothers noting, "these observations indicate that infants of alcoholic mothers are at high risk for pre- and postnatal growth and developmental failure," and suggesting that "greater attention should be given to alcoholic women during the child bearing years" [Ulleland, 1970].

When the prominent dysmorphologist, David Smith, and his associate, Kenneth Lyons Jones, examined a group of these children they immediately recognized the subtle, but important, pattern we now know as FAS. The physical and behavioral characteristics of these children were subsequently published [Jones et al., 1973], ushering in the modern era of research on fetal alcohol syndrome.

In their search for other evidence of the adverse effects of alcohol on fetal outcome, Jones and Smith discovered a paper published in 1968 in France, by Lemoine et al., [1968] describing virtually the identical physical and behavioral problems among 127 children of alcoholic mothers from Roubaix, France. The Lemoine paper had likely escaped attention because it appeared in a minor journal and was published in French [Warner and Rosett, 1975]. Subsequently, an earlier doctoral dissertation on the influence of parental alcoholic intoxication on the physical development of young babies by Jacqueline Rouquette, published in Paris in 1957, came to the attention of FAS researchers [Barrison et al., 1985]. In their second publication, David Smith introduced the name "fetal alcohol syndrome" to describe their clinical observations [Jones and Smith, 1973]. It was often the case that a new syndrome would be named after the scientists or physicians who first describe the condition (e.g., Williams's

Syndrome). The authors chose to assign the name fetal alcohol syndrome (FAS) because they believed that the name would call attention to alcohol as a teratogen, alert women to the dangers of drinking in pregnancy, and aid in the elimination of this disorder. While the name FAS does garner attention in the medical community and public, some argue that the name FAS today may actually be more problematic due to the stigma associated with alcohol problems than if a neutral name like "Smith and Jones" or "Lemoine" syndrome had been applied.

No Immediate Acceptance

Despite the Lemoine and Jones and Smith reports, much skepticism as to whether alcohol could cause birth defects existed in the 1970s. For example, if it truly existed, why did we not know about it before in this era of modern medicine? How did we know that alcohol was indeed the agent rather than nutrition, other drug use, or the "deviant lifestyle" of the alcoholic woman?

The answer to these questions required the undertaking of animal and epidemiological research and a funding agency to support that research.

The National Institute on Alcohol Abuse and Alcoholism and FAS: The Story of a Science Success

In the late 1960s, a United States Senator, Harold E. Hughes, himself a recovering alcoholic, along with a group of influential recovering alcoholics with business and political acumen and ties, began advocating for legislation to create a federal focal point for alcoholism. At this time, medicine had little if any concern for alcoholics who were seen as morally deficient, or suffering from weak wills or character defects (shades of the earlier 19th/20th centuries temperance movement). Treatment for alcoholism was mainly accomplished through Alcoholics Anonymous, and to a much smaller extent within state mental health systems (a small center for the control and prevention of alcoholism in the National Institute of Mental Health was tasked with helping to create a federal alcoholism presence mainly within the existing federal and state mental health services system).

Many early alcohol investigators noted that alcohol research was as stigmatized as alcoholism itself [Lieber, 1988]. The National Institutes of Health supported very limited alcohol research; what was supported was often disguised as something else, e.g., using alcohol as a "probe" to study other types of liver disease. Indeed, a major epidemiological study of birth defects undertaken in the late 1960s did not ask any questions on alcohol use [Jones et al., 1974]. This attitude changed with the passage of the landmark Comprehensive Alcohol Abuse and Alcoholism Prevention, Treatment and Rehabilitation Act of 1970 (P.L. 91–616) which established the National Institute on Alcohol Abuse and Alcoholism (NIAAA) and provided national visibility and funds to understand, prevent, and treat alcoholism and problems related to alcoholism. NIAAA, with its newly minted research mandate, supported the research that helped to validate the existence of FAS and what we now recognize as the full spectrum of fetal alcohol spectrum disorders (FASD).

The 1970s alcohol and pregnancy research took two forms: animal research and human epidemiological research. Animal research established the nature of FAS teratogenesis by verifying that the same deficits reported by Lemoine and Jones and Smith could be seen in animals (rodents, dogs, and later primates); and that alcohol and not other confounding factors were responsible. Human epidemiological research prospectively examining the outcomes of children exposed to alcohol in pregnancy demonstrated the range of physical and behavioral deficits in children exposed to alcohol in pregnancy. By 1977, NIAAA sponsored the first international research conference on FAS. Though not an original intent of the meeting, those attending were so impressed with the findings to date that they collectively recommended that NIAAA issue the first government health advisory on FAS.

Warning the Public

Doing anything the first time in Government presents numerous challenges. In this instance, NIAAA was attempting to have the Federal Government put its imprimatur on a warning about drinking during pregnancy that ran counter to prevailing medical and social practices. Resistance from within the US Department of Health, Education and Welfare (now the US Department of Health and Human Services), NIAAA's administrative home, and from non-Federal groups and organizations was expected. Federal skepticism was overcome primarily due to the strength of the science, and the first governmental advisory about alcohol use during pregnancy was published by NIAAA in 1977 [Warren and Foudin, 2001]. Taking a "conservative approach" this first ever advisory stated that more than six drinks a day was dangerous and recommended a "2-Drink Limit" per day. Unlike today's warnings against any use until proven safe, implicit in this first warning was the notion that alcohol use is "safe" within the given guidelines until proven dangerous.

The response was as varied (and as vocal) as expected. For example, the recommendation in the advisory was supported by the American College of Pediatrics, but not immediately by the American College of Obstetrics and Gynecology. Some medical and patient advocacy organizations criticized NIAAA for going too far, and some for not going far enough, by not recommending abstinence during pregnancy. However, the 1977 Health Advisory did focus sufficient attention on the issue of alcohol and pregnancy that Senate hearings were held for the purpose of considering legislation requiring warning labels related to alcohol and pregnancy risks. The outcome of the hearings was the call for a Report to the President and Congress on *Health Hazards Associated with Alcohol and Methods to Inform the General Public of these Hazards* prepared jointly by the Departments of Health and Human Services and Treasury [US Department of Transportation and US Department of Health and Human Services, 1980]. The report did not immediately call for alcoholic beverage labeling but did recommend the issuance of a Surgeon General's Advisory on Alcohol and Pregnancy that was subsequently issued in 1981 [FDA Drug Bulletin 1981]. Unlike the previous Advisory, the 1981 Advisory recommended that women who are pregnant or planning to become pregnant avoid alcohol. In 1988 Congress considered the issue of alcoholic beverage labeling as a means to warn of the dangers of alcohol exposure in the womb and enacted the Alcoholic Beverage Labeling Act of 1988 (Public Law 100690) which became effective in 1989. In 2005, the Surgeon General reissued an updated advisory on alcohol use and pregnancy that warned against FASD, the full spectrum of birth defects caused by prenatal alcohol exposure (US Surgeon General, 2005].

Conclusion: Promises of Current Research

Although today there is little disagreement about the existence of FASD, we are again embroiled in determinations that are as much about policy as medicine. What does a physician tell his/her patient who is either pregnant or may become pregnant? The US Surgeon General's Advisory on Alcohol and Pregnancy is clear. We do not know the dose at which we can unequivocally state that the fetus will not be harmed. It is therefore prudent advice to avoid all drinking during these time periods. Yet, there is not full agreement on this issue. Recently, for example, a medical ethicist likened this message to "medical paternalism" [Gavaghan, 2009]. As science continues to refine our knowledge of the consequences of exposure to alcohol during gestation, we are hopeful that public health policies and practice can reach closure on what advice will best serve pregnant women and their future offspring.

As concluded by Clarren and Smith, alcohol exposure during gestation "appears to be the most frequent known teratogenic cause of mental deficiency in the Western world" which "through accurate understanding . . . and widespread public awareness could be largely reduced

and, ideally, eliminated" [Clarren and Smith, 1978]. This was the goal of the early pioneers in describing FAS and FASD, and it remains the goal of committed scientists, patients, and their families today.

References

Abel EL. 1997. Was the fetal alcohol syndrome recognized in the ancient Near East? Alcohol Alcohol 32:3–7.

Abel EL. 1999. Was the fetal alcohol syndrome recognized by the Greeks and Romans? Alcohol Alcohol 34:868–872.

Abel EL. 2001a. The gin epidemic: much ado about what? Alcohol Alcohol 36:401–405.

Abel EL. 2001b. Gin lane: did Hogarth know about fetal alcohol syndrome? Alcohol Alcohol 36:131–134.

Armstrong EM. 1998. Diagnosing moral disorder: the discovery and evolution of fetal alcohol syndrome. Soc Sci Med 47:2025–2042.

Armstrong EM, Abel EL. 2000. Fetal alcohol syndrome: the origins of a moral panic. Alcohol Alcohol 35:276–282.

Barrison IG, Waterson EJ, Murray-Lyon IM. 1985. Adverse effects of alcohol in pregnancy. Addiction 80:11–22.

Boycott AE. 1923. The action of alcohol on man. Lancet 202:1055–1056.

Clarren SK, Smith DW. 1978. The fetal alcohol syndrome. N Engl J Med 298:1063–1067.

Coffey T. 1966. Beer street—Gin lane—some views of 18th-century drinking. Quart J Stud Alcohol 27:669–692.

FDA Drug Bulletin. 1981. Surgeon genera's advisory on alcohol and pregnancy. Washington, DC: FDA Drug Bulletin. p 9–10.

Fielding H. 1751. An enquiry into the causes of the late increase of robbers, etc.: with some proposals for remedying this growing evil. London: printed for A. Millar. 203 p.

Gavaghan C. 2009. "You can't handle the truth"; medical paternalism and prenatal alcohol use. J Med Ethics 35:300–303.

Haggard HW, Jellinek EM. 1942. Alcohol explored. Garden City: Doubleday, Doran and Company. 297 p.

Jones KL, Hanson JW, Smith DW. 1978. Palpebral fissure size in newborn infants. J Pediatr 92:787.

Jones KL, Smith DW. 1973. Recognition of the fetal alcohol syndrome in early infancy. Lancet 302:999–1001.

Jones K, Smith D, Streissguth A, et al. 1974. Outcome in offspring of chronic alcoholic women. Lancet 303:1076–1078.

Jones K, Smith D, Ulleland C, et al. 1973. Pattern of malformation in offspring of chronic alcoholic mothers. Lancet 301:1267–1271.

Katcher BS. 1993. The post-repeal eclipse in knowledge about the harmful effects of alcohol. Addiction 88:729–744.

Lemoine P. 2003. The history of alcoholic fetopathies (1997). J FAS Int 1:e2.

Lemoine P, Harousse H, Borteyru JP, et al. 1968. Children of alcoholic parents—anomalies in 127 cases. Arch Francaises De Pediatr 25: 830–832.

Lemoine P, Harousseau H, Borteyru JP, et al. 2003. Children of alcoholic parents—observed anomalies: discussion of 127 cases. Ther Drug Monit 25:132–136.

Lieber C. 1988. NIAAA and alcohol research: a researcher's view—National Institute on alcohol abuse and alcoholism. Perspectives on current research. Alcohol Health Res World 12:306–307.

MacDowell EC. 1922. The influence of alcohol on the fertility of white rats. Genetics 7:117–141.

MacDowell EC, Vicari EM. 1917. On the growth and fecundity of alcoholized rats. Proc Natl Acad Sci USA 3:577–579.

MacNish R. 1835. The anatomy of drunkenness. New York: D. Appleton. 227 p.

Morris C. 1751. Observation on the past growth and present state of the city of London. London.

Randall CL. 2001. Alcohol and pregnancy: highlights from three decades of research. J Stud Alcohol 62:554–561.

Rodin AE. 1981. Infants and Gin mania in 18th century London. JAMA 245:1237–1239.

Stockard CR, GNP, 1918. Further studies on the modification of the germ-cells in mammals: the effect of alcohol on treated guinea-pigs and their descendants. J Exp Zool 26: 119–226.

Sullivan WC. 1899. A note on the influence of maternal inebriety on the offspring. J Mental Sci 45:489–503.

Ulleland C. 1970. Offspring of alcoholic mothers. Pediatr Res 4:474.

US Department of Transportation, US Department of Health and Human Services. 1980. Report to the president and congress on health hazards associated with alcohol and methods to inform the general public of these hazards. Washington, DC.

US Surgeon General. 2005. Surgeon general's advisory on alcohol and pregnancy. Washington, DC: US Department of Health and Human Services.

Vallee BL. 1994. Alcohol in human history. EXS 71:1–8.

Vallee BL. 1998. Alcohol in the western world. Sci Am 278:80–85.

Varma SK, Sharma BB. 1981. Fetal alcohol syndrome. Prog Biochem Pharmacol 18: 122–129.

Warner RH, Rosett HL. 1975. The effects of drinking on offspring: an historical survey of the American and British literature. J Stud Alcohol 36:1395–1420.

Warren KR, Foudin LL. 2001. Alcohol-related birth defects—the past, present, and future. Alcohol Res Health 25:153–158.

Critical Thinking

1. To date, scientists have not been able to determine the dose level at which the fetus will be harmed by alcohol. What factors must a pregnant mother consider when deciding whether to drink during pregnancy?

2. What do you think is the best advice a doctor can give his or her patient concerning alcohol consumption during pregnancy?

3. How should policymakers approach this topic to reduce the incidence rate of FAS?

Identifying the Proper Drug-Abuse Treatment for Offenders

MARK T. SIMPSON

The criminal justice system, with respect to drug abuse treatment, has come a long way since the dark old days of "nothing works." By the late 1990s, nearly half of all adult and juvenile correctional facilities were providing some level of drug abuse treatment. By 2003, nearly three-fourths of all prisons provided such services.[1] The proliferation of drug abuse treatment for offenders extends beyond the walls of prisons and jails. It is now estimated that the criminal justice system generates nearly 50 percent of all referrals to community-based drug abuse treatment.[2] With state legislatures searching for cost-effective alternatives to incarceration, the growth in drug abuse treatment for offenders can only be expected to continue.

The Link between Drugs and Crime

So why has the criminal justice system turned to drug treatment in such a big way? Certainly, a hypothesized link between drug use and crime offers one explanation. As the theory goes, if people turn to crime to support their drug use, then treatment aimed at stopping offenders' drug use will also impact their propensity to commit crime. A reduction in the demand for drugs therefore results in a reduction in crime. Viewed from this perspective, drug treatment is a win-win situation for the offender as well as for society. How could anyone argue against this public policy strategy?

The drug-crime link, however, presupposes the notion that offenders are addicts who, absent their addiction, would live a crime-free, pro-social life. This may not necessarily be the case. To illustrate this point, offenders can be categorized as belonging to one of two groups. The first group of offenders can be thought of as living primarily a criminal lifestyle. That is, their lives are organized around criminal activity as a way of life. These offenders engage in crime as a means to obtain money, sex, material possessions and status. For these offenders, drug use is not the primary focus of their lives; rather, drugs are viewed as a means to support their criminal enterprise. The second group of offenders can be thought of as living primarily an addict lifestyle. That is, their lives are organized primarily around their use of alcohol and other psychoactive substances. Unlike offenders who manifest a criminal lifestyle, these offenders are the "true" addicts. Their crimes, whether it is simple possession, prescription drug fraud or more serious crimes such as vehicular homicide, are committed primarily as a consequence of their use of alcohol and other drugs.

Although offenders can exhibit either a criminal or addict lifestyle, it is likely that many offenders exhibit aspects of both. Although no research exists to specify the degree of overlap between these two populations, it probably depends on a variety of factors, including the type and security level of the facility in which offenders are housed (e.g., jail vs. prison, high vs. low security). Regardless, there is little evidence to suggest that illicit drug use converts nonoffenders into offenders; rather, drug use appears to intensify criminal activity among those who are already offenders.[3] As a consequence, it can be expected that a large percentage of offenders who use drugs also exhibit a criminal lifestyle.

Targeting the Treatment

What happens when these two groups of offenders are separated from their drugs of choice? Consider the case of the lifestyle addict. There is a truism in addictions treatment that individuals stop growing up emotionally when they start abusing alcohol and other drugs. This is because drugs and alcohol become the means by which substance abusers cope (or actually avoid coping) with life's problems. The earlier those individuals start relying on alcohol and other drugs as a coping mechanism, the earlier they stop developing more mature coping skills. Typically, offenders begin using drugs—particularly alcohol and marijuana—in their teen years. As a consequence, when the lifestyle addict is separated from his or her drugs of choice, what is left is an immature individual with poor coping skills for dealing with the frustrations of adult living. Drug treatment for these individuals can thus be conceptualized as a crash course in growing up. What happens when you separate the lifestyle criminal from his or her drugs of choice? You basically have a well-functioning criminal—and perhaps an even better functioning criminal, due to the fact there are no drugs in his or her system to disrupt the offender's criminal activities.

Simply stated, if drug abuse treatment is to be effective in reducing both drug use and criminal behavior, it must address the offender's criminality as well as his or her substance use. Drug abuse treatment with an offender population that does not target the elimination of criminal behavior as a primary goal of treatment runs the risk of returning offenders to the community who are more of a danger to public safety than they were prior to treatment.

Individuals familiar with the criminal recidivism literature will not likely be surprised by this message. Proponents of the risk-need-responsivity model have long advocated that treatment interventions focus on criminogenic needs—those factors such as anti-social behaviors, attitudes and social networks that support an offender's propensity to engage in crime.[4] While drug abuse is considered one such criminogenic need, psychological interventions that focus solely on offenders' drug use and do not attempt to address their criminal behavior will likely show limited success in impacting recidivism. To put it bluntly, there is no getting around the simple fact that to impact criminality, criminality must be targeted.

The good news is that evidence-based treatments exist that are effective in reducing offenders' propensity to commit crime. The bad news is correctional mental health providers and administrators are often poor consumers of research. All too often, correctional treatment providers rely either on the belief that "What I learned in school with nonoffenders will work with offenders" or, as an alternative, "If it's an interest of mine in my personal life, it must be good for them." As a consequence, counselors rely on techniques that either do not work (e.g., Rogerian client-centered therapy, self-esteem enhancement) or that target behaviors that are unrelated to criminality (e.g., pet therapy and drama therapy). Researchers Latessa, Cullen and Gendreau describe such interventions as "correctional quackery."[5] This is not to say programs such as pet therapy and the like have no place in a correctional setting; they serve to occupy offenders' time, create a more human atmosphere in the institution, and may even be beneficial to the pets. However, it would be disingenuous to suggest they will impact recidivism because they will not.

Proven Techniques

Two treatment approaches receive consistent support within the research literature as having the most promise in reducing recidivism. The first, cognitive-behavioral therapy, targets offenders' thinking and its impact on their perception of themselves and their environment. This therapy helps identify and correct the "thinking errors" they use to justify and excuse their criminal behavior. While a variety of cognitive-behavioral approaches exist to address criminal behavior, psychologists Samenow[6] and Walters[7] have developed particularly useful systems for understanding and targeting offenders' faulty and criminal thinking. These treatments directly target offenders' cognitions that support and perpetuate their criminal lifestyles.

The second treatment approach that receives consistent support in the research literature, the therapeutic community, is most commonly associated with prison-based substance abuse treatments.[8] The therapeutic community philosophy holds that substance abuse is not the main cause of the offenders' criminality, but is one symptom of a disorder of the "whole person." The therapeutic community relies on peer support within the offender treatment community to encourage each participant to act in accordance with values that are associated with prosocial rather than criminal behavior (or what is called "right living").[9] The therapeutic community approach emphasizes the critical importance of personal accountability and responsibility in choosing to give up a criminal lifestyle.[10]

While cognitive-behavioral therapy and the therapeutic community are often discussed as though they are competing treatment modalities, they are in fact complementary models that can be combined to target the behaviors most closely associated with criminal recidivism. Cognitive-behavioral approaches target offenders at a psychological level, addressing the internal cognitive mechanisms they use to justify and perpetuate their criminal behavior. In contrast, the therapeutic community approach targets offenders at a social level, targeting offenders' social networks that reinforce and support continued criminal activity. The two can be combined to address offenders' criminogenic needs at both the psychological and social level by disrupting the social networks that reinforce offenders' anti-social thinking, values and behavior. In contrast to "correctional quackery," treatment programs that combine the cognitive-behavioral and therapeutic community approaches can be expected to impact offender recidivism as well as their substance abuse.

Addressing Criminality

Two fallacies can be attributed to the lack of appreciation for the role of criminality in offenders' substance use. The first fallacy is the belief that, when it comes to drug treatment, something is always better than nothing. Unless administrators and treatment providers are prepared to offer evidence-based programs that address offender criminality, nothing may in fact be better than something. Paper programs that allow offenders to receive completion certificates without requiring that they engage in any meaningful behavioral change feed offenders' power orientation and confirm their belief that they can "beat the system." Whereas no program leaves offenders just as they are, bad programs may in fact make them worse.

A second fallacy is the often-expressed hope that drug treatment will someday replace the need for a criminal justice response to drug use. Again, this fallacy stems from the lack of understanding that criminality more often than not drives offenders' drug use, and not the other way around. It is seldom that offenders seek drug treatment out of the realization that they are "sick and tired of being sick and tired." Most often, offenders seek treatment as a means for avoiding some consequence they perceive as undesirable—such as incarceration. While under the threat of criminal justice sanction, some offenders will express motivation for treatment and offer surface compliance to program requirements. Only once the criminal justice sanctions are lifted will they reveal their true motives, as they quickly revert to their criminal lifestyle. It is often a truism in offender treatment that "People don't change because they see the light, but because they feel the heat." The criminal justice system will always play a role in providing the "heat" that motivates offenders to engage in meaningful treatment that can have a chance at impacting their propensity to commit crime. This is the rationale underlying the creation of drug courts. The question, therefore, is not whether the criminal justice system or the treatment community can best address the problem of crime and drug abuse, but whether the two systems can bridge their differences and learn to understand the role each plays in responding to this very real societal problem.

It is clear from research that, unlike drug abuse treatment in the community, drug abuse treatment in corrections must target the attitudes, values and behaviors associated with criminal behavior, as well as those associated with the abuse of alcohol and other drugs. If the criminal justice system continues to be tasked with the role of "patient identifier," then it is incumbent upon treatment providers within the system to implement evidence-based programs that truly address the patients' needs. To address only the substance abuse, and not the underlying criminality, is to ignore both the needs of the offender and public safety.

Notes

1. Taxman, F.S., M.L Perdoni and L.D. Harrison. 2007. Drug treatment services for adult offenders: The state of the state. *Journal of Substance Abuse Treatment,* 32(3): 239–254.

2. Fletcher, B. and R. Chandler. 2006. *Principles of drug abuse treatment for criminal justice populations: A research-based guide.* Bethesda, Md.: U.S. Department of Health and Human Services, National Institutes of Health, National Institute on Drug Abuse.

3. Farabee, D., V. Joshi and M.D. Anglin. 2001. Addiction careers and criminal specialization. *Crime and Delinquency,* 47(2):196–220.

4. Andrews, D.A and J. Bonta. 2003. *The psychology of criminal conduct, third edition.* Cincinnati: Anderson.

5. Latessa, E.J., F.T. Cullen and P. Gendreau. 2002. Beyond correctional quackery—Professionalism and the possibility of effective treatment. *Federal Probation,* 66(2):43–49.

6. Samenow, S.E. 1984. *Inside the criminal mind.* New York: Times Books.

7. Walters, G.D. 1990. *The criminal lifestyle: Patterns of serious criminal conduct.* Newberry Park, Calif.: Sage Publications.

8. Wormith, J.S., R. Althouse, M. Simpson, L.R. Reitzel, T. Fagan and R.D. Morgan. 2007. The rehabilitation and reintegration of offenders: The current landscape and some

future directions for correctional psychology. *Criminal Justice and Behavior,* 34(7):879–892.

9. De Leon, G. 2000. *The therapeutic community: Theory, model, and method.* New York: Springer.

10. Farabee, D. 2005. *Rethinking rehabilitation: Why can't we reform our criminals?* Washington, D.C.: American Enterprise Institute.

Critical Thinking

1. How many types of drug-abuse offenders are there and what is the best treatment recommended for each?

2. Cognitive-behavioral therapy and the therapeutic community are referred to as "complementary models." How do they complement each other?

MARK T. SIMPSON, PhD, is the psychology treatment programs coordinator in the Mid-Atlantic Regional Office of the Federal Bureau of Prisons.

Author's Note—Opinions expressed in this article are those of the author and do not necessarily represent the opinions of the Federal Bureau of Prisons or the Department of Justice.

Whose Responsibility Is Substance Abuse Treatment?

MELVIN L. WILLIAMS

In response to public outcry, U.S. lawmakers have determined that using, selling, purchasing and possessing certain drugs are criminal acts. This has created an explosion in the U.S. prison population. Punishment for these acts ranges from a slap on the wrist to life in prison. Nationwide, the prison population grew by 25,000 last year, bringing it to almost 1.6 million. Another 723,000 people are in local jails. The number of American adults is about 230 million, meaning that one in every 99.1 adults is behind bars. The U.S. is a nation of laws that concern behavior, especially when it is perceived that the behavior will infringe on the rights of others. The dilemma, then, for corrections professionals when substance abusing offenders are incarcerated is what can be done?

During the past 30 years, a whole new set of offenders has emerged as a result of the war on drugs. Since 1970, the state and federal prison population has grown nearly seven-fold.[1] Certainly most would agree that law enforcement agencies have not been successful in stopping the flow of illegal drugs into this country, nor had the public been successful in curtailing their use. This comes at a tremendous financial cost to taxpayers. According to the National Association of State Budgeting Officers, states spent $44 billion in tax dollars on corrections in 2007. That is up from $10.6 billion in 1987. With money from bonds and the federal government included, total state spending on corrections in 2007 was $49 billion. The report also revealed that states are on track to spend an additional $25 billion by 2011.

In addition to the obvious costs, there are hidden expenses. According to the Office of National Drug Control Policy, health care costs attributable to drug abuse were projected to total $15.8 billion in 2002.[2] Many practitioners estimate that as high as 80 percent of the incarcerated population are there due to drugs, whether it is possession, sale or trying to obtain funds through illegal means to purchase them. The Bureau of Justice Statistics recently reported that 53 percent of state inmates and 45 percent of federal inmates meet criteria of drug abuse or dependence, and 16.6 percent of state inmates and 18.4 percent of federal inmates committed their crimes to obtain money for drugs.[3]

With almost 2 million individuals in detention centers and prisons across the country and an estimated 6 million more under criminal justice supervision, it can be surmised that the majority are there due to drug-related crimes. Between 1995 and 2005, admissions to drug treatment increased 37.4 percent and federal spending on drug treatment increased 14.6 percent. During the same period, violent crime fell 31.5 percent.[4] There are many reasons for this drop, but it cannot be overlooked that when spending on treatment increased, violent crime fell.

The U.S. has spent billions of dollars on incarceration and treatment, but with recidivism rates in the 60 percent range, taxpayers are asking why the nation is not doing better. How specifically are corrections professionals expected to reform these offenders?

The Role of Corrections

The role of the corrections field is to protect society by rehabilitating offenders. Returning someone back to the community with improved skills and attitudes that they learned while incarcerated gives that person a better chance for success, thus protecting the community. However, the substance abuse offender population still remains a major challenge for the corrections field because once these offenders enter correctional facilities, there is no national treatment handbook or guide correctional staff can use to rehabilitate them. The silver bullet of substance abuse treatment has not yet been discovered. In addition, U.S. courts have consistently embroiled themselves in the operations of correctional facilities, demanding more responses to individual offender needs.

Certainly, however, no one is giving up. Commissioners, directors and policymakers are hard-pressed to find a proven, success model for treating drug offenders. There are many successful individual programs around the country, but they are sometimes hindered by economics and the lack of community resources available in remote locations. Thousands of treatment professionals in state, local and private programs work hard every day toward success. What is lacking, however, is the integration of these many ideas with treatment interventions and their applications.[5]

One way corrections can respond is by influencing the way in which addiction is viewed.[6] The addictions that Americans

	1995	2000	2005	Change from 1995 to 2005
Drug treatment admissions	756,269	803,632	1,039,074	+37.4%
Violent crime rate (per 100,000)	684.5	506.5	469.2	−31.5%
Federal spending on drug treatment (millions)	$2,175.8	$1,990.9	$2,494.3	+14.6%

This past decade has seen a rise in drug treatment admissions and federal spending, along with a drop in violent crime.

Source: Justice Policy Institute. January 2008. *Substance Abuse Treatment and Public Safety,* Washington, D.C.

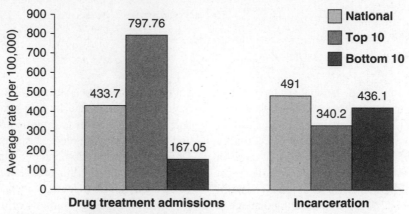

The 10 states with the highest rate of admissions to drug treatment send, on average, 150 fewer people per 100,000 to prison than the national average.

Note: The top 10 states are New York, Connecticut, Maryland, Rhode Island, Delaware, Vermont, Oregon, Washington, Massachusetts and Missouri. The bottom 10 states are Kentucky, New Hampshire, North Dakota, Texas, North Carolina, Wisconsin, Mississippi, Florida, Tennessee and Idaho.

face during treatment are both physiological and psychological. This presents many issues to those in the treatment field. Should the addiction be treated like a disease, a practice used by those in the medical field, or should addiction be treated as a behavior, a choice that one makes? Many would say it is some of both. However, instead of treating the addiction, clinicians in any setting—prison or community—must treat the individual. Offenders may do well in an enclosed treatment environment, but unless they change their way of thinking before they go back to their community, the same people, places and things will be welcoming them back to their previous lifestyles.

Due to challenging budgeting issues, many state and local jurisdictions would like to wait until an offender is close to going home before beginning treatment. However, a person's addiction should be addressed from Day 1. Increased use of drug treatment within the criminal justice system, whether it is mandated treatment through drug courts or optional treatment through transitional and aftercare programs, has been shown to reduce rearrest and new arrest rates, as well as drug use.[7]

It should be noted, then, that states with a higher drug treatment admission rate than the national average send, on average, 100 fewer people to prison per 100,000 in the population than states that have lower than average drug treatment admissions.[8] Obviously, diverting people from the criminal justice system into community or therapeutic settings will lower prison populations and lower the tax-payer burden. Many states, including New York, are working toward the reintegration model, and better preparing offenders for release. In addition, many states are diverting people from prison to treatment environments.

Many books have been written and experts have expressed their opinions, but the problem of substance abuse seems to only grow stronger. Who is responsible? Many drug offenders come from communities and neighborhoods where doing drugs is not thought of as a criminal act and where family structure is often an issue. The reasons for abuse are myriad and multiple. Often, offenders will say that it started as a pleasurable but exciting risk that soon developed into a real or perceived physical need/addiction. Many times there is no one available to warn children of the dangers of substance abuse, the health risks or the criminal justice consequences. These are the same neighborhoods and families to which the offender returns when released from a correctional facility, the majority of whom will re-offend or violate parole and return to prison or jail. The nation is willing to spend billions of dollars on incarceration, but people sometimes balk at the idea of appropriate community assistance, whether this assistance is job training, transportation assistance or day care.

The lack of national coverage and review in this area is distressing. With the vast amount of people in prison, the suffering endured by citizens and the billions of dollars spent should entice a national response.

Conclusion

Ultimately, the offender is responsible for his or her actions. The criminal justice system has made offenders accountable by arresting them for their behavior. They should also be held accountable for their decisions, which created the problem.

Treatment providers do not need to convince someone to take a minimum-wage job until they get off parole. Instead, they need to address their criminal thinking. The offender's mind-set has to change. Substance abuse programs must address the whole individual, but there must also be hope. Correctional staff's goals should be one-on-one decision-making and positive change. After all, taking illegal drugs is a choice, a decision.

Treatment providers must address the decision process that brings the offender to them. Many providers agree that the longer a person is in treatment the better that person's chance for recovery is. Treatment must continue once the offender returns to the community. Treatment also must be constant and continuous, but no change will take place until the individual is ready to change. That individual must decide to change his or her behavior. And corrections must help facilitate the thinking that will work toward that change.

Notes

1. Niman, M.I. 2000. Incarceration nation: The US is the world's leading jailer. *Buffalo Beat,* January 4. Available at www.mediastudy.com/articles/incarceration.html.

2. Office of National Drug Control Policy. 2004. *The economic costs of drug abuse in the United States,* 1992–2002. (Publication No. 207303). Washington, D.C.: Executive Office of the President.

3. Mumola, C.J. and J.C. Karberg. 2006. *Drug use and dependence, state and federal prisoners, 2004.* Washington D.C.: Bureau of Justice Statistics.

4. Justice Policy Institute. 2008. Substance abuse treatment and public safety. Washington D.C.: Justice Policy Institute. National Admissions to Substance Abuse *Treatment Services. 2005. Treatment Episode Data Set (TEDS) highlights-2005.* Drugs include heroin and other opiates, cocaine, marijuana, methamphetamines/amphetamines.

Federal Bureau of Investigation. Uniform Crime Report, *Crime in the United States, 1995, 2000, 2005.* Available at www.fbi.gov/ucr/ucr.htm.

Office of National Drug Control Policy. 2005. *National budget control policy: FY 2005 budget summary* Table 3: Historical Drug Control Funding by Function 1997–2006.

5. Connors, G.J., D.M. Donovan and C.C. Diclemente. 2004. *Substance abuse treatment and the stages of change.* New York: Guilford Press.

6. DiClemente, C.C. 2006. *Addiction and change—How addictions develop and addicted people recover.* New York: Guilford Press.

7. Inciardi, J.A., S.S. Martin and C.A. Butzin. 2004. Five-year outcomes of therapeutic community treatment of drug-involved offenders after release from prison. *Crime and Delinquency,* 50(1):88–107.

8. Alaska, New Mexico, West Virginia and Wyoming were excluded from these calculations due to incomplete treatment admissions data. The 23 states with higher drug treatment admission rates than the national average had, on average, an incarceration rate of 354.43 per 100,000. The 23 states with lower than average drug treatment admission rates had, on average, an incarceration rate of 454.43 per 100,000.

Critical Thinking

1. Do you believe money could be more effectively spent on substance abuse treatment? If so, in which areas could it be spent?

2. Who should take the lead in substance abuse treatment, and are there any groups/institutions who you believe could take a bigger role in substance abuse treatment?

MELVIN L. WILLIAMS is superintendent of Willard Drug Treatment Campus in Willard, N.Y.

Test-Your-Knowledge Form

We encourage you to photocopy and use this page as a tool to assess how the articles in *Annual Editions* expand on the information in your textbook. By reflecting on the articles you will gain enhanced text information. You can also access this useful form on a product's book support website at www.mhhe.com/cls

NAME: DATE:

_____

TITLE AND NUMBER OF ARTICLE:

_____

BRIEFLY STATE THE MAIN IDEA OF THIS ARTICLE:

_____

LIST THREE IMPORTANT FACTS THAT THE AUTHOR USES TO SUPPORT THE MAIN IDEA:

_____

WHAT INFORMATION OR IDEAS DISCUSSED IN THIS ARTICLE ARE ALSO DISCUSSED IN YOUR TEXTBOOK OR OTHER READINGS THAT YOU HAVE DONE? LIST THE TEXTBOOK CHAPTERS AND PAGE NUMBERS:

_____

LIST ANY EXAMPLES OF BIAS OR FAULTY REASONING THAT YOU FOUND IN THE ARTICLE:

_____

LIST ANY NEW TERMS/CONCEPTS THAT WERE DISCUSSED IN THE ARTICLE, AND WRITE A SHORT DEFINITION:

We Want Your Advice

ANNUAL EDITIONS revisions depend on two major opinion sources: one is our Advisory Board, listed in the front of this volume, which works with us in scanning the thousands of articles published in the public press each year; the other is you—the person actually using the book. Please help us and the users of the next edition by completing the prepaid article rating form on this page and returning it to us. Thank you for your help!

ANNUAL EDITIONS: Drugs, Society, and, Behavior 11/12

ARTICLE RATING FORM

Here is an opportunity for you to have direct input into the next revision of this volume.
We would like you to rate each of the articles listed below, using the following scale:

1. **Excellent: should definitely be retained**
2. **Above average: should probably be retained**
3. **Below average: should probably be deleted**
4. **Poor: should definitely be deleted**

Your ratings will play a vital part in the next revision.
Please mail this prepaid form to us as soon as possible.
Thanks for your help!

RATING	ARTICLE	RATING	ARTICLE
	1. History of Alcohol and Drinking around the World		24. Caffeinated Energy Drinks—A Growing Problem
	2. Did Prohibition Really Work?		25. Issues in Correctional Care: Propofol and Intravenous Drug Abuse
	3. Tackling Top Teen Problem—Prescription Drugs		26. College Students' Cheap Fix
	4. Smoking, Drugs, Obesity Top Health Concerns for Kids		27. Availability of Websites Offering to Sell Psilocybin Spores and Psilocybin
	5. San Diego State U. Defends Its Role in Federal Drug Sting		28. Youth Use of Legal Drugs Eclipses Illicit-Drug Use, Annual Survey Reports
	6. Reflections on 40 Years of Ethnographic Drug Abuse Research: Implications for the Future		29. The Problem with Drinking
	7. Mexico Drug Cartels Extend Reach in U.S.		30. With Cars as Meth Labs, Evidence Litters Roads
	8. A Pill Problem		31. Los Zetas: The Ruthless Army Spawned by a Mexican Drug Cartel
	9. Drug Addiction and Its Effects		32. The Role of Substance Abuse in U.S. Juvenile Justice Systems and Populations
	10. Family History of Alcohol Abuse Associated with Problematic Drinking among College Students		33. Catch and Release
	11. Biological Perspectives- Antimethamphetamine Antibodies: A New Concept for Treating Methamphetamine Users		34. Drugs: To Legalize or Not
	12. Medical Marijuana and the Mind		35. Do No Harm: Sensible Goals for International Drug Policy
	13. Scripps Research Team Finds Stress Hormone Key to Alcohol Dependence		36. It Is Time to End the War on Drugs
	14. The Genetics of Alcohol and Other Drug Dependence		37. New Drug Control Strategy Signals Policy Shift
	15. Role of Cannabis and Endocannabinoids in the Genesis of Schizophrenia		38. Beyond Supply and Demand: Obama's Drug Wars in Latin America
	16. Movement Disorders and MDMA Abuse		39. Feature: Twenty Years of Drug Courts—Results and Misgivings, Drug War Chronicle
	17. An Update on the Effects of Marijuana and Its Potential Medical Use: Forensic Focus		40. Crime and Treatment: Overcrowded Prisons and Addicted Inmates are a Tough Challenge for Lawmakers
	18. Methamphetamines		41. Fetal Alcohol Spectrum Disorders: When Science, Medicine, Public Policy and Laws Collide
	19. Crystal Meth: The Dangers of Crystal Meth		42. Identifying the Proper Drug-Abuse Treatment for Offenders
	20. Binge Drinking and Its Consequences Up Among American College Students		43. Whose Responsibility Is Substance Abuse Treatment?
	21. Public Lands: Cartels Turn U.S. Forests into Marijuana Plantations Creating Toxic Mess		
	22. Pseudoephedrine Smurfing Fuels Surge in Large-Scale Methamphetamine Production in California		
	23. Adolescent Painkiller Use May Increase Risk of Addiction, Heroin Use		

BUSINESS REPLY MAIL
FIRST CLASS MAIL PERMIT NO. 551 DUBUQUE IA

POSTAGE WILL BE PAID BY ADDRESSEE

McGraw-Hill Contemporary Learning Series
501 BELL STREET
DUBUQUE, IA 52001

ABOUT YOU

Name   Date

_____

Are you a teacher? ❐ A student? ❐
Your school's name

_____

Department

_____

Address   City   State   Zip

_____

School telephone #

_____

YOUR COMMENTS ARE IMPORTANT TO US!

Please fill in the following information:
For which course did you use this book?

_____

Did you use a text with this ANNUAL EDITION? ❐ yes ❐ no
What was the title of the text?

_____

What are your general reactions to the Annual Editions concept?

_____

Have you read any pertinent articles recently that you think should be included in the next edition? Explain.

_____

Are there any articles that you feel should be replaced in the next edition? Why?

_____

Are there any World Wide Websites that you feel should be included in the next edition? Please annotate.

_____

May we contact you for editorial input? ❐ yes ❐ no
May we quote your comments? ❐ yes ❐ no

NOTES

NOTES

NOTES

NOTES

NOTES

NOTES

NOTES

NOTES